The Good Spy

The Life and Death of Robert Ames

KAI BIRD

B\D\W\Y
Broadway Books
New York

Published in the United States by Broadway Books, an imprint of the Crown Publishing Group,
a division of Penguin Random House LLC, New York.
www.crownpublishing.com

Broadway Books and its logo, B \ D \ W \ Y, are trademarks of Penguin Random House LLC.

Originally published in hardcover in slightly different form in the United States
by Crown Publishers, an imprint of the Crown Publishing Group,
a division of Penguin Random House LLC, New York, in 2014.

Library of Congress Cataloging-in-Publication Data
Bird, Kai.
The good spy : the life and death of Robert Ames / by Kai Bird.
pages cm
Includes bibliographical references.
1. Ames, Robert, 1934–1983. 2. United States. Central Intelligence Agency—Officials and employees—Biography. 3. Intelligence officers—United States—Biography. I. Title.
JK468.I6B549 2014
327.12730092—dc23
[B]
2013049480

ISBN 978-0-307-88976-8
eBook ISBN 978-0-307-88977-5

Printed in the United States of America

Book design by Chris Welch
Cover design by Darren Haggar
Cover photography by George Baier IV; (eyes) UMAM Documentation and Research, Beirut;
(Robert Ames) courtesy of Yvonne Ames; (Ali Hassan Salameh) As-Safir newspaper, Beirut;
(Georgina Rizk) Associated Press; (Yasir Arafat) As-Safir newspaper, Beirut

First Paperback Edition

Praise for
The Good Spy

"A rich, nuanced portrait of a man who, in the CIA's term, had a high tolerance for ambiguity ... One of the best accounts we have of how espionage really works."

—Mark Mazzetti, *New York Times Book Review*

"Cool and authoritative ... The book's understated pleasures come from reading a pro writing about a pro. Mr. Bird has a dry style; watching him compose a book is like watching a robin build a nest. Twig is entwined with twig until a sturdy edifice is constructed. No flourishes are required.... Mr. Bird's style is ideal for his subject."

—Dwight Garner, *New York Times*

"A well-researched, engagingly presented biography ... *The Good Spy* is a fascinating book that sheds much-needed light on one of the murkier corners of CIA—and Middle Eastern—history."

—Max Boot, *Wall Street Journal*

"Full of great morsels and details ... *The Good Spy* succeeds on the basis of Bird's considerable research skills, his interviews with intelligence officials, his access to Ames's letters home, and, above all, his ability to spot and put together an engrossing biography."

—*Washington Post*

"[Bird] spent years researching this terrific biography of one of America's most important covert operatives. It was worth every minute."

—*Seattle Times*

"In his riveting, illuminating account of Ames's life and ultimate death in the 1983 embassy bombing in Beirut, Bird pulls back the thick black curtain on the world of clandestine intelligence affairs. A."

—*Entertainment Weekly*

"Engrossing . . . This absorbing book suggests that even the best of intentions, and the best of spies, aren't enough to bridge the chasms in the Middle East."

—*Los Angeles Times*

"Bird captures the acrid taste of regional politics and offers a perceptive portrayal of the internal workings and interplay of personalities within the CIA at the time. . . . An enthralling read."

—*Houston Chronicle*

"With its pacy narrative, exotic locales, and colorful cast of CIA and Mossad agents, Palestinian and Iranian revolutionaries, Lebanese operators, and even a winner of the Miss Universe contest, the book has all the ingredients of a first-class thriller. Kai Bird writes well enough to be a novelist, too, but his sentences have the additional virtue of being true."

—*Times Literary Supplement*

"One of the best nonfiction books ever written about the West's involvement in the Arab world."

—*The Spectator* (UK)

"All of this is engrossing for those fascinated by the machinations of the people and politics of the Middle East . . . but this book should appeal to a wider audience. It underlines the need for intelligence-gathering by humans as well as by machines, and illustrates the gap between spying and policy."

—*The Economist*

"Long after you put it down, the story continues to haunt you."

—*The Daily Beast*

"A lucid, thorough, fascinating biography."

—TIME.com

"It is a reflection of the drama of this patch of history as well as Bird's skill in rendering it that the book is as compelling a read as most spy novels."

—*National Interest*

"Bird is a master storyteller. . . . The narrative is heightened by Bird's meticulous and prodigious research. . . . There is no denying the power of the story, which is only enhanced by the fact that it is true."

—*Foreign Service Journal*

"More exciting than le Carré's George Smiley or Fleming's James Bond, Bird re-creates the life of CIA superspy Robert Ames. . . . Bird's meticulous account of Ames's career amid an ongoing Mideast climate of caution and suspicion is one of the best books on the American intelligence community."

—*Publishers Weekly* (starred review)

"Kai Bird has produced a compelling and complex narrative that must be read on many levels—including as a detailed account of the immense influence that a truly good man can have on an agency as cynical as the CIA and as a reminder of a myriad of losses."

—Seymour Hersh, Pulitzer Prize–winning author of *The Price of Power*, *The Dark Side of Camelot*, and *Chain of Command*

"Kai Bird has delivered two miracles—the best day-by-day account of a secret intelligence career in the CIA and the best book about the murderous intelligence war between Israel and her enemies, with America smack in the middle.... Bird has written a powerful and revealing story that leaves the reader with a troubling question—how did America get trapped in this war it can do nothing to end?"

—Thomas Powers, Pulitzer Prize–winning author of *Intelligence Wars* and *The Man Who Kept the Secrets: Richard Helms and the CIA*

"Well-reported, even-handed, compelling reading—one of the best books ever written about the CIA."

—Joseph Kanon, *New York Times* bestselling author of *Los Alamos* and *The Good German*

"Beautifully written and researched, *The Good Spy* is the best book I've ever read on espionage. It perfectly captures the CIA at its best. What's more, it's a book you can't put down, right to its tragic end. I need to add this: while Bob Ames's career and mine crossed paths over the years, it's Kai Bird who has finally put the story together for me. Reading this, I wondered at times if Kai somehow pulled off a black bag operation to get into the Agency archives."

—Robert Baer, former CIA operative and *New York Times* bestselling author of *See No Evil*

"[This] book could not be more timely in showing us the perils and advantages of clandestine actions in the name of national security. *The Good Spy* gives new meaning to the adage that truth can be stranger than fiction."

—Robert Dallek, author of the #1 *New York Times* bestseller *An Unfinished Life: John F. Kennedy 1917–1963*

"If John le Carré were a nonfiction specialist, he surely would feel the lure of writing the story that is at the heart of *The Good Spy*. Kai Bird works the seam between history and espionage. He has produced an arresting book—one that is knowing, and masterful in its rendition of a time when the United States cast a huge shadow across the Arab world. Robert Ames, the spy in Kai Bird's title, is a figure of unusual poignancy because his guile and innocence run side by side."

—Fouad Ajami, the late author of *The Syrian Rebellion*, *The Arab Predicament*, and *The Dream Palace of the Arabs*

DEDICATED TO SUSAN.

AND FOR YVONNE AMES,

who lost the father of her six children in Beirut.

AND IN MEMORY OF MY MOTHER,

Jerine Newhouse Bird (1926–2012).

THREE STRONG WOMEN.

CONTENTS

AUTHOR'S NOTE

When I began the research for this book, I visited the CIA's headquarters in Langley, Virginia, and met with George Little, then head of the Agency's Office of Public Affairs. We met for exactly one hour: I did most of the talking, trying to describe the kind of book I hoped to write about Robert Ames. I also explained that I would welcome the opportunity to sit down with one of the CIA's in-house historians and check basic facts about Ames's career. I was hoping that the CIA would declassify some materials related to Ames and his work in the Middle East. Mr. Little eagerly expressed the hope that the Agency would be able to give me some kind of limited assistance. But after repeated requests in the months and years to come, I never heard back from the Agency. CIA directors Leon Panetta and David Petraeus never replied to my e-mails. So I wrote this book without the cooperation of anyone inside the CIA.

Fortunately, I found more than forty retired officers, both clandestine officers from the Directorate of Operations and analytical officers from the Directorate of Intelligence, who generously shared their memories of Bob Ames. Some of these individuals were willing to speak for the record, but many spoke not for attribution. I have given aliases to those sources who did not want to be named. These aliases appear in the narrative in italics. This is also the case for a number of retired Mossad officers who agreed to be interviewed.

I knew Bob Ames when I was an adolescent. He and his wife, Yvonne, were our next-door neighbors from 1962 to 1965 in the small U.S. consulate compound in Dhahran, Saudi Arabia. So I have vivid memories of this tall, handsome young man who liked to play basketball with the consulate's squad of U.S. marine guards. I was unaware at the time that Bob was a CIA clandestine officer. I thought he was just another Foreign Service officer, like my father. Decades later, I approached Yvonne to say that I was writing a biography of her late husband; she remembered me. And though she'd never spoken to a reporter about her husband's life, she graciously agreed to talk and to share her small collection of photographs, correspondence, and a family scrapbook.

I also found a few declassified documents in the National Archives and the Ronald Reagan Presidential Library pertaining to Ames. But most of this book is based on interviews in Washington, D.C., Beirut, Amman, Tel Aviv, and Jerusalem. I wrote it in Barranco, a suburb of Lima, Peru.

CAST OF CHARACTERS

Robert C. Ames: A CIA officer in the Directorate of Operations and later chief of the Near East and South Asia Division of the Directorate of Intelligence.

Yvonne Blakely Ames: The wife of Bob Ames and mother of his six children.

Frank Anderson: Chief of the Near East and South Asia Division of the CIA's Directorate of Operations.

Ali Reza Asgari: Iranian Revolutionary Guard intelligence officer.

Anne Dammarell: A U.S. Agency for International Development officer stationed in Beirut.

Robert S. Dillon: U.S. ambassador, Beirut.

Phyllis Faraci: A CIA administrative officer working in Beirut.

Bashir Gemayel: A Maronite Christian warlord and president-elect of Lebanon.

Kenneth Haas: The CIA station chief in Beirut. Haas had a Ph.D. in philosophy from Syracuse University.

Deborah Hixon: A thirty-year-old CIA officer in Beirut on a temporary-duty assignment.

Frank J. Johnston: A CIA officer in Beirut, married to Arlette, a Palestinian-Israeli woman.

James F. Lewis: The deputy CIA station chief in Beirut. He was the last POW released from a North Vietnamese prison, in October 1975.

Monique Nuet Lewis: A Vietnamese-born, naturalized American citizen. She was the wife of James Lewis. Monday, April 18, 1983, was her first day on the job as a CIA administrative officer.

Sgt. Charles Allen Light Jr.: Assistant commander of the Marine Security Detachment for the U.S. embassy in Beirut.

William McIntyre: Acting director of the U.S. Agency for International Development mission in Beirut.

LCpl. Robert ("Bobby") McMaugh: The U.S. marine on duty at Post Number One in the U.S. embassy in Beirut on April 18, 1983.

Henry Miller-Jones: A CIA officer who served with Ames in Aden and Beirut.

Imad Mughniyeh: A Shi'ite Lebanese, recruited by Ali Hassan Salameh into the PLO's Force 17 and later associated with a long list of kidnappings, air hijackings, and car bombings.

Stuart H. ("Stu") Newberger: A senior partner at Crowell & Moring, a Washington-based law firm, who has pioneered civil suits on behalf of victims of international terrorism.

Georgina Rizk: Miss Lebanon and Miss Universe, 1971. Rizk became Ali Hassan Salameh's second wife in 1977.

Ali Hassan Salameh: Chief of the PLO's Force 17 intelligence unit.

William R. Sheil: A contract CIA officer and former Green Beret.

Janet Lee Stevens: Freelance American journalist in Beirut, a model for John le Carré's *Little Drummer Girl*.

Mustafa Zein: A Shi'ite Lebanese businessman and friend of Robert Ames in Beirut. Zein became the intermediary in Ames's relationship with Ali Hassan Salameh.

"Espionage, properly conducted, never announces itself. 'Stolen' information remains in its accustomed place; the 'spy' is a trusted civil servant; the spymaster betrays no sign of special knowledge."

—Thomas Powers, *The Man Who Kept the Secrets*

The Good Spy

PROLOGUE

Monday, September 13, 1993

I t was a bright blue, cloudless September day in Washington, D.C., a day of hope for the peoples of the Middle East after decades of cyclical wars, massacres, and spectacular acts of terrorism. But Frank Anderson—the Central Intelligence Agency's ranking clandestine officer in the Arab world—was nevertheless somehow annoyed that morning. He knew something extraordinarily good was about to happen. At fifty-one, Anderson had spent half his life working on the Middle East. After joining the CIA in 1968, Anderson had risen rapidly in the ranks of the Agency's clandestine services, learning Arabic in Beirut and specializing in the war-torn Middle East. By 1993, he was chief of the Near East and South Asia Division of the CIA's Directorate of Operations. That morning he had every reason to believe that peace was finally coming to a region to which he had dedicated his entire career. He should have felt elated, but he was quietly miffed.

Israeli prime minister Yitzhak Rabin and Yasir Arafat, the chairman of the Palestine Liberation Organization, were to sign a peace accord at the White House. President Bill Clinton had invited three thousand people to witness the historic moment on the South Lawn of the White House—and Anderson suspected that not a single CIA officer had been invited. Anderson thought that was wrong. Someone in the White House had forgotten how this peace process had started as an intelligence operation. Anderson believed the CIA, through its careful cultivation of clandestine sources, had created the opportunity for the Oslo Accords, which were to be signed that morning. He knew it had all started decades earlier when a young CIA officer named Robert Clayton Ames had cultivated the first highly secret contacts between the United States and the Palestinians. Ames had paved the way for the peace accords—and for his dedication to his spy craft and his work as an intelligence officer, he'd been murdered in Beirut on April 18, 1983, in the first truck-bomb assault on a U.S. embassy. He had happened to be in the wrong place at the wrong time. The horrifying attack had killed sixteen other Americans—including seven other CIA officers—and forty-six Lebanese civilians. Anderson thought that on this special day someone should remember what Ames had done for the peace process.

So when he arrived at his office at Langley's CIA headquarters that morning, Anderson convened a regular 9:00 A.M. meeting of his top officers. "It was noted that this was a big day for the peace process," recalled Charles Englehart, another clandestine officer, who'd worked with Ames. "We were all quite optimistic in those days that *this* time the Israelis and the Palestinians would get it right. Someone asked who was representing the CIA on the occasion: the director? A quick check indicated that there was no CIA representation at the ceremony."

After an awkward moment of silence, Anderson turned to his assistant, Bob Bossard, and said, "Okay, let's get a bus and go visit our dead." Anderson quickly spread the word that he wanted to take dozens of young, newly minted clandestine officers—and a few analysts— out to Arlington National Cemetery. They would walk to Ames's gravestone and say a few words in his memory. "I'm proud to say that it was my idea," Anderson said many years later. It was a spur-of-the-moment decision. By 10:30 A.M. a CIA bus was waiting at the southwest entrance. "We filled the bus," said Anderson, "probably thirty or forty people." Anderson wanted the younger officers there because he thought of the visit as a "values transmission opportunity."

When they arrived at Ames's gravesite on a gentle hill near a clump of oak trees, Anderson and his colleagues stared across the Potomac River toward the White House. They knew that at that moment, at 11:43 A.M., Israeli and Palestinian officials were signing a Declaration of Principles on Palestinian self-government in the Israeli-occupied territories of Gaza and the West Bank. Rabin said in his formal remarks, "We the soldiers who have returned from the battle stained with blood, we who have fought against you, the Palestinians, we say to you today in a loud and clear voice: 'Enough of blood and tears! Enough!'"

The *New York Times*'s correspondent Thomas Friedman reported that as soon as the documents were signed, President Clinton "took Mr. Arafat in his left arm and Mr. Rabin in his right arm and gently coaxed them together, needing to give Mr. Rabin just a little extra nudge in the back. Mr. Arafat reached out his hand first, and then Mr. Rabin, after a split second of hesitation and with a wan smile on his face, received Mr. Arafat's hand. The audience let out a simultaneous sigh of relief and peal of joy, as a misty-eyed Mr. Clinton beamed away." It was an awkward moment, but "hope" had seemingly "triumphed" over history.

"We were at Bob's gravesite," Anderson later recalled, "at the moment of the handshake—as planned." The chalky white gravestone read simply, "Robert Clayton Ames, Central Intelligence Agency of the United States of America, March 6, 1934–April 18, 1983." Nearby were the graves of veterans from the Civil War and America's wars in Europe, Korea, and Vietnam. A rear admiral born in 1876 was buried behind Ames. But Ames's was then the only gravestone in Arlington to identify a clandestine officer of the CIA. Standing near the grave, Frank Anderson spoke briefly of Ames's career and how Bob's clandestine relationship with Arafat's intelligence chief, Ali Hassan Salameh, had brought the Palestinians in from the cold. Ames, Anderson explained to the novice officers, was one of the CIA's fallen heroes, a man who was good at forming clandestine relationships in a dangerous part of the world. "He was no Lawrence of Arabia," said Henry

Miller-Jones, another clandestine officer. "He had little patience with pretentiousness or patronizing 'Arabophiles' and fanatic adventurers. He was never naïve about the Middle East, a cockpit of power politics. He understood the personalities and motivations of the revolutionary left in the Arab world as much as he appreciated the rituals of the Sheiks."

Ames had understood that a good CIA officer must have a curiosity about the foreign other—and a certain degree of empathy for their struggles. As Miller-Jones put it, "He came to know kings, emirs and princes as well as revolutionaries and terrorists, goat herders and penthouse commandos." He was adroit at making his way through the wilderness of mirrors that was the Middle East. He was naturally reserved, a man who easily kept secrets. He inspired trust, even in the company of men with bloody pasts. But he was also an intellectual, who later in his career could brief a president or a secretary of state about the intricacies of Middle Eastern politics and history. He was a model intelligence officer. "Everyone credited Ames with getting the peace process started," recalled *Lindsay Sherwin,* a CIA analyst.

"There was a moment of silent prayer," recalled Englehart, "as we all stood on the grass around the grave. I remember wondering why, after all we had done for this, President Clinton would not recognize our contribution—but it wasn't politically expedient. We should have known that, but it still stung."

After a few minutes, Anderson led his colleagues over to the nearby grave of William Buckley, the CIA Beirut station chief who'd been kidnapped in March 1984; he had been severely mistreated in captivity and had died fifteen months later, probably of pneumonia. Next they visited the gravesites of James and Monique Lewis, both of whom had died with Ames on that terrible day in April 1983. Both were CIA employees. And then they walked to the gravesite of Kenneth Haas, the CIA station chief in Beirut at the time. He too had died with Ames. Finally, they found the gravesite of Frank Johnston, yet another CIA officer who'd died that day in Beirut. All had been buried in Arlington. It had been a heavy toll—the worst in the Agency's history.

The visit to the cemetery was a sobering moment. But there was also a feeling of exhilaration—as if these sacrifices had been vindicated. "We were all quietly excited," Englehart recalled. "For those of us who spent our working lives in the Arab-Israeli firestorm, it was positive. After all, everybody would get what they wanted [with the Oslo peace accords], or what they thought they wanted. I had a definite feeling at the time that the sacrifices of our dead were not in vain, that the Israeli people and the Palestinian people could at last let go of each other's throats and understand that they are all brothers and sisters."

It was not to be.

Israeli prime minister Yitzhak Rabin hesitates for a moment before the iconic handshake with PLO chairman Yasir Arafat, September 13, 1993.

CHAPTER ONE

The Making of a Spy

I love you now and ever more
And promise to be true.
> —Robert Ames

Robert Clayton Ames was a very good spy. Everyone at the Central Intelligence Agency who knew him thought he was good at his work precisely because he was so very disarming and innocent. He was a classic American—idealistic and good-hearted and open as a Jimmy Stewart character. There was nothing phony about him, nothing cosmopolitan or pretentious. To the contrary, as another CIA officer later observed, he exuded a "rock-bottom American-ness that was neither Ugly nor Quiet." Foreigners invariably liked him.

Bob Ames was born on March 6, 1934, in Philadelphia and grew up in Roxborough, a largely white, working-class neighborhood in the northwest part of the city. People prided themselves in caring for the row homes that lined the streets. Fairmount Park, Wissahickon Creek, and the shops along Ridge Avenue were all within walking distance, and Roxborough residents had multiple bus routes to take them into downtown Philadelphia. Ten churches graced the neighborhood. Life in Roxborough was sheltered and comfortably predictable. Bob spent his entire childhood in the same plain, two-story row house at 4624 Pechin Street. His father, Albert Clayton Ames, was a steelworker who spent thirty-two years with SKF, the Swedish-owned ball-bearing plant. His paternal grandfather, Albert Beauregard Ames, was a Philadelphia policeman. Albert "Bud" Ames's job at SKF was to inspect the quality of ball bearings; it was tedious, low-paid work. Bob's mother, Helen Frances Amorose, was a homemaker. Bob was the second of three children. He had two sisters, Patricia, who was three years older, and Nancy, who was two years younger. The family got by, but modestly. Albert Ames lived from paycheck to paycheck. He was a union man, a member of the United Steel Workers—and every two years, around Christmastime, the union would take him out on strike. Albert would then sometimes go door to door, selling Christmas wreaths. A soft-spoken man, he never complained. He never raised his voice or his hand against the children. There were hard times, but Albert's son, Bob, grew up feeling as though he was a part of the American dream.

Helen was a second-generation Italian. She was the avid reader in the family—and also the disciplinarian. "She had her way," recalled Nancy Ames. "You did what you were told." Helen kept the house immaculate. Mondays were washdays, Tuesdays ironing days. Every child had chores and regular homework hours. Helen was a lapsed Catholic. She'd married a Methodist, so the children went to their father's Methodist church every Sunday. Though the Ameses were a working-class family, they were registered Republicans, like most of their neighbors in Roxborough. "My mother didn't think much of FDR," recalled Nancy. "She was a very smart woman. She listened to the radio news every day and read the newspapers. She was the kind of Republican who liked Ike."

Bob took after his mother. He was an avid reader. "He used to de-vour books," Helen later said. When Bob turned ten, his Uncle John gave him an encyclopedia—and many months later Bob came down-stairs one night and announced that he'd read it from cover to cover. He was mild-mannered and personable. "He didn't like confrontation of any kind," recalled his sister Nancy. "He was very private and quiet. Not a talker." Like most boys in the neighborhood, he was a Cub Scout and later a Boy Scout. Though his father liked to hunt and fish, Bob took no interest in his father's guns. As the only son, he got away with things. If his mother asked him to do the dishes, he'd stand at the sink and start whistling a tune. He loved to whistle, but he knew his mom hated it—and inevitably she'd dismiss him from doing the dishes. In school, he was known as the class prankster. When Bob was in sixth grade, a teacher thought he was so bright that she recommended he be sent to Penn Charter, a local private school. "There was no money for that," recalled Nancy.

Bob was always meticulous. His bedroom in the Pechin Street house was tiny. There was room only for a bed, a small bookcase, and a desk. So maybe he *had* to be neat. But his handwriting was also remarkably tiny and perfect script. "At dinner," remembered Nancy, "all his food had to be separated; nothing was ever to be mixed. The gravy had to be poured exactly in the center of his scoop of mashed potatoes."

One evening when Bob was thirteen or fourteen years old he was given tickets to see the Harlem Globetrotters perform in an exhibition game. He was enthralled by the show. That Christmas his parents bought him a basketball. It became his prize possession. "In Roxborough," recalled his sister Nancy, "if you owned your own basketball, you were special."

Bob and the girls attended Roxborough High School, just a few blocks from their home. By then, he stood six feet three inches. He was a strikingly handsome teenager with brown hair and hazel eyes—and a prominent, squared-off chin. His smile was broad and infectious. He was a spiffy dresser. Despite all these attractive qualities, he never dated in high school. His mother later observed that her son was "never one to travel in crowds." He either kept to himself or socialized with a few friends who enjoyed basketball.

During his summers "Big Bob" worked as a lifeguard at Wildwood Crest, a small beach community on the Jersey Shore. Wildwood was almost a second home. His mother's parents—Vittorio and Agnes Amoroso (later changed to Amorose)—owned a summerhouse at Wildwood. An Italian immigrant, Victor had done well in the furrier business. He boasted that his clientele included the wives of Dupont chemical company executives. Like most everyone, he'd lost money during the 1929 crash, but he was still well off enough to own a beach house and a small apartment building on the Jersey Shore. Helen Ames refused to take any money from her father, but every summer she and the children vacationed in the Wildwood beach house.

Bob's passion was still basketball, and even at the Jersey Shore he played the game at a local gym. One evening at Wildwood's Kenny Gym night court he was introduced to a young man named Tommy Gola, who he soon realized was a truly phenomenal player. "Bob was always talking about Gola," recalls Jack Harmer, a friend who lived a block away from the Ames house. "Bob played basketball year round. We had a dirt court at the end of my street where the neighborhood kids played. I would hear Bob dribbling his basketball past my house on the way to the court, and I'd join him to shoot baskets. In the winter mornings the ground would be frozen, but later it would thaw out and your hands and the ball would be coated in mud." Harmer thought Ames was a "quiet fellow, and a little hard to get to know on an inti-mate basis . . . but very likable."

Ames loved the game, and by his senior year he was the team's leading scorer. This earned him a four-year athletic scholarship to La Salle College, an all-men's Catholic college in Philadelphia run by the Christian Brothers. He also had a scholarship offer from Gettysburg College, where he would have been a starter on the basketball team. But he knew Tommy Gola was going to La Salle, and he wanted to play ball with Gola. Bob was the first and only member of his family to attend college. To save on expenses, he lived at home throughout his college years.

Ames did well academically. He majored in sociology but also took quite a few courses in psychology and philosophy. He knew he had an aptitude for languages. (He'd taught himself some Spanish during his summers at Wildwood.) In college he excelled in French. He had a vague notion of someday becoming an FBI agent. He knew the Bu-reau hired many lawyers, so he also took prelaw and kept a 3.06 grade average. And he played basketball every single day. He was a terrific outside shooter. At Roxborough, he had been the star player—yet at La Salle he mostly warmed the bench. That's how good La Salle's team was. "Ames was a great player," recalled Fran O'Malley, one of his teammates. "I don't know why he didn't play more." The star of the team was Tommy Gola. (Gola later played professionally for the Philadelphia Warriors and the New York Knicks. He was so good that Yogi Berra of the New York Yankees once described him as "the Joe DiMaggio" of basketball.) The coach for La Salle's team, the Explorers, was Ken Loeffler, a Yale-trained lawyer who led the team in 1954 to an NCAA (National Collegiate Athletic Association) championship. It was a magical season for La Salle; the team won nineteen of its last twenty games. When the boys returned in triumph from Kansas City that spring, they were greeted at the airport by ten thousand fans. Bob even saw a few holding placards emblazoned with "Ames." It was an exhilarating moment.

Yet Coach Loeffler had kept him on the bench for much of that championship season—even though he maintained the highest shooting percentage on the team. He was nevertheless intensely proud of his time with the Explorers. (During the 1953–54 season he played in fourteen out of thirty games, averaging two points and a rebound in each game.) For the rest of his life he kept prominently displayed in his home an NCAA plaque honoring the Explorers. He carefully saved in his scrapbook newspaper clippings and even the TWA baggage-check stub from the trip to Kansas City. Still, he'd always remember that Coach Loeffler hadn't let him play in that one glorious championship game. Years later, he wrote a thinly disguised short story in which he had the coach tell him, "I'm not talking to you to say that I am sorry that I didn't play you tonight. As I said, I'm never sorry for what I do. . . . You took all I could give you and you took it like a man. It's the hardest thing in the world to be a sub."

If Ames chafed at being a sub, his demeanor was always genial. He was always a team player. Basketball taught him discipline and persistence. "The other sports can be fun," Coach Loeffler once explained. "But the truth is that most of them are elementary compared to basketball. None involves such speed and intricacy of tactics. None demands such fast-moving, fast-thinking and all-round athletic skill." Ames would shoot baskets for the rest of his life.

■

After graduating from La Salle in June 1956, Ames headed to Orange, Texas, where he worked for the Catalytic Construction Company. Like most young American men in the 1950s, he expected soon to be drafted into the army. But in the meantime he needed the money.

The army inducted him on November 8, 1956. After thirteen weeks of basic training, Ames was assigned to the U.S. Army's Middle East Signal Communications Agency. He shipped out to Africa in the early winter of 1957. His assignment was to work as a signal-supply specialist at Kagnew Station, an army listening post just outside the town of Asmara in what was then the Ethiopian province of Eritrea. Ames had to look up the location in an atlas to see where he was going. In the Eritrean language, *Kagnew* means "to bring order out of chaos." Gen. William Westmoreland once visited the listening post and remarked, "I do not believe we have a more remote station of our Armed Forces than Kagnew Station."

Kagnew was home to the Fourth U.S. Army Security Agency. Ames was a member of the 9434 Signal Corps. Getting to this isolated spot entailed a four-day trip in a Douglas C-47 two-engine propeller plane. The flight took him first to Bermuda and then to the Azores for refueling. He had to spend one night in Tripoli, Libya, and another night in Dhahran, Saudi Arabia. These stopovers gave him his first glimpse of the Arab world. He heard Arabic spoken for the first time. Then the next morning he caught another C-47 for the flight to Eritrea.

Located close to the equator at an elevation of 7,300 feet, Kagnew was one of America's most valuable Cold War listening posts. It housed several thousand American soldiers and technicians employed by the U.S. military, the Central Intelligence Agency, and the National Security Agency. They called it their "island in the sky." The Americans operated a 2,500-acre "antenna farm" to intercept radio communica-

tions from all over Africa and the Middle East. Because of its location
and high altitude, the spot was ideal for "listening." The station's primary mission was to intercept the military and diplomatic communications of Egypt and other Arab governments. As a practical matter,
everyone at Kagnew Station was working for the National Security
Agency, America's electronic eavesdropping agency. So Ames, like everyone else, was accorded one of the highest security classifications—
Top Secret Codeword.

It was merely an accident of army life that Ames was chosen for
this signal intelligence duty. But for whatever reason, the assignment
to Kagnew opened Bob's eyes to the world of intelligence. It was a
very technical world. Kagnew's antenna intercepted radio waves and
recorded the intercepts on reel-to-reel tape recorders. If the data were
encrypted, then trained cryptographers had to decipher the codes.
Russian, Arabic, and other linguists had to translate the material. It
was all very classified. Yet Ames's personal duties were mundane. He
and his army buddy John Wilson, a young man from Oklahoma, were
assigned to a supply company responsible for keeping track of spare
parts for the transmitters and receivers.

Ames had first met Wilson in a signal-supply classroom at an army
base in Georgia. The classroom instructor announced that Private Wilson would be the squad leader for their group. Ames promptly shot his
arm in the air; he wanted to know why Wilson had been chosen. The
instructor replied that Wilson had scored the highest on the aptitude
test. Afterward, the instructor called Wilson and Ames to the front of
the class and explained that Ames had scored only two points lower.
Ames was clearly ambitious, but he and Wilson nevertheless became
close friends.

At Kagnew, they lived in a second-story squad room with ten other
soldiers. Ames and Wilson had facing lower bunks. "Ames was closer
to me than either of my two brothers," Wilson later said. Their daily
routine was spent entirely together. They showered at the same time,
walked together to the mess hall, and worked at their desks facing
each other. Ames, the city boy from Philadelphia, enjoyed reading the

newspapers Wilson received through the mail from his small town in Oklahoma. Their work was not onerous. And life in the barracks was simple and easy. Tending each squad of a dozen men were two Eritrean "houseboys" who made the beds and cleaned up after the Americans and shined their boots.

Kagnew was equipped like a summer camp in the midst of Eritrea's dirt-poor villages. It boasted a chapel, commissary, snack bar, and post office. The mess hall—"Mom's Place"—served mediocre food, but when the men were off-duty they could buy ten-cent beers at the Oasis Club. The 320-seat Roosevelt Theater showed decent movies. There was a bowling alley, a softball field, and an indoor pool. The men sometimes took day trips down to the Red Sea beaches. Ames was once again the star of the basketball court, winning a trophy in the autumn of 1957 for being the post's leading scorer. "Ames played every game like it was the most important thing going," recalled Wilson. Ames may have had the opportunity to visit Arabia a second time because Kagnew's basketball teams were occasionally invited to compete with teams at the U.S. air base at Dhahran.

The social life at Kagnew was intense. The young, crew-cut men worked long shifts—they called them "tricks"—and they played hard as well. But while others spent their off-duty hours in Asmara's bars drinking beer and paying for the services of local women, Ames abstained. Wilson remembers how Bob preferred to stay in the barracks, reading books or working out in the gym. "Ames spent a lot of time in the gym working out with weights," Wilson recalled. He was never much of a drinker. Neither did he play poker like many of the men.

Bob Ames was a serious young man—far more serious than most army recruits. Kagnew Station changed him in many ways. He met a Catholic priest, probably one of the army chaplains, who persuaded him to convert to Catholicism. Back home in Roxborough, Bob's sister Nancy remembered being told by their mother that her brother had become a Catholic. Nancy was surprised—though later in life both she and her sister, Pat, also converted. The Church was in the family's ancestry. Bob knew that his mother, Helen, had been raised a Catholic—and he knew that his Italian-born grandfather, Vittorio Amoroso, and his Irish-born grandmother, Agnes Egan, had been Catholics. So it was in the blood. But the Church also suited Ames's personality—and it suited his future profession.

During his occasional trips to downtown Asmara, Ames made a point of visiting St. Joseph's Cathedral, an ornate Romanesque-style church built by the Italians in 1922. Wilson would wait for him while he spent a few minutes in the confessional booth.

Many of the men at Kagnew Station worked out of uniform. It was a very informal army post. But Ames was different. "Ames was very meticulous about his clothing," remembered Wilson. "His fatigues always somehow looked like new. His khaki cap, however, was worn enough for the sweatband to show." But Ames never laundered his cap because to do so one had to remove the wire band threaded at the top of the cap. The caps never kept their shape after laundering.

On the other hand, Ames didn't take the U.S. Army too seriously. One day the soldiers had to put on dress uniforms and pass inspection prior to a parade in honor of Ethiopia's Emperor Haile Selassie, who was visiting Asmara. As the commanding officer passed down the line of men standing at attention, he suddenly stopped in front of Wilson and commented, "Fine-looking soldier!" At that, Ames snorted loud enough that Wilson thought the two of them would be reprimanded. "I don't think Ames really ever had the soldiering spirit," recalled Wilson.

Ames was a steady, solid character, but there's also evidence that he was impressionable. One day he happened to be in the Oasis Club when a local hypnotist came to entertain the men. The performer chose Ames as his subject, and to the astonishment of everyone, he hypnotized Ames and had him riding an imaginary bicycle on the stage. "I never thought he would give up control to that extent," said Wilson.

One extraordinary thing happened during Ames's stint at Kagnew Station. In December 1957, the cryptographers in the classified Operations Company launched a virtual mutiny to protest the post commander's decision to institute compulsory inspections and parade duty. The men grumbled that as they were getting off their long shifts they were forced to get ready for an inspection. "After a week or so of this bullshit," recalled one Kagnew veteran, George E. Matthias, "they rebelled." The Morse code intercept operators claimed that there was too much static and they couldn't hear anything; the automatic Morse code and telex operators claimed they couldn't find the network that they were monitoring. In effect, it was a work stoppage—unheard-of in the army. After about a week, the National Security Agency headquarters realized what was happening and immediately dispatched a group of new officers to relieve Kagnew's commander.

After this incident, Kagnew's chaplain announced that he was organizing a morale-building trip to the Holy Land. "Ames talked me into going," Wilson said. "I'm still very grateful." They managed to spend several days in Jerusalem, walking through the narrow lanes of the Old City, visiting the Church of the Holy Sepulchre and the Dome of the Rock, one of Islam's most sacred sites. On the flight back, the plane had to land in Cairo, and the airline put the men up in a hotel and arranged a tour of the Pyramids of Giza. Ames and Wilson got to ride a camel. The entire trip took less than a week, but it left a deep impression on young Ames.

Toward the end of his assignment, he began to study Arabic. It was a curious choice. "Sometime before we were to leave Africa," Wilson recalled, "Ames began to learn Arabic. I don't know whether he had outside help or not, but I remember him sitting cross-legged at his footlocker, using it for a table, and making those Arabic characters." He had heard the guttural but melodious language spoken during his brief visits to Jerusalem, Cairo, and Dhahran. In addition, he had certainly heard Arabic spoken in the streets of Asmara. (Tigrinya and Arabic were the official languages in Eritrea from 1952 to 1956.) Perhaps this was enough to motivate him to tackle Arabic—one of the most difficult languages for an English speaker to learn. It was a fateful decision.

After one year, one month, and three days at Kagnew Station, Ames was flown back to America. His two years of service were up, and he expressed no interest in an army career. He was no longer the boy from an insulated working-class neighborhood in Philadelphia. He'd seen a bit of the world, and the exposure to life overseas had implanted the idea that maybe he could have a career in the State Department. He left the army on November 7, 1958, with an honorable discharge and a good-conduct medal.

Back home in Philadelphia, Ames got a job with Allstate Insurance Company, and in the evenings he began studying to take the State Department's Foreign Service written exam. He told his parents that he "could not spend his life stuck behind a desk." He wanted to travel "and see the world." The insurance company had its offices in the Gimbel Building in downtown Philadelphia. Bob went through a training program to become an underwriter for Allstate. It was tedious and repetitive work. But the company's six-foot-three rookie was charming and he could get the job done. After lunch one day in the spring of 1959, Ames was walking back to work when he spotted a pretty blond, blue-eyed young woman whom he recognized as someone who worked as a secretary in the insurance company. He made a mental note to himself that she was far too beautiful for him—and that she must have a dozen men after her already.

Yvonne Blakely had been born on June 21, 1937, in San Diego, California, where her father was stationed with the navy at the time. But like any navy brat, she had moved around. She ended up spending her high school years in Groton, Connecticut, graduating in 1955. Instead of college, she enrolled in the Katharine Gibbs Secretarial School in Boston and learned stenography and typing. "Gibbs girls" were considered to be class A secretaries; every student was required to wear a formal hat and long white gloves. "You were virtually guaranteed to get a job," Yvonne recalled. She graduated in 1956 and followed her parents to Honolulu, where her father was stationed at Pearl Harbor. She spent two years working for a shipping company until 1958, when her father was transferred once again, this time to the navy yard in Philadelphia.

For her part, Yvonne, twenty-two, had noticed Ames. She'd already heard through the office rumor mill about a new employee, a handsome and very tall bachelor. "I was going back to work," she recalled, "and I saw this giant of a man. I decided right away that he wasn't for me because there were already too many girls after him."

But one day they found themselves together, walking to catch a bus on Chestnut Street. Bob introduced himself. "One of the first things he talked about was his love of Arabic," Yvonne said. "He wanted to go to the Middle East." Yvonne thought he was not only attractive but worldly. By then, he'd taken to smoking a pipe—and even when he was not actually smoking he often had it clenched in his teeth.

Ames took her out on their first date on April 11, 1959. They went to a movie theater. "Bob was not a big winer and diner," Yvonne recalled. But by July 30 they were engaged. "His parents were wonderful about it," Yvonne said. "My parents hesitated because of Bob being Catholic." Yvonne had been raised in the Lutheran Church—and when her father retired from the navy in 1961 after twenty-nine years of service, he enrolled in a Lutheran seminary and became an ordained pastor. The Blakelys were serious Lutherans.

There was also a big class difference. Yvonne's father, Robert Graham Blakely, had been born in San Bernardino, California, and raised in Idaho. His parents were from Ireland and Scotland. During World War II he'd been a submariner—dangerous duty. But he'd survived and spent the rest of his career in the navy. By 1960, he had risen to the rank of a navy commander. He was somebody, and young Bob Ames from Roxborough had no pedigree other than his association with a winning college basketball team. But he was charming, and he was clearly in love.

Later that summer Bob wrote a love poem to Yvonne:

There are so many loving things I'd like to say to you.
That even in a million years I never could get through.
I'd like to tell you how I feel when you are by my side.
And how you always fill my life with happiness and pride.
But there are not sufficient words to glorify a star.

Or any phrase that can describe how wonderful you are.
So after all is said and done
I say these words to you.
I love you now and ever more
And promise to be true.
Love,
*   Bob*

Yvonne was a truly stunning woman. She had dirty-blond hair, icy-blue eyes, and the prominent, high cheekbones of her mother's Norwegian ancestors. (One of Bob's friends later remarked that she bore a strong resemblance to the Norwegian movie actress Liv Ullmann.) She walked with a quiet elegance that came naturally. She knew how to dress stylishly, but without great expense. She possessed the polite poise of a navy officer's daughter. There was something formal about her demeanor, but it wasn't pretentious.

They were married on April 30, 1960, in a Lutheran church. "Bob was excommunicated by the Catholic Church," Yvonne said. "He just accepted it; he didn't have a problem with it." He was Catholic, but he chose Yvonne over the Church. It was an easy choice.

Immediately after their marriage in the spring of 1960 Bob took the written Foreign Service exam—and soon learned that he'd failed it. Still determined to have a career in the Middle East, he decided to apply to the Central Intelligence Agency. In late June he and Yvonne made a quick trip to New York City, where he had his first Agency interview. In New York, the couple took the opportunity to see Alfred Hitchcock's newly released thriller *Psycho*. By mid-August, Yvonne was pregnant.

CHAPTER TWO

The Agency

Helms and Ames were very much alike. Both were real gentlemen who valued a certain decorum. They were not soldiers of
fortune like some of the guys in operations.

— *Lindsay Sherwin, CIA analyst, Directorate of Intelligence*

L ate in 1960, the CIA offered Ames a job. They hired him at
a salary of more than $5,000 per annum. That was serious
money for the young man from Philadelphia. Bob and Yvonne
moved down to Washington, D.C., right after the Christmas holidays
and rented—for $150 a month—a small apartment at 1400 South
Twenty-eighth Street in Arlington, Virginia. They arrived in Bob's red
Fiat, his first car. They called it the "tomato can."

Bob had been told that he couldn't tell anyone whom he was working for. Ostensibly, that meant even his wife. But in practice most CIA
officers told their wives. Yvonne knew. But other relatives usually had
only a vague notion of what they were doing in Washington. When one
of Ames's future colleagues, Clair George, joined the CIA a few years
earlier, he wrote home: "Dear Mom, I have been offered about $4,500
per year or so to do something for Uncle Sam, exactly what I'm not
sure. Nor do I know where, when, how, or why. So think it over and
remember the child of 1955 has [a] strange and sometimes tortuous
path to follow." Bob probably told his parents what he was doing after
CIA officers came by to interview them and various neighbors for his
background check. Helen and Albert then told his sisters that he'd
joined the CIA. "Initially, I couldn't picture him as CIA," said his sis-

ter Nancy. "This was not the brother I knew. Bob didn't seem like the kind of person who would put himself in danger. But later we all told ourselves that this was the perfect job for him. He was very private and he knew how to keep a secret."

It was an exciting time to be in Washington. Jack Kennedy was about to be inaugurated as president. Bob and Yvonne were both registered Republicans, but after watching the Kennedy-Nixon televised debates they decided to vote Democratic. "Nixon looked horrible," Yvonne recalled. "I tended to vote Republican, but I never voted a straight party ticket." Bob rarely talked politics with his wife. He had very conventional views about women: he thought they belonged at home.

That winter Ames was inducted into the Agency as a junior officer trainee (JOT) and assigned to Operations Course-11. (The Agency had been founded in 1947, but this was the eleventh year in which the yearlong Operations course had been offered.) There were forty-four other men in this class—and, unusually, one woman.* Everyone in the class was slated to work in the Directorate of Plans (DP)—which later became the Directorate of Operations (DO) and today is called the National Clandestine Service. DP was the Agency's branch for the collection of intelligence by covert means. If the JOTs survived the DO's nearly two-year-long training program, they could become case officers, usually assigned abroad to work in U.S. embassies or consulates under diplomatic cover. While ostensibly listed as Reserve Foreign Service officers, their actual job would be the recruitment of foreign agents and the collection of covert intelligence from foreign sources. Operations Course-11 would teach them basic tradecraft: how to spot and assess potential agents and then how to recruit and manage them. Ames was surprised by how much of it entailed "sitting behind a desk." It was a bureaucracy. Initially, the trainees had to memorize a one-page

---

* Harriet Isom was a physically imposing, six-foot-tall young woman who had a graduate degree from Tufts University's Fletcher School of Diplomacy. Isom survived the JOT program, but at the end of the course the CIA did not offer her an operational slot, so she resigned and subsequently joined the State Department, where she became an ambassador many years later.

list of cryptonyms identifying the Agency's various departments and functions. Classes were held in a row of dilapidated white clapboard, barrack-like buildings thrown up during World War II as "temporary" office space. Years later, in the early 1960s, the CIA was still using the spartan structures, located on Ohio Drive along the Potomac River. One could see the ground between the gaps in the floorboards. All day long, the trainees were subjected to a parade of speakers from various parts of the Agency, each more eager than his predecessor to regale the new recruits with the virtues of his particular expertise. "It got old, fast," recalled one of Ames's classmates.

Because the Agency barracks were located so close to National Airport, there was a sign at the back of each classroom, facing the speaker, that read, "Pause for Planes." The roar of the planes taking off was close enough to rattle the windows.

By 1961, at the dawn of President John F. Kennedy's New Frontier, the CIA was already a large, unwieldy bureaucracy, numbering some sixteen thousand employees. The Agency was about to move into its new seven-story quarters in Langley, Virginia. Allen Dulles, veteran Wall Street lawyer and former Office of Strategic Services (OSS) officer, was the Agency's director of central intelligence. But he was also head of the entire intelligence community and the president's principal intelligence adviser. The new recruits got so tired of being told that Dulles wore "three hats" that some took to coming to work wearing more than one hat. No one seemed to get the joke. One day a speaker in class was surprised to be greeted with groans and boos when he casually boasted, "At this time, I am actually wearing two hats." Ames and his fellow Operations Course-11 classmates quickly acquired a reputation for their public unwillingness to suffer such pretentiousness without a display of derision.

The men snickered when more than one speaker was heard to say, "We'll run this up the flagpole and see if anyone salutes it." And they sat nonplussed when another officer admonished them, "Do not clog the intelligence stream with the luxuriant water hyacinth of trivia."

But they were impressed when a group of four or five men from the

Agency's School of International Communism came to address them. They were cigar-smoking, hard-drinking intellectuals, all with doctorates in political science or history. They explained that it was their job to keep themselves well informed on the intricacies of the international communist movement. They talked about the doctrinal disputes and the various personalities who led one faction or another in the world of communism. Ames and his colleagues were surprised to learn that communism was less than monolithic.

There were rules in the game of intelligence, and then there were rules to be broken. Some years later the Agency hired some psychiatrists to profile the qualities of a good covert operative. One of the characteristics identified was "a high tolerance for ambiguity."

Ames quickly made new friends, discovering early on that one of his classmates came from Philadelphia. Socially, the group split between those who were married and those who were still single. "The institution of the cocktail party was still alive, and we all supported the institution," recalled one of Ames's classmates. "Mixed drinks were very much still in vogue, and beer and wine might accompany a meal, but they never preceded it."

In late March of 1961 Ames was sent to the CIA's "Farm"—a ninethousand-acre training ground at Camp Peary, located on the York River in Virginia's Tidewater region near Williamsburg. Army MPs stood guard at the gates, part of the site's cover as an army base. Officially, Camp Peary was known for "Armed Forces Experimental Training Activity." But everyone referred to it as "the Farm." The trainees were housed in Quonset huts; everyone had individual rooms, but they had to share common latrines and showers. Upon arrival, they donned khaki shorts and shirts. That first evening they attended a cocktail party hosted by an army colonel whom they never saw again. Every day there were morning reveille and evening retreat announced with bugle calls on loudspeakers. There was an auditorium shaped like a small Roman coliseum with a speaker's well at the bottom. They called it "the Pit." Everyone ate together in a central mess hall, and after dinner an officers' club opened in the evening where the men could drink beer. The club had a pool table, a Ping-Pong table, and a television. A small movie theater screened a different film each evening for ten cents. It might have been a rustic country club.

But over the next twenty-two weeks Ames and the other men received paramilitary training in the use of firearms and demolitions. They learned to fieldstrip an AK-47, an early version of the M-16 rifle, pistols, and other weapons. They practiced firing these weapons on a target range but also in moving cars and at night. They learned how to maneuver and land a small motorboat and engaged in hand-to-hand combat exercises. They ran through an obstacle course of barbed wire, chain-link fences, and trenches set up to simulate a border. "We gained a respect for the borders that can both be protected and breached," recalled one trainee. They were taught to handle explosives. "It was the first time I learned that ordinary fertilizer could be used to blow stuff up," recalled fellow DO officer Henry Miller-Jones. "They blew up a barn for us using fertilizer." Recruits took a course in map reading and went on uncomfortable marches through the forest at night. It was physically exhausting—but not as rigorous as a marine boot camp. Some sixteen years later another young recruit went through a similar paramilitary training course at the Farm. "The course was a relic from the OSS, which really did fight in World War II," Robert Baer wrote in his memoir, *See No Evil.* "But the DO existed to run agents, not defend battle lines. As far as I could figure out, the only reason the DO kept the course going was to engender an esprit de corps in its new officers—a reminder that we didn't work for the pinstriped crowd down at the State Department."

Soon after coming to the Farm, on the morning of April 17, 1961, the trainees were called to the Pit and told that a Cuban rebel force supported by the CIA had landed at the Bay of Pigs. They were given regular updates throughout the next few days. "We cheered initially," said one of Ames's classmates, "but became increasingly quiet as the scope of the disaster unfolded. Everyone was pretty despondent." One

trainee, Ben Ramirez—a Mexican American and a former marine—
revealed that a few months earlier he'd briefly had an interim assignment with the Agency in Miami. His job had been to help with the
training of some of the Cuban volunteers. Ramirez was devastated that
so many good men he'd trained had probably died in the operation.
There was no guilt, but there was a profound sadness.

A few weeks later, Lyman Kirkpatrick, the Agency's inspector
general, came to the Farm to brief everyone on what had happened.
Kirkpatrick was one of the Agency's highest-ranking officers. He'd
contracted polio during a trip to Bangkok in 1952 and was still confined to a wheelchair. But he sat at the bottom of the Pit and briefed
the members of Operations Course-11 at length on the Bay of Pigs.
When he was finished, he announced that he'd be available for further
questions in the bar of the officers' club after dinner. He stayed in the
bar until closing hour, taking questions. Kirkpatrick made it clear that
he didn't blame President Kennedy or the Agency. He characterized
the Bay of Pigs as a professionally planned and executed operation that
had gone terribly awry. He explained that he'd be leading a vigorous
investigation of what was obviously one of the Agency's most embarrassing debacles. Ames and his classmates were impressed that someone of Kirkpatrick's stature would spend so much time with them.*

Three weeks after the Bay of Pigs, Ames was given permission to
rush home to see Yvonne, who was about to give birth to a baby girl.
On May 11, 1961, Catherine was born. A few days later, he had to report back to the Farm. Bob never told Yvonne what he was doing at the
Farm—only that he was undergoing some kind of training.

---

* Kirkpatrick's subsequent classified report was highly critical of the architects of
the Bay of Pigs operation, and specifically of Richard Bissell and Tracy Barnes. President Kennedy fired Bissell in early 1962. Richard Helms replaced him as deputy director
of plans—and in 1966, when Helms became director of central intelligence, he fired
Barnes. Kennedy also dismissed Allen Dulles as director in November 1961 and replaced
him with John McCone, a Republican businessman. But before leaving the Agency,
Dulles managed to have nineteen of the twenty copies of Kirkpatrick's scathing report
destroyed. The one surviving copy remained classified for nearly forty years.

After Ames got back from seeing his newborn daughter, he was finally exposed to the Farm's core purpose: learning how to recruit and handle agents. (The paramilitary training might seem glamorous, but it would rarely, if ever, prove useful in Bob's future career as a case officer.) One morning he and his fellow trainees reported to the Pit. Everyone was handed thick briefing books for what was called a "live problem scenario." Ames was told to imagine that he'd been posted to a CIA station in a fictional country. The briefing books named this fictional country and gave it a history, a geography, a currency, a cultural life, a government—everything that a CIA officer might expect to encounter in a real country. Government leaders and opposition-party members were identified. These fictional characters had detailed biographies that the trainees were told to memorize. Senior military and intelligence officials were named. "The live problem scenario was to become very real to us," recalled one trainee, "and the degree to which each of us was able to immerse himself in it had a great deal to do with our eventual performance at the Farm."

The trainees were divided into five or six groups, and each team was assigned an individual mentor from the Farm's training staff. The mentor guided the trainees through imaginary scenarios; the mentor played the role of a station chief in a CIA post abroad, and the trainees acted as case officers. Everyone was given individual assignments. There was no pretense of teamwork—because in reality case officers act alone.

Everyone was assigned the same pseudonym—John O. Thorne—to be used in official correspondence. The only female trainee was assigned a similar pseudonym: Jane O. Thorne. (After a while, it occurred to the trainees that the initials of the pseudonym, JOT, stood for "junior officer trainee.")

One of Ames's fellow JOTs later explained the elaborate game:

> Although we became almost intimately familiar with many of the Scenario characters and their life stories, we were never to meet them. We were, however, to meet other, lesser individuals who either knew or had other access to the characters, or who worked

in some of the various government ministries and offices. This was our first contact and experience with agents. We initially met our agents, either in turnover meetings in which a departing case officer brought us in as his replacement, or in cold meetings making use of an established re-contact plan, complete with appropriate signals and paroles. All of this involved, as we proceeded to grasp them, increasing use of the principles and techniques of clandestine operations, included in that all-encompassing term that was quickly becoming integral to our lives: tradecraft.

The trainees were taught that the hardest part of their job was recruitment. Not many CIA officers are good at this, because recruitment is simply very hard and improbable. It is a slow dance, a subtle exercise in peeling away an individual's loyalties and transferring them from one "cause" to another. It happens rarely, usually when the recruiter can make it seem only natural and fitting that the target should be talking to his case officer. Invariably, recruited spies want to be recruited. Most of them, in fact, are walk-ins—meaning they volunteer to serve in some fashion. Otherwise, a genuine recruitment happens via a form of intellectual seduction. The case officer shows his empathy and solicits the heartfelt views of his target. He takes him or her to dinner and eventually offers small, even innocuous material rewards. And one thing leads to another. The goal is to get the "source" to sign up as a knowing agent with a written agreement. It is a psychological dance. Once the target of recruitment has given his "views" or "information" in return for some benefits, material or otherwise, the game is in play. "But the other side of the coin," observed an officer who went through the Farm and later worked with Ames, "is the target's own conscience and sense of what he is doing. Sometimes you know what he feels; often not. Most people will rationalize their way out of anything that makes them feel bad, whatever the objective evidence. And others will feel guilty on very flimsy evidentiary bases. Both are exploitable."

The JOTs met their "agents" in clandestine meetings outside the

Farm in restaurants or shops in nearby Williamsburg and Richmond. Each encounter was carefully planned. One had to make sure that one hadn't been followed to the meeting point. Ames learned how to set up a safe house and how to make sure that neither he nor his controlled "agent" was subject to surveillance. The trainees were taught how to communicate with agents through "dead drops"—a hole in a tree or a loose floor tile—and how to set up a clandestine meeting in a safe house. They also learned that a mountain of mundane paperwork was associated with any recruited agent. Payment varied widely. It could be as little as several hundred dollars a month, or, in extraordinary cases, it could go into the six figures. Typically, a bank account had to be established, sometimes in the United States. Occasionally, an agent would be given a life insurance policy. And often an asset would be required to sign a "certification . . . stating briefly that U/1 [the abbreviated cryptonym of this particular agent] understands that no federal or state or social security taxes would be withheld from his RTACTION [the cryptonym for the CIA] compensation during this period of employment." A copy of this signed certification was to be filed away in Langley just in case "any questions arise as to his compliance with the IRS regulations with regard to his RTACTION compensation." Even spies have to pay their taxes if they are U.S. citizens or green card holders!

Later, the training staff that played the roles of agents sat down with the trainees and graded them on their tradecraft. Ames was taught that after each encounter with a foreign source, one had to write up a "Contact Report" of how the meeting was arranged, what was said, and what "intelligence" was conveyed, if any. Writing things down accurately was essential. Arranging and evaluating these encounters with agents required methodical planning and the meticulousness of a scientist. But Ames soon realized that his new profession was much more of an art than a science. Or it was an imprecise science. The hardest part of these human relationships was the introduction. He was taught that the relationship between a case officer and his agent was fraught with ambiguities and even deceptions. As a general rule, the agent knew his case officer only by his alias. But it was a real relationship. The agent needed to feel that his case officer was somehow empathetic with his circumstances, with his cause, and indeed, with his life. There had to be trust—but the kind of trust that left the agent entirely dependent on the case officer for his security and well-being.

Forming a new relationship was a delicate proposition. But it was almost equally difficult to "turn" a source or agent over to a new case officer. The relationship between a case officer and a paid or knowing source was not worth much in the end if it could not be sustained from one case officer to another. But turning over a source to a new case officer required intimate knowledge of an agent's personal biography. "At the end of our twenty-two weeks," recalled one JOT, "we were either to turn the agents over to a new case officer or establish with them a re-contact procedure. None of the cases came to a resolution, and this, too, was an excellent early taste of what our professional lives, for the most part, were to be like. Very seldom was a clandestine activity ever to come to a neat, orderly, successful and satisfactory conclusion."

Ames did very well on his live problem scenario, scoring the highest grade in his group of forty-six Operations Course-II JOTs. He won a reputation for a cool demeanor combined with a low-key, common-sensical approach to problem solving.

He also gained a degree of notoriety during one of the Farm's night-time exercises. At dusk one evening, all forty-six trainees were given a flashlight and a compass and told that they needed to navigate their way through several miles of wooded fields. To make sure that no one cheated by walking on the roads instead of cutting through the woods, they were told that Agency guards in jeeps would be patrolling the roads, armed with pistols and submachine guns loaded with blanks. The trainees boarded a school bus to take them to a drop-off point in the forest. But along the way, someone proposed that they turn the tables on the instructors. Instead of walking through the woods, everyone agreed to ambush the armed guards, disarm them, and then use their jeeps to get to the target point. After months of grueling work, this would be their mock insurrection. As the bus bounced along to their destination, Ames remarked, quite loudly, "My strength is as the strength of ten because my heart is pure." It was very uncharacteristic of him to say something so boastful. But everyone was exhibiting high spirits, and as each trainee was dropped off every fifty yards near the woods, they shouted out some epithet. "*Abajo* [Down with] Fidel," exclaimed one trainee. An Irishman called out, "Erin go bragh!" But when it was Ames's turn, he cried out in French, "*Vive le soixante-neuf*"—in celebration of the joys of a certain oral sexual practice. "It was so un-Ames-like," recalled one of his friends, "that all of us on the bus simply broke up in laughter."

The "insurrection" went according to plan. Most of the men went off individually through the woods as they'd been instructed. But a smaller group, including Ames, ambushed a jeep. One trainee lay down in the road as a jeep approached and feigned injury. The jeep stopped and a guard got out to see what was wrong, leaving his machine gun in the jeep. Three trainees then jumped the driver from behind, got him in a choke hold, and disarmed him. The other guard was wrestled to the ground and made a prisoner. Several more jeeps were similarly ambushed and captured. A few hours later, Ames and the other insurrectionists triumphantly arrived at the target point, armed and in possession of both jeeps and their prisoners.

Those involved had hoped to be congratulated on their operational planning and execution. But they were sadly mistaken. The Agency was a bureaucracy like any other, and while some of the instructors privately expressed praise for the audacity of their escapade, the Farm hierarchy was not amused. "We were roundly and soundly excoriated on the spot," recalled one of the mutineers. "This became the outstanding event in which we were reminded, not gently, that not only were we not yet officers, we were junior trainees."

Despite the reprimands, the story of what happened that night began to circulate through the corridors of Langley. Membership in Operations Course-11 became a badge of honor, particularly among those involved in the planning and conduct of clandestine operations.

Though Ames's graduation ceremony may have been subdued, in the end, the "insurrection" didn't hurt his career.

After graduating from the Farm all trainees had the option to volunteer for additional paramilitary training at the Jungle Warfare Training Center at Fort Sherman in Panama's Canal Zone. Not everyone in Ames's class volunteered, but Ames did. The "Jungle Operations Course" included further weapons training and jump training. The latter required a minimum of five parachute jumps from an Agency C-47. The final exam, as such, required a three-day solo exercise in which the trainees were flown into a Panamanian jungle, given a knife and a compass, and told they had to find their way out on their own. It was a very demanding exercise, but Ames passed with flying colors. He had his last parachute jump in October and graduated on November 22, 1961.

Most of Ames's classmates were assigned to work in the Soviet Union or Western Europe. Some of the men had already gone through Russian-language training in the army. The Soviet Union, of course, was the Agency's primary target for the collection of intelligence and the recruitment of agents. But early on Ames advertised his interest in the Middle East. Everyone knew that he'd already begun to study Arabic and that he wanted to learn more. It was a natural fit, and he had no problem being assigned to the Near East Division, which was then headed by James H. Critchfield (1917–2003), a legendary CIA officer who was known as one of the Agency's powerful "Barons." Critchfield once described the CIA's operations in the Middle East during the 1950s as "the cowboy era." He was determined to end that swashbuckling culture and bring a greater degree of knowledge and sophistication to the Agency's activities in the region.* In the wake of World War II, Americans had remarkably little professional knowledge or

---

* Critchfield gave CIA support to the 1963 coup that killed Iraq's president, General Abdul Karim Kassem, and brought the Ba'ath Party to power. This paved the way for Saddam Hussein's rise to power five years later.

experience in the Arab world. Duane R. Clarridge, a veteran CIA clandestine officer who later became one of Ames's bosses, observed that
Washington "was terribly dependent on the missionaries and the oil
crowd for first hand knowledge."

The Agency's Middle East operatives in the 1950s and early 1960s
were men with large, outsized personalities. Though they were supposed to be clandestine officers, many created public personas. Men
like Archie Roosevelt (and his cousin Kermit Roosevelt), Miles Copeland, Wilbur Crane Eveland, and James Russell Barracks spent many
years wandering through the back alleys of Beirut, Damascus, Baghdad, and Cairo—yet they were known to the working press. Copeland
was once described by *Time* magazine correspondent Wilton Wynn as
"the only man who ever used the CIA for cover." Copeland thought
of intelligence as a sport, and he later wrote a book about his exploits
entitled *The Game of Nations: The Amorality of Power Politics.* Similarly,
Eveland more or less advertised his intelligence credentials and later
wrote his own book, *Ropes of Sand,* in which he described his involvement in bribing Syrian generals to stage coups. But in retrospect none
of these clandestine officers, who confidently posed as if they were
playing a virtual board game of Risk, were very good spies.

None of these men possessed a deep knowledge of the history
and culture of the Arab world, and most spent their careers helping
conservative military dictators and kings to maintain the status quo.
Moreover, few of these Middle East "experts" actually spoke any
Arabic—and the handful who did, such as Ray Close and his brother
Arthur, and William Eddy, were the sons of American missionaries
who'd learned the language as children.

By the time Ames joined the Near East Division in 1961, it was
thought to be an "elitist" arm of the Agency. Partly this was just because learning Arabic was hard and so only really dedicated officers
stuck it out. "People tended to go there and stay there," recalled Peter
Earnest, a veteran case officer who served in Europe and the Middle
East for twenty-five years. At the end of 1961, Ames was told that he
would soon receive an overseas posting. In the meantime, he studied

Arabic for six months. Then in the early summer of 1962 he was posted to Dhahran, Saudi Arabia. It was, to say the least, a hardship post. But Ames was pleased. He was all of twenty-eight years old.

■

When the CIA was established in 1947, fully one-third of its early recruits were veterans of the recently disbanded OSS. A preponderance of these OSS men were upper-class gentlemen, graduates of Ivy League schools like Yale and Harvard, and many had some experience on Wall Street—or their fathers came from Wall Street. The former head of the OSS, William "Wild Bill" Donovan, was himself a Wall Street lawyer, and he had recruited men with similar pedigrees into the wartime OSS. When Donovan and other leading lights of the early postwar American foreign-policy establishment, such as the ubiquitous Rockefeller family lawyer, John J. McCloy, finally succeeded in persuading President Harry S. Truman to form a civilian centralized intelligence agency, they naturally sought out young men who had similar backgrounds. The early CIA therefore was well populated with those having elite Establishment credentials—men like Allen Dulles, William Bundy, John Bross, Kermit Roosevelt, Desmond Fitzgerald, Tracy Barnes, Frank Wisner, Richard Bissell, and Mike Burke. All were gregarious extroverts who embraced the "Great Game" of intelligence with a fearless exuberance. Many were graduates of Groton, the elite preparatory school, and went on to get degrees from Yale, Harvard, or Princeton. (If they went to Yale, they invariably were tapped for Skull and Bones, one of the university's most exclusive secret societies.) They not only believed in America but confidently believed that they could work America's will abroad with the adroit use of cloak-and-dagger operations—and a little cash. And in the 1940s and 1950s they successfully toppled regimes in Guatemala and Iran with splashy covert operations.

These were not the kind of people Bob Ames had known growing up in Philadelphia. Not at all. He wasn't a blue blood, but he was smart and ambitious. And while he shied away from pretentiousness, he exuded some of the qualities valued by the Establishment. John McCloy, the son of a poor hairdresser, had also grown up in a working-class Philadelphia neighborhood (on Twentieth Street in North Philadelphia, just a block from where Ames's maternal grandfather lived). Like Ames, McCloy was a scholarship boy, but he went to Amherst College and then Harvard Law School. He'd risen in the ranks of the Establishment despite his origins. McCloy had a reputation for common sense; his clients were reassured by his ordinary reasonableness. Over time, he positively began to exude gravitas.

Bob Ames was not a John McCloy. He would never wield that kind of power. But he had some of the same down-to-earth qualities. And coincidentally, Ames's ranking CIA superior in 1962, Richard Helms, was another Philadelphia boy. There's no reason to believe that Helms had yet met this novice case officer, but Ames certainly knew of Helms. He knew Helms was his boss. An immediate consequence of the Bay of Pigs fiasco was that Richard Bissell—another Boston Brahmin—lost his job as deputy director of plans. Dick Helms replaced him in early 1962, becoming chief of the Agency's covert operations.

Helms had always made it clear that he was skeptical of paramilitary operations. Experience had taught him that the collection of secret intelligence was an all-important task—and that high-visibility covert-action operations were usually not conducive to that task. Helms had a cohesive philosophy about intelligence that would greatly influence young Bob Ames. In just a few years, he would become a mentor and friend who would shepherd Ames's rapid rise through the ranks of the Agency. Bob Ames would become one of Dick Helms's most promising protégés. "Helms and Ames were very much alike," recalled *Lindsay Sherwin*, a veteran intelligence officer. "Both were real gentlemen who valued a certain decorum. They were not soldiers of fortune like some of the guys in operations."

Dick Helms was an enigma to many who worked with him. His official pseudonym inside the Agency was "Fletcher M. KNIGHT." (Agency etiquette required the surname of any pseudonym to be capitalized so as to be identified as a pseudonym.) In some ways he was very much old school. He had a patrician, reticent demeanor. Unlike Ames, he came from a solid upper-middle-class family; he was very cosmopolitan. His father was a business executive with Alcoa. Born in 1913, Helms grew up in South Orange, New Jersey—but his parents sent him to boarding schools in Europe for two of his high school years. He spent one year at Le Rosey in Switzerland and another year at the Real gymnasium in Freiburg, Germany, where he learned fluent French and German. In 1935 he graduated from Williams College, a highly selective liberal arts college in Massachusetts. Thereafter he got a job in Germany working as a reporter for United Press International. At the age of twenty-three he covered the 1936 Summer Olympics, and that autumn he found himself with several other reporters in Nuremberg Castle interviewing Adolf Hitler.

After two years in Europe, Helms returned to America harboring the ambition to someday own a newspaper. To that end, he got a job as the national advertising manager for the *Indianapolis Times*. Just as he was getting to know the business side of running a newspaper, Japan attacked Pearl Harbor. Helms quickly joined the navy—but a year later he was recruited into the OSS. He was given paramilitary training on an OSS farm in Maryland. It was very similar to what Ames later experienced at the CIA's Farm: hand-to-hand combat, weapons training, and intelligence tradecraft. Like Ames, he was a tall, physically fit young man. But over the course of the war he was to learn that much of what he'd been taught was irrelevant to the actual business of espionage. He would never have to fire a gun in combat or use a knife on an adversary. As his biographer Thomas Powers later wrote in *The Man Who Kept the Secrets*, "From the outside, espionage and covert action may seem all of a piece, but in fact they proceed in a quite different spirit. Paramilitary teams or covert political operatives necessarily draw attention to the people they support, if not always to themselves. . . . But espionage, properly conducted, never announces itself. 'Stolen' information remains in its accustomed place; the 'spy' is a trusted civil servant; the spymaster betrays no sign of special knowledge."

Helms learned this from hard experience running OSS operations from Scandinavia, trying to glean information from agents who had contacts in wartime Germany. These weren't covert "actions" but the careful parceling together of bits of information bought or solicited from businessmen, journalists, and low-level civil servants. Talking was what mattered.

Powers wrote of Helms, "Friends said he carried away two abiding impressions: that secret intelligence matters, and that paramilitary derring-do doesn't." Human beings, not machines, could steal secret documents. But even government documents are sometimes just pieces of paper. "Just because a document is a document," wrote the legendary Soviet spy Kim Philby, "it has a glamour which tempts the reader to give it more weight than it deserves. . . . An hour's serious discussion with a trustworthy informant is often more valuable than any number of original documents." Philby hastened to add, "Of course, it is best to have both." But if human intelligence was essential, it required the simple art of conversation—and that could be a most complicated skill.

After the war, Helms briefly tried to return to the newspaper business, but he soon realized that he'd never have the money necessary to own a paper. He needed a job, so when the CIA was created in 1947, he became a ranking officer in the Office of Special Operations. At the age of thirty-three, he was running agents in Germany, Austria, and Switzerland. Throughout the early Cold War, Helms fought a bureaucratic battle inside the Agency, arguing for the primacy of espionage and quiet intelligence gathering over the splashy pyrotechnical covert operations run by Frank Wisner's team.

Helms was a political moderate, a Cold War anticommunist—but certainly no ideologue. He was cool and opaque, and an astute and pragmatic bureaucratic player. When asked one day, "Just what are the prerogatives of a chief of station?" Helms gave the enigmatic reply, "To do the best job he can unless and until recalled for cause." He avoided making arguments that delved into what he called "the soggy mass of morality." On those rare occasions when someone in the room suggested assassinating an errant agent, Helms always dissented. Violence, he said, was usually impractical, ineffective, and costly. Lethal covert operations usually got into the newspapers, thus drawing attention to the Agency. This, he thought, made the Agency's job of collecting secrets much harder. On the other hand, Helms knew he was working in a dirty business. He liked to say, "We're not in the Boy Scouts. If we'd wanted to be in the Boy Scouts we'd have joined the Boy Scouts." He participated in the planning of scores of covert ops— but he was invariably the one man in the room who asked the hard questions that compelled his colleagues to scale the operation back, to make it more cautious, less visible, and more subtle in its execution. For some in the room, he was always an irritant.

He lost many bureaucratic battles in the 1950s, and his career was often sidetracked. It was impossible, for instance, to discount the sheer volume of raw intelligence produced by Richard Bissell's high-altitude U-2 spy planes. The photos of Soviet military installations were invaluable. "Our best Russian agents, [Pyotr] Popov and [Oleg] Penkovsky," said Helms, "suddenly seemed pale and inadequate." And so Helms was not terribly surprised when Allen Dulles passed him over for the job of deputy director for plans in the autumn of 1958 and gave the job to Bissell. As Helms later explained it, "The collectors with technical gadgets began to disparage the efforts of the human collectors. The new cry from the gadgeteers was, 'Give us the money and leave it to us.' And indeed, why take risks running spies when gadgets would tell you what you wanted to know? But therein lay a fallacy. . . . Gadgets cannot divine a man's intentions." He knew the pendulum would swing back.

The Bay of Pigs was a turning point. After that debacle, Helms's priorities became the Agency's priorities—at least for the next two decades, until the pendulum once again swung away from human intelligence (HUMINT) and back toward expensive high-tech intercept intelligence and paramilitary covert ops under the administration of President Ronald Reagan and his CIA director, William Casey.

CHAPTER THREE

Arabia

He was one of the best spooks I ever met.

—*David Long, State Department Bureau*
of Intelligence and Research

I n 1962, the year that Bob Ames undertook his first assignment abroad as a CIA case officer, the Agency's culture was gradually shifting to one that put a high value on the kind of officers who could develop human sources. It was that part of the Agency's culture that valued bland anonymity, discretion, and ironclad secrecy. A case officer had to have patience and restraint; one couldn't hurry the cultivation of a source. One had to be methodical, keeping a minute record of what was said and what went unspoken during each encounter with a potential agent. A good case officer had to have commonsensical powers of observation. Ames was a natural.

"Bob was a very complex person," recalled David Long, a State Department intelligence analyst who met him in the 1960s in Jeddah, Saudi Arabia. "He was self-effacing and not afraid to speak up, a cynic and an idealist, a good old boy and an intellectual, a moralist and a problem solver. Put it together and he was one of the best spooks I ever met." *Harry Simpson*, a senior CIA officer who knew Ames at the time, thought he had a "magnetic" personality. "He was able to show empathy to just about anyone—if it was in his interest to do so," said *Simpson*. "It didn't hurt that he was a physically imposing human being."

Bob, Yvonne, and baby Catherine flew into Dhahran, Saudi Arabia, early in the summer of 1962. As they stepped out of the plane, they felt the sting of hot, humid winds on their faces. With temperatures hovering at 120 degrees Fahrenheit in the summer, it was an Arabian oven. They were driven four miles to the U.S. consulate compound. This fifty-five-acre facility had been built in 1947–51 at a cost of $600,000. It contained the consulate offices, the consul general's two-story residence, and about a dozen other block stone homes. The compound had its own electric generator, water tower, and septic tank. A four-foot rock wall surrounded the compound, purportedly to keep out the camels and goats of nomadic Bedouins who sometimes pitched their black tents nearby. A squad of five U.S. marines guarded the outpost. Altogether, the compound housed about thirty-five Americans, including eight Foreign Service officers, secretaries, code clerks, and their families.

Bob Ames was one of only two CIA officers; his boss was Robert Carlson, who'd previously served in Damascus and Beirut. Dhahran was such a small post that the CIA deemed it a "base," not a "station." Carlson's title was chief of base (COB). The Agency's station at the time was located in the port city of Jeddah because the Saudis refused to allow any foreign legation to situate an embassy in the capital of Riyadh. That city lay in the heart of the Nedj, the Saudi royal family's homeland, dominated by the most conservative Wahhabi tribes. The Saudis would not allow foreigners to reside there until the 1970s.

In Dhahran, Ames was listed in the consulate phone directory as the commercial officer. This was his official cover. Carlson was identified as a "consul-political officer." (A year or so later, Carlson was replaced by Harold M. Young Jr.) Their job in the Dhahran Base was to collect political intelligence about both Saudi Arabia and the Trucial Coast emirates—the present-day United Arab Emirates. But the larger purpose, of course, was to provide intelligence on anything that might affect America's access to Arabian oil and its special relationship with the House of Saud. Like all CIA officers, Ames was assigned a pseudonym to sign reporting cables he sent back to Langley. For the rest of his career he would be known in writing as Orrin W. BIEDENKOPF. Agency officers sometimes even used their pseudonyms to refer to each

other orally—but Ames's Germanic pseudo was a mouthful, so over
the years some of his colleagues informally referred to him as RAMES
instead of BIEDENKOPF. But everyone soon came to recognize the
author of a cable signed by BIEDENKOPF. The communications were
always snappy, tart, and well informed.

The CIA's cramped quarters in Dhahran were located at the opposite end of the building from the consul general's office. There was
no special cage or even a locked door. The base's secretary was a vivacious Lebanese American woman in her midforties named Martha
Scherrer. Her desk was next to Ames's. There was barely enough room
between them for Bob to squeeze by. Carlson, a former marine who'd
seen combat service, had his own office next door with dark, rough-
hewn stone walls. It wasn't a very pleasant work environment, but neither Ames nor Carlson spent much time inside the office.

Dhahran was even more isolating than what Ames had experienced
at Kagnew Station. But in terms of his career, he was fortunate in his
first tour abroad to be able to work directly under one other officer.
In such a tiny base he received close supervision, and he was exposed
to all facets of the work. If Ames had been sent to a large station,
he would have been forced to specialize and would have received less
hands-on experience. Headquarters sometimes singles out a junior officer as particularly bright and "fast-tracks" him by sending him to a
small Agency base. This may have been true for Ames. In any case,
Ames would call Dhahran home for nearly four years.

Bob and his family lived at house number 8, a small, three-bedroom
stone-block structure with a glassed-in front porch. As it happened,
I lived across the street. My father was a Foreign Service officer also
stationed in Dhahran, so Bob and Yvonne were our neighbors for three
years when I was eleven, twelve, and thirteen. I just remember him as
a tall, handsome man who had a very pretty young wife and baby. I had
no idea he was a CIA officer.

Their house, like ours, was furnished with worn, ten-year-old fur-
niture and a tiny refrigerator and a propane gas stove. There were no

locks on the doors because the consulate's administrative officer said there was no crime in Arabia. Many years later I wrote about Arabia in a memoir and described the compound:

> All we could see for miles was flat desert interspersed with the occasional *jebel* (hill) and a bit of scrubby vegetation. The only greenery in the compound was a few scrawny eucalyptus trees and two dozen baby Washington palm trees, planted the previous year, that lined the one paved road up the hill from the Consulate to the consul general's residence. A solitary thirty-foot date palm—resembling the Saudi national emblem—stood in the circular driveway in front of that residence. Scattered about the compound were a few bougainvillea bushes that added a touch of color in the winter months—the only time it ever rained. Gas flares burned night and day in the surrounding *jebels*. The distinctive whiff of sulfur was often in the air.

Dhahran was a true "hardship" post. The only justification for the consulate's existence lay one mile down the road. The "American Camp" housed some six thousand American oil workers inside a one-square-mile compound surrounded by a chain-link fence. Inside was a slice of Texas. It looked like a typical American suburb, with brownish-green lawns and neat ranch-style homes with pitched roofs and screened porches. It contained a school, a commissary, swimming pools, a movie theater, a bowling alley, and a baseball field on "King's Road." When Mary Eddy, the wife of the veteran OSS and CIA officer Bill Eddy, first saw the American Camp, she wrote home, "The oil town at Dhaharan [*sic*] is just like a bit of USA."

This was the home of the Arabian American Oil Company (Aramco), a consortium of four American oil companies. Oil had first been discovered in March 1938 at Jebal ("Hill") Dhahran. A quarter century and millions of barrels later, oil wellhead Dammam No. 7 was still producing over a thousand barrels of oil per day. By the 1960s,

Aramco was selling millions of barrels of oil daily for the European and American markets.

The Aramcons pretty much kept to themselves. Bob thought they lived an unduly insular life in the American Camp. When President Kennedy was assassinated, he was shocked when he ran into an Aramcon who offered him "condolences for *your* president." They'd learned of the tragedy in the middle of the night, Dhahran time. Yvonne went back to bed, but Bob couldn't sleep; he spent the rest of the night pacing the house. Yvonne had few friends other than the half-dozen or so other wives on the consulate compound. She didn't mind Dhahran; her life was Bob, baby Catherine, and the house.

Bob absolutely loved Arabia. On some muggy evenings he would walk out to the basketball court across the street and shoot baskets with the consulate's marine guards. During the winter of 1963 he led the consulate's basketball team, the Dhahran Bears, to a championship win against all the Aramcon teams. He worked on his Arabic, taking private lessons. During long road trips with a young vice-consul, Ralph Oman, he talked about his fascination with the Bedouin tribes. "He said that he had plotted out a career path," Oman recalled, "that would keep him on the Arabian Peninsula for thirty years—at which point he would retire a happy man." Someday he hoped to have postings to Jeddah, Kuwait, Muscat, and Yemen. On one trip he and Oman spent a day searching for ancient pottery shards at the alleged site of the ancient city of Gerrha (ca. 650 B.C. to A.D. 300), near the bay of Dohat as Salwa, about fifty miles east of the oasis of Hofuf. They didn't find much worth taking home, but Oman vividly remembers how Ames gave him an impromptu lecture on the history of the region. He pointed out that they were standing on the very site where the Kingdom's founder, Ibn Saud, had signed the Uqair Protocol with the British. The 1922 treaty, he explained, had set the borders between the new Saudi kingdom and its neighbors to the north.

Oman remembers being amazed by Ames's grasp of the history. The young CIA officer obviously read a lot. "The Saudis loved him," Oman recalled. "He was terrific in one-on-one conversations. He was tall, handsome, respectful, and soft-spoken, with an engaging smile and a lively twinkle in his eyes. He had very broad shoulders that made him almost loom over the Saudi men he was talking to, and, as a rule, Saudi men are not short. He always addressed them with the honorific 'ya sheikh.' They always insisted that he was too kind." Early in his Dhahran posting, Ames persuaded one of Aramco's Saudi desert guides to teach him how to track herds of camels. These expeditions took him out into the desert and could be physically grueling. But for Ames, the reward was meeting the Bedu. "When the Arabs did not know him well," wrote one of his fellow Agency officers, "they held him in slight awe for his size. When they got to know him, they loved him for his humor, his Arabic, his knowledge of their ways, his heart."

During the month of Ramadan, the eight consulate officers were often invited on Thursday nights to a large dinner hosted by the governor of the Eastern Province, the crusty old emir Bin Jiluwi—whose father had fought side by side with the Kingdom's founder, Abdul Aziz ibn Saud, at the 1902 battle of Masmak Fort in Riyadh. Old Bin Jiluwi's spear was still stuck in the door of the fort, a stark reminder of this signature battle for the unification of Arabia under the House of Saud. Emir Bin Jiluwi ruled the Eastern Province with an executioner's sword; he was widely feared as "Head-Chopper Jiluwi." But at these Thursday evening affairs he usually made a point of serving Arabic coffee to the American diplomats in his private reception room before attending to his other guests.

"We entered the reception room in order of rank," recalled Oman. "Bob and I, both junior officers, would be last in line, with Bob second to last and me last. I always had to cool my heels for an extended period before shaking Bin Jiluwi's hand, because the emir would always grab both of Bob's hands and have an extended conversation with him, which they both enjoyed, talking about the camel crop in the Eastern Province, and the date harvest in al-Hasa."

After coffee, the Americans filed into a great hall where dinner was being served to more than a hundred guests. Each diplomat sat at a different low-lying, circular table that seated twelve men. In the center was a four-foot-wide platter with a huge mound of rice mixed with dates and raisins, surmounted by a whole roasted goat or sheep. "Among the Saudis," said Oman, "Bob was a sought-after table companion, because he spoke perfect Arabic, he could tell jokes, he loved the food (which was delicious), he could eat deftly with his hand and a knife, and he seemed to really enjoy himself with the food and the good company."

On rare occasions, Yvonne and Bob would invite a few people to dinner. They did not like large mob-scene parties. "The house was small, and Bob was big," recalled Oman, "so he seemed to dominate the room more than ever, but in a very nice way. He was an attentive and charming host, welcoming us to his home. Thinking back, he was a gracious Bedouin, welcoming strangers into his tent, treating them with traditional Arab hospitality, and making them feel very special. No wonder he was so good at what he did."

Ames didn't spend much time socializing with other Americans, particularly the Aramcons in the American Camp down the road. He was a case officer, and as such his job was to cultivate Saudi contacts. The one exception was an Aramcon who worked in the oil company's Government Relations Department. Ronald Irwin Metz was himself a veteran of the OSS and the CIA. A tall, ruddy, gregarious man with a hearty laugh, Metz had a colorful résumé. During World War II the OSS had parachuted him behind enemy lines in China. By the end of the war he spoke fluent Mandarin. Like many OSS veterans, he soon went to work for the CIA, which sent him for Arabic language studies at the American University of Beirut. Upon graduation with a master's degree in Middle Eastern studies in 1954, he was hired by Aramco and dispatched to Riyadh as the company's key liaison with King Saud, the eldest son of the Kingdom's founder. (Abdul Aziz ibn Saud had died the previous year.) Metz thus had unusual access to the Saudi royal family. By the mid-1950s, he was one of the king's drinking companions and quite possibly his closest foreign confidant. When Ron visited the royal palace the king would greet him in his audience chamber. Servants would bring trays of sweet black tea. After a few moments,

Saud would curtly dismiss the servants, toss the tea, and pull out a bottle of scotch.

It was Washington's policy then, as now, to support the Saudi royal family, if only to safeguard American access to Saudi oil. Metz's relationship with King Saud was thus a useful conduit for conveying political intelligence about what was going on inside the palace and the Kingdom as a whole. Metz tutored Ames in the intricacies of Arabian tribal politics and no doubt helped to polish his Arabic. They had an easygoing and fruitful relationship. After hanging around Metz, Ames could talk at length about the intricacies of palace politics and, in particular, the power struggle that was then taking place between King Saud and his half-brother Crown Prince Faisal al-Saud.

Ames spent a lot of time just wandering the desert in his jeep. He loved to stop at Bedouin encampments and strike up a conversation with the tribesmen. He later told a fellow officer, Henry Miller-Jones, that he was sometimes invited to honorific dinners that took place inside the Bedouins' black tents. Sitting on layers of Persian carpets, he would eat lamb roasted over an open fire. Inevitably, as the guest of honor he'd be offered the tastiest morsel of the lamb, its eye. Bob said he hated eating the eye.

"Ames' interest in the Bedu was not just cultural education," said Miller-Jones. "He was seeking contacts among them who would be sources of information on the growing Arab nationalist movement and other subversive elements. He educated me on the threat to the Saudi government posed by the Shi'a of the Eastern Province, and the Shi'a relationship to Iran. Bob always considered it a minor but not insignificant concern, but one the hyper-Sunni Saudis fretted over inordinately. At that time, he was more concerned about Arab Nationalism, and growing Soviet inroads among some of the Arab intelligentsia in the Arabian Peninsula in general."

One day in late 1964 the consul general in Dhahran, Jack Horner, called Ames into his office along with a brand-new vice-consul, twenty-two-year-old Patrick Theros. Horner explained that he'd received an invitation from the Emir Saud bin Jiluwi to attend a head chopping.

Horner said he wasn't in the mood to attend an execution, but he wanted Ames and Theros to go in his place. "Bob thought it would be an excellent opportunity to develop some local contacts," recalled Theros. "He was very matter-of-fact about it." On the appointed day the two men drove nine miles north to Dammam's central square, where a large crowd had gathered for the spectacle. Bearing rifles, members of the feared Saudi National Guard lined the square. The condemned prisoner was soon escorted into the square. He was an alleged pederast who'd been convicted of raping and murdering a small boy from a notable family. The families of both the murder victim and the murderer were present in large numbers. Emotions were high because of the notoriety of the crime. The Emir Bin Jiluwi himself was presiding over the event. Breaking with tradition, Jiluwi announced that he would allow the eldest brother of the murdered boy to carry out the beheading. As Ames and Theros watched from the back of the crowd, the executioner's sword was handed to the brother. Instead of taking aim at the neck, the brother swung the sword and brought it down on the condemned man's back, severely wounding him. He had deliberately botched the execution. Angry cries erupted from the members of the wounded man's family—and the National Guard troops began to finger their rifles. At this point, Ames calmly turned to Theros and said, "I think we should leave." They turned and walked quickly up an alley away from the square. A moment later, they heard a single shot. A National Guard officer had stepped forward and killed the wounded murderer with a shot to the head. Theros remembers how unemotional and nonjudgmental Ames was in the wake of witnessing such a grisly event. Bob was cool. This was just the way justice was handed out in Arabia.

Theros saw a lot of Ames during his stint in Dhahran. Saudi Arabia was Theros's first posting abroad as a newly minted Foreign Service officer. He knew Ames was CIA because that was how he'd been in-

troduced at the consulate's weekly country team meetings. It was a
very small post and everyone knew everyone else's brief. Theros was
stamping visas. But Theros and Ames were the only two consulate officers who regularly traveled to Bahrain and the Trucial sheikhdoms to
the south. Ames flew to Bahrain frequently to liaise with his counterparts in British intelligence. So sometimes he and Theros flew together.
It regularly fell to Theros, as a lowly vice-consul, to make the run to
Bahrain, where he would buy a suitcase full of Ballantine whiskey and
smuggle it into "dry" Saudi Arabia. The Saudi authorities at Dhahran airport knew full well that Theros was bringing in the consulate's
monthly stash of booze, but they'd been instructed to ignore this diplomatic smuggling.

In the summer of 1965, Theros was asked to make another booze
run to Bahrain and bring back an extra-large shipment of Ballantine
for the consulate's Fourth of July party. After the landing in Dhahran,
a Saudi porter picked up the heavy bag before Theros could grab it—
and the porter promptly dropped it. The sound of broken glass echoed
through the terminal, and the whiff of alcohol left no doubt about what
had happened. Theros was told to leave the bag and return late that
night when the terminal would be largely empty. Theros was only five
feet eight inches tall and weighed a mere 165 pounds. Thinking he could
use someone with more brawn, he persuaded Ames to assist him. They
arrived at about 10:00 P.M. and found the suspicious bag hidden away
in a storage room. "Bob was a muscular fellow and weighed over two
hundred pounds," recalled Theros. "So he grabbed the bag and swung
it over his shoulder—and then suddenly dropped it. He had thrown his
back out. I'm afraid this was the source of his persistent back pain in
the years to come."

Despite this unfortunate injury, Ames and Theros became good
friends. "Bob tended to see humor in every situation—however bad,"
Theros recalled. Bob and Yvonne didn't socialize much in their home,
which was rapidly becoming a nursery. On June 13, 1963, Yvonne gave
birth to a new baby girl, Adrienne. She was born in the local hospital in Al-Khobar, a very rudimentary town a few miles away from

the consulate compound. And just a year later, Yvonne was pregnant again. Kristen was born in Al-Khobar on February 6, 1965. So now there were three baby girls in house number 8. There was little time for dinner parties. "But Yvonne decided that I was one more child to feed," Theros said. "So I came by pretty often for dinner and sometimes I baby-sat the girls. Bob and Yvonne—well, it was as tight a family as I had ever seen."

In the summer of 1966, Bob and Yvonne packed up their household goods in Dhahran and shipped them off to Beirut, where Bob was slotted for a full year of intensive Arabic language training. Meanwhile, Aramco told Ames he had a standing offer to join the oil company; he would have made a lot more money, but he turned them down. He liked being a CIA case officer; he thought of it as public service. That summer he and Yvonne went on home leave to Philadelphia and Boston to see their parents and other relatives. By September they were settled into a lovely apartment in West Beirut, two blocks from the seaside corniche and within walking distance of Pigeon Rock Bay, one of Ras Beirut's iconic landmarks. Ras Beirut was the most cosmopolitan part of the city, home to a multicultural population of middle-class Christians, Druze, and Muslims. In 1966, there were still several thousand Jewish Lebanese. It was also home to the American University of Beirut, founded a century earlier. And it boasted chic boutiques, cafés, and cinemas showing films in French, English, and Arabic. Bob studied Arabic during the week, but on weekends he and Yvonne often took the kids up to the Dhalamayeh Country Club in the mountains to the east of Beirut. When they couldn't get away, Bob contented himself with reading the many books on Middle Eastern history and biography that he bought cheaply from Khayyat's, Beirut's oldest bookstore, located near the university on Rue Bliss.

Soon after his arrival in Beirut, one of Bob's colleagues took him to the bar at the St. George Hotel. It was inevitable. The St. George was

Beirut's premier hotel in the 1950s and 1960s and well into the 1970s. It was where visiting dignitaries stayed, and its famous bar was the watering hole for two generations of diplomats, journalists, and the agents of various intelligence services. Surrounded by the Mediterranean Sea on three sides, the St. George offered its clientele a beautiful view of both the sea and the snow-capped mountains to the east. It employed 285 staff to service only 110 rooms. "I felt as if my clients were running the Middle East, occasionally the world," said Jean Bertolet, the hotel's manager in the 1960s. Bankers and financiers such as John J. McCloy, J. Paul Getty, and Daniel Ludwig stayed at the St. George on their business trips to Beirut. Journalists like Joe Alsop and NBC's John Chancellor were regular visitors. The legendary British spy for the Soviet Union, Kim Philby, drank his gin and tonics at the St. George— until he fled to Moscow on January 23, 1963. Philby later wrote in his memoir, "Beirut is one of the liveliest centres of contraband and espionage in the world." He loved the city. "It was an amazing listening post," recalled the London *Daily Mail*'s Anthony Cave Brown. "Everything and everyone passed through it." Like many foreign correspondents, *Newsweek*'s Loren Jenkins used the bar as his "mail drop."

The St. George's longtime concierge was Mansour Breidy, a Maronite Christian. "He knew everyone," said Jenkins. Around noon each day Lebanon's most connected journalist, Mohammed Khalil Abu Rish—more commonly known as Abu Said—arrived to cultivate his sources over lunch. Abu Said had once worked for the *New York Times*, but by 1966 he was working for *Time* magazine. Abu Said knew just about everyone connected to this exotic labyrinth, including the CIA station chief and the Egyptian intelligence chief. It was an era when a reporter like Abu Said discreetly traded information with various intelligence services and in return was given useful nuggets for his reports in *Time*. Over the years, rumors dogged him that he was an agent for the CIA. He always firmly denied this. Certainly, he was openly pro-American and gladly passed along his observations to the CIA. "It was clear to me that Abu Said had never been anybody's agent," wrote

Wilbur Crane Eveland, a CIA operative in the Middle East in the 1950s. "He happened to believe that Americans were friends of the Arabs."*

Abu Said's grown son Said Aburish was then a reporter for Radio Free Europe, and later the author of many revealing history books about the region. In 1989, he wrote a book about the St. George: "For those of us lucky enough to have known the St. George Hotel bar in the fifties, sixties and seventies, life will never be the same again; the bar will always be with us, an invisible, hallowed component of our existence which we celebrate wherever we may be."

But though Bob Ames certainly knew some of these St. George bar regulars, he was not one of them himself. Aburish never met him. Ames was studying Arabic in 1966, not cultivating agents. But neither was he a barfly. He preferred to spend his free time either practicing his Arabic in the *suq* or doting on his girls.

---

* Many years later, however, a retired CIA officer claimed that Archie Roosevelt had recruited Abu Said as an agent in the late 1940s. This source said that Abu Said was assigned the cryptonym PENTAD. This was corroborated in 2010 when Abu Said's son Said Aburish confided to the Norwegian journalist Karsten Tveit that his father had confessed to him that he had indeed been an agent of the CIA.

CHAPTER FOUR

Aden and Beirut

He didn't share secrets, so that made life normal.

—*Yvonne Ames*

By the spring of 1967, Ames was told he was scheduled for a posting in Sana'a, North Yemen. As Yemen was still embroiled in a brutal civil war, it was unlikely that Yvonne and the children would be allowed to move with him. But then yet another Arab-Israeli war broke out, on June 5, 1967. A month prior to the war, as tensions escalated, the Israelis sent an intelligence estimate to the Johnson administration warning that they could be defeated. Within six hours the CIA's top analysts produced a counterestimate that predicted, "Israel could defeat within two weeks any combination of Arab armies which could be thrown against it no matter who began the hostilities." Dick Helms thought the Israelis were just trying to get President Johnson to green-light a preemptive attack—and authorize American arms shipments. When a skeptical President Johnson asked Helms to review the estimate—or, in his words, to have it "scrubbed down"—the Agency analysts revised their prediction: the Israelis would win any war within one week. As it happened, the Agency's estimate was off by only one day. Within six days Israeli forces swept into East Jerusalem and occupied both the West Bank and the entire Sinai Peninsula.

The June War was a defeat for the entire Arab world—but specifically for Gamal Abdel Nasser's brand of secular Arab nationalism. It was a humiliation that disillusioned an entire generation of Arabs. But it also circumscribed American influence in the Middle East. In its aftermath, twenty-four thousand American expatriates working in the region were expelled. Anti-American demonstrations swept through Cairo, Damascus, and Beirut. Egypt and most other Arab states broke diplomatic relations with Washington. Ames's posting to North Yemen was canceled, and instead he was posted to Aden in the British protectorate of South Yemen.

Yvonne was already pregnant again. That summer Bob had completed nine months of intensive Arabic language study. The family spent much of that summer in Washington and Boston—where baby Karen was born on August 30, 1967. Bob came up to Boston from Washington, D.C., to see his new baby—their fourth child. And then in early September he flew off to Aden. Yvonne and the girls weren't permitted to join him. And for good reason. Aden was a war zone.

Before heading off to Aden, Ames was required to take a routine polygraph. He thought it a waste of time. He told the technician administering the test, "Why don't you ask me the one question that matters: Have I had an illicit contact with a foreign agent? And then we can be done with this." The technician was not amused.

Ames flew to London in late September and had a couple of nights in the Cumberland Hotel near Hyde Park. He chose this hotel because he knew it was within walking distance of Francis Edwards, an antiquarian bookseller dating back to 1855. He found many books he wanted to buy, but he wrote Yvonne that he had "no honey to convince me that I should buy them." He later regretted this. "When I think of all the good maps in them I get mad at myself, but that's me. Mr. Indecision." Bob was instinctively too careful with his money.

On the evening of Monday, October 2, 1967, he flew to Tripoli and then Nairobi, finally landing in Aden at 9:15 A.M. Bob was startled to see that as his plane rolled to a stop it was quickly surrounded by British troops with rifles cocked. A helicopter hovered overhead, providing additional security. Armed with a green diplomatic passport, he walked rapidly through customs, to be greeted outside by Consul General William Eagleton and another Foreign Service officer. As they exited the airport, they drove past a sandbagged machine-gun nest manned by two British Tommies wearing their trademark berets. "Everywhere you look there are soldiers with guns," Bob wrote home. "Kind of creepy." The streets were mostly deserted and plastered with political graffiti. Aden had been built on forbidding volcanic rocks. Its paint-flecked, fortresslike houses now were pockmarked with bullets. Ames could see, off in the distance, the blue and turquoise waters of the harbor. He and his companions drove directly to the waterfront offices of the U.S. consulate general in Tawahi, just down the street from the Aden Port Trust. There, Bob was introduced to Arthur Marsh Niner, the Agency's chief of station. Niner was the product of an East Coast prep school. He wore casual wrinkled seersucker suits and Brooks Brothers shirts and ties. He'd married a pretty German woman just before arriving in Aden. His cover in the consulate was as a political officer. Ames's cover would be as a commercial officer. He was one of only seven officers in the tiny post.

A few weeks after Ames arrived in Aden, *Dick Roane*, another junior CIA officer, was walking back to his apartment when he noticed that he was being closely followed. Fearing a kidnapping or worse, he hastily made it to his apartment gate and locked the door. The following day Niner issued 9mm Browning automatic pistols to everyone in the station. Ames decided not to walk around with a gun. "If they get you here," he wrote Yvonne, "it is in the back or when you're not looking, and a gun wouldn't do much good."

On October 14, 1967, Ames witnessed his first full-fledged street battle. It was the fourth anniversary of the National Liberation Front's uprising against the British; a general strike was declared, and then at about 9:30 A.M. Ames heard machine-gun fire. He looked out his office window and saw British troops running for cover. "I saw one Brit get wounded about a block and a half away and the firing was so fierce that it was about five minutes before his buddies could get him."

The Brits had to bring in armored cars to suppress the firing. When it was over several hours later, one Arab had been killed and four British soldiers were wounded.

A few days later a visiting Danish sea captain walked out of the Port Trust building and headed past the U.S. consulate. Someone walked up quickly from behind him and shot him in the head, leaving him dead in the street. The Dane was the first nonmilitary, non-British civilian to be assassinated since the outbreak of the rebellion. A week or so later a senior British official from the Governor-General's Office was walking up the steps to the entrance of the Crescent Hotel when he was sprayed with machine-gun fire from a passing car. Grievously wounded, the man survived. In late October, Bob wrote, "The situation in Aden becomes worse each day." After these brazen attacks, life in Aden for any of the expatriates became much more restricted. Henry Miller-Jones recalled the extreme security precautions he had to take on his way to work in the consulate: "Each morning, Niner instructed me that I was to ensure my 9mm was loaded and I was to open the gate in the wall that surrounded our 4-story apartment building that faced out onto the main street running from Ma'alla to Tarshyn. While I was doing this, gun in hand, my roommates would drive the car from its parking space in front of the building behind me with the rear door open. As the car passed through the gate on my all clear signal, I would jump in the back seat, and off we went to the office, right around the block, no more than three minutes away." Miller-Jones had arrived in Aden a month after Ames. He was on a three-month temporary-duty assignment. Fresh off the Farm, he'd never been abroad to anywhere except Europe. "I was pure raw material for Ames's self-appointed mentoring," Miller-Jones recalled. "Niner was no help."

Aden was then in the middle of a three-way civil war. Southern Arabia was still a British protectorate. But British forces were fighting an insurgency waged by both the National Liberation Front (NLF) and the Front for the Liberation of Occupied South Yemen (FLOSY)— both of which were in turn engaged in a bloody struggle for power against each other. FLOSY was the guerrilla faction supported by Nasser's Egypt. The NLF was a more leftist organization, an offspring of the Arab Nationalist Movement (ANM). From his time in Dhahran, Ames was familiar with the ANM. But the NLF was an entirely different story. Some of their cadres had been trained in Moscow. In the last year, the NLF had taken to assassinating foreign civilians. Several British wives had been killed by sniper fire along Ma'alla Straight, where many of the British lived in new high-rises. This stretch of road became known as "Murder Mile." Rebels sometimes seized the rim of the Crater district, which gave them a bird's-eye view of the city from a thousand feet above. From there, they lobbed mortar or grenade rockets randomly into the city below. The Crater and its narrow, meandering streets in the Arab Quarter became a no-go zone for any foreigners.

In such circumstances, the colonial representatives of the fading British Empire were just hanging on, trying to negotiate an orderly transfer of power. The June 1967 War had closed the Suez Canal, making Aden's port of transit far less strategic to British maritime interests. That month the British evacuated most official families, and Governor-General Sir Humphrey Trevelyan announced that he intended to pull out all British forces entirely by January 1968.

Thus, by the time Ames arrived, much of the European Quarter was deserted. Within a week of his arrival, Bob reserved a furnished three-bedroom house in the Khormaksar neighborhood. It had a lovely view of the Arabian Sea and came with a large roof deck equipped with an outdoor grill and bar. Quarters for two servants were located above the detached garage. But until Yvonne and the kids arrived, it didn't make sense to move into a large house. For the first month, Bob had a hotel room in the Rock, a modern high-rise with a glassed-in rooftop restaurant. He found it to be pretty confining and lonely. The Rock was also Aden's best-known watering hole; Niner and the rest of the station spent a lot of time in the Rock. But not Ames. "It's a good thing," Bob wrote Yvonne, "I'm not a drinker because that seems to be the favorite pastime." He preferred root beer and a bowl of pretzels. He was still smoking a pipe, however, and in Aden he discovered a forbidden pleasure—Havana cigars. "I bet you'd like to be sitting in my office now," he teased Yvonne in a letter. "I'm smoking a big smelly Cuban cigar!"

Later that autumn, he and *Dick Roane*, who became Bob's best friend in Aden, decided to share a small flat near the consulate. *Roane* was a bachelor. "He won't have to worry about my cramping his style—there are just no girls here," Bob wrote to Yvonne, and, in another letter, "Except for the aura of terrorism that now exists, I think I'd like Aden, and I'm sure you would. There are nice beaches and plenty of clubs and things to do—that is, in normal times." Aden had evolved over the past century as a coaling station for freighters and tour ships passing through the Suez Canal on their way to or from India. The European Quarter of the city was relatively clean, and the city had the usual colonial amenities, including the British-run Gold Mohur Beach Club at Steamer Point, a duty-free market in the port area, and several good bars and hotels.

"Bob wasn't the kind of guy to go out drinking with the boys," recalled one colleague. "He could be brusque and he didn't suffer fools." Ames and Niner didn't get along. The chief of station "could be very imperious." Niner was Germanic—like his German wife. He was a stickler for regulations. The chemistry between the two men was sour. They had what one case officer called an "ugly relationship."

But Bob didn't care what his station chief thought, and he made no effort to cultivate Niner. Instead of hanging out at the Rock drinking, Bob spent his time reading and wandering the *suq*. On a typical day, he'd get into the office at 7:30 A.M., do some paperwork for two hours, and then walk to the *suq*, where he'd sit and chat with the merchants for several hours. "Most of them are quite friendly," he wrote Yvonne, "when they learn I'm American and speak to them in Arabic. . . . What fun the *Suq* is here—you'd go wild."

One quiet weekend, he took time off and went for a swim at the Gold Mohur Beach Club, a very colonial British institution that welcomed American and European expatriates. Arabs were not allowed to join the beach club. Henry Miller-Jones remembers having his first long conversation with Ames, standing knee-deep in the Arabian Sea. Ames pointed out to him the nets strung across the mouth of the bay to prevent sharks from attacking bathers. "Ames admonished me to avoid socializing with the Western and American expat colonies," recalled Miller-Jones. "He urged me to mix with the locals and other Arab targets where there was more likelihood of finding a potential source of any value. This was good professional advice, but I believe Bob also considered the social life among the expat communities not to his taste; he thought it pretty boring and superficial and maybe a bit too social." Ames never joined the Gold Mohur Beach Club and instead eventually paid for a family membership at the less fancy Italian Beach Club. The latter had a clientele that included diplomats from communist and many Third World countries.

The British naturally dominated the social scene in Aden. And though he was always cordial, Ames clearly didn't care for the Brits. They were the colonialists, and Ames believed them to be both insensitive to Arab mores and ill informed about Yemeni politics and history. During his visits to the *suq*, Ames noticed sandbagged machine-gun nests at every corner, and British soldiers patrolling the narrow alleys. "The soldiers are arrogant and forever harassing the Arabs," he wrote. "No wonder they're hated."

In his spare time, Ames read anything he could find on Yemeni history. "I really feel frustrated that there are no bookstores in Aden," he wrote Yvonne. "You know how I like to ramble through them." He particularly admired the works of Wendell Phillips (1921–75), the American explorer and adventurer who wrote about traveling through southern Arabia in the 1950s. His best-known book was *Qataban and Sheba: Exploring the Ancient Kingdoms on the Biblical Spice Routes of Arabia*, published in 1955. Phillips was a self-taught archaeologist and pistol-packing "Indiana Jones" adventurer. In 1950–51, he persuaded Yemen's monarch to let him excavate the ancient city of Marib, thought to be the queen of Sheba's ancient capital. While he was digging at Marib's circular Moon Temple, a Bedouin raiding party attacked his encampment; the archaeologist survived to write *Qataban and Sheba.* Around the same time he wrangled oil concessions from the sultan of Muscat and Oman. By the 1960s, he was worth a reported $120 million. His fellow explorer Lowell Thomas once called Phillips the "American Lawrence of Arabia."

That Ames was attracted to the life and work of a modern-day Arabian explorer like Phillips is evidence of a certain kind of romanticism. But he was not guilty of the shallow Orientalism skewered by the late professor Edward Said. "He fully grasped the irrationality, fecklessness, bravado and rhetoric of the area," observed his friend Henry Miller-Jones. He was an Arabist with a genuine curiosity and affection for Arab culture and in particular the culture of the Arabian Peninsula. He prided himself on his growing knowledge—and he was not afraid to be dismissive of those he thought ignorant. One day that autumn a cable arrived from the CIA station in Sana'a reporting the sensational news that Russian pilots were now flying combat missions in North Yemeni airspace in support of the Republican regime. Their evidence came from a recently downed MiG jet fighter: the body of the pilot had been recovered and he had red hair, so clearly he must be a Russian. Ames read the cable and burst out laughing. The dead pilot's "red hair," he knew, was just evidence that the pilot was a good Muslim who had probably recently returned from a pilgrimage to Mecca, and so, like thousands of other Hajjis, had dyed his hair red with henna. The dead pilot was the usual Egyptian, not Russian. Ames fired off a highly dismissive cable to Langley; senior analysts in Headquarters read it and decided to kill the earlier report.

On October 28, Ames accompanied Consul General Eagleton on a trip to the Sultanate of Muscat and Oman. "This is one of the most inaccessible kingdoms and a place I've always wanted to visit," he wrote to Yvonne. They flew in a U.S. Air Force plane to Salalah, where Sultan Said bin-Taymur lived in an otherworldly mud palace. Ames later told a friend that it looked like something right out of Sir Richard Burton's *Arabian Nights.* "You'd love Muscat (I think), and Salalah too," Bob wrote Yvonne. "The people are real friendly and full of the real Arab hospitality. . . . In the barren hills behind Salalah you can find the frankincense tree—the only place in the world it is found. Dhufar is the Ophir of the Bible and the land from which the wise men came. I got some frankincense which I'll send home some day, hopefully by Christmas." The sultan was without a doubt the Middle East's most medieval ruler. "We had an audience with the Sultan and his son Qaboos," Bob wrote. "They are both very charming." But Ames also noted that the sultan and the emperor Haile Selassie of Ethiopia were probably the last two complete despots in the world. "Nothing is done without the Sultan's personal approval."

After the royal audience, the sultan's twenty-seven-year-old son Qaboos bin Said took the visiting Americans on a tour of the royal gardens and "dined us royally." Qaboos confided in Ames that his father was keeping him under virtual house arrest. Qaboos had been educated at Britain's Sandhurst Military Academy. Ames was startled to hear that Qaboos was allowed only a few books and some classical Western music records. Qaboos had to send notes across the courtyard, asking permission to see his father. Obviously, this was an untenable situation for the son. "The Sultan, of course, will succumb to nationalists one day," Ames predicted. "But it's a shame that the ruler, who is father to all his subjects, must be overthrown by men who have no respect for family or the old Arab traditions, preferring instead the new testament and ten commandments of [Egypt's] Abd-al-Nasir. There I go romanticizing. I should know that progress can't be stopped—it's just too bad that progress in the Arab world usually brings into play the worst of both worlds."

Ames was right to think the sultan wouldn't last. Three years later, Qaboos bin Said staged a palace coup and seized power from his father. He did indeed modernize his kingdom, introducing schools, paved roads, and all the accouterments of modernity. But Qaboos is still an absolute monarch.

Aden was one of the most dangerous places to live in 1967. Soon after Ames returned on November 1, the city was rocked by another round of assassinations. A German broadcaster with the Süddeutscher Rund-funk was shot at close range as he walked out of the Tawahi post office around noon. He'd just sent a telegram to his new Lebanese bride. The assassin was caught—and to everyone's shock he was identified as the Yemeni announcer on the local evening radio news show. "They've caught the killer," Ames wrote, "and it seems he is the one who did all the recent killings . . . and one of the fellows he killed was the Brit who taught him to be an announcer. How do you figure a person like that out?" The assassin had evidently been a secret member of the NLF all along. But that he had targeted a non-British foreigner, and a journalist at that, was ominous. "A great quiet has fallen on our part of the city," Ames wrote. "No cars on the streets, no people, shops closed. This is the eye of the hurricane."

A few days later, the British suddenly announced that their military forces would all be out of Aden by the end of November—a full month or two before London's planned withdrawal. The Brits had decided they just couldn't take any further casualties. This precipitated a final blowout between the NLF and FLOSY forces. "We have a full scale civil war going on about five miles away from us," Ames wrote. "At last count, there were over 100 killed and 300 wounded with many more kidnapped and assassinated." The NLF controlled most of the countryside outside Aden—and some, but not all, of the key districts inside the city. "The Tawalhi, Steamer Point and Ma'alla area is now NLF since the NLF slit the throats of all FLOSY people in those areas."

In the event, the NLF won the civil war. "Well, it looks like the NLF all the way," Ames wrote. "NLF flags are everywhere and it looks as if the Brits will turn over the government to the NLF. . . . There is a holi-day mood in the air. I actually went down to the *suq* today and shopped around for two hours. I also got a much needed haircut."

In the midst of this chaos—civil war, assassinations, and general insecurity—Ames was worrying about his personal finances. And rightly so. He had about $1,000 in his stateside bank account. He reluctantly warned Yvonne, "I'm afraid some things must be put off because of lack of funds . . . so please portion out your expenses for the time being—just spending on the real necessities." Bob was living in Aden entirely on his daily expense account and saving his paycheck. But with a wife and four children it was still hard to make ends meet on a government salary. On the other hand, he was so careful about money that he was never in debt.

Bob hated to be separated from his wife and girls. He was counting the days. By October 22, 1967, because of home leave and his business travels, he'd seen Yvonne only 20 of the past 141 days. "I'm sure I'll be a stranger to them when we're together again." He had photographs of his smiling girls displayed on his office desk, but he wrote Yvonne, "What good is a picture?" His letters home always began, "Dear Bonnie [Bob's nickname for Yvonne] and babies," and they always ended with the phrase "God love you all." He looked forward to the day when they could live as a family again, and he even asked Yvonne, "Ready for #5?" But he worried about their security. "I love you and miss you so very much. . . . I won't bring you out until I'm sure of your safety." As Christmas approached, he wrote Yvonne, "Give the girls a hug from daddy and tell them, just like Santa Claus, daddy really does exist."

Ames viewed the British departure ceremony from aboard a British aircraft carrier, the HMS *Albion*. He was glad to see the Brits leave. Independence was officially declared on November 29. Crowds surged into the streets to celebrate. Cardboard and plywood arches were constructed and festooned with palm fronds and the red-, white-, and black-striped NLF flag. In the backs of pickup trucks racing through the city were gun-toting rebels who shouted slogans against the British. More than fifty thousand people attended the independence rally and heard speeches by the new president, Qahtan al-Sha'bi, and other NLF leaders. "The new government appears to be quite leftist," Ames wrote, "and many feel it is deeply infiltrated by Communists. Certainly, the Communist press corps got the best treatment." On the other hand, Ames pointed out that the new president appeared to be "sincere and hard working."

Ames stood in the hot sun for several hours, taking notes on the speeches. Astonishingly, he was the only consulate staffer who spoke enough Arabic to understand the speeches. "I've been living and breathing the Arabic language for the last three days," Ames wrote Yvonne. Consul General Eagleton and the other Foreign Service officers were completely dependent on him—and this annoyed Ames. "After sixty straight days of work," he wrote Yvonne, "I'm getting kind of tired and a bit cranky. Sometimes the acidity of my tongue surprises me, but there is so much incompetence and lack of organization on the State [Department] side that I find I can take [only] so much." Ames was particularly annoyed that his Foreign Service colleagues would quiz him for what was being said in Arabic and then run off to the consulate to give the consul general "their news" without crediting him. Ames thought it "pathetic.... But when I think of myself as a taxpayer, I get kind of sick."

Ames also believed the consulate's staff had no empathy for what was taking place in Aden. He thought "the whole independence bit was kind of exciting—the enthusiasm and jubilation of the people over being free after 138 years of British rule was contagious.... It was only when I returned to the confines of the Consulate that I felt depressed. Here the freedom and independence that pervaded the new state was lost on the obsequious individuals who compose our Consulate staff."

During the busy transition period to independence, Ames was designated to serve as the consulate's "press officer." This allowed him to attend the new government's press conferences and mingle with local reporters and a few foreign correspondents. Among others, he met CBS broadcast reporter Winston Burdett and the New York Times's Dana Adam Schmidt. Ames found the press people he met "interesting." He also served as Consul General Eagleton's translator in meetings with NLF officials. "My Arabic is improving even if my patience and stamina are not." Ames thought the consulate was "one disorganized mess and our office is no exception—and you know how I am about neatness and organization."

In the ensuing weeks, Aden came back to life. "People are cautiously sticking their heads out of their hiding places," Ames reported, "and finding they're not getting shot at now." He resumed his visits to the *suq*, where he bought Yvonne a beautiful pearl necklace—and, on an uncharacteristic whim, got himself an expensive Akai tape recorder. He wrote guiltily to Yvonne, "I got it for under $250 [worth $610 in the U.S.] and we still have $750 in the bank. Hope you're not too upset, what with your pinching pennies, but you know that spending is good for the soul." He wanted it so he could play music in his room. Bob had been confined to his apartment and office for weeks on end, complaining, "Our contacts are so restricted." He was looking forward to getting out and doing his real job—recruiting some agents. "So far, I haven't made any real close Arab friends," Ames wrote, "but that is because they are conservative by nature and are still not sure what the new government feels about contact with Americans." With the independence festivities behind him, he was eager to be "lost in the obscurity which I enjoy so much."

The new NLF government gradually restored a semblance of security, and it became safe enough for Ames and other consular officials to travel into the countryside. Ames drove to Lahej, a day trip north from Aden. Bob loved getting out into the rugged countryside, driving past old Arab forts, camel trains, and dusty mud villages. He later also took the opportunity to travel to the Hadramaut, South Yemen's exotic but very isolated province in the far east—and the ancestral home of Osama bin Laden.

Ames was rarely seen in the Agency's consular offices. Despite the dangers on the street, he spent most of his time cultivating contacts among the locals, using his commercial-officer cover story. "I have been all over Aden in places I wouldn't dare to have entered a few days ago." He made himself approachable, dressing casually in his standard polo shirt, blue trousers, and chukka boots. At six feet three inches, Ames stuck out. His size impressed the Arabs and he was aware of that. Word got out that the tall American was approachable and simpatico. "I don't recall a lengthy or active list of agents on Bob's payroll," said Henry Miller-Jones. "He was not an aggressive recruiter across the spectrum of potential assets, rather more the type who developed meaningful personal relationships with significant people of real potential value and, if appropriate, brought them gradually into a paid or otherwise compromised agent relationship. It was his knowledge of the area and culture that enabled him to draw real intelligence out of such contacts, rather than a more formal business-like relationship. He was more interested in the subject matter than 'adding coonskins' to his belt." Stephen Buck, a young Foreign Service officer who arrived in Aden in 1968, admired Ames's grasp of Arabic and of Yemen's complex tribal politics. "I used to say that Bob forgot more about Yemen than the rest of us ever learned."

One expatriate institution Ames made sure he frequented was the Catholic church. He was, after all, still a Catholic. He sometimes attended Mass at St. Anthony's Church, built by the British in 1839, the year they seized Aden and made it a protectorate of the British Empire. The Franciscan order had built a church at Steamer Point in Aden. The church operated several Catholic schools. Ames easily got to know some of the priests associated with these institutions. A thirty-one-year-old priest, Father Ambrose, became a regular dinner companion. Bob described him as "a real down to earth fellow who knows more jokes and appears to be anything but a priest." Father Ambrose came from the same order of priests Ames had known in Asmara a decade earlier.

If you socialized in Yemeni society, that inevitably meant learning to chew qat, a mildly narcotic leaf that Yemenis languidly chew every afternoon for hours while sipping sweet black tea. Qat makes people loquacious. It is the perfect drug of choice for a case officer cultivating agents. So perhaps Ames met Abd'al Fatah Ismail while chewing qat in someone's living room. Born in 1939 in North Yemen, Ismail had been educated at the Aden Technical College. He became a schoolteacher and then a labor-union activist. He was a dogmatic, bookish Marxist. Ismail was only twenty-eight years old when he met Ames. Four years earlier, Ismail had been a founding member of the NLF. Ames later told CIA director William Casey that he had befriended this budding young revolutionary. At the very least, he got Ismail to confide in him. Yemen's brutal civil war was finally winding down; the British were soon leaving. Ostensibly, South Yemen was about to become a republic. In reality, it was a feudal backwater, a nation with a high illiteracy rate steeped in Islamic traditions and bogged down by petty tribal feuds. Ismail explained to Ames that he wanted to change all this. Casey gave a speech in May 1985 in which he explained:

> Abd'al Fatah told Bob of his experience in the higher Komsomol school that the Soviets maintain in Moscow for training young revolutionaries. . . . Abd'al Fatah explained that he had been taught in Moscow that he would need 20 years—a generation—to consolidate his revolution. He would have to control the education of the youth. He would have to uproot and ultimately change the traditional elements of society. This would mean undermining the influence of religion and taking the young people away from their parents for education by the state. He was taught that to control the people he would have to establish block committees . . . and a powerful secret police.

Ames was a patient listener. He'd already confided to his own colleagues his disdain for the British Raj. So it isn't inconceivable that he'd express to someone such as Ismail his empathy for Ismail's anti-colonial struggle. By December he'd already met many of the regime's new cabinet ministers. "Most of them are just about my age," he wrote, "and I must say that I'm impressed with their sincerity and desire to get their country on the road of progress. Perhaps this, more than any other factor, has given me confidence in the new state." Ismail was named minister of culture in the new NLF government. The right-wing faction of the NLF purged him in March 1968; he was arrested and then sent into exile. But then in the summer of 1969 he orchestrated a "correction" in NLF party doctrine—essentially an internal party coup—and by the summer of 1969 was secretary-general of the NLF and a member of the Presidential Council. As such, he was South Yemen's de facto leader.*

"Ames told me," Casey said, "that as he looked back, Abd'al Fatah—with Soviet bloc help—had done just as he'd been taught. He captured and subverted a legitimate war of independence in his own country. He killed or drove into exile those members of the movement who believed in democracy, and then went about the work of consolidating a Communist regime."

Ames's colleagues back in Langley noted that he'd been able to cultivate a future head of state. Getting to know the right people was the definition of good spy craft. It was all about getting close to influential or powerful actors. It's hard to see in retrospect what Ames or Washington got out of this relationship in any concrete sense. And it's hard to see what Ismail got out of it. Perhaps the young revolutionary got a kick out of confiding in a CIA agent. But Ames got a chance to understand the mind of someone who became a player. It didn't matter that Ismail was an ideological opponent. It didn't matter that he was not a "controlled" source. He'd become a source nevertheless, a window onto this very foreign world called Yemen. Ames thought his government wanted him to understand what motivated Ismail and his colleagues to wage a revolution against the British. Good spying was all about empathy.

"Had Ames been a public man," wrote one of his colleagues in Aden, "he would have stood tall in his all-American shoes [cowboy boots] as a Louis L'Amour hero. But he belonged more to John le Carré's world:

---

* Ismail was a dominant figure in South Yemeni politics for nearly two decades. But in January 1986 he was mortally wounded when a gun battle erupted at a contentious Politburo meeting.

anonymous, perceptive, knowledgeable, highly motivated, critical, discreet—with a priest's and a cop's understanding of the complexity of human nature in action. More private than secret—but that too."

One day at the Gold Mohur Beach Club three Arabs swam over from another beach and approached a U.S. Foreign Service officer swimming in the cove. One of the young men asked the diplomat if he knew how to contact "Mr. Bob." The Foreign Service officer said, "Sure, you can find Bob Ames at the Caltex building." Later, Ames casually thanked the Foreign Service officer for the referral.

This young man would become one of Ames's sources. Born in Iraq in 1933, Basil Raoud al-Kubaisi had earned a B.A. from Adams State College in Colorado, an M.A. from Howard University in Washington, D.C., and a doctorate in political science from American University in Washington, D.C. His 1971 thesis was titled "The Arab Nationalist Movement, 1951–1971: From Pressure Group to Socialist Party." The 167-page thesis explored the origins of the ANM, the same organization that Ames had been told by his Langley superiors to target for intelligence during his first posting in Dhahran in the early 1960s. By 1969, the ANM would morph into the Popular Front for the Liberation of Palestine (PFLP). But in 1967–68 Al-Kubaisi visited Aden to interview sources for his thesis research. In July 1967, for instance, he interviewed Qahtan al-Sha'bi, an ANM member who later that year became the first president of the Democratic Republic of South Yemen. He had also interviewed George Habash (a medical student at the time and the principal founder of the ANM), Nayef Hawatmeh (leader of the Popular Democratic Front for the Liberation of Palestine), and Wadi Haddad, later the mastermind behind the PFLP's spectacular air piracy in the early 1970s.

Al-Kubaisi came from a wealthy and well-connected Sunni Muslim family in Baghdad. He finished high school in Baghdad and then studied political science at the American University of Beirut. Habash befriended him at the American University. Basil joined the ANM, but his political activities on campus eventually led to his expulsion. He spent his senior year at Colorado's Adam State College, graduating in 1956. Basil then returned to Iraq, where he worked in the foreign ministry. But once again his political views got him into trouble. In the mid-1960s he fled Iraq altogether and enrolled in Howard University in Washington, D.C. While pursuing his graduate studies, Basil was also a prominent leader of the ANM's activities in America, recruiting Arab students to the cause of Arab unity. After the June 1967 Arab-Israeli War, Basil went back to the Middle East to interview ANM figures for his thesis.

We cannot know what motivated Al-Kubaisi to seek out Ames in Aden, but we can know that Ames would have regarded the Iraqi academic as an invaluable source of information about a rising new generation of radical Arab political figures. "Ames was good at recruitment," recalled a former Agency officer, "because he sensed how to match up a potential recruit's interests with his own. He could make a recruit believe that 'you and I talking' was the right thing to do." Al-Kubaisi may have been just one of Ames's "sources" and not a fully recruited agent. We just know they knew each other in Aden. Al-Kubaisi was probably delighted to find someone who was willing to listen to what he was learning from his research about the ANM. "Bob was a very good listener," said the Foreign Service officer who had referred Al-Kubaisi to Ames.

That Al-Kubaisi had been educated in America presumably also made him susceptible or open to talking with an American official; he was someone who obviously understood the United States. Perhaps this made him want to help America, and Ames in particular, to understand Arab aspirations. We also know from a top-secret British Foreign Office memo that Al-Kubaisi had been a source in 1963 for information on the ANM—so he already had some experience in dealing with Western intelligence services. Al-Kubaisi's obvious sympathy for the ANM and the Palestinian cause gave him entrée to left-wing intellectual circles. And likewise, Ames's interest in the history of the ANM and his empathy for the Palestinian cause attracted Al-Kubaisi's interest in the American. They were a natural fit.

With independence and the departure of the British, it was now safe for Yvonne and the kids to come to Aden. But Bob was nevertheless forced to spend Christmas in Aden alone. He did manage to attend midnight Mass, but he called it "the most depressing and un-Christmas-like Christmas I have ever spent." The only present he got was from a colleague who gave him a meerschaum pipe from Turkey. Still, on Christmas morning he wrote Yvonne a satirical ditty taking off from Clement Clarke Moore's nineteenth-century Christmas poem. Ames's version was set in Aden, and St. Nicholas was an "agent."

> *T'was the night before Christmas and all through the town*
> *Not a rifle'd been fired nor grenade had been thrown.*
> *The checkpoints were manned, the security tight;*
> *No sleigh-driving agent would get through tonight!*

The poem had Arab gunmen intercepting the "sleigh-driving agent" and confiscating his toy guns. "So lock up this agent, his deer and his sleigh, / and double the guard through the whole holiday." Sitting in Norwood, Massachusetts, Yvonne was faintly amused. She and the four children finally were allowed into Aden in January 1968 and moved into the spacious Khormaksar house Bob had found. "Aden was spartan," Yvonne recalled. "But I loved it. I felt at home in this part of the Middle East. Beirut was a big city, and I am not a big-city girl. But in Aden I didn't feel confined." She drove the girls to the Gold Mohur Beach Club and frequently shopped in the duty-free shops in the Port Authority. She had a cook—who turned out to have tuberculosis and infected one of the girls. Yvonne also hired an Ethiopian *ayah* to help her take care of the girls. Bob was out and about every day, but he always spent his evenings at home. "He didn't share secrets," said Yvonne, "so that made life normal."

Even in Aden it was the sixties, and Bob Ames, the CIA case officer, was not immune to popular culture. He still considered himself a conservative Republican, but he loved pop music, particularly the Beach Boys. He'd also listen to Petula Clark and Glen Campbell. But the Beach Boys was his favorite band. He could sing some of their classics, hitting all the falsetto high notes.

Bob was still the occasional prankster. He could make his little girls squeal with delight by speaking to them in a Donald Duck voice. But he'd never perform his Donald voice on command; he'd only do it spontaneously. One evening at the dinner table he showed the girls his "thumb apart" magic trick. The Ethiopian *ayah*, a woman named Hewit, was feeding baby Karen when she saw Bob "separate" his thumb. "Her eyes got wide, she threw the spoon up to the ceiling and went screaming out of the room," Bob wrote. "The kids were hysterical and that was the end of dinner." By then, the four girls ranged in age from four months to six years. They were a handful. Yvonne had to boil their diapers in a pot over a kerosene burner. She had a wringer washer machine—but no dryer. Every morning the three older children were dressed in white school uniforms and sent off to the convent school run by an order of nuns. Late in November 1968 a very pregnant Yvonne flew alone to Asmara, leaving Bob to look after the girls. The medical facilities at Kagnew Station were thought to be superior to anything in Aden. "Please hurry the baby on its way," Bob wrote facetiously. "Sit-ups are the best thing, so that you can get home to your family." A betting pool was established among Aden's expatriate community on whether Yvonne would have yet another girl. "I think half of Aden is waiting!" Bob wrote on December 3. "The betting has been brisk." Six days later, Yvonne gave birth to their first son. They named him Andrew Thomas Ames.

Later that year, Marsh Niner left Aden, and Ames replaced him as chief of station (COS), a significant accomplishment for someone only thirty-four years old. *Dick Roane* was promoted to be his deputy chief of station. *Roane*'s Arabic was not yet as good as Ames's, but he was on his way to becoming very fluent. They were a good team. *Roane*'s previous post had been just to the north in Sana'a, where his job had largely been to collect intelligence on SOVMAT—Soviet weapons pouring into the country. He'd spent a lot of his time crawling under Soviet-made tanks and other military equipment, copying down their serial numbers so that analysts back in Langley could build a database on Soviet arms shipments. It was dangerous work, and one day he was kidnapped on the road from Sana'a to Hudaydah. The U.S. government had to pay a sizable sum to ransom him. Despite this experience, *Roane* loved Yemen. He and Ames shared an interest in Middle Eastern history, and they worked well together over the next two years.

Relations between the U.S. consulate—now upgraded to an embassy—and the new government of South Yemen were difficult. In retrospect, it is somewhat extraordinary that the U.S. mission even existed in Aden, given the radical nature of the regime. But finally, on October 24, 1969, the South Yemeni regime broke relations, denouncing the Nixon administration's decision to sell Phantom jet fighters to Israel. The U.S. chargé d'affaires, William Eagleton, was given twenty-four hours to get out. The seventeen other embassy staff and their dependents were allowed forty-eight hours to leave the country. "A female police officer arrived at the house and stood in the kitchen while we packed up our things," Yvonne said. "And then we were escorted to the airport by armed soldiers." On October 26, 1969, Bob, Yvonne, and their five children boarded a chartered flight for Asmara.

Soon afterwards, Ames flew off to Washington for debriefings at Langley, leaving Yvonne stuck in an Asmara hotel with the children (and their pet cat). When Christmas arrived, they were still camping out in the hotel. Finally, after ten long weeks in the hotel, the Agency arranged for them to move to the army base at Kagnew Station, where at least they could eat all their meals in the army cafeteria. There they sat until late in the spring of 1970, when Ames received travel orders to move his family to Beirut. In the meantime, Bob had spent much of the past year commuting between Washington, Beirut, and Asmara. Yvonne was greatly relieved when in mid-May she finally moved into a nice apartment on Rue de Californie, just west of the American University of Beirut and within eyesight of Ras Beirut's landmark lighthouse. The kids were enrolled in the American Community School—well within walking distance. "I let them walk alone," Yvonne recalled. "I felt safe." On some evenings they could walk to Uncle Sam's Diner, a student hangout at the corner of Rue Jeanne d'Arc and Rue Bliss. Faisal's Restaurant, also on Rue Bliss, right across the street from the American University's main gate, was another nearby landmark. And Khayyat's Bookstore was just down the street.

Beirut was not without its hazards even in these pre–civil war days. A Druze Lebanese family lived across the street, and one day Yvonne went to the window when she heard a young woman screaming. She saw the woman struggling with her brother. A moment later shots were fired and Bob hastily pulled Yvonne into the hallway. When they next looked, they could see the woman's body lying in the street. She had been shot dead. The young woman had "dishonored" the family by having a love affair. A few minutes later, a taxi arrived to whisk the murdering brother away. After the body was removed, there was still blood on the street. "We told the kids the next day," Yvonne said, "that a truckload of ketchup had accidentally overturned."

Yvonne had given birth to five children in less than a decade. But she was not yet done. By late November, she was pregnant again. Bob kept very regular hours. "Most of us case officers worked at night, to see our agents," observed a CIA case officer who knew Ames. "Not Bob. He was devoted to his family. He would come home, go to his study and decompress a bit by reading, and then he'd have dinner. He saw his agents during the day."

Another CIA case officer, Sam Wyman, once asked Ames how he found the time to read books. "Oh, I always make time to read—at least an hour a day," Bob replied. Wyman was another of the Agency's few Arabists. (At any one time, the CIA had only twelve to thirteen Arabic speakers in the Directorate of Operations.) Wyman's father had been an army intelligence officer stationed in Cairo—where Wyman spent part of his childhood after World War II. Wyman had gone to

Georgetown University and then earned a master's degree in Middle Eastern studies from Columbia University. He also spent two years studying Arabic at the University of Baghdad, so he had much more formal training in Arabic than Ames. He'd joined the CIA in 1965. But Ames was probably the more fluent Arabist. "We used to try to come up with Arabic puns and little limericks," recalled Wyman. "We had a lot of fun together playing with the language." Both men also enjoyed listening to the popular Lebanese singer Fayrouz. Wyman still has in his possession an Arabic lexicon that once belonged to Ames; the blank pages at the back of the volume are filled with Bob's neat, tiny handwriting—lists of Arabic words with his own translations.

In Beirut, Ames was working under Station Chief Gene Burgstaller, who was very much an old-school veteran case officer. He'd served in Berlin and later was chief of station in Paris. Ames admired him and thought he'd built a good team in Beirut Station. His fellow officer from Aden, Henry Miller-Jones, was also living in Beirut. Miller-Jones studied Arabic for a full year and then was peremptorily ordered to replace another case officer assigned to recruiting agents in Syria. This was a tough job, since Syria was deemed a no-travel zone for Agency officers. Too dangerous. So Miller-Jones also was instructed to target potential agents who could pass on any information about Soviet activities in the Middle East. Ames scoffed at this mission; he thought the Soviets were a decidedly secondary target in a place like Beirut.

Richard Zagorin, another member of Beirut Station that year, lived down the street from Ames in Ras Beirut. "I was in awe of Bob," *Zagorin* said. "I'd studied Arabic, but I knew Ames knew Arabic. And I knew Ames understood the Arab world. He was a guy who knew his stuff." *Zagorin* had attended the language school in Beirut, and with the outbreak of the June War he'd joined the station. The station chief had called him in to help shred classified papers. *Zagorin* had entered the CIA because he had an acquaintance, Bill Bromell, who served in the Directorate of Operations and specialized in the Middle East. *Zagorin* admired Bromell, so when the Agency asked which division he'd like to work in, *Zagorin* said the Near East. They gave it to him.

"Beirut in those days," *Zagorin* said, "was terrific, a great operational climate. It was like a Gilbert and Sullivan show. You could do anything. There was nothing you could do that would land you into trouble. We had a team of very talented people."

The CIA station in Beirut was located then on the top floor in the left wing of the U-shaped embassy building. "We case officers," said *Zagorin,* "all worked in this bull pen. We worked hard, and we played hard. There were, I am afraid, lots of divorces. Our targets were various Arab governments, but also the Soviets." The crypt for Soviet officials in the region was REDTOP. "We called them *Realflops.*"

Ames befriended another officer in Beirut Station, the rather mercurial Henry J. McDermott III. Henry was known inside the station as the "Green Wog," partly because of his Irish ancestry and partly because he was always referring to Arabs as "wogs"—a British colonial acronym for "worthy Oriental gentlemen." *Wog* was a nineteenth-century British Raj euphemism for an Indian trying to emulate upper-class British etiquette. The word was obviously derisive, but Henry loved his "wogs" and he used the term affectionately. Henry had grown up with an abusive father, which may or may not have explained his legendary capacity for drink. One case officer in Beirut called him "a professional Irishman." But he was nevertheless admired for his brazen courage. He once famously walked into the Beirut offices of the PFLP and introduced himself as a comrade from the Irish Republican Army. The scam worked for a while and led to McDermott's obtaining information that allowed the CIA to prevent a planned hijacking of a commercial airliner. McDermott had arrived in Lebanon in 1965, and with the exception of one year spent in Iraq, he'd been there ever since. He was a good Arabist—and a very convivial spirit. "Henry was an aggressive, talented, street smart and gutsy officer," recalled Henry Miller-Jones, who knew him well in Beirut. "He was willing to take big risks and his Irish charm took him a long way." Like Ames, McDermott was working the Palestinian target. "This called for some serious bravery," said Miller-Jones. "Bob was pretty tough himself and appreciated someone who could act on his bravado, and Henry had a productive ops imagination."

Ames and McDermott made for an improbable friendship. They were opposites. The one thing they had in common was their Catholicism. Both men regularly attended Mass at St. Francis, a Catholic church on Hamra Street. But the steady, reliable Ames enjoyed the company of the mercurial, hard-drinking McDermott. "They really were very close," recalled McDermott's wife at the time, Betty, "and Henry, as much as he was able, loved Bob and respected him enormously." Henry nicknamed the six-foot-three Ames the "White Whale."

McDermott lived in an apartment building near Ras Beirut's landmark lighthouse. Loren Jenkins, *Newsweek*'s bureau chief in Beirut from 1970 to 1973, was a neighbor. "Henry was a character," recalled Jenkins. "He loved to throw knives at a wooden board. He'd show up at odd hours with a bottle of whiskey, and then he'd try to get me drunk so he could pump me for information. But I could hold my liquor better than Henry, so I would turn the tables on him and pump him for stories about his tradecraft. He was the only CIA officer who ever tried to recruit me."

Beirut was a vibrant, cosmopolitan, chaotic city in 1970–71, and a playground for a score of rival intelligence services. Things happened. "There was a period," said *Zagorin*, "when I was given a recruitment pitch by a Soviet officer—and in the days afterwards, I felt threatened. So I arranged with Bob to have a mutually agreed-upon signal, so that if I got wind they were trying to take me or something, he would come to my rescue. He was armed and ready."

In late 1969—soon after his evacuation from Aden—Ames met a twenty-seven-year-old Lebanese citizen who had spent his college years in the American Midwest. Mustafa Zein would become a keystone of Ames's career. As one of Ames's CIA colleagues put it, Zein was Ames's Sancho Panza for the next fourteen years. They met in West Beirut's Bedford Hotel, where Zein lived and worked as a businessman. They spoke in English, but occasionally Ames would interject an Arabic proverb. It was his way of making a point and making sure that his Arab contacts understood that he had an appreciation for the language.

Mustafa had spent his childhood in Lebanon, the son of a moderately wealthy Shi'ite Lebanese landowner from southern Lebanon. He was born on January 22, 1942, in the coastal city of Tyre. The Shi'ites of Lebanon were then typically an underclass. Most were landless peasants who worked the rocky soils of South Lebanon as virtual serf laborers for Maronite Christian and Sunni Muslim landlords. Zein's circumstances were different. He grew up privileged and cosmopolitan. His mother gave birth to eight boys and three girls, all delivered at home. His father owned a general grocery store that sold food staples and household goods. The Zeins also owned orchards that produced olives, figs, oranges, and watermelons that they sold in Beirut. Mustafa's uncles had made a fortune trading diamonds in Sierra Leone. His maternal grandmother was the richest woman in Tyre and lived in an old palace. Mustafa adored his grandmother. Though illiterate, she was both religiously devout and tolerant. Mustafa used to read the Koran to her, and she persuaded him to help with her charitable projects. From the age of nine, Mustafa was entrusted with large sums of cash and instructed to purchase sacks of flour, rice, and sugar, which he quietly delivered on Thursday nights to the homes of Tyre's poorest residents.

Unlike most of his peers, Mustafa learned good English at the Gerard Institute, an American boarding school founded in 1881 in Sidon and run by the United Evangelical Church. In 1959 the American Field Service selected Zein to spend his senior year in high school with an American family in Naperville, Illinois, a town thirty miles southwest of Chicago. Naperville, population 12,933 in 1960, gave Zein a quintessential small-town American experience. "Bob and June Beckman became my American father and mother," Zein said, "and their two daughters and their son became my American sisters and brother to this very day." Mustafa was particularly close to June Beckman, a devout Christian Scientist. Far from being put off by the Beckmans' religiosity, Mustafa came to "greatly admire this very principled Christian community." Zein soon fell in love with all things American. "That was the year I truly became bi-national," he observed.

Upon graduating from high school in Naperville, Zein enrolled in the town's North Central College, a small private liberal-arts college founded in 1861 by the United Evangelical Church. Zein waited tables in the summer at an upscale restaurant, and later he and three friends won a contract from the college to clean dormitories. Zein was already displaying the kind of entrepreneurship that would make him both a good businessman and a facilitator of intelligence. By the time he graduated from college in 1964, he'd saved close to $12,000. He then moved to New York City, where he worked in the national headquarters of the Organization of Arab Students.

America politicized Zein. As a Shi'ite, he sympathized with the Palestinian refugees. They too were a landless people, and like the Shi'ites of southern Lebanon they had little or no political power. In 1964, he was elected vice president of the Organization of Arab Students in the United States and Canada. He was a handsome young man, his black hair neatly parted on the side. His slightly hooded eyes made him seem exotic. He spoke excellent American English, but with a definite hint of the Middle East. He was a charming extrovert.* Zein's leadership position in the Organization of Arab Students naturally brought him into contact with a similar organization, the U.S. National Student Association—whose international program was underwritten by the CIA from the early 1950s until *Ramparts* magazine revealed the CIA funding in 1967. The CIA found the National Student Association's contacts with similar foreign student societies a fertile recruiting ground. Zein was a friend of Richard "Rick" Stearns, the international

---

* As a student activist in America, Zein befriended numerous Palestinians, including Nabil Shaath, who later became a cabinet minister for the Palestinian Authority. Zein also knew men like Amr Moussa, later an Egyptian politician, and Dr. Osama El-Baz, who became a high-ranking Egyptian diplomat.

vice president of the National Student Association.* Inevitably, the
CIA took note of Zein's activities. Interestingly, when *Ramparts*'s revelations were published, Zein was unfazed by the fact that the CIA
had funded some of these student organizations. He told his friends in
Cairo at the time that the Soviet Union's intelligence service, the KGB,
was doing the same thing.

"Zein was a player in the Arab student milieu," said another CIA
officer who got to know him later. "He had built quite a network of
contacts through his work with the Arab student association. He was
very bright, very well read, and genuinely pro-American. He had very
good taste in art. My wife enjoyed him a lot."

In May 1964, Zein became embroiled in a public controversy over
a mural in the Jordanian exhibit at the World's Fair in New York City.
The mural depicted a destitute Palestinian refugee living in a camp in
Jordan. The *New York Times* reported that officials from the nearby
Israel Pavilion had dispatched a telegram to Robert Moses, who was
then running the World's Fair. They had protested that the Jordanian
mural amounted to "propaganda against Israel and its people" and
had demanded that Moses remove the offending image. When Moses
declined to censor the exhibit, some forty Jewish American protesters converged on the Jordanian pavilion and shouted obscenities. Zein
happened to witness the event—and this inspired him to send his own
telegram to Moses. Writing in his capacity as vice president of the Organization of Arab Students, Zein expressed his shock at the behavior
of the protesters. "This and many other incidents are wearing out the
patience of Arab students in the United States," he wrote. "It makes us
wonder sometimes if we are living in America or Israel." Zein pleaded
with Moses to maintain an open mind and to understand his "sincere
desire to bridge the gap of misunderstanding between the American
people and our Arab nation." Zein had become a lobbyist—a truly
American pastime.

* Rick Stearns was later a friend of Bill Clinton's at Oxford University, and President Clinton appointed him a federal district judge in Boston in 1993.

In late 1964, Zein moved to Cairo, where he enrolled in Cairo University's medical school. He lasted only a year before dropping out to devote himself to politics and business. That year, he began to acquire powerful acquaintances. He was photographed with King Hussein of Jordan in 1964. And in April 1965 he met Egypt's president, Gamal Abdel Nasser.

In 1968, at the age of twenty-six, Zein landed a job as a "special adviser" to Abu Dhabi's Sheikh Zayid bin Sultan al-Nahyan. Zein became the sheikh's strategic adviser and interlocutor with the Americans and the British, who were then competing to control the future of the oil-rich Trucial Coast kingdoms. Given Zein's history of connections to the CIA-funded National Student Association a few years earlier, it was not surprising when one day in 1968 Zein received a phone call from a visiting American. Allen McTeague identified himself as a Foreign Service officer stationed in Dhahran, Saudi Arabia. He explained that he was the commercial officer in the U.S. consulate—the same position held by Ames just two years earlier. He wanted to talk. Zein invited him to his office in the Abu Dhabi palace. They talked. McTeague gave Zein a copy of John F. Kennedy's book *Profiles in Courage* and then revealed that he was really from the CIA and simply wished to establish a channel of communication with Zein. The young Lebanese listened—and indicated that he was sympathetic. That was all. But McTeague mentioned that the next time he was in Beirut he should look up a young American named Bob Ames.

Zein met with Ames in Beirut in late 1969, just after Bob's evacuation from Aden. Ames wore a gray suit and his trademark western boots. He greeted Zein with a broad smile. He made a few jokes in Lebanese Arabic. "Bob opened the meeting by informing me that he was very familiar with my life," recalled Zein. Ames had read Zein's file. He knew about his work with the Organization of Arab Students in New York. He knew about Zein's cable to Robert Moses in 1964—which demonstrated not only that Mustafa was capable of taking the initiative to approach a powerful figure but that he was genuinely interested in "bridging the gap" between his people and America. They talked frankly. Zein told Ames that he "knew who he [Ames] was, and I did not mind a bit." But he also underlined his deep disappointment in Washington's alliances with "thugs and despots." America, complained Zein, was pushing patriots into the arms of the Soviets "by default." Inevitably, Zein brought up the plight of the Palestinians. Ames listened patiently—and largely in silence.

Ames knew from his training that recruitment was a difficult art. Failure was almost inevitable—unless the target actually had a desire to be recruited. Ames sensed that young Zein wanted to work for America because he really believed it was in the interest of his people to develop a genuine bond of friendship with the United States. "Was there ever anyone easier to recruit than me?" says Fuad, the fictional character in David Ignatius's 1987 novel *Agents of Innocence.* "I recruited myself." Ignatius's brilliant spy novel is set in Beirut in the 1970s. It is a roman à clef, and Fuad is most definitely based on Mustafa Zein. But Zein firmly says this was wrong. He was never in the employment of the CIA.* He was something else entirely.

Zein made a good living in Beirut as a business consultant. His clients eventually included such multinational companies as City Service Oil, Suma Corporation, Salomon Brothers, United States Steel, Kaiser Corporation, and Northrop Corporation.

Sometime in 1969 Ames blandly suggested that they shared mutual interests; perhaps they could work together. Nothing more. Zein always believed their relationship was based on simple friendship and shared values. "He was never a 'paid agent,'" confirms Sam Wyman, a CIA officer who later dealt with Zein. "His was an ideological recruitment. He probably did recruit himself, or allowed himself to be recruited, but he wouldn't deal with anyone he didn't like or respect.

---

* Years later, a CIA official testified in a federal district court, "Mustafa Zein never received any monies for his efforts. The basis for Mr. Zein's collaboration with the Agency has been his desire for the United States to comprehend and sympathize with the Arab and Palestinian perspective on the situation in the Middle East." Mustafa Zein, e-mail to author, August 4, 2012, and U.S. Court of Federal Claims, *Mustafa M. Zein v. The United States,* No. 99-244C, April 23, 2002, p. 5.

But he would do just about anything for those whom he did like and respect, and those who achieved the most success with him understood this." Zein was the absolute best. He was not a bought man. He didn't take orders from the Americans. He was his own man. But he was willing to do things to advance the relationship between America and his people. Bob Ames thought Mustafa was ideal. So there was no need to make him a paid agent. As Mustafa later explained, "When I met Bob in Beirut a few months later we made a pledge to be truthful to each other in a world filled with lies." In the world of intelligence this was a rare kind of friendship. It was a partnership.

Ames told Zein that he thought he was the most "qualified" Arab capable of building a bridge across the political and cultural divides between America and the Arab world. Zein knew America from his college years—and he knew the Arab world. Zein was an Arab Zelig—and like Woody Allen's Leonard Zelig, he seemed to be everywhere and know everyone. (His unpublished memoir, "Deceit with Extreme Prejudice," contains photographs of himself with King Hussein of Jordan, Egypt's president Gamal Abdel Nasser, India's Krishna Menon, the sheikh of Sharjah, Yasir Arafat, Barbara Walters, and other noted personalities.)

Bob just wanted Zein to introduce him from time to time to his broad range of friends. Normally, Zein would be called what is known in the business as an "access agent." Jack O'Connell—a veteran case officer and station chief in Amman—defined an access or principal agent as a "headhunter" for other spies. "You recruit a principal agent because he knows everybody in the town. . . . You want him to be your partner in finding spies. You might match his salary, pay him $10,000 a year, or $1,000 a month—enough for his time and loyalty." Zein was a very good access agent—but he refused any money and refused to sign a contract.

"I was very fond of Mustafa," said one CIA officer who worked with him. But he knew Zein had an "obsessive personality." Zein observed the proprieties in Arab society; he dressed stylishly but conventionally. He frequented Beirut's nightclubs and casinos—though he rarely drank. For a time he dated one of Beirut's most famous and beautiful casino dancers. He didn't care what people thought. He was a free spirit, handsome and charming. But there was a serious side to Mustafa. He was deeply philosophical, and beginning in 1963, while still in college in Illinois, he began to study Sufism, a mystical but culturally liberal tradition in Islam.

Zein knew that Bob Ames was very much married with all those kids. Bob had introduced Mustafa to Yvonne early in their friendship. Mustafa became a family friend of long standing. (Decades later, when one of Bob's sons got married, Yvonne invited him to the wedding. Mustafa couldn't make it.) Bob and Mustafa were not professional colleagues; they were just good friends. This was Ames's way. He recruited sources by befriending them. "Bob really wasn't that great at recruiting agents," said *George Coll*, a former high-ranking CIA officer. "Very few people are. Bob didn't see the need to formally recruit people. They just became friends."

But it was also true that Zein was capable of delivering more than the average friend. He knew how to cultivate *new* friends; he was pragmatic and quite courageous.* "He was very long on guts," recalled one Agency officer. "I saw him operating in some very dicey circumstances, particularly in Lebanon, crossing one dangerous checkpoint after another. He was very brazen." Ames began referring to Zein in his cables back to Langley as "the Prophet," partly because his intelligence was so often on the mark—but partly because Ames knew Zein was a fan of Kahlil Gibran's best-selling book *The Prophet*. And sometimes he called him "the Catalyst." It was a Sufi term. To be a catalyst one had to be "in this world, but not of it." Without the Catalyst, the Americans and the Palestinians would not have come together.

---

* Zein was once kidnapped by Abu Ahmed Yunis, the PFLP's notorious security chief, and interrogated brutally for ten days in a dank prison cell in the Palestinian refugee camp of Shatila. Zein had the presence of mind to persuade one of his guards to convey a cryptic message to a friend—who organized a rescue operation. Yunis was executed by the PFLP in 1981.

CHAPTER FIVE

The Red Prince

People expect a revolutionary to be a miserable-looking, shabby creature dressed in rags. That's the wrong notion.... As the Arabic saying goes: Better a reputation of opulence than a reputation of misery.

—*Ali Hassan Salameh*

In Beirut, Ames began to spend a lot of time with Mustafa Zein. One day in late 1969 they began talking about various personalities in the Palestine Liberation Organization (PLO), and Zein mentioned that he'd reconnected with a young Palestinian who had the ear of Yasir Arafat, the chairman of the PLO. At forty years of age, Arafat was already known as the "Old Man." Zein's friend, Ali Hassan Salameh, twenty-seven years old, was a member of Fatah's Revolutionary Council and since 1968 had worked with Fatah's Revolutionary Security Apparatus. Salameh was essentially nurturing the PLO's rudimentary intelligence bureau, later called Force 17, simply named after its telephone extension in Fatah's Beirut headquarters. He was trying to turn Force 17 into a professional intelligence organization. He was no ideologue. Soon after taking control of Force 17, he overheard one of his men accusing another officer of being an Israeli spy simply because the man could speak Hebrew and was seen reading an Israeli newspaper. Salameh interrupted to say that they all should be fluent in Hebrew. And then he dismissed the officer who had made the accusation.

Salameh was a decidedly cosmopolitan Palestinian. Zein said he was the kind of young man who broke all the social mores of the Arab world. He flaunted his modernity. Though married, he loved beautiful women and usually had one on his arm. "He was a youthful Marlon Brando, standing over six feet tall," recalled Zein. Ali Hassan was also a sixties revolutionary. That didn't mean that he was a Marxist. Like many other Palestinian revolutionaries, Salameh was just a young man with a gun who believed in the righteousness of the struggle to return to his ancestral homeland in Palestine. He drove around town in an expensive car and ate in the finest restaurants. He obviously came from money. Israeli intelligence gave him an aristocratic moniker: the Red Prince. Ames was intrigued.

At this point, Ames made a brazen pitch to Zein. He told the young Arab that President Richard Nixon himself had authorized him to "explore the possibility of contact between the USA and the PLO. . . . He [Ames] was the person designated for this task." It was a good story, an improbable story, but a perfect story. There are no declassified records in the Nixon Presidential Library to suggest that Nixon had entrusted Ames—a low-ranking, thirty-five-year-old CIA officer—to open a back channel to the PLO. But Ames told the story to inspire Zein—and to underscore the importance of their collaboration. Ames then asked Zein to go to Amman and look up his friend Ali Hassan Salameh. Zein left for Amman the very next day.

Zein told Ames that he was a very close friend of Ali Hassan's. Zein had met Salameh five years earlier in Cairo in 1964. They had been introduced by the president of the General Union of Palestinian Students, just prior to a trip Salameh was making to Europe. Salameh was off to visit an Italian girlfriend. "The man was a magnet," recalled Zein, "who literally could not be resisted by girls. Period." Ali Hassan and Mustafa instantly connected. "He was a fixture in my apartment, spending many nights in my guest room." When Ali Hassan returned from Italy he told Mustafa that he'd decided to move to Kuwait and join the PLO. In Kuwait City Salameh was interviewed by Khalid al-Hassan, the head of the PLO mission in Kuwait and a founding member of the organization. Al-Hassan was delighted to meet the young Salameh—because he knew of the young man's singular pedigree.

Zein and Salameh kept in touch even after Salameh moved to Kuwait. The Palestinian visited Zein in Abu Dhabi—and at one point Zein gave Salameh a very thin Swiss platinum watch. Salameh would wear it for the rest of his life.

Ali Hassan Salameh was born in 1942 in Baghdad, where his parents had fled from Palestine when the British Mandate authorities put a price on his father's head. His father, Sheikh Hassan Salameh, was born in 1911 into a poor Palestinian peasant family in Qula, near Lydda. By the time he was twenty-three, Sheikh Salameh was a wanted man. In 1934 he joined Abdul Qader al-Husseini's anti-British underground army, the Jihad al-Muqaddas (Holy Struggle). During the 1936–39 Arab Revolt he was a commander of a Palestinian militia in the Lydda-Ramla district. In 1938 he led a raid that blew up the Lydda-Haifa railroad tracks. British Mandate records from the Criminal Investigation Department describe Sheikh Salameh at the time as a "gang chieftain." The Haganah—the military arm of the Zionist movement at the time—created an intelligence file on Salameh that portrayed him as a hardened criminal and terrorist: "Salameh has turned Ramla [town] into a centre of disorder," the Haganah reported. "People are being murdered in the middle of the city." Whether he was a "gang chieftain" or a guerrilla resistance leader, Salameh had the backing of the grand mufti of Jerusalem. And when the mufti fled Palestine in 1939, Salameh followed him into exile to Baghdad. There he received military training in Iraq from 1939 to 1940. But soon afterwards, Salameh followed the grand mufti to Nazi Germany, where he served as his senior aide.

For Palestinian nationalists in World War II this was a classic story: the Nazis were the enemies of their enemies—the British Empire and the Zionist colonialists—so the most prominent Palestinian leader at the time, the Grand Mufti Haj Amin Husseini, considered the Nazis to be strategic allies. This would prove to be an egregious miscalculation, not only because the Germans lost the war, but also because of what the Germans did to the Jews. The enormity of the Holocaust would mean that Haj Amin Husseini's alliance—however ineffectual—would become a black stain on the reputation of the Palestinian cause. And Hassan Salameh was personally involved. He became a virtual covert operative of the Germans.

In December 1941 Haj Amin met with Hitler and suggested that German and Palestinian commandos should parachute into Palestine and incite the local population to rise up against the British. This idea languished until late in the war, when the Germans activated a covert plan—Operation Atlas—to do exactly what the grand mufti had suggested. By one account, Haj Amin Husseini persuaded the Germans to provide the commando team with poison to release into the city of Tel Aviv's water supply.

On the evening of October 6, 1944, a five-member unit parachuted from a small plane over the Jericho Valley. Hassan Salameh was one of the five. A German SS officer, Colonel Kurt Wieland, led the team. Wieland had grown up in the Templar community of Sarona, just outside Jaffa. (Templars were a small German Protestant sect whose millennial beliefs drove them to immigrate to Palestine in the late nineteenth century.) In 1936 Wieland traveled to Germany and joined the Nazi Party. He was familiar with Palestine and spoke fluent Arabic. Wieland was thus unusually well qualified, but Operation Atlas was an impossible mission. Things went awry from the moment the men jumped out of a German prototype plane powered by an experimental engine. The plane was supposed to have dropped the five-member team at a site north of Jericho. But it flew too high, so Wieland and two other team members landed south of Jericho—while Hassan Salameh and another German officer landed even farther afield. Their supplies—which included two thousand gold coins, guns, maps, radio equipment, and allegedly ten cardboard boxes of poison—were scattered over a wide region.

The parachute drop botched the entire operation. British police soon received reports that locals had stumbled across gold coins. Search parties were sent out to scour the Jericho region. Wieland and two others sought refuge in one of Jericho's caves—where they were soon discovered and arrested by British forces. But Salameh and another German escaped on foot toward Jerusalem. Salameh had suffered a foot injury during the parachute landing. He nevertheless made his way to his native Qula, near Lydda, where a doctor treated him. Despite putting a price on his head, the British never caught Salameh.

On November 29, 1947, the United Nations General Assembly adopted a resolution proclaiming that the British Mandate in Palestine would end on May 15, 1948. On that date Palestine would be divided into a Jewish state and a Palestinian state. The Jewish population of Palestine celebrated long into the night of November 29. The very next morning, however, Palestinian guerrillas firing machine guns and throwing hand grenades attacked a Jerusalem-bound bus filled with Jews, six of whom were killed. Salameh's guerrillas allegedly carried out the attack. A week later, Salameh led three hundred of his men in an attack against the Hatikva Quarter, a suburb on the eastern edge of Tel Aviv. But he lost sixty of his fighters and was forced to retreat. Salameh concluded that his militia was no match for the Haganah, so in the ensuing months he returned to attacking Jewish vehicles on the open roads. It was a deadly strategy.

Sheikh Hassan coordinated his road attacks with Abdul Qader al-Husseini, the Palestinians' most famous guerrilla leader—and a cousin of the grand mufti. Abdul Qader tried to conquer Jerusalem, while Salameh sought to control the roads leading up to Jerusalem. During the first six months of 1948, Salameh's force grew to a roving band of perhaps five hundred guerrillas. He called his men the "Mediterranean Irregulars." They specialized in roadside bombs. On January 22, 1948, seven Jewish auxiliary policemen were killed when their vehicle was blown apart as it drove past a booby-trapped carcass of a dog lying in the middle of the road. In late March 1948, Salameh boasted to a reporter from the Associated Press that his men were preparing to conquer Tel Aviv. He maintained his headquarters in a building in an orange grove outside Ramla. On the night of April 4, 1948, this four-story structure was blown up; more than twenty of his men died, but

Salameh once again escaped with his life. By then he and Abdul Qader al-Husseini were recognized as the Palestinians' two top military commanders. But not for long. On April 8, an Israeli sentry outside the village of Al-Qastal shot and killed Husseini.

On May 30, 1948, militia from Menachem Begin's paramilitary group, the Irgun, attacked the strategic village of Ras al-Ein, whose wells supplied Jerusalem with much of its drinking water. After a two-hour battle, the Irgun seized the village, including the ruins of Antipatris, a Crusader fortress. The next day Salameh led three hundred of his men to take back Ras al-Ein. After eleven Irgun men were killed and a score were wounded, the Irgun fell back. But as they retreated, they managed to fire off one more mortar round that exploded in the midst of the advancing Fedayeen—volunteer militia. Salameh's cousin was killed and a nephew was wounded. And Salameh himself suffered shrapnel wounds to his chest. On June 2, 1948, he died in a Ramla hospital. He was only thirty-seven years old. His death marked a decisive turning point in the Palestinian resistance to the newly established Israeli state.

Ali Hassan Salameh was only six years old when his father died. But he grew up with family stories of his father's exploits. Salameh was reared to regard his father as a legendary Palestinian hero and martyr to the cause—notwithstanding his association with the failed plot to poison Tel Aviv's water supply. His father had displayed audacity and courage. "We must mention two Palestinian commanders," later wrote the official historian of the Haganah. "Abdul Kader [al-Husseini] and Hassan Salameh. In spite of all the cruelty they showed in harming non-combatant Jewish civilians, they fought personally at the head of their soldiers, and both perished in battle."

Salameh was a Palestinian patriot, a guerrilla fighter, and a terrorist. He had killed civilians in the name of Palestinian nationalism. His fellow partisans would say that he only fought terror with terror. He was brazen and unorthodox and fearless. His son would become all these things.

Ali Hassan spent his childhood years in Beirut. He and his sisters,

Jihad and Nidal, were raised by their mother in a middle-class apartment in the lovely neighborhood of Ashrafiyeh. They were Palestinian refugees; the Salameh family house in Qula had been razed to
the ground. But in Beirut they did not live like refugees. Ali attended
Maqassed College, a private school. In 1956, when he was fourteen,
he was sent to a boarding school in Bir Zeit, on the West Bank. His
mother constantly reminded him of his father's legacy. "The influence
of my father has posed a personal problem to me," Ali Hassan Salameh later told a Lebanese reporter in the only extended interview he
ever gave to the press. Twelve other family members, mostly cousins,
had died in the 1948 war. "My upbringing was politicized," Ali Hassan
said. "I lived the Palestinian cause, at a time when the cause was turning in a vicious circle. They were a people without a leadership. The
people were dispersed, and I was part of the dispersion.... The problem I faced was this: whereas the family considered struggle a matter
of heritage, there was no real cause to struggle for. There was a history
of a cause, but no cause. My mother wanted me to be another Hassan
Salameh at a time when the most any Palestinian could hope for was
to live a normal life.... I was constantly conscious of the fact that I
was the son of Hassan Salameh and had to live up to that, even without
being told how the son of Hassan Salameh should live."

Ali tried for years to live his own life. "I wanted to be myself," he
said. "The fact that I was required to live up to the image of my father
created a problem for me."

In 1958 the family moved to Cairo, where Ali studied engineering,
graduating with a B.A. in 1963. The move to Cairo was made possible
by an invitation from Egypt's charismatic president, Gamal Abdel
Nasser—who had heard that the family of the famous Palestinian
martyr was living in strapped circumstances. Nasser offered scholarships to Ali Hassan and his two sisters. Afterwards, Ali did graduate
work in Germany—where he learned fluent German and acquired a
taste for expensive clothes, gourmet foods, and wine. Also women.
But all along, despite his ambivalence, he was always drawn to politics. In May 1964 Ali Hassan attended the first convening of the

Palestinian National Council in East Jerusalem, and thus he witnessed the formation of the PLO. Shortly afterwards he joined Yasir Arafat's Fatah, a secular Palestinian political party and militia. (The name is an acronym from the full name—the Palestinian National Libera- tion Movement—which when spelled backwards becomes "Fatah" in Arabic, or "opening.") Ali Hassan had finally found his cause—and how to live as the son of Hassan Salameh. "I became very attached to Fatah," he recalled. "I had found what I was looking for."

After spending a year in Cairo, Salameh was sent by Arafat to Ku- wait to be in charge of the PLO's Popular Organization Department. As chairman of the Kuwaiti chapter of the General Union of Palestin- ian Students, Salameh actively recruited students into Fatah. In 1966 Mustafa Zein paid a visit and spent a week in his home. When the June 1967 war broke out, Ali Hassan fled to Amman, thinking he could join in the fight. It was all over soon after he arrived. Afterwards, Arafat assigned him to work in Fatah's Revolutionary Security Apparatus (al- Razd), the organization's intelligence bureau. In 1968 Salameh was sent back to Cairo, where he received intelligence training from the Egyptian government. Initially, Ali Hassan specialized in counterin- telligence, vetting the security files of Fatah volunteers and keeping track of Palestinians who might have been recruited by the Israelis to penetrate Fatah. It was distasteful work, but Ali Hassan was good at it. He was methodical and patient.*

Arafat liked Salameh—despite the young man's extravagant life- style. And he was certainly drawn to Salameh's pedigree as the son of a famous Palestinian martyr. Perhaps it also counted that Ali Hassan had married well. His wife was Nashrawan Sharif, whose wealthy Pal- estinian family came from Haifa, where they'd owned property worth millions of dollars. Ali and Nashrawan had met in Cairo—and it had

---

* Another part of Salameh's intelligence job was to liaise with "comrades" from radical organizations like the Baader-Meinhof Group, a terrorist organization that oper- ated in Europe. In 1970 Andreas Baader and other German colleagues reportedly re- ceived training in a Fatah camp in Jordan. But the Germans misbehaved, and eventually Ali Hassan Salameh sent them packing back to Europe.

been a love marriage. Nashrawan was an intelligent, attractive woman who had earned a bachelor's degree in French literature.

Bob Ames knew only enough of Salameh's biographical details to know that he made an interesting target for recruitment. Accordingly, he encouraged Mustafa to approach his friend. Zein and Salameh soon met in Faisal's Restaurant on Rue Bliss, across the street from the American University of Beirut's main gate. Salameh was as clever as he was flamboyant, and he immediately understood that Zein had some special American friends. According to Zein, some months earlier Salameh had "alerted me to expect an American request for me to arrange a contact with the PLO." Salameh wanted to establish contact with some "official" Americans. But he could not meet in public. So Ames later conveyed through Zein his plan for an initial contact: Zein would meet Salameh at the Strand café at Hamra Street and Rue Jeanne d'Arc. Ames would stroll by at an appointed hour, and as he walked by their table Zein would signal that the man walking by was their contact. Salameh would respond by placing his hand on Zein's shoulder. It was a script by which Ames could know that Salameh indeed knew whom he was dealing with and was willing to play the game. They would not speak to each other; they might make eye contact. In public, they were merely passing strangers on Hamra Street. But in the future, they'd be able to recognize each other. It was designed by Ames as the first step—one that would preserve Salameh's security.

The scene is accurately portrayed in David Ignatius's novel about Ames and Salameh, *Agents of Innocence.* Both Salameh and Ames brought their own security. Salameh had a number of Force 17 commandos in civilian clothes stationed discreetly around the café. Ames had his own security team in place. As scripted, Ames approached Salameh's table at the Strand café; but instead of walking by silently as planned, Ames suddenly paused, and Salameh rose and shook his hand. "Ali looked at Bob, and then pointed to me," Zein recalled, "and said, 'This is my man.'"

Soon afterwards, Ames had Zein set up a clandestine meeting with Salameh in a CIA safe house—actually an apartment—in Beirut. A PLO source later told David Ignatius that Ames had told Salameh he'd been authorized by the National Security Council to open up a channel to the PLO. The gist of his message was: "You Arabs claim your views are not heard in Washington. Here is your chance. The president of the United States is listening." This was somewhat of a calculated embellishment. Ames would have reported the initial contact and requested permission to develop the relationship.

CIA director Richard Helms had cause to learn of Ames's operation at the end of January 1970, when he attended a meeting of the National Security Council in the White House's West Wing. Also present were President Nixon and British prime minister Harold Wilson. On the agenda was a discussion of the political challenges facing King Hussein's Hashemite monarchy in Jordan. The British handed over intelligence reports showing that Arafat had communicated to one of Hussein's associates an offer to be prime minister in a future government. Clearly, the PLO expected to soon topple the king. According to David Ignatius, who talked with a source close to Helms while researching *Agents of Innocence*, Helms went back to the Agency convinced that the CIA needed to improve its sourcing from within the PLO. After questioning some top officers in the Directorate of Operations, Helms was informed about Ames's promising lead with a top Fatah officer.

Helms thus knew about Ames's contact with Salameh within six weeks of the meeting. But at what point Helms went to President Nixon to inform him of the existence of this back channel is unknown. Helms had an awkward relationship with Nixon. They didn't meet often. So Helms probably waited until he had something of substance to report from Ames's meetings with Salameh. He wouldn't have waited too long, however, because of the political sensitivities. The PLO was regarded as a terrorist organization, and thus political contacts with its members were prohibited. On the other hand, the CIA viewed the PLO as a natural target for intelligence recruitment. Ames had not gone "rogue" by approaching Salameh. Helms knew Ames was just doing his job as a clandestine officer. His encounter with Salameh could always be seen as the first step in an attempted recruitment. But it was another matter if Ames's intention was not recruitment but the opening of a liaison relationship. That could be political dynamite if it were to leak. Helms understood that the president—and probably his national security adviser, Henry Kissinger—had to approve the operation and judge its potential rewards against the risks of disclosure. Nixon and Kissinger were probably brought into the loop by the summer of 1970, some six months after the initial contact. And this meant that at some point intelligence reports sourced to someone close to Chairman Arafat—not naming Salameh, but making it clear where the information came from—would have landed on the president's desk, perhaps in the Presidential Daily Brief. So maybe Ames's boast to Salameh was not such an exaggeration. The president of the United States was listening.

Ames and Salameh had an easy and quite open relationship. "Bob had Ali Hassan over to our apartment one time," recalled Yvonne, "but I didn't meet him." They made an odd pair. On one level, they clearly had nothing in common. Ames dressed modestly, like a conservative American businessman: cheap tan slacks, perhaps a loose-fitting polo shirt and a gray sports jacket. Nothing out of the most ordinary— except for the cowboy boots he sometimes chose to wear. Going on thirty-six years of age, Bob had a bit of a paunch. He kept his hair short and well trimmed. He was devoted to his wife of ten years and their five children. And he hated to spend money. He rarely drank. There was nothing extravagant about Bob Ames.

Ali Hassan, age twenty-seven, looked like a movie actor or a rock 'n' roll musician. He dressed his six-foot frame in black. His standard uniform was a tight-fitting black shirt unbuttoned to show his hairy chest, a black leather jacket, and black trousers. His wavy, jet-black hair was thick and brushed straight back, revealing a broad forehead. His sideburns were long and bushy, almost like a nineteenth-century Englishman's muttonchop sideburns. His stomach muscles were taut and firm, evidence of his almost daily karate workouts in the Continental Hotel's gym; he'd earned either a fourth or a fifth black belt. He was in very good shape. "He moved like a panther," recalled Frank Anderson, a case officer who worked with Ames. He spoke fluent English, German, and French. He listened to American pop music; his favorite song was Elvis Presley's "Love Me Tender." He was rumored to have an IQ of 180. Ali Hassan was not a nervous man, but rather incongruously, he chain-smoked cigarettes. He drank Scotch whiskey, but he also had a taste for expensive red wines, and though he was married and had two sons he openly dated other women. "When Ali walked in," recalled the wife of one CIA case officer, "he sucked the air out of the room." He knew people gossiped about his playboy lifestyle. But he didn't care. He once told a reporter, "People expect a revolutionary to be a miserable-looking, shabby creature dressed in rags. That's the wrong notion. . . . As the Arabic saying goes: Better a reputation of opulence than a reputation of misery."

Ames and Salameh were opposites. But they quickly established a genuine friendship. Ali Hassan joked that by hanging out with Ames he'd get a chance to practice his English. "Professionally speaking," said Anderson, "they each were the most significant person in each other's lives."

The ever-reliable Mustafa Zein always arranged their meetings. "Mustafa was a constant presence," Anderson said. "He deeply admired both Bob and Ali Hassan." Zein had cultivated a persona in West Beirut's café society as a smooth-talking radical-chic Lebanese leftist who strongly sympathized with the Palestinian cause. He seemed to know everyone.

By the summer of 1970, Ames's special relationship with Salameh had evolved to a point where the young Palestinian had become a critical source of information about the brewing crisis in Jordan. Salameh was still just a "source"—not a recruit. Nevertheless, the CIA sometimes assigns a cryptonym to a source, if only to make it easier to disseminate the source's information more widely within the Agency without compromising his identity. Salameh's crypt was MJTRUST/2. All crypts are capitalized and begin with a two-character prefix, a diagraph that signifies a country or subject. At the time, *MJ* stood for Palestinian. The originating case officer—in this instance, Bob Ames—usually selected the root word following the two-character diagraph. Significantly, Ames called Salameh TRUST, suggesting exactly what he thought of him. He was trusted. The root word in the crypt is always followed by a slash and a number. MJTRUST/2 signified that Salameh was the second member of this organization to have been identified by this case officer. "The PLO factions were the darling of Arab intellectuals and the Arab street," recalled Hume Horan, then the U.S. embassy's chief political officer in Amman. "King Hussein was extraordinarily isolated. Washington wondered how Hussein could last, with half of Jordan's population being Palestinian. . . . Every Arab under twenty thought Hussein a stooge for Zionism and Western imperialism."

Early in 1970, Ambassador Harry Symmes made it clear to President Richard Nixon and his national security adviser, Henry Kissinger, that he believed the king's days were numbered. "I didn't think the king was effectively in charge of the situation—and even if he tried to be in charge that he would succeed."

Kissinger agreed that King Hussein was "in grave peril" and was concerned that his collapse "would radicalize the entire Middle East." At the same time, he doubted that Israel would ever allow the PLO to take over Jordan.

But the facts on the ground suggested that the Hashemites could no longer be sustained in power. By June 1970, lawlessness was commonplace. Both the Fedayeen and the army committed various atrocities. That month the king's convoy of cars was attacked and Hussein personally participated in a street battle. On September 1, 1970, he barely survived an assassination attempt. The CIA's longtime station chief in Amman, Jack O'Connell (1921–2010), bluntly told the king that the time had come to mount a crackdown on the PLO's militia and seize back the streets from the Fedayeen. "I was virtually alone in believing that the king and his army would ultimately prevail," O'Connell later wrote in his memoirs. "The U.S. government was deeply divided. State was pessimistic. The Agency was split between my views in Amman and the views of Bob Ames, a rising CIA star who was stationed in Beirut and in liaison with Arafat's intelligence chief, Ali Hassan Salameh. Ames and I were rivals."

O'Connell had first arrived in Amman in 1958 when he was sent by the Agency to warn King Hussein of an army plot against his regime. O'Connell played a key role in thwarting the coup and thus earned the king's gratitude. In 1963, O'Connell was sent back to Amman as chief of station, and he quickly became the king's closest foreign confidant. O'Connell believed deeply in the "plucky little king" and believed that his Bedouin army could keep him in power—regardless of the wishes of the majority of his people.

Ames believed Salameh—who was telling him that the PLO forces were capable of withstanding anything the Hashemites could throw at them. Ames believed the Palestinians were going to win, if only because the PLO had a popular mandate and the momentum. "Bob was just very clearly anti-Hashemite—and ambivalent about Israel," recalled Dewey Clarridge, later a high-ranking officer in Arab Operations. Ames and O'Connell argued vigorously with each other, both verbally and in their cables back to Langley. O'Connell thought Ames was "misinterpreting his own personal experience with urban warfare in Aden, where the Yemeni insurgents had driven British troops from the port city in 1967." O'Connell pointed out that the British were the foreigners in Aden, while the Jordanian army was fighting on home ground. Ames countered that historically, King Hussein, the Hashemite family, and the king's Bedouin tribesmen were actually the foreigners in that they had come from the Hejaz in western Arabia during World War I. The British colonialists, Ames reminded O'Connell, had imposed the Hashemite regime on the Palestinian population. It was the Palestinians, he argued, who were on home ground, and it was the Palestinians who possessed the higher quotient of political legitimacy. O'Connell thought this was too fine a point; Ames was intellectualizing. What mattered was power, and Hussein's army had 150 tanks and plenty of artillery. "Bob was prescient," said Graham Fuller, another clandestine officer. "And like many prescient officers, he would be right about the longer time frame, and just wrong in the short term."

As civil war loomed, the PLO had around twenty-five thousand men in its militia, but all summer they'd been passing out arms to thousands of young men in the refugee camps. All told, there were perhaps as many as forty thousand Palestinians walking around with guns in their hands. Hussein's regular army numbered some sixty thousand troops, but more than half of these men—even many of the officers—were Palestinians. Hussein felt he could count on the loyalty of less than half his army. But O'Connell was right about one thing: Bedouin officers loyal to the monarch controlled the armored units, and they could prove to be decisive in any showdown with the guerrillas.

Ironically, the Israeli political and military establishment was having the same debate as Ames and O'Connell. Leading Israeli political figures were themselves divided on whether saving King Hussein's throne was good for Israel. Golda Meir, Yigal Allon, Abba Eban, and Yitzhak Rabin surmised that King Hussein might someday be persuaded to conclude a separate peace deal with Israel. "The opposing opinion," wrote Mordechai Gur, the Israeli general in charge of the Syrian-Lebanese front in 1970, "supported the transformation of Jordan into a Palestinian state. . . . They suggested allowing the guerrillas to achieve their aims and to take control over all of Jordan. In this they saw the ideal solution to the issue of the Palestinians." Ezer Weizman, Gen. Moshe Dayan, and Shimon Peres made this argument—and so too did Gen. Ariel Sharon.

Henry Kissinger claims that he knew nothing of this internal Israeli debate. But in the midst of the crisis, on September 20, 1970, he told his aides, "I'm not really sure the Israelis would mind it if Hussein should topple. They would have no more West Bank problem." And

just a few days later he read an official memorandum of a conversation
in which Israel's foreign minister, Abba Eban, speculated that Israel
might indeed be better off without the Hashemite regime:

> Foreign Minister Eban told [U.S.] Ambassador [Charles] Yost at
> the UN on September 23 that while Israel, on balance, favored
> Husayn at this time, "the world would not come to an end if he
> departed the scene." Eban said the Palestinians would become
> more responsible when saddled with the day-to-day burdens of
> government, and the long-term trend in Jordan was toward greater
> recognition of the fact that Jordan was 70 percent Palestinian.
> Yost added that Eban seemed to imply that, sooner or later, Is-
> rael has to find an accommodation with the Palestinians and that
> it might in the long run be easier if they dominated the state of
> Jordan.

Kissinger read and initialed this memorandum—but evidently
he discounted Eban's analysis. Years later he insisted to the British
scholar Nigel Ashton that "any move to undermine Hussein would
have provoked a crisis in their [the Israelis'] relations with Washington." More likely, Kissinger instinctively thought America's Cold War
imperatives—which in the Middle East usually meant blind support
for a pro-American, anticommunist, and anti-Nasserite monarch—
was a safer policy than actually addressing the Palestinian problem,
one of the region's primary sources of unrest. Ames thought this shortsighted. And O'Connell thought Ames was too much under the influence of his "Red Prince."

Some thought Ames had an overt pro-Palestinian prejudice. But
in point of fact, most CIA officers who spent any time in the region
came to sympathize with the plight of the Palestinian refugees. "Like
all of us who get to know anything about the Palestinian problem,"
said George Cave, a veteran of more than three decades in the Agency,
"you can't help but feel sympathy for them. . . . When people ask me
what to read about the Arab-Israeli problem I tell them the Old Testa-

ment." O'Connell also sympathized with the Palestinians—but he had a personal relationship with Hussein and genuinely liked the king.

■

On September 6, 1970, the crisis in Jordan was further inflamed by a brazen act of air piracy. Commandos from the Popular Front for the Liberation of Palestine (PFLP) hijacked four commercial airliners all in one day. One of the four planes, a Pan Am jumbo jet, was flown to Cairo. A hundred feet above the runway, a PFLP commando lit a fuse and informed the crew that they had eight minutes to get everyone off the plane. As the plane screeched to a halt at the end of the runway, the cabin crew blew the emergency slide chutes open and yelled at the 173 passengers to evacuate. Three minutes later, the $25 million jet blew apart on the tarmac. Miraculously, no one was injured. The hijacking of an El Al passenger jet bound for New York from Amsterdam was foiled by Israeli security guards; one of the hijackers, an American citizen, Patrick Arguello, was killed, and his companion, Leila Khaled, was detained in a British police station in London. But two of the other planes were piloted to Dawson's Field, an abandoned World War II–era desert airstrip north of Amman. The passengers were kept hostage by hundreds of PFLP Fedayeen. Three days later, they were joined by yet another hijacked plane. By then, the PFLP had 426 hostages at Dawson's Field—surrounded by hundreds of King Hussein's Arab Legionnaires sitting in armored personnel carriers.

The multiple hijackings were a piece of meticulously planned guerrilla theater, designed to focus the world's attention on the problem of Palestine. The PFLP demanded the release of more than three thousand Palestinians held in Israeli prisons in return for the release of the hostages. A year earlier, Israeli prime minister Golda Meir had famously insisted that when Israel was created in 1948, "it was not as though there was a Palestinian people.... They did not exist." Now it became a little harder to say this with any credibility. As Walter Cronkite intoned on the *CBS Evening News*, "Palestinian guerrillas, in a bold and coordinated action, created this newest crisis Sunday, and in doing so they accomplished what they set out to do: they thrust back into the world's attention a problem diplomats have tended to shunt aside in hesitant steps towards Middle East peace."

The standoff at Dawson's Field dragged on for ten days. King Hussein felt this was the final humiliation. The CIA's Jack O'Connell urged the king to order his Arab Legionnaires into action. Finally, on September 16, 1970, Hussein declared martial law. That evening fifty tanks moved into positions above the main Palestinian refugee camps of Amman. The king told the new American ambassador, L. Dean Brown, that he was "betting all his chips." It was going to be an "all or nothing showdown."

At dawn the next morning, the Arab Legion began lobbing artillery shells at guerrilla positions on Jebel Hussain and into the crowded camps of Wahdat and Al-Husseini. The bombardment was indiscriminate, hitting residential quarters in the tightly packed camps. "It was very messy," recalled the embassy's Hume Horan. "The Jordanians didn't want to send their infantry against the guerrillas in the slums of Amman. They felt the urban geography would negate the Army's edge in discipline and weaponry. So they led their assaults with armor, the infantry following close behind. Through field glasses you could see the tanks roll up toward some buildings. Lurch to a stop. Then the main battle guns would go, 'Boom!' and part of the buildings would collapse. Out would swarm some Palestinians. The tanks would chase them, firing machine guns, with the infantry also in pursuit." The result was carnage. The Royal Jordanian Air Force dropped phosphorus and napalm bombs on the refugee camps. From his bunker in one of the camps, Arafat vowed, "The fight goes on until the fascist military regime in Jordan is toppled." By his side stood Salameh, who had rushed to Amman when the fighting broke out.

Over the next ten days, the Fedayeen held their ground in Amman and even turned down a cease-fire offer. Many were able to survive by hunkering down in some 360 subterranean bunkers carved beneath the refugee camps. Most of northern Jordan was still controlled by the PLO. But not for long. The threat of American and Israeli intervention dissuaded the Syrians from providing air cover for the attacking Syrian armor that had invaded northern Jordan in support of the Palestinians. At one point in the battle, King Hussein sent a frantic message to Washington asking "for an air strike by Israel against the Syrian troops." But in the end, outright Israeli intervention was not necessary. The king's own armored forces managed to advance, the Syrians withdrew, and the PLO's guerrillas soon began to fall back. In Amman, the king ordered his army to redouble its bombardment of the refugee camps. An estimated 3,400 Fedayeen and civilians were killed. Some had to be buried in mass graves. "There were atrocities," admitted Horan. "It was a time when no quarter was asked by or given to some of these combatants." And yet, in the end, Horan believed, "The good guys won."

That is certainly not how Arafat or Salameh saw things. By the end of September, they'd been forced to accede to a cease-fire brokered by Egypt's Gamal Abdel Nasser. The PFLP agreed to release the remaining hostages from the air hijackings. And the PLO's Fedayeen had to retreat from Amman. Salameh was responsible for getting Arafat out of Amman. It was Salameh's idea to dress Arafat in the robes of a Kuwaiti sheikh; he and Salameh were then smuggled aboard an airliner, posing as part of the fourteen-member Arab Committee sent to mediate a cease-fire. Arafat arrived safely in Cairo, where he met with President Gamal Abdel Nasser and signed the cease-fire.

That autumn, King Hussein appointed Wasfi al-Tal as prime minister. A half-Kurdish businessman from Irbid in northern Jordan, Al-Tal was known for his hard-line views critical of the PLO. He now urged the king to rid the country of the PLO once and for all. In July 1971, Al-Tal ordered the army to resume its offensive against the Fedayeen. After four days of artillery and napalm strikes, at least 1,000 PLO fighters were killed or wounded and some 2,300 were arrested. King Hussein's secret police arrested another 20,000 Palestinian civilians and expelled Arafat and all other PLO officials to Lebanon. Henceforth, Jordan would be for "authentic" Jordanians—and "Jordanized" Palestinians.

Salameh was devastated by the PLO's defeat in Jordan. "It left an indelible mark on all of us," he told Nadia Salti Stephan, a reporter from Beirut's English-language weekly *Monday Morning*, in April 1976. "I am one of those who were and remain unable to imagine how on earth we were driven out."

The month of September 1970 was a national calamity for the Palestinians—and a sad month for Arabs everywhere. On the evening of September 28, 1970—just hours after Egypt's president, Gamal Abdel Nasser, had patched together a temporary truce between the PLO and King Hussein—the charismatic Arab leader died suddenly, felled by a massive heart attack. He was only fifty-two years old. Sitting in Beirut, Ames watched as tens of thousands of mourners poured into the streets, weeping and crying out Nasser's name. Some of the mourners burned tires, and men armed with Kalashnikovs fired barrages into the evening heavens. Arabs everywhere could see television images of four to five million Egyptians walking behind the six-mile-long funeral procession. Nasser had been a volatile figure. A populist leader who had genuinely tried to improve the lives of Egypt's impoverished peasantry, he had also gradually built an inefficient and sometimes bumbling police state. He was not exactly a tyrant, but neither was he a democrat. He was personally incorruptible. He was the only Arab leader of his time who could plausibly claim to reflect the broad popular will. But more than one American president had tried to dislodge him from power—and Nasser personally believed that the CIA had plotted with his domestic political enemies. Ames nevertheless was moved to write a poem the day Nasser died.

Abd-al Nasir died today:
A light went out, an era ended.
A world stood still, a gloom descended.
A nation cried today:
A river stopped, a dream lay shattered.

Abd-al Nasir died today,
   A nation cried today.

Ames was an idealist—and as this poem suggests, he felt real empathy for the millions who were in mourning for Nasser.

Back in Langley headquarters, the news of Bob Ames's meetings with Ali Hassan Salameh was still a tightly held secret. Henry Kissinger was adamant in public that the United States could not be seen as lending a terrorist organization any legitimacy. But inside the CIA, Ames's relationship was regarded as an intelligence coup. Salameh was providing raw intelligence that eventually landed on the desks of the president's National Security Council staff. (In this sense, Ames had fulfilled his promise to Mustafa Zein that the Palestinians would have a channel to the U.S. president.) Dick Helms knew all about Ames's back channel with Salameh and approved it. The CIA director later privately complained to Frank Anderson that he was "under a lot of pressure from Nixon and Kissinger to get better intelligence about Arafat's Fatah." Ames was providing that intelligence.

Yet some of Ames's superiors were unhappy that it was still only a relationship and not a formal recruitment. "Headquarters in Langley wanted Salameh to be a fully recruited agent," said Bruce Riedel, an Agency officer who later read all fifteen volumes of cables and memoranda associated with the case. "Everyone involved knew that it was an extraordinary case. And everyone was debating the messy questions about whether we should be in liaison with a terrorist organization. Of course the director of central intelligence (Helms) knew. But this also went all the way up to the president. Helms had to tell Nixon because of the potential for blowback."

Riedel and other Agency officers believe that Helms was always supportive of Ames. But the policy makers—really Kissinger—and President Nixon blew hot and cold. They wanted the intelligence. They even wanted the back channel because it only made pragmatic sense to be able to communicate with such important actors on the ground. But the policy makers would have greatly preferred that the relationship be with a controlled, paid agent—and not an independent actor like Salameh.

There were layers upon layers of ambiguity. "There is a lot that is just a matter of opinion in the business," said Henry Miller-Jones. "Mainly it is what the customer thinks of the agent's reporting that determines his overall value and it doesn't matter whether he signed a chit or not."

This was the nature of the game. It was hard to know exactly how to define the relationship. Some officers later insisted that Ames surely must have turned Salameh into a fully recruited agent. But those few people with direct knowledge of the case believe it was always a liaison relationship. "Part of the time, Salameh was probably telling Arafat that he had recruited a CIA officer," said Riedel. "And Ames probably knew this. He would have understood that there was probably some resentment inside Fatah circles against Salameh's friendship with a CIA officer. Salameh needed to tell his own people something like this for his own protection."

Late in 1970, a debate took place inside the CIA about what to do about Salameh. At the time, the chief of the Near East and South Asia Division in the DO was David Henry Blee, fifty-four, a South Asia expert, Harvard lawyer by training, and highly regarded administrator. (He was also a devout Catholic who wore a Fatima medallion beneath his shirt.) Dave Blee looked over the Salameh case file and decided it was time to make the recruitment pitch. Ames thought this unwise. "Bob would say," recalled *John Morris*, another clandestine officer, " 'You know, it would be fine to recruit Salameh, but you get what you can.'" Ames thought Salameh was not recruitable. "My best sources were never recruitable," said Graham Fuller, a fellow Arabist and case officer. Ames sensed, correctly as it turned out, that Salameh had from the beginning kept Arafat apprised of his meetings with Ames. Salameh had explained to Arafat that the PLO needed a way to communicate with the Americans—and if Washington wouldn't allow its diplomats to be seen talking to the PLO, then the next best thing was to establish a regular back channel through the CIA. Arafat agreed. The PLO chairman was running an armed liberation struggle, but at the same time he desperately wanted America to take him seriously. And from Ames's point of view, his relationship with Salameh was as useful and productive as a formal recruitment could be. Moreover, it was a two-way street in which Ames tried to influence Salameh to have the PLO act more like a political party—and less like a guerrilla organization—while Salameh tried to influence Washington, through Ames, to understand that it was unrealistic for U.S. policy makers to ignore the Palestinian cause. "Ali's ambition was to turn the back channel into a real diplomatic relationship," recalled Frank Anderson. "He wanted the relationship to evolve into a de facto recognition of the PLO. But on our side, we had to cloak the relationship as an intelligence operation. At the same time, Ali had to make it seem to his own people that this was diplomacy, not intelligence. In the end, we committed more diplomacy, and he conveyed more intelligence."

At times, Salameh and Ames traded useful bits of hard intelligence with each other, the kind of information that could save lives. "I remember avidly reading MJTRUST's file," recalled Charles Allen, an experienced DO officer. "It was unbelievably good stuff." Ames obviously thought so too. So when Dave Blee pressured Ames to take the next step and turn Salameh into a full recruitment, Ames resisted. Why, he argued, should such a valuable relationship be jeopardized just so the CIA could claim it had a paid agent at the side of Arafat? "I thought it was a mistake," recalled *Charles Waverly*, who was privy to the argument. "I thought it was out of context." Sam Wyman also sided with *Waverly* and Ames. "I was of the opinion that it was not necessary to recruit Salameh," Wyman said. "We had what we wanted."

This was an old argument in the intelligence business. "An agent does not always mean a paid agent," says *Hillel Katz*, a former high-ranking

Mossad officer. "If I had heard about this, I would have said, 'Bob, very good work. This is a good way to cultivate an agent.' As a matter of principle you have to allow your agent to have a good reason to justify what he is doing. Sometimes, he has to be able to tell himself, 'I am doing good service for my people.' It is never clean. In fact, it is best for everyone to keep it vague. Let him keep his pride."

Ames, Wyman, and *Waverly* were overruled, and Blee ordered another Agency officer, Vernon Cassin, to make the recruitment pitch. Ames nevertheless played his part. He told Mustafa Zein that Washington had agreed to initiate a dialogue with the PLO. A clandestine meeting would take place in Rome. "A CIA officer would start the ball rolling and Bob would pick it up in Beirut afterwards." Bob gave Mustafa handwritten instructions on how to meet Cassin in Rome. He told Mustafa to fly to Rome, where on December 16, 1970, he would receive a phone call in his hotel room at precisely 4:00 P.M.: "John will say he and his wife are in Rome and hope to see you . . ." Exactly one hour later, Mustafa was supposed to walk into the lobby of the Hilton Hotel with a coat over his arm. "John will carry [a] rolled Italian newspaper. You should take a seat in the corner of [the] lobby. John will approach and say, 'I think I met you in the Semiramis Hotel.' You should reply, 'I think it was the Shepard's [*sic*] Hotel.'" (Both were landmark hotels in Cairo.)

Zein did as he was told. Traveling on a diplomatic passport issued by Sharjah, Zein arrived in Rome on December 16, 1970. He met with "John"—Vernon Cassin—and subsequently made reservations for adjoining suites in the Cavalieri Hilton Hotel from December 18 through 21. Posing as a rich Arab businessman, Zein played host. Salameh arrived in Rome, along with a contingent of twenty-three security guards. His guards mostly kept out of sight. Salameh had been briefed by Zein and was under the impression that he was to meet with a high-ranking CIA official who was authorized to open a dialogue with the PLO. This was only several months after the September debacle in Jordan, and there was much to discuss. Salameh was introduced by Zein to Cassin, a tall, thin man who wore a fedora. A former station chief in Damascus and Amman, Cassin was a pretty straitlaced Agency officer. One colleague described him as "a complete professional who went by the book."

Cassin told Zein that he wanted to speak to Salameh alone. Zein immediately understood what was up, and before the meeting he took Ali Hassan aside and told him, "He is coming to recruit you. Just be cool. Listen to what he has to say and then politely excuse yourself." Salameh did as Zein advised. According to Peter Taylor, a British broadcast reporter who interviewed Zein at length, "The meeting did not go well." Salameh was offered $300,000 a month "to co-ordinate activities between your organization and our organization." Taylor later wrote in his 1993 book, *States of Terror*, that there was no proverbial suitcase stuffed with cash—just a verbal offer. After making the pitch, Cassin was pleased by Salameh's calm demeanor. No theatrics was a good sign. When Salameh rose to leave, Cassin promised they'd meet the next day for a fine meal in one of Rome's most expensive restaurants.

The next day the three men met for lunch. When Salameh momentarily excused himself, Zein turned to Cassin and said, "Ali told me everything. He said you were willing to finance the PLO to the tune of $35 million a year—and recognize the PLO. He's already sent a coded message to Arafat. The Chairman is very pleased."

Flabbergasted, Cassin hastily left the restaurant. Salameh and Zein were playing with him. He knew the attempted recruitment had failed; he reported this to Langley, but he also claimed that Salameh had angrily refused to cooperate with the Agency in combating terrorism. This was a lie, but one that conveniently explained the failed recruitment. Cassin painted Salameh as a dogmatic extremist.

For his part, Salameh was deeply offended by the overture. "It took a while to restore the relationship," said *Waverly*.

◼

Back in Beirut, Ames and Zein tried to put things on an even keel. But Ames was terribly disappointed by the fallout from the Rome fiasco.

"We, you and I," he wrote Mustafa Zein, "really tried to do something which was perhaps ahead of our time." He was also angry about the "lies and misunderstandings" told by Cassin about Salameh. "Since I have read the files on these matters I can say, unfortunately, that lies were told." Ames also had cause to worry about Salameh's safety. Soon after the Rome meeting, Salameh received a package addressed to him in Beirut. "Bob had warned us to watch out for letter bombs," Zein said. Salameh normally received all his mail through the PLO office. But one day in early 1971 a heavy manila envelope arrived at his Verdun Street apartment. Salameh had it x-rayed. Had he opened it, he would have been maimed or worse. This was almost certainly Mossad's first attempt to kill Ali Hassan.*

Ames saw Salameh intermittently over the next six months, and they met about a month before Ames was posted back to Washington in June 1971. But then Salameh seemed to disappear. "After the Rome meeting," Zein said, "Ali lost favor inside the PLO. Arafat had put him in charge of Palestinian-American relations, and now this didn't seem to be going anywhere." Ames was aware that Salameh's fortunes had dimmed precisely because of his association with the Agency. "I know he's suffered some setbacks because of his contact with me," Ames wrote Zein. "He was also ahead of his time. We really started something good and I believe history will prove that if people had been wiser and more honest much misery could have been avoided."

Just two weeks later, Ames wrote Zein again. The tone of the letter made it clear that Ames was trying to keep Zein on board, trying to persuade him that all was not lost in their venture. It was not a letter from a CIA case officer instructing his access agent. It was a letter of persuasion from one friend to another. "It sure was great to hear from you," Ames wrote in longhand, "and learn you are still in the middle of things. Life back here [Washington, D.C.] is dull by comparison—

---

* Mossad had a technician skilled in assembling letter bombs. This individual devised the book bomb that maimed the PFLP's Bassam Abu Sharif on July 25, 1972. Mossad's "Q" was reportedly responsible for more than thirty such mail bombs.

paper, politics and bureaucracy. Frankly, I miss the action and wish I were out doing something again."

Zein was then still working for the ruling sheikh of Abu Dhabi, but he was planning to move back to Lebanon. Ames told Zein that he felt indebted to him and offered to help: "Whatever you choose, I hope you'll keep in touch and if there is anything I can do to help let me know. I don't like to owe debts and I do owe a great deal to you." He said that he was planning a trip to Beirut and Amman in late October and suggested that perhaps they could meet there or in Bahrain. "I have much more to discuss when we get together later," Ames wrote. "There is much that can't be put in writing. As I'm sure you realize."

Zein was not an agent of the CIA. Ames knew that Mustafa was his own man. But Mustafa was also Bob's invaluable channel to Ali Hassan. "Regarding our friend," Ames wrote, "if you see him tell him that we are doing our best to balance things and we have achieved some success. I have a few things for him which I'll pass along via you. These items will help him regain some of the stature I know he lost because of his contact with us. I have a debt to him too which I want to pay off."

Bob signed this letter "Munir"—Arabic for "the Enlightener." This was Mustafa's affectionate, Sufi-derived alias for his American friend. Bob used his home for the return address on the envelope, but instead of his name he used the initials RCA.

Three weeks later, on September 14, 1971, Ames wrote Mustafa again about possibly setting up a meeting with Salameh. Ames was anxious to resume his conversations with Salameh, but he knew any such meeting, if leaked, could jeopardize Salameh's standing in the PLO. "Regarding our friend," Ames wrote Zein, "I believe it is imperative that you and I discuss any meeting with him prior to any firm commitment being made, if indeed we decide such a meeting should even take place. I, of course feel, personally, such a meeting would be extremely useful but what we want to avoid is any misunderstanding, such as existed in the past, and which caused all the parties concerned, especially you, so many problems. Now that he is back in his proper position, we do not want to repeat past mistakes."

Salameh's standing in the PLO had indeed suffered a setback in the spring and summer of 1971. Ali Hassan had his rivals, and Abu Iyad (Salah Khalaf) was one of them. The PLO's number-two leader had once been a mentor of Ali Hassan's. But after the disastrous outcome of the Jordanian civil war, some blamed Abu Iyad for poor intelligence on King Hussein's intentions and capabilities. Ali Hassan had once worked directly under Abu Iyad, but after September 1970 Salameh became Arafat's shadow. Abu Iyad resented Salameh's growing influence and access to the Chairman. By the spring of 1971, Abu Iyad was looking for any excuse to discredit Salameh. The perception that Salameh had somehow mishandled the back channel to the CIA had hurt his standing. But Abu Iyad also seized upon an incident in Europe on February 6, 1972, where a shoot-out involving some of Salameh's Force 17 commandos had resulted in the deaths of five men. Abu Iyad went to Arafat and complained that Salameh was out of control. Arafat placed Salameh on a three-month leave while an internal PLO investigation probed the incident. Salameh used the time to visit London and other European cities, traveling on an Algerian diplomatic passport. Upon his return to Beirut, Salameh was vindicated. Arafat's investigation concluded that the five men killed by Salameh's Force 17 operatives had been Mossad informants. As Ames had heard through his own sources, by the autumn of 1971 Salameh had been restored to his position as chief of Force 17.

The incident later became an important piece of Salameh's résumé, because in his absence Abu Iyad had created a rival organization within the PLO that became known as Black September. Salameh was not there when this happened. He thus had an alibi for not being present at the creation of Black September.

In the aftermath of the Jordanian civil war, the PLO found itself at a difficult crossroads. The defeat in Jordan had demoralized Arafat's Fatah Fedayeen and had simultaneously increased the political appeal of radicals to Arafat's left. The spectacular airline hijackings carried out by George Habash's PFLP had turned the Palestinian cause into a global issue. But now Arafat's younger cadres demanded that the "Old Man" come up with a new strategy. Arafat needed some victories lest he find himself pushed aside. His ranking deputy, Abu Iyad, urged Arafat to escalate the violence. Arafat was torn. A sharp debate took place. Khalid al-Hassan, the PLO's virtual foreign minister at the time, later explained to the British journalist Alan Hart, "I was opposed to the playing of the terror card. But I have to tell you something else. Those of our Fatah colleagues who did turn to terror were not mindless criminals. They were fiercely dedicated nationalists who were doing their duty as they saw it. I have to say they were wrong, and did so at the time, but I have also to understand them. In their view, and in this they were right, the world was saying to us Palestinians, 'We don't give a damn about you, and we won't care at least until you are a threat to our interests.' In reply those in Fatah who turned to terror were saying, 'Okay, world. We'll play the game by your rules. We'll make you care!'"

Arafat quietly authorized Abu Iyad to organize a clandestine force to bring the war to the West—and to take his revenge against the Hashemites. Abu Iyad was Arafat's oldest friend. With Arafat's blessing, he now created a covert arm of Fatah called Black September, named obviously after the bloody events of September 1970. Abu Iyad was thought to be its "spiritual godfather and chief." Black September was said to be "more a state of mind than an organization as such," but the shadowy group drew on Fatah communications and financial resources.

Arafat may have thought he could turn on terror operations—and then just as easily turn them off. But it was more complicated than that. Alan Hart later interviewed a member of Black September whose nom de guerre was Ben Bella. Hart asked him about Arafat's attitude toward its activities. "At the time," said Bella, "Arafat could not afford to speak against us in public because he knew what we were doing had the support of the majority in the rank and file of our movement. Our way was the popular way. But in private meetings he took every opportunity to tell us we were wrong. I remember an occasion when he said to some of us, 'You are crazy to take our fight to Europe.' I was angry and I said, 'Abu Amar, maybe you are right, maybe we are crazy—but tell me this: is it not also crazy for us to sit here in Lebanon, just waiting to be hit every day by Israeli fighter planes, and knowing that we will lose some ten or more fighters every day without advancing our cause. Is that not crazy too?"

Ali Hassan Salameh no doubt understood these sentiments. As the head of Force 17, Salameh supervised the men who served as Arafat's personal bodyguards. But Force 17 was also Fatah's nascent intelligence service. As such, Salameh reported to Abu Iyad—though he had his own special relationship with Arafat. If Abu Iyad served as Black September's spiritual inspiration, another senior PLO chieftain, Abu Daoud, was its tactical and operational commander. But the chain of command was murky. As head of Force 17, Salameh could hardly be unaware of the existence of this shadowy group. But according to Mustafa Zein, Salameh was not responsible for Abu Iyad's operations: "I told Ali that under no circumstances should he involve himself in spilling civilian blood."

Salameh was clearly a rival of Abu Iyad's. Both men were in competition for Arafat's affections. Citing Jordanian authorities, the *New York Times* reported that "Ali Hassan Salameh, the hard-living Fatah intelligence expert, who they say oversees Black September activities, has become a pawn in a rivalry between veteran commando chiefs." The *Times* published a photograph with this story "said to depict Ali Hassan Salameh"—but it was a mistake. The photograph was clearly not Salameh.

Black September's first target was Jordan's prime minister, Wasfi al-Tal. Salameh personally chose the assassins and organized the operation. According to Yezid Sayigh, the author of the definitive history of the PLO, Salameh was the "mastermind." On November 28, 1971, as the Jordanian prime minister was walking into Cairo's Sheraton Hotel, four Palestinians attacked him. Before his bodyguards could do anything, a young man named Izzat Ahmad Rabah fired four shots at close range. As Al-Tal's wife and bystanders watched in horror, one of the assassins, Monsa Khalifa, crouched next to the dying prime minister and licked some of his blood off the floor. As they were arrested, the assassins cried out, "We are Black September. . . . We have taken our revenge on a traitor."

Bob Ames happened to arrive in Amman that Sunday, just a few hours after the prime minister's assassination in Cairo. "The Jordanians were in an ugly mood," Ames wrote, "and you can bet that there was not a Palestinian to be seen on the streets." What he had planned as a brief informal fact-finding trip now became something more official. Two days after the assassination, Ames drove up with some other American diplomats to Irbid, where they paid a condolence call on Wasfi al-Tal's family. "It was a pleasant trip and I enjoyed the good bedu coffee," Ames wrote, "even though the occasion was solemn. . . . It was kind of fun to be in the middle of things again."

Later that week, Ames drove to Allenby Bridge on the River Jordan and crossed into the Israeli-occupied West Bank. It had been only a little more than four years since the Israelis had conquered the West Bank, but they were already intent on taking every opportunity to demonstrate that their presence was permanent. When Ames arrived at Allenby Bridge—the only crossing point from Jordan into the occupied territories—the Israelis wanted to stamp Ames's diplomatic passport with an Israeli visa stamp. Normally, as a courtesy, and to encourage tourism, the Israelis routinely gave visitors an Israeli visa on a separate piece of paper so that their passports would still be valid for travel in Arab countries. But on this occasion, the Israeli officials at Allenby Bridge made a point of trying to stamp Ames's diplomatic passport. When he refused to permit this, they delayed his passage. "They really put me through the mill," Ames wrote. "They completely took apart my suitcases, emptied my toothpaste tube, dug into my shoe polish, exposed the film in my camera . . . and they were not going to let any of my aerosol cans in—deodorant, shaving cream—they could be bombs you know."

And then someone intervened. Ames saw an Israeli army major

inspecting his passport and wallet. Upon finding some Yemeni money stuffed into the wallet, the Israeli army major turned to Ames and explained that he'd emigrated from Yemen in 1948. They'd found common ground. Ames charmed the man. "We talked about Yemen (my common language with the Israelis is Arabic) and he put all the aerosol cans back in my suitcase and let me go through."

Arriving in Jerusalem, Ames checked in to the American Colony, a quaint boutique hotel in East Jerusalem's Sheikh Jarrah neighborhood. Built in the late nineteenth century out of Jerusalem's beautiful white stone, the American Colony had served as an integral part of Jerusalem's social and political life for decades. It was a genteel expatriate haven in the midst of Arab Jerusalem. At the end of World War I another spy, T. E. Lawrence, had taken lodgings in the American Colony. Lowell Thomas, Gertrude Bell, and John D. Rockefeller were among the Colony's notable list of visitors. Even after the June 1967 war, its bar and grand dining hall served as a cosmopolitan salon for Jerusalem's diplomats, journalists, and intellectuals. In the evenings, dozens of expatriates and Palestinian intellectuals mingled in the "big salon," sitting in overstuffed armchairs under an elaborate Damascene ceiling hand-painted with gold leaf. Ames loved the hotel's old-world, Orientalist charm. He liked the convenience of its location, just a few blocks from the American consulate. Also nearby was St. George's Cathedral, where Ames's old friend from Dhahran, the newly ordained Ronald Metz, was now an aide to the Anglican bishop of Jerusalem. Metz had left both the CIA and Aramco for the Church. But his political work for the bishop focused on aiding the Palestinian residents of East Jerusalem in coping with all the difficulties they faced living under the Israeli occupation. (The Israelis had annexed East Jerusalem in 1967, but neither the Palestinians nor the international community regarded the annexation as legal.)

Despite all his sympathies for the Palestinians, Ames could sometimes empathize with the other side. In Jerusalem he visited the Old City, entering through Jaffa Gate in the Jewish Quarter. He walked to the Wailing Wall. "Today is the Jewish Sabbath," he wrote home, "so there was a large turnout at the Wall, and I must say this was impressive. Most of the visitors to the Wall were Oriental/Orthodox Jews dressed in their traditional garb. One goes away with the feeling that these people should not be denied access to the Wall no matter what the final solution is."

Ames could see that the Israelis had imposed some modernity on the Old City. Hebrew signs adorned every street. The garbage was picked up routinely, and the city was just better organized than when the Jordanians had ruled it. But Ames was a bit of a romantic, and he "missed the oriental dignity that was Jerusalem." He wrote Yvonne that he "kind of liked the old chaos—it made you feel a little closer to the time of Christ."

Ames also disapproved of what the Israelis were doing to encircle East Jerusalem with Jewish neighborhoods. "I can look out my window [from the American Colony] and see all the high rise apartments the Israelis are building on the hills that surround Jerusalem. Somehow that doesn't seem right. . . . You certainly get the impression that the Israelis are here to stay."

After seeing a few contacts, both Israeli and Palestinian, Ames returned to Washington in time for the Christmas holidays.

CHAPTER SIX

Secret Diplomacy

If you can keep your head when all about you
Are losing theirs and blaming it on you

— Rudyard Kipling, 1895

Home was now Reston, in northern Virginia, not far from CIA headquarters. Bob, Yvonne, and the children had left Beirut early in the summer of 1971. Yvonne was pregnant again. On home leave that summer, they first went to Jackson, Mississippi, to visit Yvonne's parents. Her father had retired as a navy commander and become a pastor with the Lutheran Church, Missouri Synod. And then they moved into a furnished apartment for a few weeks near Washington, D.C., while they went house hunting. On August 3, 1971, they bought their first home, a single-family, split-level brick-and-wood house at 2304 Short Ridge Road in Reston, Virginia. It was nestled on a cul-de-sac at the bottom of a gentle hill, surrounded by dense forest. Sometimes they spotted deer grazing in the woods. They paid $48,950. With four bedrooms and three baths, it was small for a family of seven—soon to be eight. The children had to share one bathroom. It was a decidedly unpretentious suburban American home.

On August 21, 1971, Yvonne gave birth to her sixth child, Kevin. After nine years abroad, Yvonne was happy to be back in America. Bob was assigned a desk job in Langley. The children could play unattended outside; they never locked their doors. Bob's twelve-mile commute to Langley was no more than twenty minutes. Yvonne loved the normalcy of it all.

In Beirut, Yvonne had become a convert to Catholicism. This certainly discomfited her ardently Lutheran parents. But she did it for Bob, who had regularly attended Catholic Mass in Beirut. Three of the children had been baptized in the Catholic Church. But three others were baptized in the Lutheran Church, including baby Kevin. Life in Reston was like nothing they'd experienced in Dhahran, Aden, Asmara, or Beirut. It was Pleasantville, USA. A meticulously planned residential community, Reston had been built in 1964 on a seven-thousand-acre piece of farmland on the outskirts of Washington. The architects zoned ten acres of parkland for every thousand residents. Bicycle paths, twenty swimming pools, and other recreational facilities were available to everyone. It was designed as a self-contained community with its own schools, cinemas, restaurants, and shopping centers. When the Ameses bought their home in 1971, Reston had a population of fewer than six thousand. And because Langley was so close, many of their neighbors were CIA officers.

Bob left for Langley at eight o'clock in the morning and, if he wasn't traveling, was always home by six. Before dinner he sat in an Ethan Allen rocking chair and read a book while listening to music through a pair of stereo earphones. He rarely drank—at parties he might nurse a gin and tonic. "He didn't like what alcohol did," said Yvonne. But she sometimes sipped a Manhattan—a cocktail made with whiskey, sweet vermouth, and bitters—while she cooked dinner. They rarely entertained at home. Their living room was decorated with Persian carpets, Arab brass coffeepots, and a few paintings depicting Bedouin life. They owned a Kuwaiti chest that had once belonged to the legendary Arabian explorer Harry St. John Philby—the father of MI6's notorious double agent Kim Philby. The bookshelves were stocked with Middle Eastern history. "He had a fantastic library of books about the Middle East," recalled Sam Wyman. "I was very impressed." Ames also owned a Modern Library collection of the one hundred greatest books of all time. Bob rarely read fiction. But he liked poetry. His favorite poem was Rudyard Kipling's "If."

> *If you can keep your head when all about you*
> *Are losing theirs and blaming it on you;*
> *If you can trust yourself when all men doubt you,*
> *But make allowance for their doubting too:*
> *If you can wait and not be tired by waiting,*
> *Or being lied about, don't deal in lies,*
> *Or being hated don't give way to hating,*
> *And yet don't look too good, nor talk too wise . . .*

Kipling's 1895 poem has become an emblem of British Victorian stoicism. Perhaps Bob thought its sentiments spoke to his own conservative instincts. He also liked to quote John Donne's line "No Man is an island, entire of itself." Charles Englehart, a twenty-nine-year-old CIA officer, remembers coming over to Ames's Reston house for dinner one evening. Books were strewn everywhere—and toys. "Bob was reading five books at any one time," said Englehart.

On weekends, Bob sometimes shot a few baskets near the garage. On Saturday he spent hours watching basketball games or other sporting events; he liked to yell at the television. The girls were on the local swim team, and when the boys were a little older Bob was most definitely their basketball coach. For idle diversion, he loved to drop by the local Fair Oaks Mall—he punned it the "Medium Maples Mall"—and buy a Heathkit electronic hobby product, perhaps a stereo clock radio or some other electronic gadget that would take hours to assemble.

On Christmas morning Bob would get out of bed no earlier than usual, walk the dog, and shave. "He would draw the whole thing out," recalled his daughter Adrienne. "He would not allow us children to come down before he was quite ready to open presents." Bob was the designated disciplinarian. If the boys needed spanking, he could scare the hell out of them by walking down the hallway toward their room snapping his belt. He was a very old-fashioned father.

And on "career day" at the local school, Bob would dutifully show up and introduce himself as a Foreign Service officer who worked at the State Department. The children did not know otherwise. "He didn't talk much about himself," recalled Adrienne. "Everything I learned about him I learned after he died." Only one neighbor, Ron Simmers Sr., knew that Ames worked for the Agency. "He was a quiet, solid neighbor," recalled Simmers. "Everyone liked him." Ames once gave Simmers a Yemeni dagger, a gift from one of his trips to Yemen.

In 1971, Bob Ames was a GS-13, earning less than $20,000—about $95,000 in current dollars. This was a very fine middle-class salary at the time, but with a family of eight, they didn't save anything. "Bob didn't tolerate debt," Yvonne recalled, "so we lived within our means. We didn't go out to dinners; we didn't have a savings account, and we didn't take vacations. Wherever home was, that was my domain. He let me run things; I paid the bills. And I watched the budget. Money was always tight." Yvonne drove a used Chevy station wagon, and Bob drove to work in a sporty four-door Fiat with leather seats that he had bought in Beirut and shipped home. The Fiat proved to be a nuisance, hard to maintain and unreliable, so he eventually sold it to his neighbor Ron Simmers, and thereafter drove around in a white Ford Pinto, a two-door subcompact. The Pinto was Ford's cheapest possible car, designed to compete with the low-end European imports of the era. Bob nevertheless dreamed of someday owning a BMW.

Life in Reston was pretty ordinary, even prosaic. And very middle-class. "Everyone in our neighborhood lived pretty much as we did," Yvonne said. "Or at least, it felt like it." On weekends, Yvonne sang with the Sweet Adelines, a four-member female barbershop-style a cappella music group. She liked the ordinariness of this time in her life—but it wouldn't last long.

In late May 1972, Bob was posted to Sana'a, Yemen, on a short-term temporary-duty assignment (TDY). He flew to Paris, stopped in Rome, and finally landed in Bahrain, where he had a meeting with his CIA colleague and friend from Aden *Dick Roane*. He spent the day exchanging briefings with *Roane* and then caught a flight for Beirut via Dhahran. "It seemed all the planes took off at midnight and landed about 5:00 A.M., so there was little sleep to be had." He had a four-hour meeting with "the boys" in Beirut and then flew to Athens, where he caught a connecting flight to Asmara. He spent a few days in Asmara, seeing some old friends. Finally, on May 25, 1972, he flew to Taiz, Yemen. From there he had to drive two hundred miles up into the mountains to Sana'a, a city that stood at 7,500 feet. "That road is really scary," Ames wrote. "They had to pry my fingers from the car when I arrived in Sana'a." Altogether, it had been a grueling trip.

He would stay in Sana'a for two and a half months, standing in for the chief of station, Graham Fuller, another newly minted Arabist. It was a one-man station. Sana'a was then still a mostly walled, medieval-looking city of stone-block and mud-brick "skyscrapers," often rising four, five, or six stories. Scores of minarets dotted the skyline. In 1972 it had a population of only 125,000. Men walked its narrow alleys dressed in belted robes and turbans. Virtually every Yemeni man above the age of fourteen wore a *jambiya*, a short, curved, double-edged dagger stuck beneath his belt, and many young men also carried a Kalashnikov rifle slung over their shoulder. Every afternoon, the men and women of Sana'a adjourned separately to the top-floor sitting rooms of their homes to sip sweet black tea and chew *qat*. Sana'a was a much more traditional society than Aden. North Yemen's traditional tribes dominated the conservative regime in Sana'a—whereas Ames's former acquaintance Abd'al Fatah Ismail was still the de facto ruler of the Marxist regime in South Yemen. Border incidents between the two Yemens were on the rise.

"There's lots of activity going on these days and, as usual, I'm right in the middle of it," Bob wrote home to Yvonne. "There appears to be a concerted effort underway to get rid of the bunch in Aden and most of the plotting seems to take place in my house." He had six "guests" the evening of June 18 and three more the following night. "It sure is interesting, but tiring. They seem to really want to do something now, but when I asked one of the leaders if he thought they would succeed, he answered only 'We're Arabs!' Which translated means, if anything can go wrong we Arabs will make sure it does! At least he is being realistic."

The CIA was encouraging political refugees from Aden to organize a coup against the left-wing regime in Aden. But Ames was skeptical: "I hear all sorts of gory tales about what's going on in Aden and if only half of them are true it's a disaster. Despite all their acts of terrorism, however, Abd'al-Fatah and his boys appear to keep right on going while the exiles in North Yemen sit around and chew qat and talk about how they're going to overthrow the government. I don't think the Adenese will ever change—qat comes before all. The only way they'll ever move is if someone threatens to cut off their qat supply."

That October, tensions between the two countries erupted into armed clashes followed by a desultory armistice. The CIA would certainly have liked to see regime change in Aden, and actually tried to bring it about in the early 1980s, in a clumsy effort that failed completely, but the leftists hung on to power until the collapse of the Soviet Union, when the two Yemens were finally united.

Ames hated Sana'a's filthy air. "Here everything is dust," he wrote. "The only thing I like about this place is the people." His cover job was as a consular officer. He had never had to process visas before and found the work tedious. "This working seven days a week and constant use of Arabic wears you down after a while," he wrote. He figured out that in the past three years he'd taken only about fifteen days of vacation. And in the year since returning to Reston, he'd been abroad for nearly ninety days of TDYs. "It's about time I relaxed a little and that's just what I'm going to do when I get home."

Yemen was a hardship post. Ames was house-sitting for the Fullers in their spacious Yemeni home. Ascetically beautiful, Yemeni architecture did not accommodate Ames's six-foot-three-inch-stature. "I still crack my head on these low doors," he complained. The house had "water problems, dust problems, electricity problems and gas problems—so I've got problems." The Fuller home was also cluttered with magazines, books, and tape cassettes. "I honestly can't stand the mess," Ames wrote. "I just can't sit down and read until I at least get the stuff out of sight." Every day he had to prepare his drinking water by boiling a large pot and then pouring the water through a filter. He cooked with butane gas and shopped for himself in a meagerly stocked cold store. His meals were simple: Arabic bread and Tang for breakfast; more Arabic bread, butter, jam, and powdered Nestle's milk for lunch; and a dinner of tough, gristly meat and vegetables. One evening he wrote Yvonne, "I just had some canned spaghetti and vegetables, but it was the best meal I've had in Sana'a." He disliked North Yemeni food—gristly boiled mutton and rice—and greatly preferred the spicy fare of Aden. (He also missed his American root beer and pretzels.) Ames typically rose at 6:30 A.M. and spent his mornings in the embassy's CIA station, then moved to the consular section in the afternoons. He read in the evenings—or sometimes he had to go out to meet contacts. But mostly he read: "Well, it's getting late for me (10:30 P.M.) and I've only read one book today." It was lights-out by 11:15 P.M.

The life of a CIA case officer in a place like Yemen was exotic but certainly not glamorous. "I won't be bored," he wrote, "just lonesome." He lived frugally, spending no more than his government TDY per diem allowance. "I'm just an old homebody now," Ames wrote, "who wants to be with his wife and kids (you've all kind of grown on me) and not wandering around the world. . . . Keep reminding the kids that 'Yes, there really is a Daddy.'"

In an effort to combat his isolation, Ames listened to the *BBC News* each morning on a shortwave radio. He also read the *Economist*, delivered each week through the embassy's pouch mail. On very rare occasions, he might see a copy of the *International Herald Tribune*. "One good thing about being in Yemen," Ames observed, "is that you are far away from the Israeli-Palestinian problem. You never hear it mentioned at all."

Yemen was still a dangerous place to be in the early 1970s. A brutal civil war had ended just a few years earlier. But because the country was still divided between a conservative regime in the North and a radical, leftist government in the South, tensions were high. Assassinations or kidnappings were common. So were roadside mines. Occasionally, the Sana'a government carried out executions of South Yemeni saboteurs who had been caught planting roadside mines. After a short, almost perfunctory trial, these young men would be shot by a firing squad in the main town square. Shortly before Ames had to drive from Sana'a to Taiz, two people were killed when their car struck a mine. So on the day of his trip to Taiz, Bob decided he should wait until 7:30 A.M. — "so there would be cars in front of me, before I went on my way. The trip was uneventful, if any ride on that road can be uneventful." Near the end of his TDY he wrote home, boasting of his travels all over Yemen: "Well, I've driven everywhere there is a road in Yemen, so that must be some kind of record."

In addition to his drab consular work interviewing Yemeni visa applicants, one day he had to deal with a mob of more than two hundred applicants lined up outside the embassy, all wanting visas to America. The consular work was part of his diplomatic cover, but it sometimes could also lead to productive sources of information. Ames was putting in long hours, as usual, developing sources and writing up contact reports. His assignment was to keep tabs on developments in Aden, but he also found time to report on political developments in North Yemen. "The thing is," he wrote, "as far as Yemen is concerned you can get all the info you want just by asking." Ames made a point of asking, meeting with government officials, tribal leaders, and even shopkeepers in the Old City's *suq*. After returning from an exhausting day trip to the isolated mountaintop village of Kawkaban (elevation 11,300 feet), he got home in the evening only to receive a string of phone calls: "People wanted to see me. It was late at night and that meant the next day would be a busy day writing." In the first two months of his TDY he wrote more than twenty-five reports back to Langley: "If I put out ten more reports, I'll have produced more in these past two months than [the station has] in the first five months of the year." Bob was nothing if not competitive.

Ames finally returned to America on Sunday, August 13, 1972, in the midst of a presidential campaign. President Richard Nixon won reelection in a landslide in November 1972 and soon afterwards he decided to fire Richard Helms as CIA director. Helms was surprised and only later realized that Nixon was worried that Helms might know too much about a scandal that would come to be known as Watergate. Nixon asked Helms if he'd like to be appointed ambassador to Moscow. Helms told the president he thought the Russians wouldn't like the notion of a former CIA chief residing in Moscow. On a whim, Helms said, "Tehran might be a more plausible choice." Nixon thought this a good idea, so by early April 1973 Helms found himself in Tehran.*

Helms took with him one of the Agency's senior Iranian experts, George Cave, who agreed to serve as deputy station chief under Art Callaghan. But Helms also asked for the services of Bob Ames. Helms said that Ames and Cave were "two of his best case officers" and he wanted them both in Tehran. Ames was an odd choice; he was an Arabist and not a Farsi speaker. He'd never spent time in Iran. But Ames deeply admired Helms and quickly acceded to his request. He arrived in Tehran that spring, and Yvonne and the six children followed shortly afterwards. They even shipped their dog, Hansje, a Hungarian Vizsla. The poor dog was temporarily lost during transit in London but eventually made it to Tehran.

Though based in Tehran for what he expected would be a two-year assignment, Ames traveled a lot that summer. In late May, Helms wrote to Henry Kissinger and urged the national security adviser to "try to find time for a few minutes with Robert Ames of the Agency who is assisting me here on Persian Gulf problems."

---

* Before leaving Langley on February 2, 1973, Helms made sure to destroy the tapes on which he had recorded hundreds of conversations in his seventh-floor office (William Colby, cable to Helms, January 31, 1974, Helms Papers, CIA, Center for Intelligence Studies; Tim Weiner, *Legacy of Ashes: The History of the CIA* [New York: Doubleday, 2007], p. 324).

Whether in Washington or Tehran, Ames continued to work on Palestinian-Israeli affairs. Over the next few years, he traveled constantly between Washington, Tehran, and Beirut. Black September's terror exploits were beginning to push the Palestinian problem to the front page of newspapers around the world. The 1971 assassination of Wasfi al-Tal was only the beginning. Over the next two years, Black September was allegedly responsible for numerous other attacks:

- March 15, 1971: the sabotage of a Gulf Oil refinery in Rotterdam.
- December 15, 1971: the attempted assassination in London of Jordan's ambassador, Zeid al-Rifai.
- February 6, 1972: the gunning-down of five Palestinians, suspected of being Mossad agents, in Cologne.
- May 8, 1972: the hijacking of Sabena Flight 572 to Lod Airport in Israel, where it was stormed by Israeli commandos. Two of the four Black September operatives were killed, along with one passenger.
- August 4, 1972: the destruction of oil-storage tanks in Trieste, Italy.
- Autumn 1972: the killing of Israeli agricultural counselor Ami Shachori in Britain by a letter bomb.
- December 28, 1972: the capture of the Israeli embassy in Bangkok by four Black September operatives. The operation collapsed when Thai police surrounded the embassy and the Fedayeen surrendered.
- January 1973: the smuggling of a handful of ground-to-air missiles into Rome. Black September agents were within minutes of firing them at a plane carrying Prime Minister Golda Meir when Mossad officers intercepted them.
- March 4, 1973: the rigging of three car bombs in New York City, timed to explode upon the arrival of Golda Meir. The bombs failed to explode, and the Black September operative, Khalid al-Jawary, escaped only to be arrested in 1991 in Rome. Deported to the United States, he was convicted and imprisoned until 2009.

Ali Hassan Salameh more or less confessed to his complicity in some of these attacks.* He explained to a reporter, "We had no choice but to strike back at the Jordanian regime, or at least at the people who were behind the events of September 1970. . . . This gave birth to [the] Black September [organization], which undertook several operations against the Jordanian regime, its men and its institutions—in Jordan and elsewhere. Some of these operations were associated with my name. It was natural that my name be singled out and that a price be placed on my head by the Jordanian authorities."

The authoritative Israeli investigative journalist Aaron J. Klein later concluded that Salameh was responsible for five operations outside the Middle East: (1) the Rotterdam oil-tank explosion; (2) the attempted assassination of the Jordanian ambassador in London; (3) the February 6, 1972, assassination of five Palestinians in Cologne who were thought to be Mossad agents; (4) the bombing of oil-storage tanks in Trieste; and (5) the attempted attack on the Israeli embassy in Bangkok in late December 1972.

Ames naturally was privy to classified intelligence about these and other PLO operations, and he feared Salameh and his associates were planning on taking their "revolution" beyond Europe and into American territory. In the spring of 1972, Ames wrote a long and candid letter to Zein explaining his concerns. "I am fully aware of the activities of our friend," he wrote, "and although I do not agree with all of them, I can sympathize with his organization's feeling that they must carry them out. Despite what our friend thinks, we are not out to 'get' his organization. Contrary to his beliefs, we are not an action group like

---

* After the 1982 invasion of Lebanon, the Israelis captured some phone transcripts that allegedly had Salameh telling a Black September operative in Rome, "Clear the apartment and take all fourteen cakes [shoulder-fired missles]" (Simon Reeve, *One Day in September* [New York: Arcade, 2000], p. 172). The Israelis interpreted this as evidence of Salameh's involvement in the assassination plot.

his group is. It is because of misunderstandings like this that I value my talks with him. We were always frank and I think the talks were beneficial even though they never reached the level we both sought. I don't think that wasn't because he and I, with your help, didn't try. It was just because our superiors were too inflexible."

Ames then conveyed a strict warning:

> As things now stand, the only area where our two organizations will clash is when his group chooses to carry out operations in our territory as they are now planning. I know the frustration his group is currently facing. I also know that his group has many men willing to be martyrs. However, sending men here is not sending them as martyrs but as sacrificial lambs, and I mean that sincerely. His group has made many errors recently. I know most of them were not his fault as he was out of power for a while. Also his parent organization [the PLO] has made many errors.... Blaming other people and groups is not going to solve his problems. He must first put his own house in order. Our friend has, in the past, always been able to differentiate between his organization's rhetoric and the facts of life. I hope that he never loses that ability.

Ames was trying ardently, perhaps desperately, to use all his powers of empathy to get Zein to persuade Salameh to reestablish contact with the Agency. Bob must have assumed that Mustafa would show this letter to Ali Hassan. The letter contained blatant flattery—but also candid threats. He was also disarming. He was ingratiating himself with the intelligence chief of Force 17, an entity that Washington's ally in Tel Aviv labeled a terrorist organization. Bob was putting in writing things that if leaked could have created a media firestorm. But he trusted Mustafa and he trusted MJTRUST/2.

Flattery: "Our friend should know that he still has friends in high places, and so does his cause."

A threat: "His activities in Europe, which are fully documented, and his plans in our territory, which we know of completely and will hit hard and expose to his organization's embarrassment, are the only points on which we disagree."

A plea: "If he works for his own immediate goals there will be no problems and no conflict. I sincerely wish we could talk things over. A great deal has happened in the past year and a good long talk would settle many issues."

Logistics: "I know our friend cannot travel much, particularly to Europe. I also know why. I know that he can travel safely to Lisbon and I could arrange safe travel to any other European point, if he so desires. It would be useless for me to travel to Beirut as there are people who might link us together and damage both our positions at this point."

And finally, a personal warning: "Give my best to our friend and tell him I said that he should move his family from Beirut, if he has not already done so."

Ames obviously knew that the Mossad was targeting Salameh. Mustafa immediately understood that Bob was warning their "friend" to move out of his apartment on Verdun Street. That spring Mustafa showed Bob's March 26, 1972, letter to Ali Hassan. But he also showed it to Arafat. The PLO chairman scoffed at the veiled warning and suggested that the CIA officer was passing on disinformation just to rattle the Palestinians. "Bob never lies to me," Mustafa told Arafat. But Salameh ignored the warning and stayed put in his Verdun Street apartment.

Mustafa thereafter decided to take his own precautions on behalf of Ali Hassan. One evening, he dropped by the bar at the Commodore Hotel, where many of Beirut's foreign correspondents traded stories. (A Palestinian family, a financial supporter of Fatah, owned the Commodore.) Mustafa knew the barman, George, a Christian Palestinian who was in fact a member of Salameh's Force 17. That evening Mustafa spotted sitting at the bar a reporter from the London *Daily Mail*, a man who he knew was one of Mossad's reliable sources in Beirut. Mustafa was not a drinker, but that night he told George, "Forget the Heineken, bring me a whiskey." George poured Mustafa what looked to be whiskey but was actually black tea—and Mustafa pretended to get tipsy. Slurring his words and speaking loudly, he turned to *Time* magazine's Abu Rish and said, "I will tell you a secret. We have information that the Israelis are going to hit Ali Hassan's apartment on Verdun Street. But the Israelis don't know that Ali has a double layer of security outside the building; he's got a second unit of men hidden in the lobby. Mossad will be in for a big surprise."

Less than a year later, on the evening of April 9, 1973, sixteen Israeli commandos slipped into black Mark 7 rubber rafts from the deck of an Israeli missile ship. They were two miles off the coast of Beirut. Led by a future Israeli prime minister, Lt. Col. Ehud Barak, their mission—code-named Operation Spring of Youth—was to land at a private hotel beach, drive five miles into the heart of Beirut, and kill three prominent PLO leaders in their Verdun Street apartments. Muhammed Youssef al-Najar (Abu Youssef) was a lawyer who in 1973 was regarded as Fatah's number-two commander. Kamal Adwan was a petroleum engineer and a member of Fatah's central committee. Kamal Nasser, the PLO's chief spokesman, was a charismatic poet. Adwan and Nasser lived in the same high-rise apartment building on Verdun, not far from the American embassy. Abu Youssef happened to live in an adjoining apartment building. All three men died that night in a hail of bullets. So too did a seventy-year-old Italian woman who opened her apartment door at the wrong moment. Numerous Lebanese policemen also died in a short gun battle as the Israelis departed.

The Palestinian leadership was shocked. Arafat himself had spent the night in a nearby apartment. Arafat survived only because one of his bodyguards heard men talking softly in Hebrew in the street below. The bodyguard, knowing what this meant, quickly hustled Arafat down the back stairwell and pushed him into a waiting car. It was a very narrow escape. Abu Iyad, the Black September chief, had recently spent the night in one of those apartments. Half a million mourners attended the funerals of the three Palestinian leaders.

Ali Hassan Salameh was as stunned as anyone by the brazenness of the Israeli assassination team. He told a Lebanese reporter for *Monday*

Morning that the assassinations were "the result of complete careless-ness, which is typical of the Oriental mentality, the fatalistic mentality. My home was about 50 meters from the late Abu Youssef's home. The Israeli assassins didn't come to my home for a very simple reason: it was guarded by 14 men." He knew the Israelis were looking for him. "In the 'spook battle' between us and the Israelis," Salameh insisted, "we have been able to score several victories." But the reality was that the PLO was always outgunned and always on the defensive.

Mustafa had no idea that three other high-ranking PLO officials lived on the same street as Salameh. After the assassinations, the Mossad escape cars sped right by Ali Hassan's apartment, traveling at ninety miles per hour. Mustafa later reminded Arafat of Ames's warn-ing to Salameh to move his family—and he told Arafat to check with George, the barman at the Commodore Hotel, about the story he had passed on to the London *Daily Mail* reporter. Mustafa was sure he had saved Ali Hassan's life. Arafat grudgingly told him, "Okay, whatever Bob says from now on, it is like it is written in the Koran."

Black September's Munich Olympics operation changed everything. In early July 1972, Abu Iyad was sitting in a Rome café with several colleagues when he learned from reading a newspaper that the Inter-national Olympic Committee had disqualified any Palestinians from competing at the Summer Olympics, scheduled to commence in late August. Israelis would be allowed to compete, but no Palestinians be-cause, obviously, they didn't have a country. Abu Iyad was incensed. And then it occurred to him that a billion people around the globe would be watching the Olympics. It would be the first Olympics tele-vised live. Black September, he decided, should force itself onto this world stage. As he later explained to Éric Rouleau, the French journal-ist who coauthored his 1981 memoir, an attack on the Olympics would serve three purposes: "(1) to present the existence of the Palestinian People to the whole world, whether they like it or not; (2) to secure the release of 200 Palestinian fighters locked in Israeli jails; and (3) to use the unprecedented number of media outlets in one city to display the Palestinian struggle—for better or worse!"

It was Abu Iyad's idea to attack the Olympics, but he turned the details over to other men. Mohammed Oudeh—otherwise known as Abu Daoud—was the chief architect of the operation. He organized the smuggling of weapons into Munich. He traveled to Munich himself and gave the eight chosen Black September commandos their final instructions. But many others were involved, including Fahkri al-Omri, who served as Abu Iyad's deputy in Fatah. According to Aaron J. Klein, a Jerusalem correspondent for *Time*—and a former intelligence officer in the Israeli Defense Force—Al-Omri "picked up the keys and collected the weapons from the lockers in Munich." Klein's book, *Striking Back: The 1972 Munich Olympics Massacre and Israel's Deadly Response,* is perhaps the most authoritative account of the Munich operation and its aftermath. Klein estimates that some one hundred accomplices—many of them Palestinian students or exiles living in Europe—assisted Black September that summer.

Before sunrise on September 5, 1972, eight Black September commandos stormed the dormitory rooms housing the Israeli Olympics team. Two Israelis were shot dead in the initial invasion. Nine were seized as hostages. Initially, the commandos told German authorities that they would release the hostages in exchange for the release of 234 Palestinians imprisoned in Israeli jails. Later, the commandos demanded an airplane to fly the Israeli hostages and themselves to Cairo. The Germans agreed—and then carried out a woefully ill-planned ambush. As German soldiers advanced on the Black Septemberists, the commandos turned on the nine Israeli athletes and killed them with grenades and machine-gun fire. Five of the Palestinians were killed, and after an hourlong hunt, the three surviving Palestinian commandos were arrested.

Munich was a bloody tragedy, but it was also a perfect example of unintended consequences. Abu Iyad later called it "a tragedy for the

Israelis and us." He had planned a public relations extravaganza on the world stage. He had not planned a suicide mission, and neither had he expected the Israeli athletes to be killed. Abu Iyad and Abu Daoud had hoped the Black September cadres would fly out with their hostages and later orchestrate a prisoner exchange. Instead, the operation had become a stain on the honor of the entire Palestinian people. In the eyes of the world, the Palestinians were now all bloody terrorists waging war on innocents.

Brian Jenkins, an American expert on terrorism, once famously quipped, "Terrorism is theater." What he meant was that usually terrorists "want a lot of people watching and a lot of people listening and not a lot of people dead." In this sense, Munich was bad theater. It got the Palestinians the wrong kind of publicity. And it killed innocents.

Munich prompted the Israelis to retaliate. Three days after the tragedy, Israeli air strikes on Palestinian refugee camps in Lebanon killed and wounded as many as two hundred Palestinians, mostly unarmed civilians. That was only the beginning. Another forty-five Palestinians were killed by Israeli ground forces in southern Lebanon. On September 15, 1972, Prime Minister Golda Meir authorized an assassination program called Operation Wrath of God; Palestinians even remotely associated with Black September and Munich would be targeted for killing. Israel had used assassinations as a counterterrorism policy in the past, but over the next year ten Arabs ostensibly responsible for the Munich killings were systematically killed in Paris, Nicosia, Beirut, Athens, and Norway. Black September had initiated a very personal war.

By many accounts, Mossad placed Ali Hassan Salameh at the top of its list of people who deserved to die because of their responsibility for the Munich murders. Writes Klein in *Striking Back*, "Dozens of senior ex-Mossad and ex–Military Intelligence officers emphasized, over the course of our conversations, [that] the intelligence pointing to his involvement was both very strong and diverse." But Klein also writes that both Abu Daoud and Tawfiq Tirawi, once a senior aide to Abu Iyad, dispute this. They agree that Salameh was involved in five major attacks in Europe and elsewhere, but they deny that he played any role in Munich.

Other accounts differ. Simon Reeve, the British author of *One Day in September,* places Salameh at a Munich railway-station restaurant on the evening of September 4, together with Abu Daoud, giving the eight commandos their final instructions. Afterwards, Reeve reports, Salameh left Munich and traveled to East Berlin, where he set up "a forward command post in a flat ... with the connivance of the East German government." Reeve's source for this story is his interview with one anonymous Israeli intelligence source—and Michael Bar-Zohar and Eitan Haber's 1983 book, *The Quest for the Red Prince.* Bar-Zohar and Haber's book contains no citations, but they obviously had the cooperation of many unnamed Israeli intelligence sources. Written in 1982, their account was the first to establish Salameh's legend as "the Red Prince." They portray him as the real operational commander of the Munich attack, reporting that he "was wide awake at his hideout in East Berlin when the operation launched." And they have Yasir Arafat warmly embracing him upon his return to Beirut: "You are my son, I love you as a son!" Bar-Zohar and Haber may have embellished this part of their story—but it was certainly an accurate reflection of what Mossad wanted to believe about Ali Hassan Salameh.*

The evidence is circumstantial. Later in the 1970s, Israeli intelligence officers told Western journalists that they had in their possession telephone conversations intercepted by the German government between Salameh and one of his operatives in Berlin—proving that he'd been there at the time of Munich. "Not to my knowledge was Ali Hassan in Munich," said *Meir Harel,* a Mossad officer at the time who later became director general. "But for sure, he was among the plan-

---

* The allegation that Salameh was at Munich and planned the operation first appeared in a book by *Time* magazine reporter David Tinnin with Dag Christensen called *The Hit Team* (Dell, 1976). Tinnin's book contains no source notes. But his book is clearly the source for many of the stories about Salameh in Bar-Zohar and Haber's *The Quest for the Red Prince.*

ners. I don't have any doubt of that. But here is the interesting point. On the one hand, Ali Hassan was talking to the Americans, and on the other hand, he was in on the planning of such an operation. His adrenaline must have been rocketing."

Some people in the CIA who had contact with Salameh also believed what Mossad believed. Sam Wyman—who later took over from Ames as Salameh's case officer—categorically says that Salameh was involved. "Ali Hassan was the tactical planner," Wyman said. "He went to Munich and organized the casing out of the Olympic Village. Abu Daoud was the strategic planner. It was his idea. But Ali Hassan made it happen. Bob Ames knew that Ali Hassan was involved with Munich. And Ali Hassan knew that I knew he was involved in Munich—but we just didn't talk about it."

Wyman may be mistaken. He never confronted Salameh about Munich. But then he can't recall discussing the issue with Ames either. He may have assumed that the legend surrounding Salameh and Munich was true because many Americans and Israelis in the business believed it. Mustafa Zein has another story. "Initially, Bob thought Ali was behind the Munich operation, and so he thought he could never see Ali in a million years. But later he learned otherwise from sources inside the PLO. This intelligence persuaded him that Ali was not personally responsible." Zein insists, "Ali's role was to hunt the Mossad; Force 17 had nothing to do with Munich." Writing in his unpublished memoir "Deceit with Extreme Prejudice," Zein explained, "I am not trying to portray him [Salameh] as St Francis, but what I am trying to make clear is that Ali had many operations, [some] extremely deadly, but they were very focused to make sure they did not harm innocent civilians."

Salameh never talked publicly about Munich. But his sister Nidal later told the British journalist Peter Taylor that she'd confronted her brother about it. "When I heard about Munich," she said, "I asked him right away. I'd heard in one way or another that he was behind it, but I couldn't believe it. So I asked him, 'Were you behind the Munich massacre?' He said, 'No.'" Taylor also reports that Ali Hassan's mother asked him about it and he denied it: "He said he was against killing any civilian and didn't believe in it."

But Munich nevertheless became a part of his legend. And he must have realized that it forever made him a target. As George Jonas, the author of *Vengeance*—yet another book about the Munich tragedy— wrote in 1984, "In counter-terrorism, as in terrorism itself, military objectives often took second place to symbolic acts. In a sense, assassinating Salameh became the equivalent of capturing the enemy's flag."

Salameh became a living reminder of the Munich murders. He was an iconic figure for both Palestinians and Israelis. And inside Mossad the quest for his death became an obsession. Israeli intelligence officers demonized him as a "man with the imagination of the devil and the determination of the believer." Salameh himself was unapologetic. He explained that Black September's operations were a desperate but necessary response to the Palestinian defeat in Jordan in 1970–71. He was very candid about their thinking: "At the time, we were subjected to a blackout—a terrible blackout. We had to overcome this blackout, and we did. We did burst out on the world scene. We overcame the blackout and were able to tell the world: 'We are here, even though we have been temporarily ousted from Jordan.' The world looked at us as terrorists. It didn't look at us as revolutionaries. . . . But the truth is that we are waging a revolutionary struggle." In Salameh's view, "revolutionary" terrorism worked. It made global headlines and made it clear that the Palestinians were not giving up.

But it is also true that Salameh believed that his "revolutionary struggle" someday had to end at the negotiating table. Long before Munich, sometime in the late 1960s, he and Mustafa Zein were arguing one day about the armed struggle. "What is the end game?" Zein wanted to know. Ali Hassan replied, "It has to be resolved in a political settlement that is just and fair between us and the Israelis."

■

Incredibly, not long after the Munich tragedy the CIA made another pass at recruiting Salameh as a full-blown agent. Ames was not involved in the second recruitment attempt, but there was a witness to the clumsy effort—none other than Salameh's wife, Nashrawan Sharif, who told Peter Taylor: "I saw somebody give him [Salameh] a cheque without any amount written in, telling him, 'You write in the number you want.' My husband was mad, very angry at the time, because it was very insulting to him. He threw the cheque back and left. He couldn't be an agent for anybody, not only the Americans. He used to tell me, 'Nobody in this world could give me anything my revolution is not giving me.' He didn't mean by that the money; he meant the satisfaction and pride he got from fighting for his country."

The CIA officer who made the pitch left Beirut empty-handed. Salameh had once again made it quite clear that he was his own man. Salameh was decidedly annoyed. It seemed to him that the CIA's only agenda was recruitment.

Ames had not given up on restoring their friendship and regular contacts, but he knew the clumsy offer of a blank check to Ali Hassan only complicated his delicate attempt to reopen the channel. His superiors had been stupid. By once again offering Ali Hassan crass dollars the Agency had only offended the Palestinian. But Ames also understood that his agency had endangered Ali Hassan's life. Ames knew full well that an organization like the PLO was extremely vulnerable to foreign intelligence. Arab, Soviet, and Israeli intelligence agencies undoubtedly had sources planted within the PLO who could report on Salameh's various contacts. And that could mark him as a CIA source, and thus a traitor to the revolution.

Late in 1972, just weeks after the Munich fiasco, Ames met with Zein in Beirut and got an earful. Zein was angry. Things seemed to be slipping away, and Zein was venting. Ames left unhappy. In February 1973, after months of silence, he finally wrote Mustafa a long letter. "I won't try to explain my silence these past months in any detail. I still consider you a friend, and friends do not have to apologize for things that happen beyond their power. Also, there is not much one can put on paper and commit to the open mails." Bob then complained that he thought "some of the things you conveyed in Beirut were unfair, but I understand why you did it."

Ames was still disturbed by what he had learned in the aftermath of Munich. "What hurt deepest were the comments of Ali," Ames wrote Zein. "I thought we understood each other. We are both professionals in our trade, but I have a personal loyalty to friends that transcends business."

Ames then confessed, "I have written much about Ali as I'm sure he has done about me for his organization. What I wrote was intimate and detailed because I wanted our people to understand him, his motives and his organization. What was written was written at the time we all had great hopes. Unfortunately, we never saw those hopes come into fruition and, in frustration, we went our separate ways. However, I never gave up my hopes and still have them today."

But then Bob acknowledged that Munich had happened. And that had changed everything. "I came back here [to Washington] ready to do things and I actually was making some headway. Then came September [the Munich operation]. Leave aside the motives for this act, and my own feelings. The fact of the matter is, this act so alienated all the people here that the damage is irreparable. It was the timing and place, not the act in and of itself that did the damage. After that act no one would listen anymore. All sympathy was gone. The only thought was that this should never happen again."

Munich had led to an upheaval at Langley. The game had changed. The horrendous casualties—innocent Israeli athletes killed on global live television—had forced the CIA to share more intelligence with Mossad. Ames was shocked by what he saw. "I happened to see many files on Ali," he wrote Mustafa Zein, "particularly from the southern company [Mossad] and believe me the details were amazing, particularly since they included much on me which could only have come from his organization! I'm sure much of our files were passed to other companies although I cannot be sure of that. Ali is not exactly unknown."

A leak had occurred. Ames obviously thought it had come from within the PLO, suggesting that Mossad had informants inside the PLO who were able to pass on information about Salameh and his contacts with Ames. Zein insists that only Arafat himself knew Ames's identity. But it was also possible that CIA sources had shared information about the Ames-Salameh back channel with their Mossad counterparts. Perhaps a leak had been inevitable.

But in any case, by February 1973, the back channel was virtually dormant. Ames had not seen Salameh since May or June 1971, shortly before his transfer back to Langley. Their only communication was through Zein. Ames had tried repeatedly to resuscitate the relationship. Munich had put even these efforts on hold. Having convinced himself that the Munich killings could not be blamed on Salameh, Ames was pushing hard to see Salameh. But Ali Hassan was clearly fearful of resuming any contact. He feared yet another recruitment attempt. Worse, he feared that perhaps in lieu of recruitment the Agency might be out to "get" him. Ames tried to address this fear directly in his February 10, 1973, letter to Zein: "If he [Salameh] believes that I or my company is out to get him personally, he is wrong and he should know this without my having to say so. In spite of all that is in the fiction books, my company does not 'get' people. Sometimes I think we're foolish in this respect, but it is, nonetheless, true."

Ames told Zein that he planned to be in Beirut around February 24 and again on March 9. "There is much I would like to tell you which I cannot put on paper. Also, I'd be willing to meet Ali any place he chooses and answer any questions he might have personally. If he then wants to 'get' me he can, although I hope we are above such things."

Sometime in the second week of March 1973, Ames finally reestablished contact with Salameh. They met in Beirut shortly after five Black September operatives invaded the Saudi embassy in Khartoum, interrupting a farewell party in honor of American chargé d'affaires George Curtis Moore. The American ambassador, Cleo Noel Jr., was wounded as the Black Septemberists stormed the embassy. They held everyone hostage for a day, demanding the release of Abu Daoud from a Jordanian prison. Abu Daoud had recently been captured by Jordanian intelligence and brutally tortured. The Jordanians ignored Yasir Arafat's demand for Daoud's release, so on March 2, 1973, Ambassador Noel, Curtis Moore, and a Belgian diplomat were taken to the basement and machine-gunned to death. The killings garnered worldwide condemnation.

Ames must have been shocked by the coldhearted brutality of the Black September murders in Khartoum. An American ambassador and his chargé had been executed in cold blood. But this did not stop him from seeing Salameh. He believed Salameh had not been personally responsible. Salameh was in Kuwait at the time, not Khartoum. Zein later told him that it had been a kidnapping plot, organized by Abu Iyad, to extract millions of dollars from the Saudis.* But this couldn't have mollified Ames. PLO thugs had murdered American diplomats. We don't have a full account of the Ames-Salameh meeting. Perhaps strong words were exchanged. Or more likely, Ames quietly listened to Salameh's explanation.

We do know that Salameh told Ames, "Khartoum has made its point of causing the USG [U.S. government] to take Fedayeen terrorist activity seriously." According to a memorandum Ames later wrote about this encounter, Salameh implicitly defended the Khartoum operation as a necessary evil. He said, "No blackmail was intended, the men would have been killed in any event." But he also assured Ames that Khartoum would not be repeated: "The Fedayeen have no plans to go after individual Americans or American interests."

Some Americans may be astonished that a CIA officer chose to meet with a man like Salameh so soon after his organization killed two American diplomats. Peter Taylor once asked a CIA officer who later dealt with Salameh if America as such was "dealing with a terrorist." The officer replied, "I suppose we were. But then we deal with all sorts

---

* The U.S. government later concluded there was good evidence that Arafat had personally approved the operation. A March 13, 1973, State Department cable reported, "Fatah leader Yasser Arafat has now been described in recent intelligence as having given approval to the Khartoum operation prior to its inception."

of people." Surely it is a gray area, but just as surely, this is what CIA agents do—deal with bad guys. "You sup with the devil," said one clandestine officer, "but you use a long spoon."

Sometimes the bad guys can offer useful intelligence. In the early 1970s, the CIA received unconfirmed intelligence about what was described as a PLO plot to assassinate President Nixon. Ames passed an urgent message to Salameh, inquiring about the plot. Salameh investigated and later told Ames and Beirut chief of station Gene Burgstaller in a meeting in Beirut's Bedford Hotel that it was merely a scam by a Libyan businessman named Al-Khudairi, who had been caught smuggling fifteen kilograms of pure heroin in Rome. According to Force 17's Mohammed Natour (Abu Tayeb), the Libyan had fabricated a story in a gambit to get himself out of jail: "The Libyan told Italian intelligence that Ali Hassan Salameh was planning to assassinate President Nixon during his coming trip to Europe." Salameh explained that he indeed knew Al-Khudairi as a millionaire businessman who lived in Switzerland. Al-Khudairi, he said, had invested $200,000 in the Diplomat Restaurant, a venture owned by Force 17 in Rome. Salameh's story checked out.

In the meantime, the Israelis were striking back at Black September with a vengeance. "After Munich," says one Mossad officer, "we had a lot of people who were to be given passports to hell. I admit some of them were not very important people. But they paid the price." On October 16, 1972, two gunmen shot and killed Abdel Wael Zu'aytir, allegedly the PLO's representative in Rome. On December 8, 1972, Mahmoud Hamshari was killed in Paris by an exploding telephone. On January 24, 1973, Hussein al-Bashir, a Fatah representative, was killed in Nicosia by a bomb planted under his bed. Accounts by the *New York Times* and other press outlets at the time implied that all three men had "played undercover roles" in the Munich massacre. In fact, we now know that none of these men had any connection to the Munich operation.

The case of Zu'aytir seems particularly troubling. Writing in his

2005 book, *Striking Back,* Aaron J. Klein convincingly portrays Zu'aytir, thirty-six, as an intellectual, a lover of music and books. At the time of his assassination he was working on an Italian translation of *One Thousand and One Nights.* He was a part-time translator at the Libyan embassy in Rome and was paid so poorly that his telephone had recently been disconnected. Born in Nablus, he was naturally sympathetic to the Palestinian cause—but the extent of his political activism was turning out for the occasional political rally. Mossad had but one piece of circumstantial evidence linking him to an actual operation, the August 16, 1972, explosion in the baggage compartment of an El Al flight from Rome. The pilot had safely returned the aircraft to Rome without any injuries. But afterwards, hundreds of Arabs living in Rome had been picked up for interrogation—and Zu'aytir was one of those questioned and summarily released. This slim fact persuaded Mossad that Zu'aytir was guilty of something.

"Over the years," Klein wrote in *Striking Back,* "Zu'aytir's guilt came to be taken as fact." But in 1993, Maj. Gen. Aharon Yariv, Prime Minister Golda Meir's personal adviser on terrorism, told the BBC, "As far as I remember, there was some involvement on his [Zu'aytir's] part in terrorist activities; not in operations but in terrorist activities: supplying, helping, let us say 'support' activities. You must remember the situation. Activity continued on their part and the only way we thought we could stop it—because we didn't have any interest in just going around killing people—was to kill people in leadership roles. And it worked in the end. It worked." Klein flatly concludes that there was no link between Zu'aytir and Munich. Zu'aytir had publicly denounced the use of violence. His assassination was, writes Klein, "a mistake." Mossad was using the right of "vengeance" for Munich as an excuse to strike out blindly at Palestinians whose worst crime was sympathy for the Palestinian cause. Mossad was combatting terror with its own brand of targeted terror.

Next on the Israeli hit list was Basil al-Kubaisi, the young Iraqi whom Ames had met in 1967–68 while stationed in Aden. Ames had cultivated Al-Kubaisi. They shared a mutual interest in the history of the Arab Nationalist Movement. Perhaps Ames had tried to recruit Al-Kubaisi. But more likely, they had just become friends. Ames would have described it as a relationship with a knowledgeable source. And he no doubt would have reported what he had learned from this source in cables back to Langley. Al-Kubaisi would have been assigned a cryptonym.

Al-Kubaisi had earned his doctorate in 1971 from American University in Washington, D.C., and then moved to Beirut, where for a while he taught as a part-time lecturer at the American University of Beirut. He'd joined the Popular Front for the Liberation of Palestine, and George Habash regarded him as one of the Front's most promising young intellectuals. "Basil was an Arab nationalist, but certainly not a violent man," said his doctoral adviser at American University, Dr. Abdul Said Aziz. "He was a mild-mannered young man, always focused and attentive, but not verbose."

Now forty years of age, Al-Kubaisi wore impeccably tailored suits; he spoke fluent English, French, and Arabic. He traveled under his own name. He was unarmed and not undercover. That spring the PFLP sent him on what was essentially a public relations mission to Paris. According to one source, Al-Kubaisi was "on a tour in Europe to acquaint the European left with the views of the PFLP." He was a suave, sophisticated academic—a man who could represent the "civilized" face of the PFLP. He lived modestly; by one account, in Paris he walked around the city, avoiding taxis to save money. Unbeknownst to him, he was being followed by Israeli agents, who tracked him down to a Paris hotel. In the late evening of April 6, 1973, two Israelis confronted him near the Church of the Madeleine, a block from his hotel, and pulled out long-barreled Berettas fitted with silencers. Al-Kubaisi cried out, "La! La! La!"—Arabic for "No!" But the Israeli agents pumped nine .22-caliber bullets into his chest and head. And then they calmly walked away. French police said the murder was "carried out with a dexterity and precision that one can only call professional." The *New York Times* cited an Iraqi embassy official who described Al-Kubaisi as "a revolutionary avant-garde intellectual known for his anti-Zionist positions." The *Washington Post* quoted a police spokesman saying that it "looks very much like the execution of a secret agent." Police found $1,000 in cash in Al-Kubaisi's hotel room, and nine different passports. He'd traveled extensively in recent months to Canada and Europe.

Mossad was probably unaware that they'd assassinated someone who might have still been an active CIA source. Basil Raoud al-Kubaisi was known to the Israelis as an operative for George Habash's PFLP. By one account, they thought him to be a "quartermaster" for PFLP operations in Europe. Al-Kubaisi was certainly a member of the PFLP—and in the eyes of Mossad that was enough evidence to label him a terrorist. After his murder, a Palestinian news agency in Beirut reported that he was a leading member of the PFLP and was "on a mission" in Paris to talk with a French government official. Some newspaper accounts called him Habash's "roving ambassador."

But even Israeli sources seem to agree that he had no role in the Munich affair. Klein writes that Al-Kubaisi "was probably not affiliated with Fatah's Black September and certainly had no hand in the Munich Massacre." Klein nevertheless reports that Mossad's file on Al-Kubaisi was "one of the thickest." This raw intelligence implied that Al-Kubaisi might have been involved in a long list of terrorist attacks. The Israelis thought that in 1956 he had somehow been associated, at the age of twenty-three, with a failed plot to assassinate Iraq's King Faisal II. Maybe. More recently, Mossad thought he'd aided the PFLP in smuggling arms and explosives into Europe. Maybe. And just a month before he was killed, Mossad thought he might have been involved in the March 4, 1973, planting of three car bombs in New York City, timed to explode on the same day that Israeli prime minister Golda Meir arrived at New York's JFK airport. Maybe. But all Klein can do is report what he was told by his Mossad sources about what was in Al-Kubaisi's file. We really don't have any evidence of how Mossad would have known these things. And the allegation that Al-Kubaisi was involved in the March 1973 New York car bomb plot seems particularly implausible. That was a Black September operation, carried out by a Fatah operative named Khalid al-Jawary, who was extradited to the United States in 1991 and convicted of the car bomb plot. (The bombs failed to explode.) Al-Jawary was sentenced to thirty years in prison, but he was released in 2009 and extradited to Sudan. No evidence emerged from the Al-Jawary prosecution that implicated Al-Kubaisi. If the evidence was murky, so too was Al-Kubaisi's life and death.*

Al-Kubaisi was not a man of the gun. So why was he targeted? One of his friends, Dr. Fadle Naqib, a Palestinian economist, had a premonition that he would be assassinated. In July 1972, when the Israelis killed Ghassan Kanafani—the PFLP's spokesman, but also a well-known novelist and literary critic—Naqib wrote to Al-Kubaisi that he feared his friend would be targeted next. Naqib later observed that the Israelis did not seem to be targeting men with guns. "The Mossad was not after the muscle of the Palestinian revolution," wrote Naqib, "but its soul. . . . Basil was a prominent leader of the Arab Nationalist Movement. . . . He was different from other Arab intellectuals or militants. He was well educated, with a Ph.D. in political science. But he was not interested in an academic career."

Al-Kubaisi was an intellectual emissary for the PFLP—and perhaps a secret asset of the CIA. We don't know if Al-Kubaisi was an active CIA asset at the time of his death. If so, this was the first time Ames had lost an agent to assassination. "Kubaisi rings a bell," said George Cave, the officer who worked with Ames in Iran. "But since I was in Islamabad when he got zapped, I don't know much about him. Bob developed a lot of contacts among the various Palestinian organizations but did not formally recruit them. They were assigned cryptonyms for communication purposes." So Al-Kubaisi might have been one of these unrecruited sources that were nevertheless assigned a crypt. "Mr. K was a chattering contact not a spy," says Dewey Clar-

---

* At the time of his assassination, Al-Kubaisi was married to Nadera Khodari, a university professor. They had three children. Khodari and her children were all killed in a plane crash near Damascus two years later.

ridge, "for Bob was not a closer." Whatever his status, Al-Kubaisi was certainly in a position to provide the Agency with a great deal of information about the PFLP. His death was a loss for the Agency. "I know," said Graham Fuller, "there was a lot of anger among officers that the Israelis seemed to be deliberately gunning down our assets who could provide influential info on the Middle East other than via Mossad channels." Fuller went on to observe, "Most Agency case officers working in the Middle East at that time did not view Mossad as friendly, or working to the same goals at all. Rather, Mossad was seen as in competition or antipathetic to the work and reporting of Agency officers. That's because most Agency officers had a view of Palestinian realities that were both based on realities that we were close to, and that we knew were not generally listened to at the Washington policy level—due mainly to Israeli or pro-Israeli domination of all such info at the policy level."

In late June 1973, Salameh sent Ames a letter in which he said that he urgently needed to see him again. So in early July Ames flew into Beirut from Tehran. The two men met on July 9 and 10 in a CIA safe house. They had a long agenda. Salameh gave Ames his assessment of the situation in Lebanon and said that Arafat had instructed his forces to avoid any confrontation with the Lebanese army "at all costs." He also complained about the Israeli assassination program. The latest victim, Muhammad Boudia, an Algerian playwright, had been blown up in his car in Paris on June 29. Salameh revealed that he had "personally recruited" Boudia to run Black September operations in France. Ames thought this was "interesting intelligence."

Two days after Boudia's assassination, in the early morning hours of July 1, 1973, Col. Yosef Alon, the assistant air attaché at the Israeli embassy in Washington, D.C., was shot and killed outside his Chevy Chase home. The murder remains unsolved, but it was reportedly the work of a Force 17 assassination team led by an operative named Abu Faris, a Palestinian of African descent who wore an Afro hairstyle. Their intended target was Ambassador Yitzhak Rabin, but because Rabin's personal security was so tight, the assassins instead targeted Colonel Alon. The next day a Voice of Palestine radio broadcast out of Cairo claimed that Colonel Alon had been killed in retaliation for Muhammad Boudia's assassination in Paris: "His is the first execution operation carried out against a Zionist official in the U.S." If it was a Force 17 operation, Ali Hassan Salameh must have known about it. Indeed, Mustafa Zein believed that Salameh himself "had ordered the execution of the Military Attaché." Ames reportedly sent an urgent message to Salameh after the assassination, demanding to know if Force 17 was operating on U.S. territory. We don't know what Salameh replied, but he reportedly had the team extracted safely back to Beirut. Four years later, the CIA tipped off the FBI that the Agency had learned from a "Fedayeen senior official" that "the Black September Organization" was responsible for the assassination. Perhaps this information came from Ames, and perhaps the "Fedayeen senior official" was Salameh.

Salameh was obviously involved with some Black September operations. He no doubt considered himself a guerrilla soldier, fighting a war to restore Palestine to his people. If he was involved in Colonel Alon's murder, he would have considered him to be a legitimate "military" target. Mossad was killing civilians like Boudia and Al-Kubaisi in the streets of Paris. Black September was retaliating. This is how Salameh would have viewed it. But if it had also become known that such a man was regularly talking with a CIA officer, well, the controversy in the media would have been the least of the Agency's problems. But at the same time, Ames must have believed that talking with Salameh was the right thing to do.

And indeed, during their talks on July 9 and 10 in the CIA's Beirut safe house, Ames learned that Salameh had something to say of extreme importance. Ali Hassan said that he'd been instructed by Arafat to initiate a major overture to the Americans. Arafat was "gratified" that a recent Nixon communiqué with the Soviet Union's Leonid Brezhnev had included a brief but telling mention of "Palestinian interests" in the Middle East. Salameh told Ames that significant changes had taken place in the Palestinian movement since the two had last seen each other in early March 1973. Arafat wanted the U.S. government to know that he'd "put a lid" on any Fedayeen operations targeting Americans—and that "the lid would stay as long as both sides could maintain a dialogue, even though they might have basic disagreements. This was not a threat—i.e., talk to us or else—but a recognition that talking was necessary." Arafat could not guarantee Americans "complete immunity from terrorist acts" because "no one can stop a determined individual gunman," but there would be no PLO operations against Americans.

The PLO's inner circle had settled on a new strategy. Munich might have put Palestinian grievances in the media spotlight, but Arafat had decided that going after European and American targets was counterproductive. He was going to turn off the terror spigot. Henceforth, Salameh said, the Fedayeen would confine their operations to Jordan and Israel. The Hashemite Kingdom would be priority number one. Why? Salameh explained that Arafat had persuaded his comrades to alter a key plank in Fatah ideology. They now recognized that "Israel is here to stay." So the "establishment of a democratic state of Muslims, Christians and Jews in what is now Israel is just not realistic." Nevertheless, the Palestinians had to have a home, and "that home will be Jordan."

As Ames put it in a long memo to Helms dated July 18, "Arafat claims to have the agreement of all Arab states, including Saudi Arabia in principle, to the replacement of the Hashemite Kingdom by a Palestinian Republic. Jordan, therefore, will be the prime target of the Fedayeen, with acts of terrorism against Israel maintained to sustain the movement's credibility. . . . Arafat wants a real state or nothing."

Salameh then asked Ames if he could get Washington to answer the following questions:

What does the USG mean when it says Palestinian interests?
How does the "Peaceful Solution" take into consideration Palestinian interests?

Is there any consideration being given to the Palestinians in the
plans for a partial or interim solution? If so, what are they? How
can any solution be meaningful while Jordan exists?

Ames said he couldn't predict how Washington would respond to
"such provocative questions," but he'd pass them on. He did.

In late July Ambassador Helms flew from Tehran to Washington,
D.C., and told Kissinger about Salameh's approach to Ames. Arafat
wanted a dialogue with the Americans, a dialogue based on two prem-
ises: that "Israel is here to stay" and that a Palestinian state should
replace the Hashemite Kingdom.

Helms and Ames certainly believed that a dialogue with the PLO
was worthwhile. After all, Arafat's first premise—that "Israel was
here to stay"—was a dramatic concession to reality. This was a real
breakthrough. His second premise was provocative, but the future
and nature of the Hashemite regime in Jordan could be negotiable. In
reality, Jordan was a de facto Palestinian state, since a majority of its
population was Palestinian. Helms bluntly told Kissinger, "The issue is
whether you want to have policy talks with Fedayeen or not."

Kissinger agreed that this was the question, and according to his
memoirs, he told Helms he would think about it. "My reflections were
unlikely to be positive," he later wrote. "I considered King Hussein a
valued friend of the United States and a principal hope for diplomatic
progress in the region." Kissinger also wrote that he thought any Palestinian state run by the PLO would become irredentist and that any
Palestinian entity in the West Bank would be used as a launching pad
for attacks on both Jordan and Israel. Kissinger thought that the Palestinians would never relinquish their desire to return to all of Palestine.
"To them," he wrote, "a West Bank mini-state could be only an interim step toward their final aims." The Palestinians wouldn't be satis-
fied even if the Israelis returned to the 1967 borders and gave back East
Jerusalem. And besides, Kissinger wrote in his 1982 memoir, "There
were few who thought this [an Israeli withdrawal] in the realm of possibility." Basically, Kissinger didn't believe the Israelis would give up

the occupied territories—and he didn't believe Arafat when the PLO leader said, "Israel is here to stay."

So on August 3, 1973, Kissinger told Helms that he had "a nothing message" by way of reply. At least, that is how he characterized the message in his memoir. But in the spring of 2008 the CIA declassified some of Richard Helms's papers. Among them was an unsigned and untitled document that addressed Arafat's questions. This memo was the first formal diplomatic communication between Arafat and any U.S. administration. It was probably conveyed to Arafat through the Ames-Salameh back channel—and it was not "a nothing message": "When the USG says that an Arab-Israeli settlement must take 'Palestinian interests' into account, it has two points in mind: First, there has to be a far-reaching solution of the refugee problem, and the U.S. is prepared to participate actively in a major program to help these people reestablish normal lives. Second, it is apparent that some Palestinians have an interest in political self-expression of some kind."

Kissinger's reply concluded, "Exactly how Palestinian interests reach an accommodation with those of others in the region is best decided by negotiation. If the Palestinians are prepared to participate in a settlement by negotiation, the U.S. would be pleased to hear their ideas. The objective of overthrowing existing governments by force, however, does not seem to be the most promising way."

Kissinger was, in fact, inviting the PLO to the negotiating table, signaling that Washington would fund a major program to resettle the refugees, but also conceding that the Palestinians had a right to some kind of "political self-expression." His only caveat was the warning that they could not expect to achieve their aims by the forcible removal of King Hussein.

This was a classic Kissinger gambit. In 1973 Kissinger was saying publicly that the PLO was a terrorist organization and that no American official could talk with its representatives. But privately, he was using what he disparagingly called in his memoirs "low-level intelligence channels" to explore how to bring this terrorist organization in from the cold. Maybe this was both devious and brilliant.

On August 13, 1973, Kissinger received another feeler from the PLO, this time through Morocco's King Hassan, who passed on the same three questions conveyed by Salameh to Ames. Perhaps there hadn't been enough time for Salameh to receive Kissinger's August 3 reply—but the fact that the PLO was knocking on another door was evidence of its seriousness. The message this time was given to Lt. Gen. Vernon A. Walters, then deputy director of the CIA, who happened to be visiting the king in Casablanca. Kissinger told Walters to keep the door open to a possible meeting. In early September 1973, Ames sent Salameh an encouraging message: "My company is still interested in getting together with Ali's company. The southern company [Israel] has investigated. I've seen a lot of their files, and they know about our contacts." Kissinger dispatched General Walters to Rabat with instructions to listen to the PLO representatives—and also warn them that any further attacks on Americans wouldn't be tolerated. Walters hesitated for a moment and then said, "Dr. Kissinger, I must be No. 8 or 9 on their hit list." Kissinger responded in his Germanic accent, "But Valters, I'm No. 2, so you're going."

On November 3, 1973, Walters and the CIA's station chief met in Rabat with two high-ranking PLO emissaries, the brothers Khalid al-Hassan and Hani al-Hassan. They assured Walters that the PLO was not targeting Americans—but that King Hussein was still regarded as an obstacle to Palestinian aspirations. Walters responded—on Kissinger's instructions: "We regard the King of Jordan as a friend." But in the context of a comprehensive settlement, Washington would expect the Palestinian movement and the Hashemite regime to "develop in the direction of reconciliation." Walters told the Al-Hassan brothers, "There are no objective reasons for antagonism between the United States and the Palestinians."

The Palestinians responded with not much more than a sermon about the plight of the Palestinian people. They insisted that the West Bank was too truncated for a Palestinian state and that it followed that King Hussein would have to step aside to make way for a Palestinian republic. The important implication of all this was that the PLO representatives were still talking under the presumption that "Israel was here to stay." Kissinger was unimpressed. He still didn't think the Palestinians were serious: "The dynamics of the movement made it unlikely that such moderation could be maintained indefinitely."

In his 1982 memoir, Kissinger downplayed the significance of this Rabat meeting, but he also quietly acknowledged that the talks had gained something concrete for Washington: "After it [Walter's Rabat meeting with the PLO], attacks on Americans—at least by Arafat's faction of the PLO—ceased." Salameh had, in fact, delivered on his promise to Ames the previous summer that Americans would no longer be targets of the Fedayeen. Ames's back channel to Salameh had created a virtual nonaggression pact between the U.S. government and Arafat's Fatah guerrillas.

At the time, of course, Kissinger could not publicly acknowledge that he was dealing with the PLO. But he was. And he understood that such a clandestine negotiation with the PLO was "potentially too explosive to risk its uncontrolled leakage." So to protect himself and Nixon, he quietly informed King Hussein, Egyptian president Anwar Sadat, and other Arab leaders of the very preliminary talks. He also made sure Israel's ambassador in Washington, Simcha Dinitz, was briefed on Arafat's approaches. The Israelis, of course, were shocked and would now do everything they could to keep Washington from further talks with the PLO.*

Yitzhak Hofi, Mossad's director general from 1974 to 1982, was outraged when he later learned of Kissinger's dealings with the PLO. And he became apoplectic when he learned that it was Ali Hassan Salameh—whom he regarded as a mastermind of the Munich tragedy—who had initiated the talks. Even worse, he thought, was the intelligence that Arafat had designated Salameh as the PLO's

---

* The Israelis had an ally inside the CIA in the figure of counterintelligence chief James Jesus Angleton, who, according to Thomas Powers, was convinced that the "KGB was in complete and utter control of the Palestine Liberation Organization" (Thomas Powers, *The Man Who Kept the Secrets: Richard Helms and the CIA* [New York: Alfred A. Knopf, 1979], p. 327). Ames thought this ridiculous.

liaison to the Americans. Hofi was livid to think that the Americans were talking to a man that his own Mossad officers had recently tried to assassinate.

On July 21, 1973—just eleven days after Ames had met with Salameh—a Mossad hit team in the Norwegian resort town of Lillehammer gunned down a Moroccan waiter, Ahmed Boushiki, in the mistaken belief that he was Ali Hassan Salameh. Six of the Mossad officers were arrested and convicted of murder, and some spent two years in prison. The botched assassination brought an abrupt end, for the moment, to Mossad's Operation Wrath of God attempts to kill Black September operatives.

When the innocent Moroccan waiter was killed in Lillehammer, Salameh was somewhere in Europe. News of the arrest of the Mossad officers was splashed across Scandinavian newspapers. "When they killed Boushiki," Salameh later told the Lebanese weekly newspaper *Al-Sayad,* "I was in Europe.... Boushiki was a swimming pool employee. His face and figure did not fit my description." Salameh then boasted that he was still alive, "not so much because of my skills, but rather because of the weakness of Israeli intelligence." He pointed out that Mossad was "supposed to be capable of hitting everywhere."

The scandal was a major embarrassment to Mossad. But the fact that the CIA had opened up a liaison relationship with the Palestinian intelligence chief was even more troubling than the Lillehammer affair. The CIA talking to Salameh established a precedent; in Jerusalem it was seen as the first step to recognition of the PLO. Mossad's Hofi protested directly to General Walters and demanded the CIA cancel its unofficial "nonaggression pact" with the PLO. According to Gordon Thomas, the author of *Gideon's Spies,* a history of Mossad, "The CIA deputy director said it was not possible and warned Hofi that Washington would regard it as an 'unfriendly act' if news of the pact became public."

Despite Israeli protests, Kissinger allowed General Walters to meet with the Palestinians again on March 7, 1974. By then Kissinger, as secretary of state, was engaged in shuttle diplomacy, trying to turn the cease-fire from the October War into a semblance of real peace. (He wouldn't be successful.) The PLO envoy—not Salameh—who met with Walters reminded Walters that when Kissinger had flown into Beirut on December 16, 1973, it had been Ali Hassan Salameh who'd thwarted a plot by the Abu Nidal Organization—the nihilist terrorist group responsible for killing numerous Westerners but also some PLO figures—to shoot his plane down. In his memoirs, Kissinger said he was unimpressed. But the reality was that U.S. diplomats in Beirut were beginning to rely on Salameh and Fatah's Fedayeen for their security.

Kissinger was still skeptical about the PLO and still wedded to his alliance with the Hashemite monarchy. The Americans felt comfortable with their "plucky little king"—but in reality the Palestinians were becoming a political force that could not be ignored. King Hussein himself had decided that as a matter of self-preservation he had to make his own deal with Arafat. By mid-1974 the PLO was rapidly moving away from a strategy of armed struggle and morphing into a political movement seeking international legitimacy. Salameh had said as much to Ames a year earlier. And now it was happening. On June 8, 1974, Arafat revealed that the Palestinian National Council had voted overwhelmingly to adopt a new "Ten Point Plan." Couched in purposefully convoluted language, the plan stated that the PLO would seek to establish a Palestinian state over any portion of Palestine that might someday be "liberated." This was code for the West Bank and Gaza, the territories occupied by Israel in 1967—and that remained occupied by Israel. The plan was the first hesitant step toward a two-state solution. It was a formal acknowledgment of what Salameh had told Ames the previous summer: Israel was here to stay.

Simultaneously, the Ten Point Plan was an implicit concession that the Hashemite regime was also here to stay. The PLO was abandoning the goal of attempting to overthrow King Hussein and turn Jordan into a Palestinian republic. This opened the door to the possibility that King Hussein could forge a reconciliation with Arafat and the PLO. And it became inevitable when, on October 28, 1974, the summit of Arab heads of state in Rabat formally designated the PLO as the "sole legitimate representative of the Palestinian people." The United Nations quickly followed up with an invitation to Yasir Arafat to address the UN General Assembly on November 13, 1974. Arafat arrived in New York—accompanied by Ali Hassan Salameh and a team of other aides and bodyguards. Salameh traveled under the alias Rafik Behlouli, using an Algerian diplomatic passport numbered 2092 A 73. But the Americans knew exactly who he was. Before departing for New York, U.S. diplomats at the Beirut embassy had spent four hours haggling with Salameh over the terms of the visit. The Americans tried to restrict the size of Arafat's delegation—and they insisted that no one in the PLO delegation could arrive in New York with their sidearms. "Salameh begged for understanding and flexibility," according to a classified telegram describing the negotiations. Salameh said all he could promise was that any arms "will absolutely not be visible." But in exasperation, he wryly observed, "Have you ever seen a picture of Abu Ammar [Arafat] without a pistol?"

The Red Prince waited in the wings as Arafat, wearing an empty holster, addressed the General Assembly. With a flair for the dramatic, Arafat ended his speech by saying, "I have come bearing an olive branch and a freedom fighter's gun. Do not let the olive branch fall from my hand." The Israeli diplomats—who boycotted the session— were outraged that the international community had given Arafat such a prominent soapbox.

That same day Salameh met with *Charles Waverly*, the newly designated CIA station chief in Beirut, in a suite the PLO had rented at the Waldorf Astoria Hotel. Ames had arranged the meeting. Mustafa Zein was there to introduce Salameh to *Waverly*. Security was tight. The PLO delegation was given three floors of the luxurious hotel; Arafat, Salameh, and other senior aides occupied the middle floor, and their security details lived below and above them. Guards armed with submachine guns were posted at the end of each hallway and on all the staircases. They spent the night in the Waldorf, traveling to the UN headquarters and back in armored limousines.

David Ignatius of the *Washington Post* later wrote an account of the negotiations between the CIA and Salameh. Ignatius reported that according to one source who was in the room, "Arafat and his Fatah wing of the PLO would seek to halt international terrorist operations outside Israel, with the understanding that Arafat couldn't be held responsible for the actions of every Palestinian. In exchange, the United States said it was prepared to recognize the legitimate rights of the Palestinians." A former CIA official had a slightly different take: "The PLO was generally going to lay off Americans, especially official Americans. In return, we would be attentive to some of the security concerns that the PLO had." Zein, *Waverly*, and Salameh spent four hours together, ironing out the details of this security agreement. Zein told Salameh that Bob Ames had told him to emphasize that if the PLO wanted to be accepted as a state, "the PLO must conduct itself as a member state to join other states of the world." (They also agreed that the CIA and the PLO should cooperate against any common enemies, such as the Abu Nidal Organization.) Finally, at 3:00 A.M. the meeting ended, and Salameh left to accompany Arafat on a flight to Cuba, where they were scheduled to see Fidel Castro.

Before leaving New York, Salameh bought a postcard picturing the Waldorf Astoria. He drew an arrow pointing to one of the suites on the upper floors and then wrote on the back, "The PLO at the Waldorf Astoria!" And then he mailed the postcard to his family in Beirut.

In retrospect, the evolution of the PLO in 1973–74 was a watershed. By the end of 1973, Arafat had closed down Black September. Arafat also deployed his men, as agreed at the Waldorf Astoria talks, against Abu Nidal. Salameh's deputy in Force 17, Mohammed Natour (Abu Tayeb), later explained, "We in Force 17 were requested by Arafat to attack Abu Nidal's headquarters in Libya, and we killed all who were there planning operations to kill PLO representatives in Europe. . . . Many terrorist operations were disrupted and stopped dead in their tracks. No terrorist act was ever allowed to reach the shores of America. All Americans and Western nationals were protected in Lebanon by Force 17."

Fatah did not give up entirely on armed struggle, but henceforth its targets were confined to Israel and the occupied territories. After the Lillehammer fiasco in Norway, Mossad's assassination program came to a halt. The war of spooks petered out.* The Palestinians had taken far more casualties, but a few Israelis had been assassinated as well. In London a letter bomb killed an Israeli diplomat—and in Madrid Black September assassinated a Mossad agent. Major General Yariv later insisted that Israel's wave of retaliatory assassinations "persuaded the PLO leaders to stop the terrorism abroad. This proves that we were right to use this method for a certain period." Yet Mossad's assassination program did not stop attacks from non-Fatah groups like the PFLP and the Abu Nidal Organization. More persuasive is the argument that Arafat and Salameh understood that Black September's spectacular attacks had indeed captured the world's attention. Everyone understood now that there was a Palestinian problem. But they realized that continued terrorism would make more people less sympathetic to the Palestinian cause. Even more important, they realized they could not keep the CIA's back channel open if Black September continued to attack Western targets. By mid-1973, Arafat could see that the channel that went through Bob Ames to the CIA leadership and ultimately to the White House offered him the potential opportunity to gain America's recognition for both the PLO and the rights of the Palestinian people to self-determination and nationhood. In this sense, Ames and the CIA had planted the seeds of a peaceful settlement. "I'm just a middle man in all this," Ames wrote to Zein in June 1974—just days before Arafat had persuaded the Palestinian National Council to ac-

---

* Oddly enough, Mossad had assassinated some Palestinians who had no responsibility for Munich—yet the tactical mastermind of Munich, Abu Daoud, died of natural causes—kidney failure—in 2010 (Trevor Mostyn, "Mohammed Oudeh [Abu Daoud] Obituary: Mastermind Behind the Attack on Israeli Athletes at the 1972 Munich Olympics," *Guardian*, July 4, 2010). At least one of the three surviving Black September commandos at Munich is also still alive.

cept the idea of a Palestinian state on a portion of Palestine. "Middle
men often spend much time waiting. It seems to me there is a famous
saying, which goes, 'He also serves who stands and waits.' That's us,
you and I. Tell our friends to be patient."

Ames was very pleased that Washington had allowed Arafat and Salameh to visit New York. He felt that his off-and-on dialogue with
Salameh—a delicate relationship cultivated over five long years—
had finally led to a concrete diplomatic achievement. After the October 1974 Rabat Arab League summit, when the PLO was recognized
as "the sole representative of the Palestinian people," Ames wished
that Washington could have followed suit. Arafat for a moment really
thought the Americans were going to recognize him as a legitimate
leader. But Kissinger balked and insisted that Arafat had to recognize
Israel's right to exist and fully endorse UN Resolution 242—which implicitly recognized Israel's pre-1967 borders. Arafat couldn't bring his
own constituency along that far—not yet. Ames thought that this stalemate was unfortunate and that more could have been done to bridge
their differences. He thought it essential to U.S. national interests that
the Palestinian conundrum be resolved. Ames's secret diplomacy with
Salameh had opened a back door to a peace settlement—but the policy
makers, Kissinger in particular, had missed an opportunity to reach for
a truly comprehensive peace settlement. Kissinger's "step-by-step" diplomacy was wasting time; it allowed the Israelis to postpone making
the hard compromises necessary for peace—and gave them more time
to create new facts on the ground in the occupied territories. Ames
was thus both proud of what he had done and also frustrated.

And even if Salameh wasn't exactly a fully recruited agent, Ames
felt that he'd been at least partially responsible for bringing this particular Palestinian in from the cold. It was a step in the direction of political legitimization and a step away from the terrorism. It was an open
secret inside the CIA that Bob Ames had helped to make this happen.
Some of his colleagues knew of Ames's cultivation of MJTRUST/2,

and those who didn't nevertheless knew that Ames was somehow a rising star. They also knew that the thirty-nine-year-old Ames was a protégé of Dick Helms. That alone marked him as special.

■

Throughout these momentous events in 1973–74, Ames had been posted first in Tehran, serving under Ambassador Helms—and later in Kuwait. He had flown frequently into Beirut to see Salameh. But at the same time, his job in Tehran required him to acquire a new expertise on things Iranian. He disliked the sprawling concrete city and thought the Persians pretentious and faux-cosmopolitan—at least those who populated the pampered inner circle of the Pahlavi dynasty. "In Tehran," recalled another CIA officer, "we were completely cut off from Iranian society. The CIA station had to rely for everything on SAVAK [the shah's secret police], and they were very condescending about the Arabs. Ames was no doubt annoyed by this attitude. Besides, these SAVAK guys were all liars. It was tiresome. They would lie to me about what they ate for lunch." In private Ames liked to mock the shah's imperial pretentions, calling him in a Farsi accent the "shah-in-shah-shah." A few colleagues in the embassy shared his sentiments. That summer, one Foreign Service officer wrote Ambassador Helms a long skeptical assessment of the shah's regime: "The Shah in his early years tried to behave like a constitutional monarch and to implement the democratic ideals which he is said to have acquired at Le Rosey [an elite boarding school in Switzerland].* Whether or not this is true (and I must say that Le Rosey seems to me a most unlikely place for anyone to acquire democratic ideas), it is clear that in the early 1950s, especially after the Mossadegh episode, the Shah determined to rule as well as reign." The officer then described Mohammed Reza Shah Pahlavi's governance style: "The system is simple and crude, but complicated in

---

* The author of this "secret" memo knew, of course, that Helms himself, for the last two years of his secondary education, had attended Le Rosey, where he had crossed paths with the eleven-year-old shah.

use, rather as primitive languages are said by linguists to have the most complex grammars. Every important organ of government is managed by a few men who must be kept in a state of intense rivalry and distrust of one another. All power comes from the Shah."

The Pahlavi regime was nevertheless a close ally, so Washington would quietly ignore the regime's inherent weakness and unpopularity for another six years—until the Persian "emperor" was overthrown by a violent and unforgiving revolution.

In the autumn of 1973, just six months after arriving in Tehran, the CIA rewarded Ames with a significant promotion to be chief of station in Kuwait. Ambassador Helms orchestrated the transfer. Ames welcomed the new posting; he was happy to get back to Arabia. Neither was Yvonne unhappy about the sudden change in orders. They were still living out of suitcases in temporary quarters in Tehran when the Kuwait assignment came up. When they arrived in Kuwait in the early autumn of 1973, their household effects were still on a ship bound for Iran.

Initially they lived in the Hilton Hotel, not far from the American embassy. But in short order they found a traditional walled house near the Persian Gulf. From the roof, one could see the sparkling turquoise waters that the Kuwaitis called the Arabian Gulf. The children attended the local American School. Yvonne bought them mail-order clothes from JCPenney and Sears Roebuck catalogues. There was no television then in Kuwait, but the children could walk to the beach and go swimming nearly every day. Bob relished being back in Arabia. He again took to driving through the desert, stopping occasionally to talk with the Bedouins. One evening the whole family was invited to a Kuwaiti neighbor's house for dinner. A Bedouin-style black tent had been pitched in the garden, and their hosts brought out a whole roasted lamb on a tray piled high with rice. After that memorable evening the Ames girls all became vegetarians. Even today, Adrienne won't touch meat.

That autumn, Ames cabled "Fletcher M. KNIGHT"—Ambassador Helms's official CIA pseudonym—and gave an enthusiastic report on their new life in Kuwait. "KNIGHT" replied, "Glad things have worked out so well." Bob liked his overseas assignments; the work was more interesting than attending meetings in Langley, and the pay was better. The Agency paid the family's rent in Kuwait; Bob had access to official cars, and he was given an entertainment allowance. Naturally, any expenses from clandestine meetings with agents were reimbursed. He had two other Agency officers working under him, and between the three of them they typically produced about twenty intelligence reports a month.

While in Kuwait, Ames recruited a Palestinian agent who seemed to be very knowledgeable about both Kuwaiti and Palestinian politics. This agent's cryptonym was MJVOICE/1, and he had close contacts in the Popular Democratic Front for the Liberation of Palestine. Ames relied on MJVOICE/1's reporting. "Bob frequently produced long think pieces on the Palestinian question," recalled *David Reeve*, a CIA case officer then stationed in Beirut. *Reeve* had known Ames in Beirut and liked him. But he grew to have misgivings. Ames's reporting made it seem as if MJVOICE/1 was an astute analyst with unique insights. But when *Reeve* met the agent in Beirut he was not impressed. "I used Bob's reporting to try to get him to open up about what was transpiring in Beirut," recalled *Reeve*. "I never found him to be very forthcoming. He certainly did not provide information on the scale that he did with Bob." *Reeve* wondered whether "Bob might have been using this source as a vehicle to get his point across. The source never struck me as that intelligent." *Reeve* knew this was an occupational hazard, but he thought it wrong to embellish your reporting with your own opinions; he thought Ames had crossed the line. For his part, Ames must have heard complaints from MJVOICE/1 about his meetings with *Reeve*. So Ames sent a back-channel cable to the Beirut chief of station, John Seidel, suggesting that another case officer be used with MJVOICE/1. Seidel refused.

A few of Ames's peers in the Agency thought he had sharp elbows.

"Bob had a keen instinct for the jugular," said Graham Fuller. Fuller admired Ames and thought they had a lot in common. But on one occasion, he felt blindsided by Ames. Fuller had confided in him, frankly sharing some of his doubts about how he was handling some of his recruits. A few weeks later, Fuller was shocked to receive a cable from Ames criticizing his work. The criticism was based wholly on what Fuller himself had revealed to Ames. "I had a feeling that my honesty with him had been turned against me," Fuller said. "After this, I was wary of him. You know, I couldn't quarrel with his judgment on matters of substance, but inside the Agency he could play these cat-and-mouse games. After this incident, I couldn't quite trust him anymore."

Ames was clearly ambitious. Some ambitious men muffle their opinions and keep their head low. Not Ames. He had certitudes, and he wasn't shy about expressing them. "He once told me," Yvonne Ames said, "that anyone working with him needed to take his ideas and make them work."

At the same time, Bob could be faultlessly loyal to those he considered his friends. Working with Ames in Kuwait was his colleague from Beirut, Henry McDermott. Bob liked the decidedly irascible McDermott, and he did everything he could to protect Henry from his foibles. "Henry was a mess," recalled Yvonne, "but Bob had patience and he could see past the problems. Henry, with all his faults, was easy to be around." When Henry had an affair with the station secretary, Ames disapproved but chose not to say anything. (McDermott had been separated from his wife, Betty, since 1970.) By then, Henry's drinking had become a serious problem. "His pugnacious Irish temperament was always pissing people off," recalled Henry Miller-Jones. After McDermott's Kuwait assignment, no one wanted to work with him. Langley wanted to cashier him but instead sent him to counseling for his drinking. At this point, Ames interceded and asked Gene Burgstaller, who by then had been named chief of station in Paris, if he could find a place for McDermott in the Paris station. Like Ames, Burgstaller had a soft spot for Henry, who he knew had pulled off more than one risky operation during their time together in Beirut. So Burgstaller agreed to shelter him.

But then several years later, McDermott found himself sitting next to an attractive young woman on a flight to Paris. Taking advantage of airline liquor, "Henry got juiced," recalled *Bill Fisk*, another clandestine officer who worked with McDermott, "and he started telling her stories about terrorist gangs in Paris. He was just trying to impress the woman." Unbeknownst to McDermott, the woman was an aide to national security adviser Brent Scowcroft. She complained to Scowcroft, and soon thereafter McDermott was forced to accept an early medical retirement. He became a potter and lived on a boat in Belmar, New Jersey.

A chief of station posting usually runs three years. But Kuwait was considered by Washington to be a hardship post, so many officers stayed only two years. In any case, Ames was pulled out of Kuwait in the summer of 1975 after only two years on the job. "Please let me know," he wrote Ambassador Helms in Tehran, "if there are any last minute things you want me to do before I start closing up shop here."

He may have been pulled because in early 1975 his name and job title had been published in *CounterSpy* magazine, a left-wing publication critical of the CIA. Yvonne still thinks they had to depart prematurely—but Bob never talked about these things, so she's not sure what happened. In December 1975, after they'd moved back to their Reston, Virginia, home, the CIA station chief in Athens, Richard Welch, was gunned down outside his home. Welch had been named in the same *CounterSpy* article as Ames. (Welch was assassinated by gunmen from the Revolutionary Organization 17 November, a Greek underground group opposed to the military dictatorship in Athens.) This first assassination of a chief of station naturally shocked everyone back at Langley. "His murder is a gruesomely fitting climax to a year of insanity," said Bill Nelson, a senior CIA officer, in a cable to Dick Helms.

CHAPTER SEVEN

Headquarters, 1975–79

Ames had his quirks, his cowboy boots and his tinted aviator
eyeglasses. But when Bob walked into the room you didn't get
the sense . . . that he was a needy person.

—*Lindsay Sherwin, senior analyst, Directorate of Intelligence*

U pon his return to Reston in the autumn of 1975, Ames was
promoted to chief of the Near East/Arabian Peninsula Branch
inside the Directorate of Operations. This put him in charge
of all covert operations in Saudi Arabia, the Yemens, Kuwait, and the
rest of Arabia. It was a significant promotion, with a pay grade of
GS-14—roughly equivalent to a lieutenant colonel in the army. At the
time, the Agency had more than 20,000 employees, but only about
2,500 of these were officers in the clandestine service, the DO. Landing a management job at Ames's level was very competitive.

Ames realized that he was coming back to a CIA very much under
siege. After Dick Helms had left as director in early 1973, President
Nixon ordered his replacement, James Schlesinger, to purge the Agency.
"Get rid of the clowns," Nixon said. "What use are they? They've got
40,000 people over there reading newspapers." Schlesinger lasted
only seventeen weeks as director, but by the time he left he'd fired
more than five hundred analysts and a thousand veteran clandestine
officers. William Colby replaced Schlesinger. Morale inside Langley
naturally plummeted.

And then, on December 22, 1974, Seymour Hersh published a
front-page story in the *New York Times* with the headline "Huge CIA

Operation Reported in U.S. against Anti-war Forces." That President
Nixon had used the CIA to spy on his antiwar critics rapidly became
a national scandal. The House of Representatives and then the Senate
opened congressional investigations into the CIA's activities over the
past few decades. Eventually, the Church Committee—named after
Senator Frank Church—published fourteen volumes of testimony
and documents. Scores of witnesses were called to testify. The most
sensational report focused on the CIA's "Alleged Assassination Plots
Involving Foreign Leaders." Americans learned that the CIA had been
involved in plots to unseat Chile's Marxist president, Salvador Allende, the Congo's Patrice Lumumba, and Cuba's Fidel Castro. Oddly
enough, congressional investigators largely ignored the Agency's activities in the Middle East. The House of Representatives' "Pike Report" criticized the Agency for having incorrectly assured Washington
that Egypt's Anwar Sadat had no intention of launching a war in the
autumn of 1973. "We predicted the day before the war broke out that
it was not going to break out," said William Colby. But otherwise, the
CIA's Near East division escaped any scrutiny. Ames was never asked
to testify.

At the time, Colby was bitterly criticized inside the Agency for giving away the family jewels, and for being too cooperative with the
congressional investigators. He thought he had no choice. "In the context of the politics of the time, we had just had Watergate, you really
weren't going to get away with stonewalling them. It just wasn't going
to work." Like most case officers, Ames was not a fan of Colby's—and
he was dismayed by the ordeal. "The Congressional investigations,"
admitted Colby in 1976, "were like being pillaged by a foreign power,
only we had been occupied by the Congress with our files rifled, our
officials humiliated and our Agency exposed."

The Church Committee revealed many of the Agency's worst intelligence failures. There came a moment when some thought the whole
CIA was going to be put out of business. Helms warned President Gerald Ford that if the congressional investigations were allowed to continue, "A lot of dead cats will come out. I don't know everything that

went on in the Agency. Maybe no one does. But I know enough to say that if the dead cats come out, I will participate." Helms meant that he thought he'd be forced to reveal national security secrets.

He was all too prescient. Eventually, the Church Committee revelations concerning the coup d'état against Chile's Allende caused Congress and the press to scrutinize Helms's testimony in his 1973 ambassadorial confirmation hearings. Helms had categorically denied under oath that the CIA had tried to overthrow Allende. Over the next four years—throughout his tenure as ambassador to Iran—Helms had to fly back to Washington thirteen times to testify before various congressional committees. Ames thought his old boss was being unfairly treated, and he made a point of taking Helms out to lunch. But Helms eventually had to plead nolo contendere to two misdemeanor counts for lying to Congress. The judge imposed a $2,000 fine and a suspended two-year jail sentence. Helms's lawyer, Edward Bennett Williams, told reporters that Helms would "wear this conviction like a badge of honor." Helms emphatically agreed.

Funding for the clandestine services shrank rapidly during the 1970s. Partly this was simply a result of the Vietnam War winding down. But the pendulum had swung, and the collection of human intelligence fell out of favor with policy makers. The business of cultivating human sources was time-consuming, uncertain, and ultimately just plain exasperating for most politicians in Washington. Once again, Washington was falling in love with high-tech spying: satellites, wiretaps, and intercepts.

Still, the CIA always had far more resources than the State Department. Ames once told my father, a regular Foreign Service officer, "If we could, we'd bury you." He said it in a manner both jocular and boasting. But it reflected a certain reality about the business of foreign policy. "In my experience," wrote Richard L. Holm, a veteran CIA officer, "agency officers and foreign service officers rarely saw eye to eye. Those differences spawned a mutual lack of trust and confidence that consistently marred our exchanges." By the late 1970s there were only about 2,300 Foreign Service officers posted abroad, with another

1,600 stationed in the State Department's Washington, D.C., head-quarters. (The Foreign Service had another 5,000 administrative staff at home and abroad.) These men and women were the public face of American diplomacy. But they were far outnumbered by the CIA's workforce, numbering more than 18,000 officers and staff with a budget of over $5 billion, which dwarfed that of the State Department.

In 1975, Ames's immediate boss was Duane R. Clarridge, deputy chief of the Near East for Arab Operations. "Dewey" Clarridge was not an Arabist. His first posting as a young case officer had been in Kathmandu, Nepal, and he'd worked in Turkey, but he knew nothing about the Middle East. He boasted about this, and much later in his memoirs he admitted: "I am sure there were those in the division who were appalled that I was given this assignment with no experience in the Arab world." But for Dewey the Middle East was just a culture based on "a seminal Hellenistic cultural root, with strong overlays of various forms of Islam and Christianity.... In a generic sense, it's all the same."

Ames thought this attitude reeked of ignorance and arrogance. His Arabs were in no sense "generic." Ames was also annoyed by Clarridge's casual use of the term *wog*. Clarridge was always talking about the "wog factor," suggesting that one could never predict what these inexplicable foreigners would do next. To be sure, Clarridge wasn't the only CIA officer who used the derogatory term, but it grated on Ames's ears.

Clarridge was flamboyant in a way Ames could never be. He wore white linen suits to the office. He was rambunctious and always wore his opinions prominently displayed on his sleeve. To be sure, Ames stood out, with his cowboy boots and tinted, aviator-style glasses. (He had three pairs in three different shades: yellow, dark brown, and pink.) But Ames was not a cowboy. Dewey was hot to Bob's cool. "Bob played with a pipe and his worry beads," observed Henry Miller-Jones, "but he never looked nervous."

Inevitably, Bob and Dewey clashed. The chemistry was not good. Bob was the consummate, learned "Arabist," while Dewey was the can-do, hands-on operational guy who wanted to get things done. Clarridge thought Ames had an academic view of the world. "Ph.D.s don't do well in the espionage business," said Clarridge. "They are trained to see the gray. So they never pull the trigger in terms of recruiting somebody." Clarridge felt a certain amount of frustration with Ames; he couldn't understand why Ames wouldn't at least try to pull the trigger with Salameh. "If you can't ask the question," said Clarridge, "you shouldn't be in the business."

Clarridge had developed doubts about the Salameh channel. If the Palestinian couldn't be recruited, maybe something else was going on. He eventually questioned whether even having a "liaison relationship with this murderer" (Salameh) was worth it. He wondered if "we, the CIA, were being had by Fatah." Perhaps, he thought, Arafat was manipulating the "Salameh setup and [we] were being fed information— which in reality was precious little—to influence U.S. policy and nothing else." Clarridge knew that the CIA had virtually no penetration into the PLO. That meant there was a lot of pressure within the Agency to believe that the Salameh channel was worthwhile. But Clarridge thought Salameh's intelligence was inflated.

"In the 1970s," Clarridge said, "we had no agents inside the PLO, none." There was one brief exception: a German national code-named "Ganymede." And even "Ganymede" had not been recruited by a CIA case officer. "Ganymede" was a simple "walk-in." Still, Clarridge regarded him—in contrast to Salameh—as the genuine article, a fully recruited agent. "Ganymede" has since told his story to a team of reporters from *Der Spiegel*. He is Willi Voss, a onetime petty criminal who in the early 1970s found himself working for Fatah's Abu Daoud. A few years later, he offered his services to the CIA. His case officer was Terence Douglas. "Willi was a very cool guy," Douglas told *Der Spiegel* in 2013. "He was creative and a bit crazy—we spent a very, very intense time together." Voss was given some minimal training. He was taught how to use a miniature camera to copy documents.

He was warned against carrying any incriminating "pocket litter" and was given a few lessons about dead drops, brush passes, and telephone security. And he was willing to sign receipts. For Clarridge, signing a "receipt" was the touchstone. It meant that the source was a fully recruited agent. On at least one occasion, Voss provided to the CIA photographs of PLO documents. While Voss was staying in the apartment of a ranking PLO official, he photographed some random documents while the Palestinian was out of the apartment. But Voss couldn't read Arabic, so he had no idea what he was photographing. "The intelligence was valuable," recalled Douglas, "in identifying participants in this chap's cell."

In January 1976, Clarridge and Douglas met "Ganymede" in an Athens hotel room. They discussed a plan whereby Voss would attempt to lure Ilich Ramírez Sánchez—otherwise known as the notorious terrorist Carlos the Jackal—into the hands of the CIA. Clarridge writes in his memoirs that he'd discussed the operation in Langley prior to his departure for Athens. A senior clandestine officer had told him, "If the agent [Voss] can set up Carlos to be taken by a security service, it would be a boon for mankind. . . . If Carlos is killed in the process, so be it." In the subsequent Athens meeting Voss initially agreed to the mission, but he eventually "lost his nerve." And soon afterwards, Clarridge learned that on February 18, 1976, President Gerald Ford had promulgated Executive Order 11905, banning assassinations. Clarridge was disappointed.* "Ganymede" was an active agent only from about 1974 to 1976. But he was the kind of penetration agent Clarridge thought Ames should have been able to cultivate. Clarridge wanted Ames to persuade Salameh to "sign receipts." He would be disappointed.

Clarridge eventually came to think of Ames as not a really good fit in the DO—despite his reputation for having cultivated the Salameh back channel to the PLO. "He and I got along well when he was my

---

* Carlos the Jackal wasn't apprehended until 1994 and is now serving a life sentence in a French prison.

deputy in Arab Ops," Clarridge later insisted. "And I admired his insights into Middle Eastern problems, but they were no better than [Charlie] Waterman's or Barnes' and others in the DO and certainly not the caliber of Philby the Elder [Harry St. John Bridger Philby], [Sir Richard Francis] Burton [1821–90] or Colonel [William] Eddy [1896–1962]"—the legendary English and American Arabists.

Clarridge just didn't think of Ames as a DO guy. He wasn't one to go out drinking with the boys after work. And since he didn't drink, how could he recruit anyone? Clarridge wondered. Alcohol, he wrote, "plays a major part" in developing an agent. Dewey always thought Bob's career as a DO officer was "mediocre."

On the other hand, few DO case officers *ever* recruit anyone. It's an extremely rare event. A CIA survey of the DO covering the three decades prior to 1985 concluded that less than 5 percent of DO case officers ever recruited someone capable of producing protected, significant information. "Recruiting agents is very hard," Clarridge observed. "If only 5 percent of all case officers in their careers ever recruit an agent—well, in my time there were no more than two thousand case officers, so that suggests the Agency had recruited no more than one hundred agents over a period of twenty-five years."

Alternatively, many unrecruited "sources" were assigned cryptonyms, ostensibly so their information could be disseminated without revealing their identities. This sometimes had the effect of misleading policy makers, who might easily assume that the reports attributed to a crypt came from a fully recruited and controlled agent. According to Clarridge, this became an inside joke. Then again, he said, if every case officer had recruited even one agent in a two-year tour, "the Agency would have been awash in spies."

Ames was certainly aware of these realities, and by all accounts he just didn't take Clarridge's criticisms seriously. He knew he had lots of contacts and good sources of information, particularly among the Palestinians. And some of them, like MJTRUST/2, were assigned crypts. Moreover, Ames thought Clarridge was one of those DO officers who too often acted like a cowboy. Clarridge was a magnet for strong opinions, both pro and con. "Dewey is a brilliant intelligence officer," said Clair George, one of his colleagues in the DO, "who suffers from one problem: he likes to see his name in the newspaper."

"Dewey was an ass, a showboat," recalled one colleague, an analyst in the Directorate of Intelligence. "I mean, Ames had his quirks, his cowboy boots and his tinted aviator eyeglasses. But when Bob walked into the room you didn't get the sense, like you did from Dewey, that he was a needy person."

Ames liked to yank Clarridge's chain. One day on his way out of the office to meet with a source in New York City, Ames turned to a colleague and said, "If Dewey asks where I've gone, tell him I've gone to New York to meet a guy in the oil business about a possible job." He knew this would tick off Clarridge, but he didn't mind. It wasn't just Clarridge. "He once told me," wrote Henry Miller-Jones, "that he thought he would never rise above middle management in the Agency because he was too argumentative and outspoken. Indeed, he could have stormy battles with his superiors over personnel choices, or how to handle an agent (often one he'd recruited), or over a significant political trend."

Ames's other boss in the mid-1970s was Alan Douglas Wolfe, chief of the Near East and South Asia Division (NESA) in the DO. Wolfe was a peculiar man for the job. "Alan looked like a shorter and ruddier version of Peter O'Toole in *Lawrence of Arabia*," recalled Henry Miller-Jones. Born in 1928 in New York City, Wolfe had graduated from Columbia University and then joined the CIA. His first posting abroad was to Karachi, Pakistan, in 1951. Some thought Wolfe had a Napoleon complex, and Wolfe himself once complained that he certainly would have risen to become director of the CIA—if only he'd been as tall as Bob Ames. "He had a low threshold for the dim-witted," wrote Clarridge. "[Wolfe] made little effort to hide his opinion of those he felt lacked common sense and operational know-how." He thought he knew a lot about the Middle East, even though his only posting in the Arab world was a short stint in Jordan in 1956. Wolfe was a specialist in South Asia; he had just come from being chief of station in

Pakistan—where in July 1971 he had served as the advance man for Henry Kissinger's secret trip to China. He was not an Arabist. In fact, he did not believe in language training. He once famously said that no case officer needed to speak anything but English because anyone worth recruiting in the Near East would speak English. "Learning a wog language," he said, "was a waste of time." He was prickly and egotistical. He had way too much confidence. The few women in the DO thought Wolfe was sexist. "He was a crude individual," said one female CIA officer.

Wolfe was very opinionated and very ambitious. "Wolfe was the kind of man who was deliberately not endearing," recalled another high-ranking officer. One evening in early 1975 Wolfe was introduced to the Israeli chargé d'affaires at a diplomatic reception in Washington, D.C. This was just after CIA director Bill Colby had finally decided to take the Israeli desk away from James Jesus Angleton*—the legendary counterintelligence chief who'd run Israeli affairs as if it were his private fiefdom—and put it where it logically belonged: in NESA. The Israelis regarded NESA with profound suspicion. Tel Aviv had lodged an official protest, arguing that they shouldn't be lumped with the Arab world—and shouldn't have to liaise with the Agency's Arabists, whom they regarded as "Orientalists," liable to be critical of Israel. So upon meeting Wolfe, the Israeli diplomat asked, "Alan, I understand you will have the Israeli account?"

"Yes," replied Wolfe, "and it is about time."

"Well," said the Israeli chargé, "I understand that you are an anti-Semite."

"That's damn right," Wolfe shot back. "I've dealt with all those Semites and none of you are worth a damn."

Wolfe rubbed a lot of people the wrong way. But he had nevertheless

---

* When Angleton was dying of lung cancer in the spring of 1987, he told Mossad's Efraim Halevy, "I have a confession. I trusted you Israelis, but not fully, so I penetrated you." The senior Mossad officer who related this story wryly remarked, "He was planting suspicion even from his deathbed." This officer recalled that the CIA had tried to recruit him on two different occasions.

risen rapidly in the ranks of the Agency. His small office had a window perched directly above the main entrance to the CIA headquarters in Langley, Virginia. Oddly enough, behind his desk was a framed color poster of a muscular Amazon beauty in a ragged, sexy outfit grasping an AK-47, leaping through the air, and proclaiming. *"Eh, maintenant, mes amis, aux barricades!"* Over the next few years Ames would learn not to trust Wolfe's judgment.

Like Dewey Clarridge, Wolfe didn't understand why Ames didn't make more of an effort to recruit his "friends." One day when Mustafa Zein was visiting Washington, Ames took Wolfe to see Zein in his hotel room. "Right away," recalled Zein, "Wolfe wanted to know why I was doing all this without any money. I told him, 'If I get paid for what I say, you are not going to respect me or believe the information.'"

Wolfe responded, "All agents are motivated by profit, not by seeking the truth."

"Mr. Wolfe," retorted Zein, "I am a seeker of truth."

As chief of covert operations for the Arabian Peninsula, Ames was on a management track. And by all accounts his immediate subordinates liked him. "Clandestine officers are usually extroverts," said Charlie Allen, a CIA officer who met Ames in 1973. "They can be supersalesmen. But Bob wasn't like that. There was something solid about him. He was just a remarkable clandestine officer, the best I've ever seen."

Ames was the kind of boss who always came out from behind his desk and sat down with people to talk one on one. "Bob had a nice personality," recalled one colleague. "He came across as a very balanced person. He was skilled with people, so it wasn't surprising that he was skilled at recruitment. He had a way of inspiring confidence."

He kept a clean desk. It was practically bare. "I think sloppiness is contagious," Ames once told Yvonne. "And if you are sloppy in the office, it will carry over to all things." He typed his own memos on a manual typewriter—and a few years later, on an IBM electric typewriter. He never learned to type with more than two fingers. He liked to write on a yellow legal pad with green ink. Only books, not paper, cluttered his office.

Though his purview was the Arabian Peninsula, Ames never relinquished full control over his back channel with Ali Hassan Salameh. Ames continued to believe in Salameh. He liked the man, especially his laid-back manner and his sense of humor. "Salameh was perceived by all of us," said *Charles Waverly*, who a few years later took over from Ames as his case officer, "as more open-minded, and Bob carefully nurtured this." At some point, Ames decided it would be a nice gesture to give Ali Hassan a personal gift. But he thought it would have to be something meaningful, something Ali Hassan would treasure. Ames knew Ali Hassan was not just a parlor revolutionary. He walked around with a pistol in a holster on his belt. So he came up with the idea that he should give Ali Hassan a fine American pistol. For this, he knew he would have to get authorization from Langley. Headquarters didn't like the idea. This crossed some invisible ethical line. The Agency could have dealings with a terrorist, but it would be unseemly to make a gift of a gun. Cables flew back and forth. Ames pressed the issue. He wouldn't give up on it. Finally, Headquarters said, "Okay, why don't you give him a replica of a gun? A neutered gun?" Ames fired back a cable saying no way. Ali Hassan would be insulted. Eventually Ames had to give up on the whole idea.

Perhaps Ames hadn't given up on the notion of a full-blown recruitment. His attempt to give Ali Hassan a gun is evidence of this. He just understood that if it were ever to happen, it would take time and a long history of proven friendship. The line between recruitment and a liaison relationship is always subtle. "Ames no doubt often tried to peel MJTRUST/2's loyalties away from Arafat," recalled Miller-Jones. Ames would do this by trying gently to solicit from Salameh his personal opinions and analysis. He'd encourage Salameh to talk about what *he* thought—as opposed to Arafat or the official PLO line. "He would seek his 'out of school' take on an issue," Miller-Jones said. "Wherever it crossed a line and differed from Arafat in a significant way, well, Salameh would really have been risking his job, at the very least, and maybe worse. And whenever he took any kind of material reward from Ames, he would be vulnerable to charges of spying for the Americans, especially if he did not report it to his Fatah bosses. Therein lies the subtle difference in nomenclature between recruited or not."

Salameh, however, seemed to understand the game all too well, and he walked a very fine line. He knew how to play it. "They were constantly trying to recruit each other," said Jack O'Connell, the chief of station in Jordan. Ames and Ali Hassan had a genuine friendship. "They tell you in the CIA never to fall in love with your agent," recalled Miller-Jones. "But everyone does, and those few who don't rise to senior management." Ames was different. It was an open question in 1975 about how high in the bureaucracy Ames would ever rise. He was known for his strong opinions and passions. Some thought his passions would block further promotions. On the other hand, he was efficient and effective. Earlier that year, during one of Ames's frequent trips from Kuwait to Beirut, Ames got Salameh to pledge that his Force 17 would provide security for the embassy—which was located in PLO territory in Ras Beirut. Force 17, of course, was the same security apparatus that provided personal security for Yasir Arafat. As part of the security arrangement negotiated between Ames and Salameh, the Agency agreed to provide Force 17 with some limited training. To put it bluntly, the Agency was now in the business of training Arafat's bodyguards.

With the end of the Vietnam War in April 1975, the CIA's heavy investment in covert operations in Southeast Asia came to an end. But although the overall number of covert ops had declined in the early 1970s, clandestine operations still accounted for 37 percent of the Agency's total budget. And a large portion was being spent in the Middle East. That was where the "action" was in terms of operations. Whereas Berlin had been the spy capital of the early Cold War, Beirut was now the place to be if you were in operations. So when Clair George was offered the chief of station job in Beirut, he regarded it as a plum assignment.

But soon after George's arrival in Beirut, the Lebanese began killing one another in a brutal sectarian civil war, pitting competing Maronite Christian militias against a loose coalition of Druze, Sunni, and Shi'ite militias. "I never thought of Lebanon as a country," wrote Said Aburish, the Palestinian journalist who spent much of his career in Beirut. "I always thought of the place as an idea, essentially a good idea." Until 1975, Lebanon had indeed been a good idea for the whole Middle East, a model of how a mosaic of religions and ethnicities could nevertheless flourish in a multicultural and mostly civil society. And then it all fell apart. One could say it began on April 13, 1975, with the "Bus Massacre" in which some twenty-seven Palestinians and Lebanese Muslims were killed by Maronite Phalangist gunmen. This egregious massacre had no doubt been incited by any number of previous, less bloody incidents. But for most historians this was the spark that began a civil war that would last for fifteen years. At least 130,000 people were killed, and some estimates range as high as 250,000. The Maronite Christian militias fought to defend their vision of a Lebanon dominated by the Maronite elite—even though by the 1970s this ancient Christian community was a decided minority compared to the Druze, the Sunni, and the rapidly growing population of Shi'ites. The Druze, Sunni, and Shi'ite communities were aligned together, but they all acquired their own militias. The refugee Palestinians, represented by the PLO, gradually became drawn into the civil war and fought against the Maronites and their dominant militia, the right-wing Phalangists. The Syrian army eventually intervened, initially against the Maronites, but then against the Palestinians and their Druze and Sunni allies. It was, needless to say, a bloody mess of a war, characterized by shifting tribal and sectarian loyalties.

Beirut became a combat zone as the civil war spiraled out of control. "In Beirut everyone has an agenda and a gun," George told a friend. "And the agenda can go in any direction, and the gun can shoot in any direction." But as things got worse, Salameh's value to the Americans rose. He became essential to the security of the American embassy. This was underscored in June 1976, when U.S. ambassador Francis Meloy and his economic counselor, Robert O. Waring, were assassinated. Despite the obvious dangers, Ambassador Meloy decided he needed to keep an appointment with Lebanese president Elias Sarkis in East Beirut. He and Waring got into the armored ambassadorial limousine and were driven by a longtime Lebanese chauffeur toward East Beirut. Incredibly, no armed security guards accompanied them. As they were about to cross into Christian-controlled East Beirut, unknown gunmen halted the car and seized them. Their bodies—including the chauffeur's—were found in a garbage dump a few hours later. According to Jonathan Randal, the *Washington Post* correspondent at the time, that particular stretch of the road from West Beirut into the Christian sector of East Beirut was controlled by a Lebanese militia calling itself the Socialist Arab Labor Party. They were loosely affiliated with the PFLP.

The specific identities of the murderers and their motives remain unknown. In any case, it was not Fatah who killed the ambassador and his aide, and they were not assassinated while under the security umbrella of Fatah. On June 20, 1976, the bodies of the two American diplomats had to be extracted from Lebanon via a convoy of cars over the mountains into Syria. The airport was closed, and even a seaside departure was deemed too dangerous. Salameh supervised the security arrangements for the embassy convoy. "I will get you through the Palestinian lines," Salameh promised Sam Wyman, the case officer responsible for extracting the bodies out of Lebanon. "Sure enough," said Wyman, "as soon as we passed out of PLO-controlled territory, we ran into a firefight between the Syrian and Maronite Christian forces. But Ali Hassan got us out. We were good friends. He was smart, well read, and not unrealistic."

After the evacuation from Lebanon of 263 private American citizens, President Gerald Ford publicly thanked the PLO for providing security for the operation. Kissinger even sent Arafat an official letter thanking him for his cooperation.

Salameh was no longer sending his operatives abroad to target Israelis or Westerners in Europe. He was, however, still an enforcer. "I asked him once," said *Charles Waverly*, "about a guy we thought was involved in terrorism. But when I mentioned his name, Salameh said, 'Oh, I killed him two days ago.'" Another case officer stationed in Beirut in the mid-1970s recalls going to see Salameh with a complaint. "I told him that we had some intelligence that some of his people were about to do something bad in Germany. Salameh reached for the phone and called someone. And then I heard him yelling, 'What is this shit? Stop it!'"

In the early days of the Lebanese civil war, *Waverly* was trying to have a conversation with Salameh in one of the Agency's safe houses. They could hear the sound of mortars being fired nearby. "It is a little hard to hear," *Waverly* said. Salameh pointed at the desk and asked, "Does that phone work?" When *Waverly* nodded his head Salameh picked up the phone and dialed a number from memory. In a moment, *Waverly* heard Salameh saying, "Yah, Bashir—*khallas* [enough]." He was talking to Bashir Gemayel, the Christian warlord and one of the PLO's main enemies. The shelling soon stopped.

Bashir Gemayel was considered to be pro-American. He certainly had close connections to the Americans. Clair George thought Bashir was a "barbarian" and a murderer. Ames called him simply "our brutal warlord." (Years later, Bob Woodward reported that Bashir Gemayel had been on the CIA's payroll, but Sam Wyman—who was in a position to know something like this—says that Woodward got this wrong.)

Gemayel and Salameh were enemies, but fellow warlords. In Beirut's surreal world, they had a grudging admiration for each other. Said K. Aburish once unkindly described Gemayel as a "pimply-faced, overweight hooligan who merits the teenage epithet 'greasy.' . . . [Salameh] competed with Bashir Gemayel as to the number of undone buttons on his shirt." Aburish was a harsh critic of both men and wrote of Salameh: "He had the mental makeup of an Italian harbor boy and his emergence as a celebrated leader of Palestinian fighting men casts serious doubts on Arafat's judgment of men." In March 1976, Mossad brought the Christian Phalangist warlord to Herzliya, a seaside resort town just north of Tel Aviv, to share intelligence and iron out the details of the Israeli alliance with the Lebanese Phalange. At one point, a Mossad officer took Gemayel aside and asked if he could share with them the details of Salameh's daily routine and itinerary. Bashir nodded and indicated that would be no problem. But Mossad reportedly never got anything. Gemayel apparently thought Salameh might someday be useful to his own political ambitions. And he understood that if the Israelis killed Salameh, a less astute player would simply replace the Palestinian.

In the midst of the seesaw civil war, Salameh sometimes tried to signal that the Palestinian community trapped in Lebanon—some 250,000 refugees—did not wish to involve themselves in Lebanese politics. "Being outside Palestine," Salameh told a reporter from *Monday Morning*, an English-language Lebanese weekly tabloid, "we get involved in problems which distract us from what is going on inside our homeland. That is what is happening in Lebanon." In another interview with the daily *Al Ziat*, he said, "We made mistakes. . . . We treated the Lebanese right-wing [the Phalangists] as the enemy camp and many of us thought that we shouldn't try to seek understanding and cooperation with it. I was among the very few who believed that we can reach understanding with them." He told another reporter, "There are no permanent enmities or permanent friendships."

This was not just talk. When Dany Chamoun, the chieftain of the Christian right-wing Tigers militia, was captured in Beirut by PLO forces, Salameh intervened and arranged for his release. Salameh was clearly trying to cultivate a pragmatic persona. And there is good reason to believe that he was doing so as a result of his relationship with Ames and the CIA.

Salameh's star was rising inside the PLO. By 1976 the intelligence chief and head of Force 17 was thought by some to be a possible successor to Arafat in the event of the death of the "Old Man." Salameh made a point now of conducting himself as a kind of envoy. He was no longer a foot soldier. "Salameh played a large part in winning the hearts and minds of the U.S. for the PLO," said Bill Buckley, a Beirut CIA station chief—who was later abducted and killed. "He was charismatic and persuasive and knew when to argue and when to listen." Sam Wyman believed Salameh was Arafat's natural heir apparent. "I spent a lot of my time coaxing him to go in the direction of responsible policy—and to understand that if you are going to have a peaceful solution, you have to come down from the barricades."

Salameh's primary conduit to the Agency was still Ames—but remotely. Given that Bob was back in Washington, Wyman and *Waverly* were the two case officers who regularly saw the PLO intelligence chief. And like Ames, they used Mustafa Zein to set up their meetings. They also tried to keep Salameh under electronic surveillance. Salameh was still in love with all women. One of his lovers was a German reporter. "We had an audio operation," boasted Dewey Clarridge. "We could hear Salameh screwing her." Obviously, the Agency regarded Salameh as a valuable liaison and source. But he was also fair game for surveillance.

In April 1976, Salameh gave a splashy interview to a Beirut tabloid. He chose to sit down with Nadia Salti Stephan, a feature reporter from *Monday Morning*, the tabloid that typically ran profiles of Beirut high-society figures with the occasional serious piece of reporting. The result was a five-page spread, complete with an extensive interview and a photograph. Sam Wyman was dismayed. "I told Salameh," recalled Wyman, "'You are violating every principle of good intelligence practice. The Israelis know who you are and they know what you did, and so you should be careful.' He shrugged his shoulders. He was so casual, so cool, just very cavalier. He was acting, I thought foolishly, like he was the *abu dey*—the street chief—of all of Beirut." By 1976, Salameh had a very set routine. He traveled in a convoy, sitting in the backseat of a large Chevy station wagon. A lead car filled with gunmen led the way, while a Toyota pickup truck brought up the rear. Mounted on the Toyota's flatbed was a Doschka 22mm cannon. Wyman once asked Salameh, "How is that damn cannon going to protect you? It just announces to everyone where you are." Salameh just laughed and said, "Oh, it is good."

Salameh was given numerous such warnings. But he was fatalistic. He knew that he'd already escaped several attempts on his life. A bomb had once exploded outside his apartment door in Beirut. On another occasion he'd refused to open a parcel addressed to him from the Algerian embassy; it turned out to be rigged with explosives. And, of course, the Israelis had tried to kill him in Norway. So far, they'd failed in these attempts on his life. "They [the Israelis] are not supermen," Salameh said. So perhaps he might evade their hit teams.

He also knew that the Israelis were, in a calculated manner, adding to his notoriety, encouraging others to see him as "a playboy, a smuggler, a murderer, a blood-thirsty killer who cannot sleep at night without seeing blood. . . . The intention obviously was to pave the way for my liquidation. . . . They were, if you want, trying to make our assassination a legitimate act."

If anything, Salameh was living his life *more* flamboyantly, not less. In 1976 he was openly dating a twenty-four-year-old woman named Georgina Rizk. She was stunning. Six years earlier, she'd been crowned the most beautiful woman in the universe. Rizk had a Lebanese father and an Italian mother. Born in 1953, she'd been raised in the Greek Orthodox Church. She began modeling for local fashion shows when she was fourteen. She spoke Arabic, French, and English. Georgina was young, beautiful, and entirely apolitical. When she traveled to Miami Beach to compete in the 1971 Miss Universe pageant, the press quickly picked up on the fact that she had befriended Miss Israel, Etty Orgad. "We are here for beauty, not politics," Rizk said when asked about her friendship with the Israeli. On July 24, 1971, Bob Barker—the famous television personality and host of the pageant—crowned Rizk Miss Universe. Because she was the first Middle Easterner to win the crown, her image was splashed across the covers of numerous

Lebanese, Egyptian, and Syrian magazines. In 1975, Lebanon issued postage stamps with Rizk's image. A local newspaper proclaimed, "She is Lebanon's queen, Lebanon's goddess." So when Ali Hassan Salameh began openly squiring around Georgina, popping up at Beirut's upscale restaurants and nightclubs, the couple became a national sensation. Miss Universe and the Palestinian intelligence chief made quite an item.

In late November 1976, just after President Ford's defeat in the presidential election, Ames persuaded then CIA director George H. W. Bush to extend an invitation to Salameh to visit Washington. The PLO was ecstatic. The Palestinians regarded it as an invitation for an "official" visit. *Charles Waverly,* the CIA chief of station in Beirut, delivered the invitation. Mustafa Zein was also invited, but he declined, saying he wanted to "prove that he was not needed anymore to uphold and protect the covert American/PLO relation and Ali knew well the way to the United States without any help or the company of Mustafa Zein." Ford's departing secretary of state, Henry Kissinger, tried to veto the Salameh visit. Kissinger, of course, knew full well that this was the man who'd been the CIA's back channel to the PLO for nearly seven years. But in an extraordinary intervention, CIA director Bush approached President-elect Jimmy Carter's designated secretary of state, Cyrus Vance, and persuaded him that Ali Hassan Salameh's visit to Washington was in the U.S. national interest. "Bush would have favored Salameh's trip," observed Duane Clarridge, "partly because of what Salameh had done earlier to get Americans out of Beirut." Vance authorized the visit.

At some point, Salameh told Ames he wanted to bring Georgina Rizk to America. He explained that she wanted to visit Disneyland in California. And after California, they wanted to visit Hawaii. Ali Hassan said he was in need of a vacation. Could Ames make all this happen? Ames could, and did.

Salameh and Rizk would come to America under CIA cover. It had to be a highly secret trip. Ames arranged for alias documentation and special tourist visas. "Bringing MJTRUST/2 onto U.S. territory was quite sensitive," recalled one Agency clandestine officer. "Much of the preparation had to do with arranging aliases for the couple." The PLO paid their airfare to America, but the Agency picked up their tabs thereafter.

Mustafa Zein flew to Cairo from Beirut and met the CIA's deputy chief of station, Sam Wyman, who handed over U.S. visas for Salameh, Rizk, and one other PLO official, Ziyad al-Hout. In early 1977, Salameh and Al-Hout flew from Cairo to New York. "Everything was arranged with U.S. immigration authorities," said Clarridge, who knew about the secret trip. Rizk met Salameh in New York, having flown on a different flight from Beirut. They then traveled to Washington, D.C., where Ames escorted Salameh to see a few officers in Langley. The Israelis never learned that Salameh had visited CIA headquarters.

Charles Waverly was assigned to accompany the couple to New Orleans, then on to Anaheim, California—to visit Disneyland—and finally to Hawaii. New Orleans was added to their itinerary, partly for pleasure but also so a discreet exchange of intelligence could take place between Salameh and Agency officers. The British journalist Peter Taylor reports that Salameh met with "senior American officials" in a New Orleans hotel. Ames's ranking superior at the time, Alan Wolfe, flew down to New Orleans to meet with Salameh. Georgina later told Taylor that Ali Hassan saw this meeting as a new step in his relationship with the Agency. It was a test. "They wanted to be sure," Georgina said, "that he had the temperament and ability of a man with whom they could do business." The meeting lasted five hours. "Abu Hassan was pleased," Georgina recalled. "He had passed the test."

Ames may have gone to New Orleans to participate in this meeting, or he may have just greeted Salameh in Washington. In any case, according to Mustafa Zein, Salameh was showered with small, symbolic gifts—including a leather shoulder holster for his gun. Ames also gave

Salameh a leather briefcase that contained a hidden tape recorder—a tool for spy craft. Later, Salameh gave the briefcase to Zein, who used it often to make a surreptitious record of his conversations with various people.

Ali Hassan hated Disneyland for all the usual reasons. But he liked New Orleans, and Hawaii was a real vacation. *Waverly* tried to teach Ali Hassan snorkeling in the blue-green waters of the Pacific Ocean. "He was scared to death of it," recalled *Waverly*. "He thought he was going to drown, and finally he just gave up and told me, 'I can't do it.' I never did get him to do it. All he really wanted to do was eat oysters. He thought they were an aphrodisiac. I was in the adjoining hotel room—so in the evenings I heard the results. It was a perfect match. I think Ali Hassan really loved Georgina."

■

In late February 1977, Dewey Clarridge and Alan Wolfe asked Ames to take on another temporary-duty assignment, this time for three months in Beirut. Bob agreed. He'd grown attached to his Reston life and hated being away from Yvonne and the children, but he still harbored ambitions of rising further in the Agency hierarchy, and taking on a TDY in war-torn Beirut would be noted as exceptional hardship duty.

Ames arrived in Beirut on a flight from Paris around February 21. He was met at the airport by an embassy security officer and hustled into an armored limousine. Accompanied by several armed guards, they drove straight to the U.S. embassy on the corniche of Ras Beirut. The streets were empty and dark. Every kilometer or so, they had to stop at a roadblock where soldiers from the Arab League peacekeeping force checked their identification papers. Syrian tanks were dug in around the main Palestinian refugee camps—with their gun turrets aimed at the camps. Forty thousand Syrian troops had invaded Lebanon the previous year, supposedly as peacekeepers. "It was kind of creepy, riding in," Ames wrote. He was told that the embassy maintained a nighttime curfew, and even during the day no one was allowed to travel about the city without an armed guard. The only exceptions to this rule were the military attaché and CIA officer Bob Ames. "Obviously, I couldn't do my job," Bob explained to Yvonne, "with bodyguards around."

Ames was given an apartment in the embassy, and he ate most of his meals in the embassy's mess hall with the marine guards ($30 a week for breakfast and dinner). Everyone was eating through the embassy commissary's very depleted stock of food. In the evenings the marines usually showed a 35mm movie on a projector. Restricted to the embassy building, most of the marines and staff were thoroughly bored. But Ames was determined to get out and see what he could learn from his contacts. He rented a beat-up 1974 Toyota to drive around town. The neighborhood around the embassy—including the Hamra Street commercial district and the American University of Beirut—seemed untouched by the war. The university, however, had suspended classes that spring, and most restaurants were shuttered. The hotel district and the center city were utterly destroyed. "I think they should just level the place and start from scratch," Bob wrote. "It is really a mess." No one really knew if the war was over or Beirut was just experiencing a lull in the fighting. "Beirut is dead," he wrote. "But it's coming to life. . . . It looks like things are opening up and tension is lessening." But Bob found his new post depressing. Soon after his arrival the city was hit by a spring thunderstorm. "Lebanon needs the rain," he wrote Yvonne, "to wash away the death and filth. It has snowed heavily in the mountains and one day we had such heavy hail in Beirut that a few inches accumulated and Beirut was pure and white for a few hours."

Ames had always found the Lebanese a little too cosmopolitan, a little too chic and thin-skinned. But they'd certainly proved themselves resilient, enduring periodic mortar shelling, firefights from the high-rise apartment buildings, and endless roadblocks. "One good thing came out of this war," Ames wrote. "The Lebanese are not so arrogant any more. They realize that life is more than a Mercedes and an Yves St. Laurent tie. . . . Of course, all this can end with one bullet. Peace is a very fragile thing."

Ames was traveling frequently back and forth between Christian-dominated East Beirut and Muslim West Beirut, talking to many people from both sides. "I feel the Muslims are more eager for settlement than the Christians.... The Christians are such bigots where Muslims are concerned, and that is the root of the Lebanese problem. I don't see any real solution for a long time. The Christians want their own state, protected by the U.S., just like Israel. We don't need another Israel in the area."

He was right. The Maronite Christian establishment was not ready to give up. The civil war would soon restart and go on intermittently for another thirteen years. But in the current lull Ames found himself extremely busy as plenty of "old 'friends' are re-contacting us." That spring, a large part of his job was to reestablish agent networks that had been disrupted by the war. Three of these agents had CIA-issued radios that they used to communicate with Beirut Station. Ames put them on a schedule: each day he had to check in with his "three radio friends" at 8:00 A.M., 5:00 P.M., and 7:00 P.M. He'd slip on a pair of headphones and listen to his agents while taking extensive notes. "What a slave to the radio I've become," he wrote home. In addition, he had ten other people he had to see on a regular basis. "I've never worked harder anywhere in my life than I'm working here. It gets worse each day because the 'peace' brings more old friends out of the woodwork, and I'm sure my list of contacts will double before long." He was working twelve hours a day, seven days a week. (He took off one day, March 6, for his forty-third birthday.) Half of his meetings were conducted in Arabic.

Needless to say, there was considerable risk associated with some of these liaisons. Ames later told a friend that on one occasion he had to hide inside the trunk of a car to get to one of these clandestine meetings. On another occasion, he was driving to meet a contact when he was stopped at an Arab League checkpoint that happened to be manned by illiterate South Yemeni soldiers from what was now the People's Democratic Republic of Yemen. They searched Ames's trunk and found a contraption they'd never seen—a vacuum cleaner. Ames was intending to give the vacuum cleaner as a gift to his contact. But the nervous Yemeni soldiers were suspicious that the machine might be a bomb. As Ames tried to explain in Arabic the purpose of a vacuum cleaner, he kept thinking to himself that he was now a spy caught with a vacuum cleaner—just like the character in Graham Greene's novel *Our Man in Havana*. It was a ludicrous situation—but also dangerous. "The problem was not Bob's Arabic, which was excellent," recalled a friend to whom Ames later told the story. The problem was that the soldiers didn't have the vocabulary to grasp the concept of a vacuum cleaner. Frightened, they fingered the triggers on their guns. But Ames managed to talk his way through the situation and was allowed to go on his way. "Bob said it was high tension for a few minutes."

Initially that spring Ames was the only CIA officer stationed in Beirut. The station had been drastically drawn down in 1976 because of the civil war. But in late March 1977 Langley sent him an assistant, *Sanford Dryden*, a very junior case officer. It was *Dryden*'s second "action" assignment abroad, and he apparently got a little shook up during his first safe-house meeting. Bob commented, "I guess none of us ever lose that strange feeling in the stomach when we enter a safe-house. It's probably a good thing." Bob decided he would turn over five of his twelve cases to this novice agent. He was later disappointed to see that *Dryden*'s Arabic was not up to snuff and he "doesn't know how to write."[*]

■

Ames had lunch with, among others, Mustafa, who was still living in the same hotel, the Bedford, a block off Hamra Street. Zein had so far survived the civil war very well. He now occupied the penthouse suite of the hotel, and Bob reported that his old friend "has fixed it up as only a Lebanese male can do." Zein had bought some nice carpets and

---

[*] *Sanford Dryden* later became a good Arabist and apparently learned to write. He eventually became a principal deputy to the deputy director for plans (DDP), the chief of all covert operations.

other furnishings "dirt cheap from looters." The apartment was too cluttered for Bob's taste. "Personally, I couldn't live in the place. It's just too full and has too much contrast between old and new for me."

Ames no longer needed Zein as his cutout contact to Ali Hassan Salameh. Bob was seeing his "important friend"—always unnamed in his letters to Yvonne—every other day, "and that keeps me busy." Salameh celebrated their reunion by giving Ames a beautiful set of solid-gold prayer beads. On Sunday, March 13, 1977, Salameh and Mustafa hosted a belated birthday party for Ames, and Mustafa gave him another set of prayer beads, this time made from white coral. "I think they're trying to convert me!" Bob wrote home.

One day Zein took Ames to meet Salameh's wife, Nashrawan, and his two young sons, Hassan, twelve, and Usama, five. Ames thought Nashrawan was quite "lovely and very bright." The elder son, Hassan, was visiting Beirut on spring break from his London boarding school. When Bob whipped out photos of his children and explained that Kristen was also twelve years old, Hassan politely expressed an interest in meeting her. "Especially since she is blonde," Ames wrote to Yvonne. "Arabs are Arabs!" Bob thought the Salamehs were "a really nice family."

Ames, of course, was well aware that Salameh was having an affair. And it didn't seem to be just one of his flings. Bob disapproved. He had met Rizk, and while she was certainly attractive, Bob didn't understand the relationship. "Why he still has this thing going with the other [woman], I'll never know," Bob wrote Yvonne. "His wife is good-looking, as are his two sons, and very well educated." Salameh knew that Ames disapproved because Bob had made it clear that he wouldn't meet him in Rizk's apartment. "Everyone says that if I tell him, because he respects me, to break off the other thing, he will. I hesitate to get involved in personal things—even though this affair is ruining his reputation." Bob was thinking like a friend and a family man—not a case officer sizing up a prospective agent for his weaknesses.

Salameh and Ames were partners at this delicate moment in the course of the Lebanese civil war. They were trying to keep the lid on. Ames knew it was important work. "I'm doing something useful and something no one else can do," he wrote Yvonne. "I'm spending a great deal of time trying to keep the Palestinians calm. They are very frustrated because nothing seems to be moving. If they get too frustrated, they will get back into the terrorist business to get attention and action. I hope the USG can come up with some pressure on the Israelis to be more flexible, but I am not optimistic. At least I am keeping the Black September group calm, but the real radicals, like the PFLP, are ready now. I talked to one of the PFLP leaders who is a friend and I must say that his arguments for action are convincing, although I can't agree with the type of action."

The Palestinian problem should have been a top priority for Washington. It was the single most contentious and thorny issue in a region plagued by volatility. It was a festering source of latent anti-Americanism. Yet astonishingly the CIA had few, if any, real assets inside the Palestinian exile community.

"The bottom line," said Dewey Clarridge, "is that except for a few uncontrolled informants and a German support asset of Fatah's, we had no significant agents in any part of the Palestinian movement for most of the 1970s. Around 1977, there were two, maybe three action-type Palestinians who were used to thwart some Palestinian ops against the US Embassy in Beirut, Lisbon and perhaps another place." Ames was the Agency's only conduit into the PLO.

To say that Bob Ames was sympathetic to the Palestinian cause would be an understatement. He empathized with them deeply and admired Ali Hassan to a degree that is hard to explain. He knew Salameh had done some terrible things. "It is hard to believe our friend was what he was," Bob wrote to Yvonne. "But that's what comes of frustration. If the Palestinians could only have a country, they would be a great asset to the world. When I see some of these so-called 'nations' in Africa like Uganda and Idi Amin, I don't think it is fair. Here a very educated people are denied a home, while the Ugandese eat each other and have a vote at the U.N.! Something's wrong somewhere."

Ames was pleased when on March 16, 1977, President Jimmy Carter referred to "a homeland for Palestinian refugees." It was a calculated comment, casually made in the course of a town hall meeting in Clinton, Massachusetts, but it was the first time an American president had ever used the words. The statement made headlines in the Lebanese press, and a few days later Salameh told Ames that his people were "delighted" with the president's words. "I think we're finally making some headway," Ames wrote, "and our friend is already talking about the house he will build for us next to his in Jerusalem."

The American ambassador at the time was Richard Parker, a veteran Arabist. Ames knew Parker was also a longtime skeptic and critic of the CIA. "I think, however," Bob wrote home, "I've earned his grudging respect because I know what I'm talking about and I won't let him bully me." It probably helped that Parker agreed with Ames's assessment of the Maronites; he thought they were overreaching and arrogant. And Ambassador Parker specifically thought the Maronite Phalangist militia chief, Bashir Gemayel, was "a consummate liar and dissembler. The truth was not in him." Everyone who ever met Dick Parker agreed that he was a man of wry humor and sharp opinions. He was a refreshingly frank diplomat. Parker thought the Israelis were encouraging the Phalangists to think they could restore Maronite supremacy in Lebanon. "I got pretty pissed off with Israeli arrogance and disregard for Lebanese sovereignty," Parker said. "Between the Israelis and the Syrians, there wasn't much to choose from." Ames grew to like Parker; they shared the same crustiness and ironic sense of humor. "I think I'm getting on better with the Ambassador," Ames wrote.

Parker was extremely impressed when Ames announced that he'd found and retrieved the embassy limousine in which Ambassador Francis Meloy and his aide had been riding when they were kidnapped and killed in June 1976. Ames also got a full report from Salameh on his investigation into the assassinations. "It makes for grim reading," Ames wrote, "but now they [U.S. officials] have all the facts on one of these assassinations for the first time. And I say, with all due humility, that no one else could have done it." Bob complained to Yvonne that none of his superiors back at Langley had bothered to congratulate him on this work. "At least the Ambassador has invited me to lunch."

Ames was being very productive. After one month in the country, he'd written sixty reports—the highest output of any CIA station in the region. There was a lot to report on. On March 16, 1977, Kamal Jumblatt, the chieftain of the Lebanese Druze, was assassinated. Jumblatt was the political leader of the Druze-Muslim leftist coalition forces, known as the Lebanese National Movement (LMN). When the civil war had broken out in mid-1975, Jumblatt's LMN, allied with the PLO, had quickly seized control of more than 70 percent of the country. Jumblatt promised to reform Lebanon's increasingly undemocratic confessional system—which apportioned political representation in parliament to the Maronite Christians, the Sunni Muslims, and other sectarian religious groups on the basis of the country's first— and only—1932 census. This antiquated sectarian political system had unfairly allowed the minority Maronite Christian community to dominate the state. The civil war might have ended at this point, but then in 1976 Syrian president Hafez Assad sent forty thousand troops into Lebanon. Assad feared that Jumblatt's promised reforms would ultimately not only weaken the Maronite political machine but also threaten the legitimacy of his own Baathist Party dictatorship, a system that favored his own Alawites, an ethnic minority offshoot of Shi'a Islam.

Jumblatt had been a voice of reason and moderation. But he was also a critic of the Syrians—and President Assad almost certainly ordered his assassination. "After his death was announced," Ames wrote, "the Druze went on a rampage and killed every Christian in the Shuf [a mountainous region south of Beirut] they could find." (The Druze are an ancient sect and, like the Alawites, are an offshoot of Shi'ite Islam, dating back to the eleventh century.) More than 140 people, mostly women and children, were massacred. Naturally, these killings reinforced hard-line sentiments within the Maronite community. Ames knew from his agents in Christian East Beirut that Bashir Gemayel's Phalangist militia was taking advantage of the political vacuum to re-arm. The Phalangists were getting armaments from the Israelis, and in the spring of 1977 the Israelis were allowing Gemayel to smuggle his men by boat via Israel into South Lebanon, where they were mounting attacks on Shi'a villages and PLO positions. The Israeli goal was to create a zone in southern Lebanon free of Palestinians. Gemayel was obliging the Israelis, doing their dirty work for them, and in return he was getting the arms and financial support he needed to reassert Maronite control over the Lebanese state. Needless to say, all these machinations were to have tragic and unintended consequences.

Ames was alarmed and frustrated by what was happening in South Lebanon. "The fighting there is foolish and both the Christians and the Palestinians are being used by the Israelis and Syrians respectively to fight their battles by proxy. This is the part that is very sad. The Israelis and Syrians look on self-righteously while Lebanese and Palestinians kill each other. I know I can get the Palestinians to stop, but [the] old USG will not pressure the Israelis to stop supporting the Christians. I guess if the Israelis lead us right into WWIII, we still won't put pressure on them." When an informal cease-fire failed to hold, and fighting once again broke out in South Lebanon, Ames concluded, "Again the Christians and Israelis started it. Most of the Christians really want a separate state which they believe we will support as we support Israel."

Ambassador Dick Parker shared some of these sentiments. He was then trying to convince Bashir Gemayel that his military alliance with the Israelis was foolish. "He reported my remarks to Begin," Parker later wrote, "who then complained to Sam Lewis, our Ambassador in Tel Aviv. The working level of the Department tried to support me in these efforts, but it was clear that there was no inclination at upper levels of our government to challenge the Israeli assertion of a right of eminent domain in South Lebanon."

Not surprisingly, the fighting that spring in the south escalated. And, of course, whenever the Palestinians managed to launch an attack across the border, the Israelis retaliated with severe air strikes, causing heavy civilian casualties among both Shi'ites and Palestinians. "When this happened," Parker later wrote in his memoirs, "frightened Shia, caught in the middle, would stream up to Beirut, exacerbating the already severe socio-economic and security problems of that city and paving the way for eventual Shia dominance in west Beirut."

Ames sometimes met with Ali Hassan Salameh inside the teeming refugee camps of Sabra and Shatila, on the southern edge of the city, near the international airport. So he couldn't help but notice the growing number of Shi'ite refugees mixed in with the Palestinian residents. The combination of the civil war and Tel Aviv's attempt to carve out an Israeli security zone in South Lebanon was creating a new alliance between the Palestinians and the Lebanese Shi'ite community—the two poorest and most disenfranchised peoples in the Lebanese mosaic. In a very few years this development would create an ominous new political force called Hezbollah—the Party of God.

On April 2, 1977, Ames had a scheduled meeting with Salameh. "When I got to the usual place," Ames wrote, "he drove me into the camp and I met #1 with the beard." This was not the first time he'd met Arafat, but his only previous encounter with the PLO leader had entailed just a handshake and a few words of greetings. This time Ames had a long, rambling conversation with Arafat and Salameh. Ames wrote to Yvonne about the PLO leader that same day. "He's funny-looking as his pictures, but a very bright and sincere man. Headquarters would go into outer space if they learned about this." By all accounts, Ames's two immediate bosses, Dewey Clarridge and Alan Wolfe, ran a very tight organization; no one did anything without their knowledge. But neither knew that Ames had met with Arafat. This was at a time when the Carter administration was publicly insisting that it wouldn't countenance any dealings with the PLO. "No one in the CIA," said a senior

Agency official at the time, "was prepared to let Ames or anyone else talk to Fatah unless it was at a diplomatic function."

One Agency officer was highly skeptical that Ames could have done this: "Had Ames met Arafat or even Salameh he would have reported it. I recall none such, and obviously, I would have remembered. Ames could be off the reservation at times but not on that kind of situation. Moreover, at that time we were constrained by State from any contacts with the Palestinians, not just Fatah, that could be used by them politically. This put a damper on our ability to cultivate Palestinian sources, but did not affect ongoing ones." But Ames did meet with Arafat—and he did not immediately report it.

So Ames was taking a risk with his career. Meeting Salameh was one thing; this was a long-standing relationship with a source. For this he had authorization. But not so for Arafat. Salameh had no doubt sprung the meeting on Ames; it came as a surprise. Ames nevertheless thought it well worth it: "I think it was most useful." At the same time, Bob had come to think that there was nothing he could do that would fundamentally change American policy in the region. "Very few dull moments here, but don't get the idea that I enjoy it. I think I would if I thought it meant anything, but it doesn't. Very frustrating. We'll just never learn."

Just seventeen months later, President Jimmy Carter reluctantly felt compelled to accept the resignation of Andrew Young, his UN ambassador. Young had met in his New York apartment with Zuhdi Tarazi, chief of the PLO mission at the United Nations. "It is absolutely ridiculous," Carter wrote in his diary at the time, "that we pledged under Kissinger and Nixon that we would not negotiate with the PLO." Carter later said the ban was "preposterous, as this group was the key to any comprehensive peace agreement." But Kissinger had given the Israelis this pledge in a Memorandum of Agreement on September 1, 1975— so when Ambassador Young informed the Israeli ambassador that he'd met with the PLO official on mundane Security Council business, the Israelis promptly leaked the information, precipitating Young's resignation. Ames knew he could have suffered the same consequence; after all, what he'd done was a worse violation of the ban. He'd lacked even the fig leaf of a recruitment attempt; rather, he'd gone to see the PLO chief to exchange political views with him. If the Israelis had found out, they certainly would have made the meeting public and vigorously protested. It might have meant the end of his career.

Ames was becoming a cynic. This was not uncommon for a rising clandestine officer. "The loss of innocence comes in stages," said Graham Fuller, a clandestine officer whose career mirrored that of Ames's. "In the beginning, you find yourself exhilarated by the access to classified information, and by all the direct, hands-on knowledge you are acquiring in the field. You have this notion that all you need to do is get the right skinny, the right facts before the policy makers—and things would change. You think you can make a difference. But gradually, you realize that the policy makers don't care. And then the revelation hits you that U.S. foreign policy is not fact-driven."

Ames was working hard in Beirut "on some very sensitive stuff." In forty-five days he'd sent out over a hundred "operational" cables, a few of which he labeled "nasty-grams." He thought if he wrote too many more "nasty-grams" the Near East Division might try to get rid of him: "My heart would be broken." He tried to restrain himself, but he felt that on occasion a strongly worded cable was "the only way to get through to people." He was not getting along with Dewey Clarridge. "Maybe my sharp cables to him will mean he won't want to work with me again—horror!" Ames complained to Yvonne that he was suffering from high blood pressure that spring. He blamed it on "job pressures" and the irregular routine he had to keep in Beirut. "I'm sure Clarridge doesn't suffer from my problem," Bob grumbled. His health worried him. "I enjoy life too much not to get my full share."

Bob was hoping he might come back to a different job in Washington. "I feel I should get a promotion this year, but I won't." He felt underappreciated. He'd been a GS-14 for only about two years, but he was already impatient for another promotion. "If John MacGaffin [a younger clandestine officer whom Ames had known in Beirut] gets promoted to GS-15 I leave the Division. That would be just too much to take." Ames admired MacGaffin, but he saw no reason why the younger man should advance more rapidly than he: "I'm more and more convinced that there are just a few good men in NE and they get ridden into the ground to make others look good. Strange people."

"I hear indirectly from people on what a great job the Station is doing," Ames wrote home. "But I've never heard a word from the Division management. I think we're doing great in terms of quality and quantity—in fact, I think we're nothing short of amazing. But not a word, and then they wonder why people want to get out." Most of his work was generated from his meetings with Salameh. He spent hours with "our friend" on Saturday, April 9—the day before Easter: "I just got back from a long meeting with our friend," Ames wrote, "so I have lots to write down between now and Monday morning, so I'll probably spend part of Easter writing." An unappreciated aspect of good spy craft is simply writing down what transpires, and Ames's cables back to Langley about his meetings with the Palestinian were detailed and meticulous. (And they remain classified.)

Ames was scheduled to spend another month in Beirut to complete a full three-month TDY. But on April 23, 1977, he received an emergency phone call from Yvonne. She told him that his father, Albert, had been hospitalized the previous day—and had died that day. Albert had apparently been diagnosed with pancreatic cancer some time earlier, but he'd kept this news from his family. He'd also had emphysema—and on April 23 his heart finally gave out. "Bob took his father's death very hard," said *Sanford Dryden.* "I think they had been very close. He did cry." Ames boarded a flight home the next day, but he arrived too late for the funeral. His father had been seventy-seven years old.

■

On June 8, 1977, Salameh married Georgina Rizk, who became his second wife. He wore a white suit for the occasion. It was not a low-profile affair. Salameh was always a bit self-indulgent. As a Muslim he could decide to take a second wife. He wouldn't divorce Nashrawan, but neither could he resist the charms of Georgina. "She seduced Ali," Mustafa Zein said. "And after they made love for the first time, that was it, Ali was in love." Arafat had bluntly told Salameh, "Marry her or leave her. Leaders do not take mistresses."

A year after Salameh's second marriage, in mid-June 1978, Ames boarded a TWA plane at Dulles and flew off to Beirut. He was traveling on a newly issued diplomatic passport, No. X135101. He hadn't been back to Lebanon in a year. His immediate boss, Alan Wolfe, had asked him to stand in for Frank Anderson, then chief of station in Beirut, while Anderson went on home leave for nearly a month. Ames was ambivalent about these occasional TDYs. They earned him extra cash—and he liked the opportunity to look up his old sources. But he disliked being away from his family. The last thing he told Yvonne was that she had to promise him to write regular letters. (All his letters to her ended with the line "God love you.")

Bob arrived in Beirut on June 16 and checked into the Riviera Hotel. But then two days later he moved into Anderson's three-bedroom apartment in the El Dorado building, right on the corniche and overlooking the sparkling Mediterranean. He thought the Andersons were "lousy housekeepers," so he spent that Sunday cleaning up the apartment. In the evening he could sit on the balcony and watch the sunset. He was amused to see that the Lebanese were participating in the current worldwide rage for jogging: "It is really hilarious to see these fat Lebanese in their Dior & Yves St. Laurent sweats. . . . Will they never change? The world may be falling down around them, but they'll never be caught out of style."

Beirut had changed dramatically. The first stage of the civil war, from 1975 to 1978, had left much of Beirut and the center city looking like a war zone. On block after block stood rows of high-rise apartment buildings that were now empty shells, pockmarked by bullets and mortar rounds. The 1976 "war of the hotels" had turned the city's famous Phoenicia Intercontinental, the Holiday Inn, and the St.-George hotels into towering ruins. More recently, on March 11, 1978, a squad of eleven Fatah Fedayeen led by a woman, Dalal Mughrabi, had landed on Israel's northern coast in rubber rafts and had proceeded to hijack a bus. They had driven the bus south on the coastal highway toward Tel Aviv until stopped by an Israeli roadblock. A nine-hour gun battle ensued. Mughrabi and most of her squad were eventually killed, together with thirty-seven Israelis—including thirteen children—and a female American photographer who happened to be sitting on the beach when the Fedayeen arrived. The Coastal Highway massacre remains the single worst terrorist attack carried out inside Israel. Three days later, on March 14, 1978, more than twenty-five thousand Israeli soldiers invaded South Lebanon, seizing the southern portion of the country up to the Litani River. The Israeli invasion killed an estimated two thousand Lebanese civilians and turned another quarter million into refugees.

Lebanon was a mess. Ames nevertheless could see lots of people strolling along Beirut's seaside corniche. On Sunday, June 18, he sat on the balcony and in his neat cursive handwriting addressed a four-page letter to his family back in Reston. As was his style, he began affectionately, "Dear Bonnie, Babies & beasts . . ." The "Babies" were the six children, none of whom were any longer babies. And the "beasts" were Hansje, the Hungarian Vizsla breed of dog, and their numerous cats. "You would not believe this is a troubled country to look off your balcony." Five days earlier, on the morning of June 13, six hundred Phalangist militia—under the control of the Gemayels, a leading Maronite Christian family—had assaulted the ancestral home of the Franjiehs, a rival Maronite clan who opposed the Gemayel alliance with Israel. Their goal was to kill Tony Franjieh, the thirty-six-year-old son of the family's patriarch, former Lebanese president Suleiman Franjieh. The Phalangists killed thirty of Franjieh's bodyguards and then forced Tony Franjieh and his wife, Vera, to watch as they shot two dozen bullets into their three-year-old daughter, Jihan. The killers then shot Tony's wife—and finally executed him. "The murder was truly savage and brutal," Ames wrote home. "In spite of this, I think the masses are just fed up with fighting and killing. . . . I'm speaking logically, of course, and there is not much room for logic in Lebanon."

Ames was later shocked to read in *Monday Morning* that after the murders of Tony Franjieh, his wife, and his daughter, Suleiman Franjieh, the clan's patriarch, had taken Tony's eleven-year-old son to see the bloody scene before the bodies were removed "so he would know what his duty was." To Bob's thinking, this was sad proof that "there is enough hatred in Lebanon for the rest of the world."

The day after he arrived in Beirut, Ames had dinner with Ali Hassan Salameh. Their relationship was long past the point of meeting awkwardly in CIA safe houses. Ali Hassan welcomed Bob into his home as a friend and colleague. "Our friend sends his best," Ames wrote Yvonne. "I had dinner with his family on Friday night [June 16]. His wife [Nashrawan, his first wife], who does all the cooking despite several maids, really made some great Leb. dishes. I gorged myself so much that I only had a *Shawarma* [minced lamb sandwich] on Sat!" The two men had a lot to discuss. Over the next three weeks, Ames made it a habit to visit Salameh every other night at 6:30 P.M. Usually, he spent an hour and a half with him and then returned to the El Dorado apartment. The meetings left Bob with "lots on my mind." He'd often wake up in the middle of the night, "usually thinking how to write the info I get in my almost nightly 6:30 P.M.–8 P.M. meetings with our friend."

▪

Even before the civil war started in 1975, Lebanon had been a very complicated piece of geography. By 1978 it was a maze of inexplicable narratives and constantly changing allegiances. The Palestinians were both a factor in the escalation of the civil war and its chief victims. Initially, Arafat and the PLO tried desperately to stay out of it, but by the end of 1976 they'd inevitably thrown in their lot with the Lebanese leftist alliance of Sunni, Shi'ite, and Druze parties against the right-wing Maronite Christian militias. Salameh was trying to brief Ames on what was turning into a very bloody sectarian war. "Lebanon is still waiting," Bob wrote to Yvonne on June 25, "for the other shoe to fall after the assassinations up North and the continued trouble down South. Unfortunately, there is much outside interference in Lebanon's affairs—not to mention their own tendency to shoot themselves in the foot. The Israelis like to keep the South unstable in order to keep the Palestinians out and to give themselves an excuse to come back in. The Palestinians want a weak Lebanon so there will be no army to harass them, and the Syrians just want Lebanon."

Three days later, the proverbial shoe dropped. Thirty-three Christian Phalangist members near Baalbek were taken from their homes and executed. Their bodies were mutilated. Ames thought this massacre was probably carried out by the Syrians as a favor to their Franjieh allies—who had lost the same number in the attack on Tony Franjieh. At the same time, gun battles erupted in East Beirut between the Syrian army and the Gemayel clan's Phalangist militia. "It's getting nasty here in Beirut," Bob wrote to Yvonne on July 5, "and we had some mortar rounds just a few hundred yards from my apartment. When they hit they sound as if they are right in the room. As I write this in the office, I can hear firing breaking out again.... Electricity has been on and off (mostly off) since noon yesterday.... One doesn't go out on the streets these days unless he has to.... I love and miss you lots. God love you."

Ames was naturally frustrated and discouraged by what he was experiencing in Beirut. "It seems a paradox," he wrote Yvonne, "to say that one is both busy and bored at the same time, but I am.... I've been working as hard as I ever have in Beirut, long hours and lots of reading and writing, but I just don't have the same enthusiasm or feeling of accomplishment. I get the feeling that I've written all this and done all this too many times before. There are no changes in the situation; it's still as bad as it was and the USG does not appear to be prepared to bite the bullet and do something about it—and nothing will change until we do." It wasn't clear whether Ames was referring to the

Lebanese situation or the old Palestinian conundrum—or both. But his malaise was deep-felt.

Something else was also bothering Ames. He'd applied late that spring for a new job in the Agency, the position of national intelligence officer (NIO) for NESA. This was a new position within what the Agency called the National Intelligence Council (NIC). As deputy chief of the Near East for Arab Operations, Ames felt he had hit a glass ceiling inside the DO. He was Dewey Clarridge's number-one deputy, but he felt that both Clarridge and his boss, Alan Wolfe—chief of the Near East Division in the DO—would never allow him to rise higher in the DO. Clarridge just didn't see Ames as a real operational officer. Neither did Wolfe. "Both men acknowledged Bob's immense other talents," recalled another DO officer, Henry Miller-Jones, "and both deferred to him in his handling of MJTRUST/2 [Salameh]. But Wolfe would not back him for a senior DO management position." They knew Ames was smart and competent, but they thought he was just too bookish for the DO. And they also thought that he should have been able to turn Salameh into a fully recruited agent. In their eyes, he had failed the recruitment.

"Bob had a reputation in the DO of being too smart, too much of an intellectual," recalled *Lindsay Sherwin*, who later worked with him. Ames liked operations, and he thought he was good at it. But he believed clandestine work had to have a purpose larger than the simple "Great Game." The point was to influence the course of history—to create a better world. He really believed this. He wanted his covert intelligence to persuade the policy makers to make good decisions. By the summer of 1978, Ames felt that American policy in the Middle East had run into a dead end. His TDY trip to Beirut had brought these feelings to the surface: "I really haven't enjoyed anything about this TDY except an occasional good session with our friend [Salameh]." For all these reasons, he was anxious to hear about the new job. He thought he'd make a good fit. The new organization was not part of the DO, but neither was it in the Directorate of Intelligence (DI). The whole idea was to gather a handful of the Agency's best people—both covert case officers and analysts—and get them to think about the broad picture. They would have access to everything from both the DO and the DI. But the council would also seek out academics and journalists outside the Agency. "After you have been around for a while," said Graham Fuller, who was both a clandestine officer and later an NIO, "you come to realize that all this classified information is not as up to snuff as you once thought. The secret stuff often just doesn't help to answer the deeper questions. In fact, the questions that really matter are usually unanswerable. Policy makers want to know if the Soviet Union is going to exist ten years from now, or if Anwar Sadat can survive signing a peace treaty with Israel. To get some kind of informed answer to a question like that requires going outside the Agency and finding the most knowledgeable minds around to make an informed judgment. I'd see a lot of academics and journalists. Independent thinkers. Being an NIO is a very stimulating job. You suddenly realize that some of these people without access to any classified information know a hell of a lot."

The NIC was supposed to provide policy makers with a truly independent view of what was happening around the world. It was sort of a throwback to the Agency's very early Board of National Estimates, when Yale's Sherman "Buffalo" Kent and Harvard's Bill Langer had hired a select number of regional experts to provide Washington with global intelligence estimates. When told in 1950 that he could hire a staff of hundreds, Langer replied in his high-pitched Dorchester Boston twang, "Well, I can't possibly do the job with more than twenty-five people." Like the Board of National Estimates, the new NIC was supposed to be very elite, prestigious, and slightly academic.

Ames desperately wanted the job. "Perhaps," he wrote Yvonne on June 29, 1978, "my malaise is because I've heard nothing on the NIO business. . . . In any event, I'm sure that A.W. [Alan Wolfe] is using my absence to lobby against the assignment. Maybe taking that job would be even more frustrating 'cause I'd only have access to more indications of missed opportunities in the M.E. [Middle East]."

A week later, Ames finally received a cable from Langley saying that no decision had yet been made on the NIO job. "I gather they're looking hard to find someone other than me, but haven't come up with a candidate yet. I'm half tempted to tell them to stuff their NIO job, and try to look for something else when I get back." He was also being urged to take another assignment to Tehran as chief of station. But he'd decided to fight that assignment: "I've done my share of 'bang-bang' posts." He would have to wait to get back to Washington to hear about a new assignment.

Ames had found it difficult to wander the streets of Beirut. "I don't like to be on the streets after dark," he wrote home. "Too much kidnapping." If he wasn't meeting Salameh for dinner, he often just ate in the U.S. embassy's marine mess. On July 4 he'd walked over to the campus of the American University of Beirut and played some softball—until the mortar shells started falling. He'd brought a little money to go carpet shopping on Rue Hamra, but he found the prices exorbitant. Before finally flying out on July 11, he had another good meal with Mustafa Zein. His young Lebanese friend was as well connected as ever. They commiserated about the Lebanese morass and the general stalemate in Arab-Israeli relations.

Later that autumn, ABC News came to Beirut to film a one-hour documentary about the Palestinians. The show focused on the PLO's training of young men for desperate attacks on Israel. Narrated by Frank Reynolds, the documentary explored why these young men were willing to participate in virtual suicide missions. It was a controversial show, seen by millions of Americans. Ames was surprised to see that it featured an on-camera interview with Mustafa Zein. "Why is it so hard in the West," Zein asked his audience, "to understand the Palestinian right to regain their dignity on his own land? Any man or woman of the Jewish faith, coming from Russia or the United States, automatically has the right to settle in Israel today—because he had a certain connection to the land two thousand years ago." Why, Zein wanted to know, were people surprised that Palestinians had the same kind of attachment to the land? "Why are we expecting the Palestinians to be less patriotic than the Israelis?" The end of the program had a clip of Yasir Arafat walking through a crowd, accompanied by Ali Hassan Salameh—who was identified as one of the most "dangerous" men in the world. The program's producers obviously didn't know of Zein's connection to Salameh.

Ames returned to Washington in mid-July and soon afterwards learned that he'd won the NIO position. He was greatly relieved and completely unaware that he had secured the job through the intervention of one of his longtime admirers, a former Beirut chief of station, *Harry Simpson.* This officer had since risen to be an executive assistant in the director's office. "Despite the fact that Bob had no background in analysis," said *Simpson,* "I thought he would make a great NIO and told [Deputy Director Frank] Carlucci that. He looked into it . . . the files, interviews, the works—talked it over with [Admiral Stansfield] Turner and they gave him the job."

Simpson felt Ames was qualified, but he also thought it was high time to break down the walls between the DO and the analytical side of the Agency. It would help, he thought, to have an experienced DO officer trying to answer some of the big analytical questions. Ames took to the analytical work with a methodical zeal. In short order he was writing long situation reports and "monthly warning assessments" on such wide-ranging topics as "oil and politics," "alleged coup-plotting" in Yemen, "mutual suspicion" between Iran and Iraq, and the possibility of a Soviet "military intervention" in Afghanistan.

Ames was now a GS-15—or the equivalent of a full army colonel, earning over $100,000 in current dollars. He knew Yvonne did not want another foreign posting. The NIC had only thirteen NIOs—one for each region or specialty. Thus Ames was NIO for NESA. But there were also NIOs for topics, such as science and technology, nonproliferation, and other issues. It was a very elite position—a coup for someone who, at age forty-four, was relatively young and who, unlike

some of his fellow NIOs, possessed no graduate degrees. But he was
nevertheless chosen to be one of the thirteen NIOs on his merits.

That autumn of 1978 the CIA conducted a routine personnel security investigation of Ames. Two of Ames's listed references were
interviewed, plus his current supervisor. One of the unnamed references told the security officer that Ames "has that unique ability to
get along very well with all kinds of people and that he is definitely [a]
people-oriented kind of man who takes [the] interest of subordinates
at heart. . . . He is the kind of man who loves to listen to other people."
When asked to comment on Ames's personal life, this informant said
that Ames and Yvonne "appear to be very happily married." Ames
will "take a drink or two at parties, but certainly nothing more." With
regard to foreign contacts, the informant "noted that he believes the
SUBJECT currently is in contact with a foreign national, however this
was done at the specific request of the Chief of his Division and with
White House approval." Ames's supervisor concurred, saying that
Ames was "doing a very strong job." Bob was known "as a man who is
extremely stable and emotionally as solid as a rock."

That autumn Ames became peripherally involved in what later became
known as the case of the "vanished imam." The imam Musa Sadr, the
spiritual leader of Lebanon's Shi'a Muslims, was a highly charismatic
scholar and political organizer who'd inspired the downtrodden Shi'a
peasants of South Lebanon to stand up for their political and economic
rights. Sadr, who was of distant Lebanese ancestry, had been born in
Iran. In 1959 he immigrated to Lebanon, and by the 1970s he'd become an important political personality. In early 1975 he spoke before
a rally of seventy thousand Shi'as and told them, "Possessing weapons is as important as possessing the Koran." He was nevertheless regarded as a voice of reason and moderation, a Shi'a cleric who could
break bread with Maronite Christian businessmen, Greek Orthodox
prelates, Druze chieftains, and Sunni Muslim leaders.

But on August 31, 1978, Musa Sadr mysteriously disappeared while on a trip to Libya, where he'd been invited to meet with Col. Muammar Qaddafi. When the Lebanese government made inquiries in early September, Qaddafi's regime announced that the cleric and two of his companions had left Tripoli bound for Rome on an Alitalia flight on August 31. The imam's checked luggage had indeed arrived in Rome, but the imam himself was missing.

Two weeks after Musa Sadr's disappearance, Ayatollah Ruhollah Khomeini—then still in exile in Iraq—sent a message to Yasir Arafat asking him to help "clarify the mystery." At the same time, Ames decided to take an interest in the case. He did so for two reasons. First, he understood that Musa Sadr's disappearance could exacerbate Lebanon's smoldering civil war. And second, he knew the imam's fate was of intense interest to millions of Shi'as not only in Lebanon but also in Iran, a country that was beginning to show signs of revolutionary turmoil in the streets of Tehran. Ames sent a message to Ali Hassan Salameh about the case and asked if he had any intelligence on the imam's whereabouts. Salameh eventually replied with a detailed account.

Arafat had learned that Qaddafi had agreed to host a meeting between Musa Sadr and one of his theological rivals, the imam Mohammed Beheshti. For some years the latter had led in exile a Shi'a mosque in Hamburg, Germany. But Beheshti was also a close political ally of Ayatollah Khomeini. Like Musa Sadr, Beheshti was a scholar of some repute. But unlike Imam Sadr, Beheshti was an intellectual proponent of a theocratic Shi'ite state. Sadr disagreed, arguing that Shi'a theology prohibited clerics from directly exercising political power.

Both Sadr and Beheshti were recipients of Qaddafi's largesse, and the Libyan dictator wanted the two men to set aside their theological disputes and cooperate on a common, anti-Western political agenda. (The eccentric Qaddafi was himself a Sunni Muslim and had no interest in the arcane merits of what was essentially a Shi'a theological dispute.)

In any case, Musa Sadr and Beheshti were supposed to meet in Tripoli and iron out their political differences under Qaddafi's auspices.

Musa Sadr arrived—but Beheshti and his delegation never came to Tripoli. Musa Sadr was an impatient man, and after several days of waiting in his hotel for a meeting with Qaddafi that never materialized, he announced that he was packing his bags and leaving Libya. Arriving at the Tripoli airport, Musa Sadr was escorted to the VIP departure lounge. In the meantime, Beheshti told Qaddafi over the phone to detain Musa Sadr by all means necessary. Beheshti assured Qaddafi that Imam Sadr was a Western agent. Qaddafi ordered his security force to delay Musa Sadr's departure. Qaddafi instructed that the imam should just be persuaded to go back to his hotel. But Qaddafi's security officers accosted Imam Sadr in the VIP lounge and addressed him disrespectfully. An argument ensued, and the imam was roughed up and thrown into a car. Things had gotten so out of hand that the imam was taken to a prison.

Qaddafi was angered when he discovered what had happened, but he felt he couldn't release Imam Sadr without embarrassing himself politically. So Musa Sadr sat in a Tripoli prison for many months. Finally, Arafat directly asked Qaddafi for his release. By this time, Ayatollah Khomeini had returned to Tehran, where he and Beheshti were writing postrevolutionary Iran's Islamic constitution. When pressed by Arafat, Qaddafi reportedly said he had to make a phone call. He called Beheshti, who told him Musa Sadr was a threat to Khomeini.

Ames was told by his Palestinian sources that eventually Imam Musa Sadr and his two traveling companions had been summarily executed and buried at an unmarked desert gravesite. Ames was shocked by Qaddafi's wanton ruthlessness but also by Beheshti's behavior. It gave him his first insight into the cruel character of the newly established Islamic Republic of Iran.

Robert Ames, age eleven, with his sisters Patricia (left), age fourteen, and Nancy (right), age eight. They grew up in a working-class Philadelphia neighborhood. Their father, Albert, was a steelworker and their mother, Helen, was the homemaker—and the disciplinarian.

Courtesy of Nancy Ames Hanlon

Bob Ames, age nineteen, worked his summers as a lifeguard on the Jersey Shore. He earned a four-year athletic scholarship at La Salle University, where his basketball team, the Explorers, won the NCAA 1954 national championship. Ames would shoot baskets for the rest of his life.

Courtesy of Yvonne Ames

In 1957, Private Robert C. Ames was stationed at Kagnew Station, Ethiopia, where the U.S. Army ran a "listening post" to intercept radio signals from around the world. While at Kagnew, Ames began to teach himself Arabic.

Courtesy of Yvonne Ames

The Ames clan, December 1959. *Left to right:* Nancy Ames Hanlon, Albert C. Ames, Grandma Amorose, Helen Amorose Ames, Bob Ames, and Yvonne Blakely.

Courtesy of Nancy Ames Hanlon

In 1959, Ames met Yvonne Blakely, the daughter of a U.S. Navy commander. She was a "Gibbs girl" secretary and he was then working as a repo man for All State Insurance Co. They wed in 1960, and that summer he interviewed for a job at the CIA.

Courtesy of Nancy Ames Hanlon

In 1962, the CIA posted Ames and his family to Dhahran, Saudi Arabia, where his assignment included collecting intelligence on radical Arab nationalists opposed to the Saudi monarchy.

Courtesy of Nancy Ames Hanlon

Bob Ames in Saudi Arabia, Christmas 1964, with his daughters Catherine and Adrienne. Ames was becoming fluent in Arabic. "He was one of the best spooks I ever met," recalled a colleague.

Courtesy of Nancy Ames Hanlon

The CIA sent Ames to Aden in South Yemen in 1967. It was a war zone. "Everywhere you look there are soldiers with guns," Bob wrote home. "Kind of creepy." But he grew to love Yemen's backcountry: "I got some frankincense which I'll send home some day, hopefully by Christmas."

Courtesy of Yvonne Ames

In 1969, Ames met Mustafa Zein, a young Lebanese businessman. Zein was an Arab Zelig—he seemed to be everywhere and to know everyone in Beirut. Ames nicknamed him the Catalyst, and Zein called Ames the *Munir*—Arabic for "enlightener."

Courtesy of Mustafa Zein

Ali Hassan Salameh, age twenty-seven, was Yasir Arafat's PLO security chief in 1969 when his friend Mustafa Zein arranged a clandestine meeting with Bob Ames in Beirut's Strand Café. "Ali looked at Bob, and then pointed to me," Zein recalled, "and said, 'This is my man.'"

As-Safir *newspaper, Beirut*

CIA director Richard Helms (right) greeting President Richard Nixon in 1969. Helms was Bob Ames's mentor inside the CIA. Helms encouraged Ames to develop his clandestine relationship with Ali Hassan Salameh—even though the Nixon Administration and Henry Kissinger had banned any contact with the Palestine Liberation Organization. *Corbis Bettmann*

Caskets of the eleven Israeli athletes murdered at the September 1972 Munich Olympics by a team of Black September terrorists. "After that act no one would listen anymore," Ames wrote. "All sympathy was gone. The only thought was that this should never happen again." *Corbis Bettmann*

The PLO's Yasir Arafat addressed the United Nations on November 13, 1974. Ames played a key role in getting Arafat and Ali Hassan Salameh to New York. "I'm just a middle man in all this," Ames wrote. They stayed at the Waldorf Astoria—and before leaving, Salameh bought a postcard of the famous hotel and wrote to his son, "The PLO at the Waldorf Astoria!" *Corbis Bettmann*

Former Lebanese prime minister Saeb Salam (left) with Ali Hassan Salameh and Yasir Arafat (right) in 1976. Ames assigned Salameh the CIA cryptonym MJTRUST/2. By 1976, Salameh's fedayeen from Force 17 were providing security for the U.S. embassy in the midst of the Lebanese civil war. As-Safir *newspaper, Beirut*

Ali Hassan Salameh shaking hands with Pierre Gemayel, a Lebanese power broker and founder of the right-wing Phalangist Party. His son Bashir Gemayel (center), a Maronite Christian warlord, was elected president in 1982—but was assassinated within weeks. As-Safir *newspaper, Beirut*

Bashir Gemayel (left) and Ali Hassan Salameh were enemies who admired each other. Ames called Bashir "our brutal warlord." As-Safir *newspaper, Beirut*

The Imam Musa Sadr (far left) with Ali Hassan Salameh (right, wearing a leather jacket) in 1975. Musa Sadr, the spiritual leader of Lebanon's Shi'a Muslims, vanished mysteriously in 1978 on a trip to Libya. Ames asked Salameh to investigate the Imam's disappearance. As-Safir *newspaper, Beirut*

Georgina Rizk with Bob Barker in Miami Beach upon being selected Miss Universe of 1971. "She is Lebanon's queen, Lebanon's goddess." Ali Hassan Salameh began dating Rizk in 1976, and that year Ames arranged for the couple to visit Washington, D.C.; Disneyland in Anaheim, California; and Hawaii. *Associated Press*

Ali Hassan Salameh with his two boys by his first marriage, to Nashrawan Sharif. Ames frequently visited Salameh at his home with wife Nashrawan, and he frowned on Salameh's affair with Georgina Rizk: "This affair is ruining his reputation." Salameh nevertheless married Rizk in June 1977.

Courtesy of Mustafa Zein

In the autumn of 1978 Ames was promoted to National Intelligence Officer for the Near East and South Asia. It was a big step up and a step away from clandestine operations. "Bob had a reputation in the DO [Directorate of Operations] of being too smart, too much of an intellectual."

Courtesy of Yvonne Ames

In November 1978 Ames flew to Beirut to warn Salameh that Mossad was once again targeting him for assassination. "I know that I'll die," Salameh said fatalistically. On January 22, 1979, his convoy passed a Volkswagen packed with explosives. When it blew up, Salameh was killed together with eight other people. As-Safir *newspaper, Beirut*

Mike Harari, the head of Mossad's Caesarea clandestine unit in the 1970s, tried to assassinate Ali Hassan Salameh in Norway in 1973, but his team mistakenly killed an innocent Moroccan immigrant. Harari succeeded in 1979. Mossad officer Erika Chambers pushed the remote-control button that ignited the explosives just as Salameh's car passed her balcony.

Haaretz newspaper / credit: Dudu Bachar

Yasir Arafat (center with keffiyeh headdress) at Ali Hassan Salameh's funeral. His arm is draped across Ali's son Hassan, who is holding an AK-47 Kalashnikov gun in his hand. As-Safir *newspaper, Beirut*

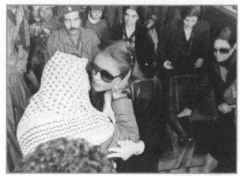

Yasir Arafat kissing a pregnant Georgina Rizk, one of Ali Hassan Salameh's two widows. "The day Ali Hassan Salameh was killed was a very bad day," recalled one of Ames's colleagues. . . . "Bob was clearly stunned when he heard the news."

As-Safir *newspaper, Beirut*

Dewey Clarridge (left), George Cave (center), and Alan Wolfe (right). All three senior clandestine officers worked closely with Ames. *Courtesy of Henry Miller-Jones*

William Casey brought to the CIA a fiery Catholicism and Cold Warrior certitudes. *Courtesy of Corbis Bettmann*

Ames (wearing his trademark tinted aviator glasses) enthralled Casey with his spycraft stories. Casey promoted him to become the CIA's chief analyst for the Middle East.

Courtesy of Yvonne Ames

Paul Wolfowitz (left), President Ronald Reagan, and Ames (second from right) at Camp David. Ames regularly briefed Reagan about the Israeli invasion of Lebanon in the summer of 1982. "It is a tricky business," recalled one of Ames's colleagues. "Do you try to stay true to your views or do you try to remain effective? At some point, people stop listening to you."

Courtesy of Ronald Reagan Presidential Library

Israeli Defense Minister Ariel Sharon (right) with his troops in Lebanon. When asked how far he intended to advance into Lebanon, Sharon replied, "As far as we have to."

Corbis Bettmann

After Arafat and the PLO were expelled from Lebanon, Phalangist militiamen massacred more than 1,000 Palestinian and Shi'ite Lebanese refugees in Sabra and Shatila. Ames was then working closely with Secretary of State George Shultz, who said, "The brutal fact is we are partially responsible."

Corbis Bettmann

Janet Lee Stevens, age thirty-two, was an American reporter who was known in the Sabra and Shatila refugee camps as "the Little Drummer Girl." She served as John le Carré's guide in the camps and spent the rest of her life investigating the massacre.

Courtesy of Kristen Stevens

At 1:04 P.M. on April 18, 1983, a truck bomb destroyed the U.S. embassy in Beirut. "The smoke had cleared, but blood and body parts were everywhere. It is a smell you never forget." *Corbis Bettmann / credit: Claude Salhani*

Sixty-three people died, including seventeen Americans and thirty-two Lebanese embassy employees. Eight of the Americans were CIA officers.

Getty Images

U.S. Marines form a perimeter around the destroyed U.S. embassy. "Bob Ames among the dead in Beirut," wrote a White House official in his diary. "We believe Iran involved. Felt very sad about Bob." *Getty Images*

President Reagan and Nancy Reagan walk by sixteen caskets at Andrews Air Force Base. "Nancy and I met individually with the families of the deceased," the president noted in his diary. "We were both in tears—I know all I could do was grip their hands—I was too choked up to speak." Ames was the only victim Reagan had known personally. *Courtesy of Ronald Reagan Presidential Library*

Yvonne Ames at Andrews Air Force Base, standing with her brother, a U.S. Navy officer. She was not told which casket contained Bob's body. "Bob's death fractured our family," she later explained. "It's like when you take a photograph and rip it. You can try to piece it back together, but it's never the same."

Courtesy of Ronald Reagan Presidential Library

Imad Mughniyeh (left) with Hassan Nasrallah, secretary general of Hezbollah. Ali Hassan Salameh recruited Mughniyeh into Force 17 in the 1970s. But by 1983 Mughniyeh was working for the Iranians in Beirut—and he was thought to be involved in the U.S. embassy bombing: "When in doubt, and we are always in doubt about this, blame Mughniyeh."

As-Safir *newspaper, Beirut*

Imad Mughniyeh with his mother. He operated in the darkest of shadows. A former director general of the Mossad described Mughniyeh as "very shrewd, very talented ... He was the liaison between Hezbollah and Iran." *Courtesy of* Al-Akhbar *newspaper, Beirut*

On February 12, 2008, Mughniyeh was assassinated in Damascus when the headrest in his booby-trapped Mitsubishi car exploded. "Mughniyeh was assassinated by the Israelis, with intelligence on his whereabouts furnished by the CIA."

Associated Press

General Ali Reza Asgari, an Iranian Revolutionary Guard intelligence officer who defected to the United States in 2007. According to Mustafa Zein, it was Asgari who recruited Mughniyeh and planned the 1983 truck bomb attack on the U.S. embassy. "At the unclassified level, I cannot elaborate on the issue," said a U.S. intelligence official.
Corbis Bettmann

The last photograph of Bob and Yvonne, Christmas 1982. *Courtesy of Yvonne Ames*

CHAPTER EIGHT

The Assassination

He [Salameh] was in a clandestine relationship with the Americans. They [the Israelis] thought such a relationship was the first step to seeing Arafat in the White House. So they would have wanted him dead just for that reason alone.

—*Bruce Riedel, analyst, Directorate of Intelligence*

Soon after Ames's return from his TDY in Beirut in the summer of 1978, an Israeli officer approached Alan Wolfe at a conference in London and asked him quite directly if Ali Hassan Salameh was a CIA asset. Wolfe brushed aside the question and walked away. But he understood the full import of the Mossad man's question. Back in Langley a meeting was convened of senior Directorate of Operations officers familiar with the case. Ames was not invited because he was by then technically no longer in the Directorate of Operations but working as a national intelligence officer in the National Intelligence Council. Wolfe was told that this was not the first time Mossad had recently asked about Salameh. There had been at least two other recent approaches. Mossad wanted to know if Salameh was out of bounds. Could they assassinate him? Or was he working for the Americans?

The questions posed a dilemma for the Agency. Salameh—or MJTRUST/2, as he was known inside Langley headquarters—was a source, but he was not an asset. "The Israelis knew full well that Salameh was our source," said Clair George, the late veteran clandestine officer. "He was a critical source. But if we had claimed him as an asset, a man under our protection, well, the Israelis would have asked us to share the intelligence we got from him. We couldn't do that. It

was a dilemma." George was not at the meeting that decided Salameh's fate, but he said he was told all about it. "There was a vigorous
debate. And in the end it was decided that we just shouldn't reply to
the Israelis. No answer was better than a yes or no."

More than one Agency officer thought this was an egregious mistake. "No answer was an answer," said *Charles Waverly*. "He wasn't our
guy, but he was an important relationship." The Agency's handling of
the problem was bureaucratically predictable. "'We won't answer the
question'—well, this is a favored CIA answer to any tough question," said
Bruce Riedel, a high-ranking analyst who'd once reviewed the Salameh-
Ames files. "They just thought answering the question would have made
matters worse. Maybe they hoped that by ignoring the problem it would
go away. But I dealt with the Israelis and I believe they viewed Salameh
as a threat in two ways. First, he was a terrorist. But second, he was in a
clandestine relationship with the Americans. They thought such a relationship was the first step to seeing Arafat in the White House. So they
would have wanted him dead just for that reason alone."

Dewey Clarridge—one of those clandestine officers who were
critical of Ames for not having made a full recruitment—nevertheless
thought it was a huge mistake. "I am sure there was a debate," Clarridge said. "And obviously, they decided to fudge it. Just stupid! They
should have protected him."

George and two other clandestine officers believed that Ames had
been told of both the Israeli approach and the Agency's decision not
to reply. So Ames knew that Salameh was in danger, and he sent him
an explicit warning. According to Frank Anderson, the chief of station
in Beirut, Ames also urged Alan Wolfe to pass an explicit statement to
the Israelis not to touch Salameh. Wolfe reportedly refused to do so.
"There was some talk of shipping him an armored car," recalled Sam
Wyman, a clandestine officer in Beirut. "But I think we did give him
some encrypted gear so he could communicate with us and upgrade his
security. I warned him. I told him, 'You idiot, they're going to get you,
the way you drive around Beirut. It is only a matter of time.'"

According to Mustafa Zein, Mossad's deputy director David Kimche approached Ames. Several retired Mossad officers confirm this. Kimche was then head of Mossad's Tevel Unit, responsible for relations with foreign intelligence services. The well-known Israeli spymaster, a veteran of Mossad since the early 1950s, flew into Washington specifically to ask Ames if Salameh was on the CIA's payroll. Kimche made it clear that Salameh was being targeted. He said his life would be spared only if Mossad was given an explicit assurance that he was working for the CIA. Ames couldn't give him an answer. But sometime in November 1978 Ames contacted Salameh in Beirut and, according to Zein, he tried very hard "to get permission from Yasir Arafat—through Ali—to tell the Israelis that Ali was working for the CIA." The two men argued. Ames bluntly warned Ali that his life was in danger—and that he was irreplaceable. Ali said that he would never change his mind. He reminded Ames that he'd rebuffed a similar effort to recruit him in Rome eight years earlier. He insisted that he couldn't be identified as a CIA asset. And probably for good reason. "If Ali Hassan had agreed to be named as an asset," said Yoram Hessel, a senior Mossad officer, "well, that would be putting a gun to his head. He knew that once he gave his consent to be called an asset, we could have launched a black psychological operation, letting it be known in Beirut circles that he was an agent." Salameh understood the dilemma, and so did Ames.

So Salameh worked for the Old Man and the revolution—and no one else. Ames did not get the answer he wanted—but he did persuade Ali to come to Washington the following month for an officially sanctioned exchange of intelligence. Perhaps Ames was hoping that the Israelis would notice such a trip—and that this would somehow protect Salameh. In the meantime, Ames arranged for the encrypted communications gear to be shipped to Beirut. It was a present for Ali Hassan that wouldn't arrive in time.

Zein was unhappy with Salameh's refusal to take more security precautions. "I knew he was dead," Zein said. He warned Salameh's wife

Nashrawan that an attack was coming. "We wanted him to move out of the Hamra area of Beirut, where it was common to see foreigners walking the streets. He really should have moved into one of the refugee camps. He would have been safe in Sabra and Shatila—but of course, you couldn't expect Georgina to live in the camps. Okay, Ali could still have moved to an upscale Palestinian neighborhood outside of Hamra. I told him it would not be forever—the Israeli hit team wouldn't wait around for long. But Ali refused to move from the Verdun apartment."

Some months earlier, Ali had been given a two-door Mercedes, a generous gift from a benefactor. Ali loved the classy sports car, but there was no room for his bodyguards. So he reluctantly gave it to Mustafa, who drove it himself, using Ali's license plate and registration. But after Ames warned Salameh about the impending attack, Mustafa decided it would be foolish to drive around the city in Ali's car. "I gave it back to Ali," Mustafa said. "I also decided to no longer ride with him in his convoy."

After the botched attempt to kill Salameh in Lillehammer in July 1973, Prime Minister Golda Meir had ordered an end to the post-Munich "war of the agents." But this decision was reversed in June 1977 when Menachem Begin, the leader of the right-wing Likud Party, was elected prime minister. Sometime in the spring or summer of 1978, Begin reauthorized the Mossad's Caesarea hit team to resume its hunt for Salameh. Perhaps Begin had never been disabused of the legend that the Red Prince was a primary architect of the Munich operation. Perhaps he thought Salameh was still running "wet" operations. But this wasn't the case. By 1979, Mossad had no evidence that Salameh was a "ticking bomb." In any case, Begin was told that Salameh was the CIA's conduit to the PLO. It's also possible that Mossad had picked up intelligence that Ames had invited Salameh to visit America for a third time, in December 1978.

In the wake of the September 1978 Camp David Accords, there

were many details to iron out between the two parties. Besides paving the way for an Egyptian-Israeli peace treaty, the Accords also included a plan to give Palestinians "full autonomy" in the occupied territories of the West Bank and Gaza. Ames had convinced Carter administration officials that it would be advantageous to bring Salameh to Washington, where he could meet various officials. Such talks with the PLO's intelligence chief would be highly secret. Washington wasn't ready to negotiate openly with the PLO. For his part, Salameh was certainly critical of the Camp David Accords. Mere "autonomy" was not a PLO goal; it wanted full sovereignty. But Ames hoped to massage Salameh into viewing the Accords as a first step, a window of opportunity for the PLO to achieve some of its aims by peaceful means. If the Israelis had indeed heard rumors of such a secret summit in Washington, this would certainly have accelerated their plans for Salameh's assassination. As it turned out, Salameh decided to postpone his Washington visit from December 1978 to April 1979.

In early 1978 officers from Caesarea, Mossad's elite operational unit, began once again to collect intelligence on Salameh's daily itinerary in Beirut. They did so with an eagerness that bordered on obsession. Aaron J. Klein, the author of *Striking Back,* reported that in his interviews with retired Caesarea officers, they described killing Salameh as a form of closure—"We want to 'close the circle.'" They knew Black September no longer existed. They knew there were other Palestinian terrorists with more blood on their hands than Salameh. But Salameh was always at the top of their hit list. Initially, they contemplated dropping a large bomb on Salameh's apartment. But architects studied the building and concluded that too many innocent lives would be lost. "We followed Ali Hassan extensively," said a former Mossad director general, "using all intelligence means. We knew his bodyguards never left him for a second."

Killing the Red Prince would not be easy. For one thing, his security was not light. Ali Hassan had stashed Kalashnikovs in every room of his apartment and office. He had a small platoon of armed men guard his apartment building off Rue Verdun in Ras Beirut. Heavy steel shutters had been installed on the Verdun apartment's windows. He always traveled in a convoy of cars with a squad of bodyguards. He rarely left Beirut.

But for all his precautions, Ali Hassan was indeed fatalistic, morbidly so at times. "I know that I'll die," he told Shafik al-Hout, the PLO's media chief. "I shall be murdered, I shall fall in battle." When *Time* magazine correspondent Dean Brelis asked him if he was worried about an Israeli assassination attempt, Salameh replied, "They're the ones who should be worried after all their mistakes. But I know that when my number is up, it will be up. No one can stop it." He told Brelis that he really needed a vacation: "Maybe a beach in Brazil or the Caribbean. But I can't just go out and get on an airplane. I don't know if I can ever fly from one country to another again."

Mossad's Caesarea chief, Mike Harari, kept looking for a gateway, a window that would allow his operatives to get close enough to Salameh to carry out the hit. Harari was the same officer who'd led the bungled Lillehammer assassination attempt against Salameh in 1973. A driven, charismatic clandestine officer, his subordinates nicknamed him "Caesar." At one point, a Mossad officer pointed out to his colleagues that Salameh had told *Monday Morning* in a 1976 interview that he loved karate. He looked fit. So did this mean he worked out in a gym? They scoured the Beirut Yellow Pages to make a list of likely gymnasiums, and then they sent agents into the various gyms in an attempt to spot Salameh. It reportedly took months, but eventually a Mossad agent found himself sitting naked next to Salameh in the Continental Hotel's sauna. Salameh, it turned out, was a member of the Continental's sports club, and he worked out nearly every afternoon. Mossad tentatively prepared a bomb that could be hidden under the sauna bench—but the plan was vetoed as likely to kill innocent civilians.

Eventually, Mossad came up with an alternative. Surveillance teams in Beirut identified the location of Salameh's apartment in the upscale neighborhood of Snoubra in Ras Beirut. This was the apartment he shared with his second wife, Georgina Rizk. And they noted the route he regularly took from his apartment to that of his mother and sister, who lived nearby in Ras Beirut. This pedestrian information—acquired at considerable cost with human agents on the ground—gave the Israelis the opportunity to mount an attack. The operation began in early November 1978. It required the deployment of some fifteen Caesarea operatives into Beirut and a considerable budget.

The first Mossad agent to arrive was Erika Mary Chambers, a thirty-year-old British passport holder. Previously, Chambers had spent four years living in Germany. But before that, she had studied at Hebrew University in Jerusalem, where Mossad had recruited her. Upon her arrival in Beirut, Chambers offered to work as a volunteer at the House of Steadfastness of the Children of Tel al-Zatar, a charity dedicated to helping survivors and orphans from the siege of the Tel al-Zatar Palestinian refugee camp. By some accounts, Chambers was introduced to Ali Hassan Salameh in Tel al-Zatar and they became friendly. (This seems somewhat improbable.) According to Peter Taylor, whose *States of Terror* contains the most authoritative account of the operation, Chambers rented an eighth-floor apartment on Beka Street; her neighbors knew her as "Penelope," an eccentric young Englishwoman who loved cats and could often be seen sitting on her balcony, painting street scenes. From her balcony, Chambers could observe Salameh's battered Chevrolet station wagon driving nearly every afternoon on Beka Street, followed by a Land Rover filled with armed guards. Salameh usually sat in the backseat of the Chevrolet, with a bodyguard on either side.

In mid-January 1979, several other Mossad officers arrived in Beirut, traveling on forged Canadian and British passports.* They checked in to different hotels and rented a Volkswagen Beetle. Two frogmen from

---

* The Canadian passport was in the name of Ronald Kolberg of Vancouver, who at the time was a biology student at the University of Tel Aviv. Kolberg later told reporters that his passport was used without his knowledge. Using the passports of third-country nationals is a long-standing Mossad tactic.

an Israeli missile boat several miles offshore delivered eleven pounds of hexagene explosives to a deserted beach, where they were picked up by other agents and packed into the Volkswagen. They parked the Volkswagen on Beka Street below Chambers's apartment. And then they waited.

A few days earlier, Salameh had been warned by a most unlikely source that Mossad was plotting to assassinate him. Bashir Gemayel, the Phalangist warlord, had heard from his Mossad sources that a hit on Salameh was imminent. Gemayel told one of his associates, Karim Pakradouni, to warn Salameh. "I think Bashir had some *crise de conscience*," Pakradouni told Peter Taylor, "and wanted to inform Abu Hassan about the operation." When Taylor asked Pakradouni why he thought Mossad wanted to assassinate Salameh, he replied: "Because he was a member of Black September and because he had a relationship with the American Embassy in Beirut. . . . The policy of Israel was to destroy any contact between the PLO and the USA. . . . So quickly the Mossad realized that Abu Hassan was not just a security threat, but a political danger because he represented the Palestinian window on America."

Frank Anderson, the chief of station in Beirut at the time, had an evening meeting with Salameh in his apartment in early January 1979. "He told me," Anderson said, "that he'd heard the Israelis were targeting him. I said he should take the warning seriously."

Salameh's sister and mother also warned him. His sister Nidal told Taylor that she knew her brother had once gone to a fortune-teller who had told him that he would die at the age of thirty-seven—the same age his father had been killed by the Israelis in 1948. Ali Hassan had just laughed. "He meant such a lot to me," Nidal said, "and I thought he was too great to die, too great to be killed. I thought he was immortal—that it was impossible for him to die."

His mother, Um Ali, told Taylor, "The last time I saw him I warned him. I told him that I had a feeling that something bad would happen to him. He laughed and said not to worry: he would live another fifty years. I told him fifty years were not enough.... As he left, I felt I would never see him again."

Mustafa Zein saw Ali Hassan on the evening of January 21, 1979. Ali Hassan knew it was Mustafa's birthday the next day, so he stopped by that evening at Mustafa's newly renovated penthouse suite in the Bedford Hotel. "He asked me how I planned to celebrate my birthday," Zein recalled. "I replied that I didn't want to celebrate. And then he walked over to my bookshelves and pulled down a book. He'd chosen *The City of Death*. I said, 'Ali, put it down.' And then I walked downstairs with him to his car and we hugged each other."

January 22, 1979, was a cold and gray day in Beirut. It was the birthday of Salameh's young niece, and Ali Hassan had promised he would stop by his mother's apartment in the late afternoon for the birthday party. He then intended to drive on to Damascus, where Arafat was expecting him to attend a meeting of the Palestinian National Council. That afternoon at 3:25 P.M. Salameh kissed Georgina good-bye—she was five months pregnant. He then got into the backseat of the tan Chevrolet station wagon. At the last moment, one of his aides, a young man named Jamal, came running up with a written message. It was yet another warning from Bashir Gemayel's Phalange, saying the hit would happen in the next day or two. One of Salameh's guards got out of the station wagon, and Jamal took his place. His driver headed out toward Rue Verdun with the Land Rover jeep following. Just a kilometer away, the convoy turned right from Rue Verdun onto Beka Street and glided past Erika Chambers's eighth-floor balcony. Just then a woman driving behind the Land Rover suddenly sped up and, passing the backup car, cut in behind Salameh's Chevy station wagon. As the Chevy came abreast of the parked Volkswagen, Chambers held her breath and pushed a remote-control switch. The Volkswagen exploded, enveloping the Chevy in a huge ball of fire. It too exploded, and so too did the car driven by the woman, a thirty-four-year-old British secretary named Susan Wareham. She died along with Salameh and his bodyguards.

"It was like hell," an eyewitness told Peter Taylor. "There was a flash, then a big bang.... So many dead people, burnt cars and young bodies littering the street. Then I saw Abu Hassan Salameh getting out of a car and falling on the ground. The people told me who he was." By sheer coincidence, Abu Daoud, the mastermind of the Munich Olympics attack, happened to be in the neighborhood and rushed down the street to see the wounded Salameh lying in the street. "His face was badly cut," Abu Daoud said.

Still alive, Salameh was taken in an ambulance by the Red Crescent (the local equivalent of the Red Cross) to the hospital of the American University of Beirut, just five hundred yards away, where surgeons tried to extract a metal splinter lodged in his brain. He died on the operating table at 4:03 P.M.

In the midst of the carnage, Erika Chambers calmly walked out of her apartment building, climbed into a rented Datsun, and drove away toward the beaches of East Beirut. Late that evening, she rendezvoused with two Mossad officers in a rubber raft who motored her out to an Israeli naval ship.*

Eight other people were killed by Chambers's car bomb: Salameh's two bodyguards and driver, the British secretary Susan Wareham, a German nun who happened to be walking on the sidewalk, and three Lebanese civilians. Sixteen people were wounded.

Frank Anderson was preparing for a meeting with Salameh when he heard the explosion. When he received a phone call from an embassy officer saying that Salameh might have been hit, Anderson drove to Salameh's apartment and only then learned what had happened.

Mustafa Zein had spent the entire day holed up in his Bedford suite. With a heavy sense of foreboding, he'd even unplugged his telephone.

---

* Chambers is today living in Israel. She was chosen for the job because in practice sessions rehearsed by Mossad's Caesarea unit the men always pushed the remote-control button a second or two late. So Mike Harari, the head of Caesarea from 1970 to 1980, decided to try a woman. Chambers was successful every time.

So a messenger had to be sent by Force 17 to tell Mustafa the news. He then rushed to the American University of Beirut hospital, but by the time he arrived Ali Hassan had died.

Early the next morning Anderson came by the Bedford and found Zein reading the Koran. Anderson sat down and took the time to write a condolence note to Salameh's eldest son, explaining what his father had meant to him.

> *Dear Hassan,*
> *At your age, I lost my father. Today, I lost a friend whom I respected more than other men. From the memory of my past loss, and from the pain of today, I share your pain. I promise to honor your father's memory — and to stand ready to be your friend.*
> *A friend.*

Frank also penned a note to one of Salameh's widows, the first wife, Nashrawan Sharif.

> *Dear Um Hassan,*
> *I, who must grieve in silence, have lost a friend. No one can compensate your loss. Still, I hope you will find some comfort in my pledge to honor your husband's memory.*

That afternoon more than twenty thousand people attended Salameh's burial in Beirut's Martyrs' Cemetery. Like his father, Hassan Salameh, Ali was dead at the age of thirty-seven. *Monday Morning* published a picture of Yasir Arafat helping to carry the casket. A poignant photo appeared on the cover of the Beirut weekly depicting a crestfallen Arafat, his arm wrapped around Ali Hassan Salameh's thirteen-year-old son, Hassan. The boy wore a military beret on his head, and a Fedayeen's *keffiyeh* was draped around his shoulders. Someone had shoved a Kalashnikov assault rifle into his small hands. It was a staged photo op. But a glassy-eyed Arafat was clearly devastated. He'd thought of Ali

Hassan as his own son. "We have lost a lion," he told reporters in Damascus. At the gravesite, he shouted out to the throngs of mourners, "We bury a martyr! We will continue to march on the road toward Palestine. Goodbye, my hero."

Mustafa Zein witnessed the chaotic scene. "It was an unforgettable day," Zein said. Arafat was a mess. He'd been in Damascus when he heard the news. A snowstorm had blocked the road from Damascus to Beirut, and it had taken Arafat and his convoy of security guards seven hours to drive to Beirut. At one point, the chairman of the PLO had to get out of his car and use his bare hands to remove snow from beneath the tires. At the funeral, Arafat came up to Zein and remarked bitterly, "Your friends could not protect my son. I gave them the most I cared for, my right hand. How could that happen?"

In an extraordinary tribute, the Maronite warlord Bashir Gemayel attended the funeral, and at the moment of burial a squad of his men saluted Ali with a volley of rifle fire in the air. "The most ardent enemies of the Palestinians were honoring the death of a Palestinian leader," Zein remarked.

The page-one headline in the *New York Times* read, "Reputed Planner of Munich Raid Killed in Beirut." In Tel Aviv that day, the widow of one of the Olympian athletes killed at Munich, Ilana Romano, told reporters that she'd waited for this day for years. "In my name, and in the name of all the other widows, I want to thank those who did it." For virtually all Israelis, the man responsible for the Munich tragedy had been justly executed.

In Langley, the CIA did not see it the same way. "The day Ali Hassan Salameh was killed was a very bad day," recalled *Lindsay Sherwin*, a senior Middle East analyst. "Everyone in the Agency knew it was a big deal. Bob was clearly stunned when he heard the news. He became very quiet, and the color drained from his face. I heard someone ask, 'Is he all right?'"

Many of Langley's clandestine officers thought Salameh's death was an egregious mistake. "I am surprised Clair George and those guys didn't try harder to keep Salameh alive," said *Sherwin*. Others labeled it a tragedy. "If Ali Hassan had lived," Sam Wyman said, "things might have gone in a different direction. He could never have been recruited, but if handled carefully he could have been a very powerful diplomatic conduit. It was a blow to our influence, and a blow to the prospects for peace." In Beirut, Chief of Station Anderson agreed: "We lost a very important diplomatic channel. We lost the capability to advance the peace process. Arafat by comparison to Ali Hassan was just a very weak man." When Anderson finally met Arafat in 1993, he came away from the interview thinking that the PLO chairman was an empty vessel. "A few weeks later," Anderson recalled, "I was having dinner with King Hussein and I began to describe how unimpressive Arafat seemed. The king finished my sentence by saying, 'There's nothing there.'"

Many in the Agency thought that Salameh should have been protected. Whatever the political risks, some spooks thought the Israelis should have been told that he was untouchable. One veteran DO officer, Charlie Allen, thought killing Salameh harmed Israel's national interest. "When Mossad killed Ali Hassan," Allen said, "it was an act of cutting off the nose to spite the face."

Herman Eilts, the U.S. ambassador to Cairo at the time, candidly told the *Wall Street Journal*, "He was extraordinarily helpful—as was Fatah—in assisting in security for American citizens and officials. I regard his assassination as a loss." Admiral Stansfield Turner, the CIA director in the Carter administration, reportedly told the president that "our man" in the PLO had been assassinated.

Some Mossad officers understood the American conundrum. "It is an enormous investment," observed Yoram Hessel. "Salameh was a ten-year intelligence relationship. So on the one hand you can see why they wanted to protect him. But there is something wrong about all this. From our perspective—the Israeli perspective—it is unthinkable that you would have anything to do with such a man. The idea that there was intelligence sharing with the Red Prince would have been anathema to us."

It was a thin red line. *Meir Harel*—later a Mossad director general— understood perfectly why Ames would have cultivated Salameh. "A backstage contact is well within the accepted rules of the game," *Harel* observed. "We knew Salameh was talking to the Americans. And I came to know later that Ames was very angry with us when Ali Hassan was killed." But *Harel* seems to think that if the Americans wanted to keep Salameh alive all they had to do was ask: "You may assume that if the Americans had told us that Ali was an asset, we would have stopped our operation." But this begs the question because Ali never would have agreed to be considered an asset. And *Harel* himself admits that he knew Ali was not an agent. "It does not surprise me," *Harel* said. "It does not make me angry that the Americans were talking to the Palestinian. It was part of the game. But it is fascinating. We suspected Ali had contacts with the Americans. We thought, however, that the relations were of a liaisonship nature and not of an agent to his control."

Another senior Israeli intelligence officer, *Dov Zeit*, recalls talking with Ames in Washington about his "close professional relations with the PLO." This must have been after Salameh's death. "He was not playing games," *Zeit* recalled. "He was being honest—even matter-of-fact. I remember my superiors were shocked by the nature of the relationship."

Virtually the entire Israeli military and intelligence establishment celebrated Salameh's death. A terrorist was dead. But aside from vengeance, what exactly did this accomplish for the Israelis? Ronen Bergman, one of Israel's most prominent national security and intelligence reporters, remains highly skeptical. "Did it solve the Palestinian problem?" Bergman asks. "No. Did it help to bring peace to the Middle East? No—and it created bloodshed from both sides in Europe. Tactically, it was successful. Strategically, it was a failure." Frank Anderson had a more cynical interpretation: "The Israelis had a policy to eliminate everyone around Arafat who had a tendency to be liberal. I know they deny this, but just look at who they killed."

To be sure, killing the Red Prince probably postponed the day when American officials would openly negotiate with Yasir Arafat. But it did not close the back channel for long. In the wake of Salameh's assassination, Anderson wanted to know who would replace Salameh as the liaison to the Agency. The PLO's Mohammed Subeh—whose wife was the sister to Salameh's first wife, Nashrawan—came to Beirut and told Anderson that Mustafa Zein would be the liaison. And indeed, Zein was called to one of Arafat's safe houses in Beirut in the middle of the night and had a long talk with the Old Man. "I want you to do this," Arafat told Zein, "even though I am asking you to put one foot in the grave. But you are Lebanese, not Palestinian, so maybe it will be easier for the Americans to meet with you." Anderson was skeptical that Zein could replace Salameh, and so too were his bosses back at Langley. But the CIA made a determined effort to keep the channel open by meeting with, among others, Hani al-Hassan, the PLO official who had met with Gen. Vernon Walters in Rabat in 1973.

Two weeks after Salameh's assassination, Zein flew into Washington. Ames visited him in his hotel room and the two men commiserated over Salameh's death. Mustafa remembers tears. Ames told him, "We want to finish the job we started with Ali."

CHAPTER NINE

The Ayatollahs

Fuck the Shah. I am not going to welcome him here when he
has other places to go where he'll be safe.

— *President Jimmy Carter*

On February 1, 1979, just nine days after Ali Hassan Salameh's
assassination, Ayatollah Ruhollah Khomeini was welcomed
home in Tehran by millions of Iranians celebrating the shah's
ouster just two weeks earlier. Over the next eleven days Khomeini mo-
bilized his supporters in the streets. By February 11, Khomeini's revolutionaries were in full command of the government. The revolution had
begun in October 1977 with a few hundred demonstrators. Protests
escalated throughout 1978, and by the late autumn it was clear to everyone that the Pahlavi regime could no longer control the streets.

After the 1979 revolution, George Cave was brought back from Saudi
Arabia to Washington, where he worked on the problem of how to deal
with a very unstable, fluid revolutionary government in Tehran. As national intelligence officer (NIO) for the Near East, Ames was working
on many of the same issues. Ever since Ayatollah Khomeini's return, a
fierce power struggle had been taking place in Tehran between moderate members of the revolutionary government and Khomeini's more
radical Islamists, who wanted to turn Iran into a fundamentalist theological state. The moderates were led by Mehdi Bazargan, a professor
of engineering from Tehran University whom Khomeini had appointed
as his interim prime minister. But while Bazargan tried to restore es-

sential government services and get a constitution written, Khomeini inflamed political passions with fiery speeches attacking foreign imperialists and corrupt, irreligious secularists at home. Throughout 1979, the ayatollah was methodically undermining his prime minister.

By the spring of 1979, Tehran was descending into chaos. Bands of radical Islamists loyal to Khomeini roamed the streets. Armed men set up checkpoints throughout the city. On March 18, 1979, the acting chief of station, Howard Hart, was out meeting a source in the middle of the night when he was attacked by a couple of men shouting, "CIA! CIA!" Beaten to the ground, Hart pulled out his gun and shot them dead. On the other hand, it was a period of postrevolutionary exuberance when a "thousand flowers were blooming." Hawkers on Tehran sidewalks were selling newspapers and magazines espousing viewpoints that ran the gamut from communist to Islamist. The Tudeh Communist Party maintained public offices, as did the People's Mujahedin Party, an armed group with a leftist Islamic program. Yet it was clear that Khomeini's Islamist radicals had the political momentum and the street muscle to prevail in any political showdown.

In this uncertain atmosphere, U.S. policy makers were under no illusions that the monarchy could ever be restored. Washington's decidedly modest goal was merely to restore some normalcy to American-Iranian relations and hope that Prime Minister Barzargan's cabinet, dominated by men of more or less moderate and modernist temperaments, could survive long enough in power to stabilize the government and write a democratic constitution—and perhaps keep the oil exports flowing to the international markets. Sadly, this goal would prove illusory. As one American official noted, "It is not easy to sleep next to an elephant that you have wounded." But Bob Ames and George Cave nevertheless made a valiant attempt in 1979 to divert the Iranian revolutionaries' relations with America from messianic nihilism to something approaching normalcy.

The obstacles in their path were truly enormous. Most Iranians were highly suspicious of American intentions. They knew that the CIA had planned the coup that put the shah back in power in 1953. They knew that the CIA had worked closely with the shah's secret police, the hated and feared SAVAK. And most Iranians assumed in 1979 that the Americans were doing everything they could to mount a counter-revolution.

In the spring of 1979, just after the revolution, the Carter administration had pulled its ambassador, William H. Sullivan, out of Tehran because he was so closely identified with the shah. So there was no ambassador, only a chargé d'affaires, in the Tehran embassy. The CIA maintained a small station with only four officers, and over the next few months the number of embassy personnel shrank from hundreds to fewer than eighty. None of the CIA officers had any experience with Iran—and, incredibly, not one spoke Farsi. Ironically, Mossad had better information about the new regime because they'd trained scores of SAVAK agents, some of whom had shed their military uniforms, let their beards grow, and joined the Revolutionary Guards.

That summer the State Department and the CIA tried to pry open a back channel to the regime. Prime Minister Bazargan had appointed his personal aide, Deputy Prime Minister Abbas Amir Entezam, to be the main liaison to the U.S. embassy. Bazargan wanted better relations with the Americans, and so with his express authority Entezam began meeting regularly with U.S. embassy officials. Entezam was a forty-six-year-old engineer and businessman who'd studied and worked in the United States. As a young man, he'd once delivered a letter of protest to the U.S. embassy in the wake of the 1953 coup. He was an Iranian patriot and dissident, a longtime member of the anti-shah National Resistance Movement, and by 1978 he was an ardent supporter of Khomeini as the figurehead of the revolution. And just coincidentally, Entezam had met Cave when the CIA officer was stationed in Tehran in the late 1950s. Cave hadn't recruited Entezam; the Iranian was not a paid asset. But Cave had known him and solicited his views about the Pahlavi regime. Cave had empathized. Unbeknownst to Entezam, the CIA had assigned him a cryptonym: SDPLOD/1. This would ruin his life, later turning him into revolutionary Iran's longest incarcerated political prisoner.

But in the spring of 1979, it made perfect sense to put Cave and Entezam back together again. And so it happened that the two men met in Stockholm on August 5 and 6. Entezam remembered Cave from their casual acquaintanceship years earlier. Cave explained that Washington wished to reestablish a friendly, working relationship with Tehran—and to that end he proposed that they set up a series of regular meetings in which Iranian officials could be briefed on various intelligence issues of interest to the revolutionary regime. Entezam agreed, and a briefing was scheduled for late August in Tehran.

Bob Ames was selected to give the first briefing. As NIO for the Near East, Ames was thought to have a broad overview. They also knew he was a good briefer. And, of course, he'd had some prior experience in Iran. He flew into Tehran from Paris, arriving on Air France Flight 168 at 10:00 P.M. on August 21, 1979. He carried with him a "courier letter" to protect his classified briefing papers—which typically would have been placed in a locked pouch chained to Ames's wrist. The courier letter under standard international diplomatic agreements exempted his bags and his person from any searches while passing through immigration control in Tehran. Ames was traveling under his own name on a diplomatic passport. But CIA cable traffic referred to him only by his Agency pseudonym, Orrin W. BIEDENKOPF. The next day he gave the briefing. Bruce Laingen, the U.S. embassy's chargé d'affaires, and Victor Tomseth, the embassy political officer, accompanied him to the meeting. The only Iranians in the room were Prime Minister Mehdi Bazargan, Foreign Minister Ibrahim Yazdi, and Entezam. Ames was told that his goal was to entice the Iranians into having regular briefings. In this he clearly succeeded. Scheduled for one hour, the briefing went on for a full two hours. Ames did not in this initial session convey any hard intelligence, but he gave the Iranians a summary of how Washington saw developments generally in the Middle East. Entezam had earlier requested information about external threats to the new regime. Ames mostly talked about developments in Iraq, Afghanistan, and the

Soviet Union. Bruce Riedel, the analyst with whom Ames was working in Washington, later explained that Ames was trying to disabuse Iranians of their long-standing suspicions of America's intentions. "Bob was basically trying to convince them that the *real* Great Satans were their neighbors in the region, the Soviet Union and Iraq." At the end of the two hours, Entezam said, "We hope your organization will improve its ties with us just as our countries are improving ties through the efforts of the Chargé [Laingen] and Dr. Yazdi." Entezam said this sitting next to Prime Minister Bazargan, who clearly understood English. Ames did not "reveal" his "RTACTION connection"—the code word for the CIA—but clearly everyone in the room understood that he was from the CIA. The meeting concluded with Bazargan stating that he "hoped similar briefings could be provided every two months." Entezam later told Cave that "they had considered" the briefing from the "NIO [Ames] as a good start."

Now that Ames had opened the channel, his job was basically done. But he lingered in Tehran for at least a few more days, trying to gauge the temper of the revolutionary regime. He managed to arrange an interview with Ayatollah Dr. Mohammed Beheshti, age fifty-one, a leading scholar and theologian who was deeply involved in writing the new constitution. This was the same Ayatollah Beheshti that Ames knew had been involved in the disappearance of Lebanon's revered Shi'a leader, Imam Musa Sadr. Ames had read the intelligence reports on Sadr's disappearance, reports that implicated Beheshti. So on every level he knew he was seeing a tough, formidable player in the Iranian revolution. Beheshti was a leading advocate of an Islamic republic and an ally of Ayatollah Khomeini's. "If Khomeini was the revolution's charismatic chairman of the board," said one Agency analyst, "Beheshti was the chief executive officer." But he was also a man who had lived in the West, having led the Islamic Center in Hamburg, Germany, for five years in the 1960s. As such, he was thought to be a little more cosmopolitan and erudite than most mullahs in the new regime. Nevertheless, he had Khomeini's ear and his respect. Beheshti had no idea that he was meeting with a CIA officer—one who was merely trying to educate himself by meeting an influential ayatollah. They met in early September, and soon afterwards Ames flew back to Washington.*

Six weeks later, in October 1979, George Cave, pseudo-named ADLESICK, came back to Tehran to convey to Foreign Minister Yazdi and Entezam some concrete military intelligence. Some analysts in the U.S. intelligence community had come to the conclusion the previous summer that neighboring Iraq might be preparing to invade Iran. Ames hadn't been authorized to convey this information in August, but now Cave came to Tehran with hard technical evidence that Iraq's Saddam Hussein was quietly positioning his vastly superior military forces in preparation for a full-scale invasion. The noted American scholar on Iranian history Mark Gasiorowski wrote about this intelligence mission: "Alarmed about the prospect of war between these two strategically important countries, [Undersecretary of State David Newsom] and presumably other top US officials decided the United States should provide intelligence on Iraq's activities to the Bazargan government so it could take steps to deter an invasion and thus prevent war from breaking out. An obvious way to do this was through the briefing series initiated by Robert Ames."

The Americans had an ulterior reason for conveying this warning to the revolutionary regime. To be sure, they wanted to establish some semblance of normalcy in their relations with the new people in control. But the CIA also wanted to persuade the provisional government in Tehran to reactivate two separate electronic surveillance systems. IBEX was an electronic system with ground-based listening posts that gathered intelligence from three C-130 aircraft flying along the Iran-Iraq border. The system could provide aerial photographs of Iraqi military movements up to seventy miles inside Iraq. In the chaos of the revolution, IBEX was no longer operational. Bazargan, Yazdi, and En-

* Ayatollah Beheshti was killed on June 28, 1981, along with some sixty other members of the Islamic Republic Party, in a bomb attack carried out by unknown opponents of the regime.

tezam had no knowledge of IBEX's existence, let alone its intelligence-gathering capabilities.

The other electronic surveillance system, Tacksman, was of special interest to the Americans because it could monitor Soviet missile tests. The CIA hoped that if it could prove the value of IBEX in providing Iran with hard military intelligence about Iraq, perhaps the new regime could also be enticed into reactivating the Tacksman missile-monitoring facilities. In 1979 the Cold War with the Soviet Union remained the Agency's number-one priority.

So on October 15, 1979, Cave gave another top-secret briefing. He bluntly told the Iranians that Iraq was preparing to invade. The Iranians were taken aback. "They wouldn't dare," Foreign Minister Yazdi exclaimed. Three days later, in another meeting with Yazdi, Cave patiently explained that if he was incredulous, he could reactivate the IBEX system and see the intelligence for himself. Yazdi and his boss, Prime Minister Bazargan, must have been swayed. The Americans were sharing hard intelligence. "We went to the degree of actually sitting down with them," said Chargé d'Affaires Bruce Laingen, "and giving them highly classified intelligence on Iraq." After Cave got back to Washington, he and Ames briefed CIA director Admiral Stansfield Turner on their Iranian missions.

By then, however, things in Tehran had rapidly deteriorated. On October 20, President Jimmy Carter very reluctantly decided to permit the exiled shah to come to New York to treat his cancer. Carter had been hounded for months by a lobbying campaign, code-named "Project Alpha," personally financed by David Rockefeller. Tens of thousands of dollars were spent on "Project Alpha." Rockefeller paid Chase Manhattan Bank employees and high-powered lawyers from Milbank, Tweed, Hadley & McCloy to pester Carter administration officials to give the shah political asylum. At one point First Lady Rosalynn Carter noted in her diary, "We can't get away from Iran. Many people—Kissinger, David Rockefeller, Howard Baker, John McCloy, Gerald Ford—all are after Jimmy to bring the shah to the United States, but Jimmy says it's been too long, and anti-American and anti-shah sentiments have escalated so that he doesn't want to. Jimmy said he explained to all of them that the Iranians might kidnap our Americans who are still there." The president's fears were all too prescient.

On October 22, 1979, the shah arrived in New York and checked into a hospital to treat his cancer. A few days later, millions of Iranians demonstrated in the streets of Tehran, protesting the shah's arrival in America. Khomeini incited the crowds with fiery statements, denouncing America and criticizing internal leftists and secularists. When several hundred students stormed the American embassy on November 4, 1979, and seized sixty-one American hostages, Khomeini praised the students. "Khomeini probably sensed that the Americans were trying to lure Iranians like Bazargan, Yazdi, and Entezam into a moderate path," said Bruce Riedel, the analyst who worked with Ames. "So when the students took over the embassy, this gave him the opportunity he needed to radicalize the situation." Two days later, Prime Minister Bazargan and his cabinet resigned. Khomeini had used the embassy seizure to purge his government of anyone critical of his vision of Iran as an Islamic theocracy.*

The hostage crisis created the pretext for Khomeini to tip political power into the hands of his mullahs. But it also destroyed the back channel created by Ames, Cave, and the CIA to Bazargan, Yazdi, and Entezam. Khomeini had not known about Ames's intelligence briefing. Neither did Khomeini know of the intelligence evidence conveyed by Cave that the Iraqis were planning an invasion. Ironically, the students who took over the American embassy found a treasure trove of thousands of classified documents—including CIA cables describing the Ames and Cave meetings with Bazargan, Yazdi, and Entezam. The classified documents—many painstakingly reconstructed from the bins of the embassy's shredding machines—were used to charge Entezam

---

* Iran's former president Mahmoud Ahmedinejad has admitted that he was one of five students who attended the first meeting to plan the embassy seizure. He claims he wanted to take over the Soviet embassy but was outvoted. Mark Bowden, *Guests of the Ayatollah: The First Battle in America's War with Militant Islam* (New York: Atlantic Monthly Press, 2006), p. 615.

with espionage. He was arrested in mid-December and eventually tried and sentenced to life in prison.* A number of CIA assets named in the documents were also arrested; Simon Farzami (SDTRAMP/1), a Jewish Iranian journalist, was executed by firing squad in December 1980. And Khosrow Qashqai (SDROTTER/4), a tribal leader, was publicly hanged in 1982.

In September 1980, as predicted by George Cave, Saddam Hussein's military launched a major invasion of Iran. The Iranians were caught completely unprepared and suffered major defeats and high casualties. The Iraq-Iran War quickly descended into brutal trench warfare and extensive use of chemical weapons. It slogged on until August 1988, by which time an estimated half a million soldiers on both sides had lost their lives. In the end, neither side gained anything.

"The tragic irony," writes Professor Gasiorowski, "is that the radical Islamists who seized the US embassy in early November [1979] did so in part because they thought US officials were plotting a coup or other nefarious activities there. In fact, US officials were warning Iran's government about Iraqi activities that culminated in the devastating invasion of September 1980."

In retrospect, there was probably nothing Ames, Cave, and the CIA could have done to change the course of this unfortunate history. Khomeini was determined to push moderates like Bazargan aside and forge a hard-line Islamic republic. He and his fellow revolutionaries were deeply suspicious of America and the West on both political and religious-cultural grounds. But Ames thought it had been worth the effort to try to keep a channel of communication open to a moderate faction of the revolutionary government.

Seven years later, on May 25, 1986, Cave boarded a chartered jet in Tel Aviv bound for Tehran on a secret mission. Accompanying him

---

* Entezam survived in prison until 1997, when he was released and then imprisoned again the following year for another eight years. He remains under virtual house arrest. In another irony, the students did *not* find Cave's memorandum in which he briefed Yazdi and Entezam about Iraq's invasion preparations. Cave had burned the embassy's copy after cabling it to Washington.

were the Reagan administration's national security adviser, Robert "Bud" McFarlane; Lt. Col. Oliver North; and an Israeli intelligence official, Amiran Nir. Their goal was to attempt to revive a back channel to a "moderate" faction of the revolutionary regime. Cave carried with him a chocolate cake made in a kosher bakery in Tel Aviv. The key-shaped cake was meant to symbolize their desire to unlock the door barring a resumption of American-Iranian relations. President Ronald Reagan authorized the trip; it was Cave's idea to bring the key-shaped cake. The mission, of course, was a failure. But it—and the cake—was a signature event of what became known as the Iran-Contra scandal.

CHAPTER TEN

Jimmy Carter
and Hostage America

Ham, they are crazy.

—*President Jimmy Carter to Hamilton Jordan, 1980*

The 444-day hostage crisis absorbed much of Ames's time. Throughout the last year of the Carter presidency, Iran was Ames's priority. As national intelligence officer (NIO) for the Near East, he was a key player in all the meetings concerning Iran and the hostages. His position as NIO gave him unique access. He was often the one individual in the room who had knowledge of both clandestine and analytical intelligence. His job title and his expertise made him a man very much in demand. Everyone realized that the Iranian revolution and the hostage crisis had taken the CIA by surprise. America was grappling with the consequences of a momentous intelligence failure. "The attacks on our embassy in Iran," said Ames's former mentor in the Agency, Dick Helms, "and the political infighting which brought on the taking of hostages were surprises born of an inadequate grasp of Ayatollah Khomeini's bigotry and zealotry.... As a country we must develop a far deeper knowledge of other peoples' culture, religion, politics than we possess today. Believe it or not, we are still essentially a provincial nation." Ames emphatically agreed.

In mid-December 1979, the ailing, cancer-stricken shah left the United States for a new haven of exile on the Isla Contadora in Panama. The Carter administration understandably believed the shah's presence in New York could only make the task of negotiating the release of the hostages that much more difficult. Sometime in early January 1980, Ames heard rumors that the White House had found a way to open secret negotiations with someone in the provisional revolutionary government in Tehran about freeing the hostages. Ames heard that Hamilton Jordan, the president's chief of staff, was the main conduit, and he thought he needed to be brought into the loop. So one day he called up Jordan and asked for a meeting. Jordan saw him right away in the White House and reluctantly revealed that two men— Christian Bourget, a Frenchman, and Héctor Villalón, an Argentinian businessman living in France—had arrived in Panama, ostensibly acting as emissaries of Iran, to request the shah's extradition. This was a formality; they knew there was no prospect that the Panamanians would execute the extradition. But then they revealed that they had another mission. They asked the Panamanian strongman Gen. Omar Torrijos to pass on a message to the White House: Iran's new foreign minister, Sadegh Ghotbzadeh, was interested in negotiating an end to the hostage crisis. But because he didn't trust the State Department, he wanted to meet with President Carter's friend and chief of staff. Jordan explained that the message had reached him and that the president had authorized him to see Ghotbzadeh. Jordan asked for Ames's advice. Did he think the politically embattled foreign minister had the clout to negotiate a release of the hostages? Was this worth pursuing? And could the CIA help arrange for any meeting to be kept out of the press? Ames explained that he hadn't met with Ghotbzadeh during his secret mission to Tehran the previous August, but he knew who the man was. He probably also explained that he'd interviewed Ayatollah Beheshti, the chairman of the Revolutionary Council, and noted that Beheshti had recently defended Ghotbzadeh when the student hostage takers had criticized the foreign minister. Ames promised to get Jordan some background intelligence on Ghotbzadeh, and Jordan promised to keep Ames in the loop. Jordan was encouraged.

Afterward, Ames assigned one of his deputies, Thomas C. Braman, to regularly check in with Jordan. Braman was delighted to get the opportunity to liaise with the White House. "This did two things," Braman later wrote. "It certainly made it quite clear to Jordan that his activities were known to the Agency, and it provided me with a personal, high-level contact who I could use in my own political dialogue between intelligence and operations officers within the Agency. A lesser officer than Bob would have kept the White House and Jordan to himself." Braman thought Ames was "the ultimate team player." Ames had brought Braman in the loop—but this did not mean that Ames cut off his dealings with Jordan.

Over the next few weeks, the CIA provided dossiers on Ghotbzadeh and his two intermediaries, Bourget and Villalón. On January 25, 1980, Jordan met with Bourget and Villalón in the White House. The two unofficial intermediaries had a plan, an intricately choreographed script that they believed would lead to the release of the hostages. First, the United Nations would create a commission of inquiry to review the historical grievances held by Iran against America. The Carter administration would criticize the idea but not block the creation of the commission. Second, the UN fact-finding commission would go to Iran and conduct a public investigation. The Iranian people would get a chance to vent. And finally, as Mark Bowden wrote in his history of the hostage crisis, *Guests of the Ayatollah*, "the commission would then have the moral authority in Iran to condemn the holding of hostages as 'un-Islamic.'" This would then give Ayatollah Khomeini the pretext he needed to order the hostages released. Jordan and others in the Carter administration were skeptical, but they thought it was worth a shot. A detailed schedule was created, delineating who would say what and when to get the charade started. But everyone agreed that this secret protocol had to be ratified by a face-to-face meeting between Ham Jordan and Foreign Minister Ghotbzadeh.

That settled, Jordan flew to Paris on the Concorde, arriving shortly after midnight on Sunday, February 17. He wore a disguise, presumably provided him by the CIA, which included a gray wig, a fake mustache, and glasses. Accompanied by a Foreign Service officer, Henry Precht, Jordan was driven to the Paris apartment of Héctor Villalón, where he met with Ghotbzadeh. The foreign minister reiterated that their meeting had to be kept highly secret. If there was a leak, he said, "First I would lose my job and then I would lose my head."

Jordan quickly got an inkling that things might not go as planned when Ghotbzadeh volunteered, not in jest, "It is easy to resolve the crisis. All you have to do is kill the shah." When an astonished Jordan said that was out of the question, Ghotbzadeh reassured him that the hostages would be released in a matter of weeks after the proposed UN commission did its work. Jordan and Ghotbzadeh came to a mutual understanding. Jordan returned to Washington, and the Carter administration announced that it would not oppose the creation of the commission. The UN commission soon began its work, and as if on script, Ayatollah Beheshti announced that he thought the commission would end the hostage crisis soon. The plan seemed to be working—until Ayatollah Khomeini gave one of his mercurial speeches and announced that the crisis would be resolved only after the election of a national *majlis* (parliament). Clearly, Ghotbzadeh did not have the backing of his ayatollah. An angry President Carter told his chief of staff, "Ham, they are crazy." Ames had had a front-row seat to the disappointing spectacle.*

Ames usually saw CIA director Admiral Stansfield Turner at least once a week. A graduate of Amherst College and a Rhodes Scholar, Admiral Turner was not popular with the clandestine division. A Christian Scientist, he never touched coffee or tea, let alone Scotch. He valued signal intelligence over human intelligence—and in 1978–79 he fired 825 clandestine officers on grounds of incompetence. Ames didn't share Turner's politics or worldview. "Bob like myself was a problem-solver, not an ideologue," observed David Long, one of his friends. "So

---

* Ghotbzadeh was arrested in April 1982 and later convicted of treason. On September 15, 1982, he was executed by a firing squad. Khomeini personally approved the execution. The revolution was eating its own children.

when we talked politics it was mainly about foreign policies, not partisan domestic politics. Both Carter and Reagan made some very excellent policy decisions and some really idiotic policy decisions. We both agreed that Carter's moralistic dislike for dirty tricks was detrimental to CIA, particularly in making Stansfield Turner the DCI [director of central intelligence]. But then, James Schlesinger as DCI under Nixon was probably worse."

Turner nevertheless admired Bob Ames and trusted his judgment. He signed promotion orders for Ames twice during his tenure, initially awarding him a rank of GS-16. Then in 1980 he elevated Ames to the elite Senior Intelligence Service (SIS) with a rank of SIS-3. This made Ames the equivalent of a one-star army general.

Ames got along with the admiral, but he was frustrated by the Carter administration's performance. Carter and his team were too often tentative and overly cautious. On the other hand, Ames admired the president's determination to get a deal done on the Camp David Accords. Bob worked many long hours, preparing the CIA's briefing book for the Camp David meetings. He was later told that Carter thought his "assessments of both Begin and Sadat were right on target."

Throughout 1979 and 1980, Ames regularly saw President Carter's Middle East man on the National Security Council, Ambassador Robert Hunter (a savvy foreign policy analyst who'd once worked for Senator Edward Kennedy). Hunter rapidly came to trust his judgment. "It was one-stop shopping," Hunter said. "I would call him up once a day, and it was all I needed to know. He could talk off the top of his head about the succession battles inside the Saudi royal family, or what was going on inside the revolutionary regime in Tehran. He knew all the intricacies. And I could trust that he was also keeping me abreast of the differences, the arguments going on inside the intelligence community. He never cooked anything. He was the most effective intelligence officer I ever encountered."

When the Soviet Union invaded Afghanistan in late December 1979, Ambassador Hunter and Ames worked together to draft a response for

President Carter to deliver in his January 23, 1980, State of the Union address. It became known as the "Carter Doctrine," and Hunter says that Ames contributed heavily to the language in the speech, but the key sentence was probably drafted by Carter's national security adviser, Zbigniew Brzezinski: "Let our position be absolutely clear: An attempt by any outside force to gain control of the Persian Gulf region will be regarded as an assault on the vital interests of the United States of America, and such an assault will be repelled by any means necessary, including military force."

Ames, the longtime clandestine officer, relished the opportunity to help make policy. But in retrospect, the Carter Doctrine seems a Cold War relic. Its purpose was to warn the Soviets not to threaten America's oil shipments through the Straits of Hormuz. It was all about oil. But the Carter administration also began a major covert operation to supply weapons to the Afghani mujahedeen. The program grew rapidly and would eventually succeed in forcing the Soviets out of Afghanistan. (That, of course, only served to usher into power a highly reactionary Taliban regime—one allied to a little-known Islamist Salafist group of dedicated terrorists calling themselves Al-Qaeda. But this particular blowback was far in the future.)

■

One day in the early spring of 1980, one of Ames's two principal deputies, Robert Earl, walked into Bob's office and said he'd heard rumors about a possible rescue mission. It was just "noise," but Earl thought something was going on. Ames knew he wasn't authorized to brief Earl on the rescue mission. "In order to preserve operational security," Earl realized later, "Ames gently deflected me. He just turned the conversation to something else. Only later did I realize that Ames had helped plan the failed Desert One rescue mission. He was one of the few Agency people who were cleared for Desert One." The rescue mission, of course, was a disastrous failure, and eight U.S. servicemen were killed when one of the eight helicopters brushed against a C-130 transport plane at the landing site inside Iran and exploded. An official investigation later blamed the debacle on poor operational coordination between the various branches of the armed services involved in the mission. But the inherent complexity of the plan probably doomed it to failure. "The effort relied very heavily on the CIA," said a State Department official. Ames was, of course, bitterly disappointed. Working through Mustafa Zein, however, he arranged for Arafat to use his contacts in Tehran to obtain the bodies of the eight U.S. servicemen. This was but a small consolation. President Carter believed the debacle heavily contributed to his electoral defeat in November 1980.

One of Ames's responsibilities as NIO was to get a consensus on each National Intelligence Estimate, an official report that goes to the president and his advisers. "Getting everybody to agree on an estimate was very hard," recalled Robert Earl. "But Bob was adept at getting some kind of consensus." Ames prided himself on his ability to write a succinct memorandum. Invariably, he'd personally write any portion of an estimate that was particularly troublesome or controversial. "He always wanted to hear people's views," said CIA analyst *Lindsay Sherwin*. "He was very good at getting experts around a table and getting them to speak their minds without any being intimidated. And by the end of the meeting he'd have produced a synthesis, hashing it out." He could do this because he never made people bristle, even when he was making a strong argument. "Bob didn't have a hard edge to him," said Robert Hunter.

As NIO, Ames was called more than once to testify on Capitol Hill before the House and Senate Intelligence Oversight Committees. But these sessions were always behind closed doors, and his testimony remains classified. Fred Hitz, the Agency's chief legislative counsel, was the Agency lawyer who helped Ames prepare his testimony on each of these occasions. Ames was well aware of how Dick Helms had perjured himself before Congress; it was a thin line. He had to know exactly how much to divulge to the legislators and how to say it. "He was much in demand," recalled Hitz. "He was very judicious. And he always managed to leave a strong impression of how tough the neighborhood was in the Middle East."

Ames's job as NIO also required him for the first time to liaise with his Israeli counterparts. They knew who he was—the man who'd created the back channel to the PLO—so they were curious to meet him. "I liked Bob enormously," recalled *Dov Zeit*, a senior Israeli intelligence officer. *Zeit*'s job in Mossad was to handle liaison relationships with foreign intelligence agencies. "Ames sought the company of revolutionaries," *Zeit* observed. "He sought out people who were going to change things. He was looking for the avant-garde." *Zeit* thought this was perfectly rational for an intelligence officer. But *Zeit* also sensed that this American spy understood the Israeli predicament: "Bob's sympathy for Israel came from his being simply decent."

By official agreement, Israel and the United States had for some years agreed to share intelligence. As part of this arrangement, a team of their respective intelligence officers would meet twice a year. The liaison meetings would alternate between Tel Aviv and Washington. "I traveled to Israel with him," recalled Bruce Riedel, a top analyst, "on his first official meeting with Mossad. The Israelis were very eager to meet this guy."

It was an awkward moment. But Ames was blunt. According to Robert Hunter, Ames spoke plainly to the Israelis. He came right out and said that killing Salameh had been a mistake. Ames told them, "Our need was greater than yours." The Israelis at the table disagreed, but they admired the chutzpah of the man and his directness. "The Israelis respected him," Hunter said. "He won their confidence." Ames had always loved a good argument, and not surprisingly, he found it exhilarating to sup and drink with Mossad officers. They were his adversaries, but they were smart adversaries. "Bob enjoyed sparring with the Israelis," said Graham Fuller. "It was like going into the belly of the beast." He was very straightforward with them. "After the Camp David Accords," said *Lindsay Sherwin*, "he told the Israelis that Egypt was now off the table. There would be no more intelligence sharing on the subject of Egypt. He could be very tough."

The Israelis had a real problem working with CIA Arabists, and the feeling was mutual. "Other than on the subject of terrorism," said *John Morris*, a clandestine officer who knew Ames well, "the Israelis have the least understanding of the broader issues and trends in the Arab world. It's surprising, since it is their neighborhood, but they just don't get it." During one of his trips to Tel Aviv, Ames was taken to a Jaffa restaurant by his Mossad counterparts. "Somehow the conversation turned ugly," said Bob Layton, an analyst who was then his deputy. "Ames got mad when one of the Israelis brashly asserted that his analysts were tilting their estimates to fit Washington's political priorities. Ames strongly chided the Israeli: 'Professionals don't accuse other professionals of cooking their intelligence.'"

Yoram Hessel, a senior Mossad officer, confirmed the story. "I was most certainly there," Hessel said. "It sounds like me." Hessel had goaded Ames into an argument, but he was nevertheless drawn to the man. "Bob was a towering, handsome man," Hessel recalled, "and he was treated with awe. He could speak out of line. He knew he was special. What endeared him to us was that he was a storyteller. He had tidbits of gossip to share. You knew that when Bob Ames came to town you would have entertainment. He had this flair. He was an American Lawrence, a Lawrence with Stars and Stripes. He was making himself into a legend." Hessel had dealt with Ames in 1978–79 when Bob was the NIO for the Near East. And he also saw him when Ames became head of the Directorate of Intelligence for the Near East. He liked Ames. But Hessel also thought Ames's expertise came with considerable baggage. "Empathy in intelligence can be dangerous," Hessel said. "An intelligence officer is not an advocate. When Ames came to Tel Aviv, his job was to listen—and to see if what he knew measured up to reality. But he was clearly emotionally involved with the Arab world. We were always aware that he was presenting things through a certain lens. We didn't see him as an adversary—but he certainly came from a different place."

Ames didn't often blow up. It was uncharacteristic. "But he understood that you do not make any inroads with the Israelis by being meek and mild," said Bob Layton. "They are not meek and mild among themselves. You could have a blowup at them and the next day everything would be okay. Still, the Israelis were perplexed on how to deal with him. They knew he had contacts on the policy side—and they knew all about his clandestine career. Ames didn't come across as a proselytizer, but he could be outspoken and he knew his shit. Anyone with a head on his shoulders would have known that he knew what he was talking about."

Uri Oppenheim, who spent a decade abroad as a clandestine officer and then worked for twenty-one years in Mossad's research division, saw Ames regularly in their twice-yearly liaison meetings. Typically, Ames might arrive in Tel Aviv with a dozen CIA officers in tow and they'd sit down with two dozen Mossad officers. "We were told," recalled one Mossad officer, "don't crack jokes in Arabic because he knows Arabic." Ames stood out. "He could tell stories," *Oppenheim* recalled, "but he wasn't a *schvitzer*—a boaster. Bob was a smiling personality." Another Mossad officer remarked that Ames seemed sympathetic to Israeli constraints: "We wouldn't be getting moralizing from Bob Ames. He understood what the traffic would bear."

Ames had a sense of humor tinged with sarcasm about the Agency's bureaucracy. "I remember one day he called me into his office," recalled *John Morris,* "and read aloud a portion of the performance report he was writing about me: 'The subject is the second-best writer in the division.' I laughed, because I knew he meant that he was the best writer." *Bill Fisk* first met Ames during the 1976 Beirut evacuation, right after the ambassador had been killed. "Bob had incredible gravitas," recalled *Fisk.* "But I had heard that as a young man he had been a throat-cutter and back-stabber. The Agency was a terribly competitive place and he was very ambitious. But once he established himself, he wasn't afraid to manage up and protect his people below him."

And while he was now at an elevated position within the Agency, briefing policy makers and testifying on the Hill, he still kept his hand in the clandestine. "He really didn't want to give up being an operations officer," recalled *Lindsay Sherwin*. "He was always out of town, seeing his sources. We joked with him that he was always away when there was a crisis.... He would imply he was in New York, but he wasn't. I just assumed he was maintaining relationships with people he had recruited."

He was juggling a lot of issues. When the Iran-Iraq War broke out, Ames was slightly incredulous. "He was very reluctant to believe that Iran and Iraq would be so stupid as to go to war," recalled *Sherwin*. But when it happened in September 1980, "We had to switch a lot of our assets to that battlefield."

In 1980, Ames was still a Republican. And he was delighted when Ronald Reagan selected George H. W. Bush as his vice-presidential nominee. Like most clandestine officers, Ames had admired Bush's handling of himself as director of the CIA under President Ford. Naturally, Ames hoped the Republican ticket would prevail that autumn. At the same time, he'd been working throughout that election year to resolve the Iranian hostage crisis, both through the aborted Desert One rescue mission that spring and later through a negotiated release of the hostages. By the summer of 1980, everyone in Washington understood that President Carter's reelection chances might well hinge on a successful, last-minute resolution of the hostage crisis. Reagan campaign strategists feared their candidate's rising prospects could be derailed by an "October surprise"—a sudden and dramatic release of all the hostages.

Ames knew that Yasir Arafat and the PLO had an open channel to the revolutionary regime in Tehran. Arafat had sent arms and men to aid in the revolution, and he'd flown to see Khomeini soon after the ayatollah's return to Iran. Arafat had also brokered the initial release of thirteen of the American hostages—all women or African Americans—in late November 1979. And that spring he'd helped the Americans retrieve the bodies of their eight servicemen killed at Desert One. Obviously, the PLO represented a potential channel of negotiations. Further, Arafat had every reason to believe that if he was successful in playing some part in obtaining the release of the remaining hostages, this intervention might open a door to Washington's recognition of the PLO.

Ames knew from his meetings that summer with the ubiquitous Mustafa Zein that Arafat was indeed trying to use his influence in Iran to solve the hostage crisis. Ames and his counterpart in the NSC, Robert Hunter, told Zein that he should do whatever he could to encourage Arafat. Ames and Hunter met with Zein more than once in the Old Executive Office Building next to the White House and briefed him on the administration's various diplomatic efforts to release the hostages. Zein understood perfectly the importance of this back channel to both the Carter administration and the PLO.

But early that summer, Zein stumbled onto what appeared to be an effort by the Reagan campaign to undermine these diplomatic efforts. As it happened, an old friend from his Naperville days, the Rev. Milo J. Vondracek, paid Zein a visit in New York. His friend encouraged Zein to look up his son, Jon Vondracek, who was then working at the Center for Strategic and International Studies (CSIS), a well-known think tank in Washington, D.C. A few weeks later, Zein happened to be in Washington to see Ames and Hunter. Afterwards, Zein had lunch with Jon Vondracek—whom he'd known from his time in Naperville—and mentioned that he'd again been to the Old Executive Office Building. The very next day Jon called Mustafa and encouraged him to meet with a friend of his who was working on the Reagan campaign. Zein asked why and was told, "This man [Jack Shaw] is slated to take over the job of Bob Hunter in the NSC if the Republican ticket wins the election." Zein's curiosity was naturally aroused, so he agreed to the meeting.

Soon afterwards, Zein met Shaw, age forty-one, for a casual lunch at a restaurant in downtown Washington. The two men began their conversation by discussing the Middle East in general terms. Shaw had served as an assistant secretary of state in the Ford administration. More recently, he'd been a vice president at Booz Allen & Hamilton International, overseeing lucrative contracts in Saudi Arabia. In 1980, he was a senior fellow at the Center for Strategic and International Studies—where Jon Vondracek was a friend and colleague. Coincidentally, Shaw had also met Bob Ames at a seminar on the Middle East sponsored by the CSIS. That year Shaw was also raising money for the Reagan presidential campaign and working with Reagan's campaign manager, William Casey. Zein recalls that he and Shaw discussed the ongoing hostage crisis—a topic that was still dominating the headlines that summer. When Zein volunteered that the Palestinians were trying to do everything they could to defuse the crisis, Shaw said that he thought the Palestinians would be better off with Reagan than Carter. As the conversation ended, Shaw invited Zein to come to his house the next day for lunch. Zein agreed, but he sensed that Shaw was going to pitch something to him. So the next day when Zein showed up at Shaw's home in a Washington suburb, he brought with him the small leather briefcase that Ames had given Ali Hassan Salameh several years earlier. This was the briefcase that contained a hidden tape recorder. Zein says that he recorded their entire luncheon conversation.

The two men sat down to a lunch of chicken and vegetables prepared by Shaw's Spanish-speaking maid. Shaw told Zein that he knew Casey well. And then he asked how Zein knew Bob Ames. Zein had nothing to hide, and he explained that he'd known Ames for more than a decade. "He confirmed to me that Casey knew about my special relation with Ames," Zein recalled. Shaw indicated that he knew from Casey that Zein was Ames's back channel to Arafat. Shaw then turned the conversation to the PLO and Arafat's relationship with the revolutionary regime in Iran. Shaw made it clear that he was aware of Arafat's role in obtaining the release of the thirteen American hostages the previous autumn. According to Zein, Shaw then asked if Arafat was still trying to secure the freedom of the remaining hostages. When Zein confirmed this, Shaw bluntly asked if Arafat could be persuaded to delay his efforts until the election was over. He argued that the "Palestinian interest lay with a strong president, like Reagan, who would push for a just and lasting peace in the Middle East." Zein asked Shaw if he wanted him to carry this message to Arafat. Did he want Zein to tell Arafat to delay his efforts until after the election? Shaw answered, "Yes." Zein promised to do so right away.

Thirty-three years later, Shaw says he has "no recollection" of the luncheon with Zein. "I wouldn't contest that such a meeting took place," Shaw said. "I know I had luncheons at that stage of the game with all sorts of people, and Jon Vondracek was a good friend who introduced me to a lot of people." But Shaw suggests that Zein misunderstood; he says he was merely voicing his personal opinion that the Palestinians would be better off with Reagan. A strong president, he said, would be more likely to bring about a real peace in the Middle East. "It is altogether possible that I would tell Zein this; it reflected my thinking at the time." But he says Bill Casey certainly didn't ask him to convey a message to Arafat, and he recalls no discussion about the hostages. "Most of my involvement with Casey that summer was purely political, talking about the campaign. I don't remember talking to Casey about the Middle East. He may certainly have known about my Middle East interests, but we didn't talk about it." But, Shaw admits, "Casey was famous for working indirectly, and I may have conveyed the message the way you described. . . . I know I was not approached directly by Casey on this, but his modus operandi was to bounce the cue ball off several billiard balls to get a job done without his fingerprints on it."

Zein insists that they talked about the hostages and persuading Arafat to suspend his efforts to get them released. Zein says he'd just come from Beirut two weeks earlier, and he was not about to fly back there on short notice to see Arafat without ascertaining that Shaw was indeed working for Casey. He wanted to be able to tell Arafat that Shaw's message was "an official request from Casey." So, soon after his lunch with Shaw, Zein looked up John Shaheen, who'd be-friended Casey when the two had worked for the Office of Strategic Services (OSS) during World War II. Shaheen was an American citizen of Lebanese ancestry who'd gone into the oil business. Casey had been one of his business partners—and Zein had met both Casey and Sha-heen earlier in the 1970s when the two men needed advice on a busi-ness proposition in the Gulf. "Shaheen confirmed to me," Zein said, "after speaking directly with Casey, that Jack Shaw was represent-ing Casey." Zein remembers that the meeting with Shaheen cost him $15,000 because Shaheen took the opportunity to solicit that amount as a campaign contribution to John Anderson's presidential campaign. (Arafat later reimbursed him for this "expense.")

In August 1980, just a few days after his meeting with Shaheen, Zein flew back to Beirut and told Arafat what this "representative of Casey" had said. He played the audiotape for Arafat. When the PLO chairman asked for Zein's advice, Mustafa wrote him a memo: "Dou-ble your efforts to release the hostages because the coming administra-tion, if the Republican ticket wins, has a devil in it. Reagan and Bush are decent men, but the maestro who is conducting the orchestra . . . cannot be trusted." But a short time later, Arafat told Zein that he'd learned from the Iranians that they'd struck a deal directly with Casey in a meeting in Spain in late July. Arafat told Zein that he should go back to Casey's man, Jack Shaw, and make him believe that the PLO was doing what he'd asked. "We wanted to earn some brownie points," Zein said, "just in case Reagan won the election." So after spending a week in Beirut, Zein headed back to Washington, where he met again with Shaw and told him the "good news": Arafat was going to hold off on his efforts to release the hostages.

Zein's story, of course, is highly conspiratorial. He insists that both the tapes and the transcripts of his conversations with Shaw and Sha-heen are stored in the PLO's archives in Tunis. But these documents have yet to be released. Shaheen died of cancer in 1985. Jon Vondracek died in 2005. And Shaw insists that whatever he may have told Zein was simply his own opinion, unprompted by Casey.

Over the past few decades numerous investigative journalists have written about a rumored meeting Casey had in Spain with a representative of Ayatollah Khomeini in July 1980. Two books have been published about the alleged October surprise. But over the years, the investigations petered out. Congress looked into the allegations against Casey and came to an inconclusive judgment. Zein says that he never told Ames about his taped conversation with Jack Shaw.* But he always thought Bob had suspected something. Bob once asked Mustafa if he thought there was going to be a last-minute release of the hostages, and Mustafa told him no.

Reagan, of course, won the election handily. He probably would have won even if there *had* been an October surprise. But perhaps Bill Casey was determined not to be surprised. Interestingly, Arafat later discussed the October surprise overtures with former president Jimmy Carter. The noted presidential historian Douglas Brinkley was present at the January 22, 1996, meeting between Carter and Arafat in Gaza City. According to Brinkley's notes, Arafat told Carter, "Mr. President, there is something I want to tell you. You should know that in 1980 the Republicans approached me with an arms deal if I could arrange to keep the hostages in Iran until after the election. I want you to know that I turned them down."

■

Like many clandestine officers, Bob Ames had a low opinion of Admiral Turner's tenure as President Carter's DCI. But the admiral nevertheless admired Ames's talents. A month before the 1980 presidential election, on Saturday, October 4, Admiral Turner took Ames with him to Middleburg, Virginia, to brief the Republican presidential candidate on Middle East issues. Ex-governor Ronald Reagan was staying for a few days at Wexford, a beautiful horse farm outside Middleburg

---

* Jack Shaw was not appointed to the NSC. The Middle East slot on the NSC went to Geoffrey Kemp. But Shaw briefly became the Reagan White House's liaison to the State Department, working under the president's chief of staff, Judge William Clark.

once owned by Jack and Jackie Kennedy. When they arrived, Turner, Ames, and two other CIA officers were taken into the large living room, where they were introduced to Reagan and his advisers. These included George Bush, legal counsel Edwin Meese, campaign director William Casey, and Richard Allen, then Reagan's adviser on national security issues. One of the participants in the session later described it as a "chaotic movie set" with chairs scattered about the room and various campaign staff constantly walking through the room. It was a noisy "circus."

Ames led the briefing with a short survey on the internal politics of Saudi Arabia and Iran. Admiral Turner talked about international oil supplies, and another officer gave an overview of developments in the Iran-Iraq War, which had broken out a month earlier when Saddam Hussein ordered an invasion of southern Iran. Afterwards, Reagan asked a few simple questions. Richard Allen made Admiral Turner uncomfortable by asking pointedly if the CIA was supplying arms to the insurgents fighting Soviet forces in Afghanistan. (The Soviet Union had invaded Afghanistan on Christmas Eve, 1979.) Turner gave him a vague answer. "The Afghan story had not yet leaked," Turner later said, "and we were scared about Pakistan's position."

The session lasted just one hour. Curiously, no one bothered to ask about the American hostages in Iran. The next day, the same briefing was given to independent presidential candidate John Anderson—who took Turner aside at one point and mentioned that he'd recently been approached by an Iranian intermediary who had suggested that perhaps the American hostages could be released in exchange for weapons Iran could use in its war with Iraq. Turner informed the State Department, but no one seems to have investigated this overture to Anderson.

After Reagan defeated President Carter, the CIA came back to brief the president-elect. The subject was again the Middle East, but this time Turner was accompanied by Martha Neff Kessler, an assistant

NIO for the Near East and South Asia Division. Kessler had joined the Agency in 1970 and had risen rapidly in the Directorate of Intelligence. She was an analyst, not a clandestine officer. She was an expert on Libya and Syria, but her real specialty was the general Arab-Israeli conflict. She went to work for Ames in the autumn of 1978, right after he was named national intelligence officer.

On November 19, 1980, Turner and Kessler met with Reagan and his staff around a dining-room table at his prepresidential headquarters on Jackson Place, near the White House. After the briefing, Reagan asked quite a few questions about the Golan Heights, Syria, and Palestinian politics. At one point, Turner was taken aback when the president-elect asked in all earnestness, "What is the biblical name for the Golan Heights?" He hadn't expected this query and had no idea how to answer this Sunday Bible-study quiz. At one point, Kessler ventured, "We could lose Sadat." This was a risky thing for a CIA analyst to say. Reagan responded, "What do you mean, 'lose Sadat'?" Kessler explained that Egypt was not invulnerable to the Middle East's general instability. Sadat, she said, could be overthrown just like the shah—or assassinated. (Less than a year later, Kessler's speculations proved prophetic with Sadat's assassination by a radical Islamist cell within the Egyptian army.)

Ames, Kessler, and other CIA briefers did not buy into the press's notion that Reagan was disconnected. But it became clear that the new president grasped information anecdotally. "You can't capture his attention," Ames told a friend, "for more than three or four minutes before he interrupts you with an anecdote." The president-elect also had certain preconceived convictions coming into office. "The problem with Ronald Reagan was that his ideas were all fixed—he was an old dog," said Peter Dixon Davis, a CIA analyst. His ideas about anything to do with the Palestinians were set in concrete. At some point prior to the inauguration, the CIA produced a memorandum to try to bring the prospective president up to speed about the Palestinian conundrum. It was complicated. The memo tried to explain the different factions within the Palestinian movement for self-determination—the radical rejectionists, the emerging consensus among those willing to settle for something like a two-state solution, and the crazy nihilists like Abu Nidal, who was from time to time assassinating any Palestinian showing any hint of a willingness to compromise with the Israelis. Reagan read the memorandum "very slowly and thoughtfully," recalled Dixon Davis. "He must have taken ten minutes. At the end he said, 'But they are all terrorists, aren't they?' My heart just sank."

CHAPTER ELEVEN

Bill Casey
and Ronald Reagan

I liked Casey. He was nuts.

—*Clair George*

When Bill Casey walked into Langley headquarters on January 28, 1981, he found himself in charge of a highly demoralized intelligence agency. Because of the personnel cuts under both Schlesinger and Admiral Turner, the CIA had shrunk to about fourteen thousand personnel with a budget of about $6 billion. "With the people fired, driven out or lured into retirement," complained Robert Gates, who'd served as Turner's executive assistant, "half our analysts had less than five years' experience. And our analysis wasn't at all sharp, forward looking or relevant. Our paramilitary capability was clinically dead. What covert action we did carry out was super-cautious and lacked any imagination." The Agency, Gates, concluded, "was hunkered down in a defensive crouch."

Ames was one of those officers who felt very skeptical about the Agency's mission. He was frustrated, gloomy, and cynical. "He was not happy with his career," said *Lindsay Sherwin*. "He said no one leaves the Agency feeling good about their career." He morbidly told one of his best friends, Bob Headley, another CIA officer, "When we're gone, they'll pass the hat for us and that will be that." Ames worried about his family finances. He hired a financial consultant, who bluntly told him that if he intended to send all six of his children to college, he was going to have to quit the government and get a job in the private sector. He told a friend that he'd stay in the Agency until 1984, when he'd turn fifty and be eligible for early retirement. He'd then leave to make some real money.

Before cleaning out his desk at the National Security Council (NSC), Robert Hunter called his successor, Geoffrey Kemp—who was slated to take over the Middle East portfolio—and told him, "Look, I just want you to know that I think Bob Ames is the most knowledgeable fellow they have at Langley on the Middle East. He is really terrific." In early February 1981, Ames came by with Chuck Cogan to introduce himself to Kemp. (Cogan was then chief of the Near East and South Asia Division in the Directorate of Operations.)

Soon after this White House encounter, Casey asked to see Ames. It was one of his earliest meetings. Casey had heard a bit about Ames's exploits as a case officer, and he wanted to take the measure of the man. Ames was at his most empathetic. He knew what Casey wanted to hear. So when Casey asked why America seemed to have so many enemies in the Middle East, Ames told his story about befriending the young South Yemeni revolutionary Abd'al Fatah Ismail, who had been trained by the Soviets and had later become head of the Marxist regime in Aden. As Casey later remembered it, Ames emphasized that in the Middle East the Soviet strategy was to undermine traditional values: "This meant undermining the influence of religion." The story, emphasizing the Soviet Union's meddling in the Middle East, struck a chord with Casey. Henceforth, Casey relied on Ames for all things Middle Eastern.

Casey was also drawn to Ames because he was an operations guy who'd made the transition to analysis. Casey wanted to break down the segregation between the Directorates of Intelligence and Operations, and Ames seemed to be a model for this new kind of officer. Ames was an experienced clandestine case officer, but he was also an articulate briefer. And Casey needed articulate people around him precisely because he was notoriously inarticulate. He was a mumbler. Early in

1981 Casey was briefing President Reagan in the White House. After the CIA director droned on at some length, Reagan quietly handed his aide Mike Deaver a note: "Did you understand a word he said?" Deaver later recalled, "It was a relief when Casey was traveling and his deputy would come to the White House instead. We'd actually know what was going on." Secretary of State George Shultz later observed of Casey, "People said he was the one guy in Washington who didn't need a secure phone to scramble."

Ames didn't know what to make of Casey. At first glance, the man was an odd choice for director of central intelligence. Sure, everyone knew he'd done stellar work in the OSS—but that was forty years ago. Casey had spent all those years making money on Wall Street and working for conservative Republicans. He was worth nearly $10 million in 1981 dollars. And he was very conservative—some might say an ideologue. But everyone agreed he was smart. John Bross, a clandestine officer dating back to the Agency's founding, thought Casey was "capable of great kindness and great ruthlessness." Dick Helms called him a "conniver." "I liked Casey," said Clair George. "He was nuts."

Casey had certitudes and an ironclad worldview. He wanted his analysts to see the world as black or white, not as wishy-washy gray: "I hate these iffy conclusions. . . . I'm not looking for consensus." He welcomed high technology as a tool, but he knew that satellite pictures and intercept intelligence rarely revealed anything about your adversary's intentions. "Facts can confuse," Casey said. "The wrong picture is not worth a thousand words."

In early April 1981 Ames accompanied Casey on a trip to Rabat, Cairo, Amman, and Tel Aviv. They flew into Tel Aviv with Secretary of State Alexander Haig. The Israelis didn't know what to make of Casey, partly because he was incomprehensible. "At the end of one meeting," recalled a senior Mossad officer, Yoram Hessel, "the note taker asked me what the hell he had said."

It was an exhausting trip. In Cairo, Casey ran out of books. Like

Ames, he was a voracious reader. One Friday afternoon after a post-lunch nap, Casey announced that he wanted to visit a Cairo bookstore. "Off we went through the streets of Heliopolis," recalled Charles Englehart, the deputy chief of station at the time. Arriving at the bookstore, they found it closed for Friday prayers. But an Egyptian security officer bounded up the steps and pounded on the door. "Soon a disheveled Egyptian appeared," recalled Englehart, "suitably terrified, and came down with the keys and opened the bookstore. Casey browsed a bit and picked out two books on Egypt." Casey was trouble.

In Tel Aviv, they met with Mossad's chief at the time, Maj. Gen. Yitzhak Hofi. Casey explained to Hofi that the Reagan administration was anxious to sell $8.5 billion worth of AWACS surveillance airplanes to Saudi Arabia. Naturally, the Israelis were uneasy about the Saudis' acquiring such sophisticated technology. Casey bluntly asked Hofi what he could do to have Tel Aviv turn down the dial on its lobbying against the AWACS deal in Congress. Hofi responded that they could use some satellite intelligence on Iraq's Osirak nuclear energy reactor. A deal was made, and two months later, on June 7, 1981, Israeli jets bombed the reactor.

On the way back to Washington, Casey and Ames had a layover in Madrid. The next morning, Ames had breakfast with Geoffrey Kemp, the NSC staffer for Middle Eastern affairs. They poured out their frustrations to each other. "One real problem of this trip," Kemp wrote in his diary, "is the failure of the principals to brief line staff—thus Ames goes to Rabat to meet Casey with very little background from [Secretary of State Al] Haig. No wonder this government gets its messages crossed. No one spends the time or effort to communicate. According to Ames, NEA [the State Department] can't stand CIA. Ergo, [the State Department] doesn't pass info to Ames. Ergo, Haig doesn't brief Casey. Ergo, Casey may say very different things than Haig. Ergo, trouble."

By then, Reagan insiders had nicknamed Haig "the Vicar." And everyone in Langley headquarters thought Haig was trying to cut the CIA out of the policy loop. Gradually, Casey came to rely on Ames to make sure that didn't happen.

Late in May 1981 Bob went back to Israel for more meetings with his Mossad contacts. Unusually, Yvonne joined him in Israel. She took a separate flight to Tel Aviv on May 30, 1981, and joined Bob there in his hotel. They'd visited Jerusalem together in 1966, driving in from Damascus, but Yvonne wanted to see the Holy City again. It was a quick and uneventful trip. They saw the major tourist sights in the Old City. Yvonne then returned to Washington on June 4, while Bob stayed a little longer to meet with his Mossad counterparts. Just before leaving for Israel, Bob thought it had come time to tell his oldest child, Cathy, about his true employment. Cathy had just turned twenty years old and was attending a local college but living at home. None of the children had known Bob was a clandestine officer for the CIA. They had all thought he worked for the State Department. It was a small but necessary subterfuge. The previous year Bob had arranged for Cathy to have a summer internship at the State Department, so he drove her every day into downtown Washington, dropped her off, and pretended to go to an office in the State Department—when actually he had to turn around and drive back to Langley. So the news came as a surprise to Cathy. "Children sense that there is something going on that shouldn't be talked about," said *Meir Harel*, a former Mossad director general who'd known Ames. "They learn not to ask too many questions. But on the other hand, they may also learn not to share their emotions." This Mossad officer was speaking about his experience with his own children. But it may be true in some sense for all children whose fathers lead a life in intelligence.

The five other Ames children were never told. They didn't need to know, but if something happened to Bob and Yvonne on this trip in the summer of 1981, at least Cathy would know where to turn for help.

With a new administration, Ames had hoped he might be given the chance to run the Near East Division for Operations. But to his bitter disappointment he was passed over. He was told that he was "too intellectual" for the job. He resented this and thought it ridiculous that being "intellectual" was a disqualification rather than an asset. He'd excelled in the clandestine work of the Directorate of Operations. Those in the know realized that he'd penetrated the PLO, creating at least two high-level sources—Ali Hassan Salameh and Basil al-Kubaisi. But most DO officers would have known these two individuals only by their "crypts" and not by their names. And of course, some DO officers, such as Dewey Clarridge, had always complained that Salameh was never a fully recruited agent—only a liaison. "I have a notion that Bob had rubbed some of the DO personalities the wrong way," recalled Bob Layton. Ames was a DO man to the core, but he'd never burrowed into the DO's peculiar culture. Bob Gates told Casey's biographer, Joseph Persico:

> You have to understand the culture of the clandestine service. It's what makes the CIA unique. They are incredibly dedicated, mission-oriented people. They are independent and self-motivated. They make tremendous sacrifices in their personal lives for a larger cause. They face risk as part of going to work in the morning. They are extraordinarily good with people. They're flexible, quick, and adaptable, sophisticated in the ways of the world. They're bright intellectually and street smart. I liken it to a priesthood. That's the positive side.
>
> Then there is the negative side of this culture.... It's a closed fraternity. Their attitude toward outsiders is like that of local people in Maine or Cape Cod toward summer people; if you weren't born there, you're always an outsider. You haven't been through what they've been through. They've put their families through hell at times. They're not able to talk about what they do. Some may eventually end up in London or Paris. But they start out in Third World hellholes without even a Western doctor when their kids get sick. They have a strong sense that almost no one understands them or what they do. So they feel defensive and misunderstood.

Bob Ames was part of this culture. But at the same time, he was an outsider as well, an anomaly. He'd never complained about being sent to Third World "hellholes." In fact, he liked them. He didn't want Paris or London. Even Yvonne preferred Aden to Beirut, and Kuwait to Tehran. So Ames didn't feel the brittle resentments of some DO officers who regarded their service as a sacrifice. For Ames, being an intelligence professional wasn't a sacrifice; it was a calling. Some of his colleagues must have sensed this difference, and it made them uncomfortable. It wasn't that Bob Ames was too much of an intellectual. It was that he loved those damned, troublesome Arabs too much. He was too empathetic.

In early September 1981, Ames received hard intelligence that a plot was afoot to assassinate Israeli prime minister Menachem Begin during his visit to the UN General Assembly. Ames called Mustafa Zein and asked him to query Arafat. Zein claims that he quickly passed the message on to Arafat, who replied that there was indeed an assassin in New York. "Arafat gave me a signed letter addressed to this man, telling him to come see [Arafat] at once." Zein reported back to Ames that the plot had been aborted. "But Bob wanted proof, so I told him, okay, on the opening day of the U.N. General Assembly, make sure you have video cameras trained on the Israeli delegation." Ames knew Zein was capable of mischief, but he did as he was told. On the appointed day, Zein went to the United Nations armed with his special UN pass that identified him as an adviser to the Arab League's UN delegation. He approached an old friend, Jimmy Ziadi, a former New York policeman of Lebanese American ancestry, who was then working as chief of security for the PLO delegation to the United Nations. Zein asked to borrow Ziadi's gun—but without any bullets. Ziadi carefully emptied the bullets and handed over the gun. Zein slipped the gun into his waistband and then brazenly walked into the General Assembly. He made his way toward the Kuwaiti delegation—seated near the Israeli delegation. The Israelis included Prime Minister Begin, Foreign Minister Yitzhak Shamir, and Minister of Defense Gen. Ariel Sharon. Zein noticed that Sharon, a large man, sat on a tiny seat at the end of the row. "I made a sharp turn," Zein recalled, "and bumped heavily into Sharon, knocking him off his perch and onto the floor. I quickly apologized and helped him to his feet. And then I shook hands with him, and then Begin and Shamir. I had caused quite a commotion. When I turned away, I made sure that the cameras caught sight of the gun shoved in my waistband."

Ames saw the whole incident on film. He later told Zein, "You practically gave me a heart attack!" But Ames also showed the tape to John N. McMahon, the deputy director for operations at the time. He explained to McMahon that Zein had just reenacted how the aborted assassination could have taken place.

In the autumn of 1981, Casey decided on an internal coup. He was unhappy with the wishy-washy analysts in the Directorate of Intelligence (DI) but also unhappy with what he viewed as an overly cautious culture in the DO. He wanted more action and less talk. The man who headed operations was John McMahon, a thirty-year veteran of the Agency. McMahon was solid and competent, but Casey thought that in the wake of the Church Committee investigations he was overly protective of the Agency's reputation. Casey wanted as chief of the DO his own man, Max Hugel, a businessman with no experience in intelligence. To that end, he persuaded a reluctant McMahon to head up the DI instead. It was unprecedented for an operations veteran to lead the DI. But McMahon was liked and trusted by most everyone. (Hugel proved to be a disaster and soon resigned.)

At the same time, Casey and his executive assistant, Robert Gates, found themselves in an ongoing dispute with Helene Boatner, the director of NESA in the DI. Gates and Boatner exchanged a series of tough notes that led to Boatner's firing. A trained economist, Boatner was probably the Agency's highest-ranking female officer. But some thought her brittle and "an acquired taste." In any case, late in the autumn of 1981, Gates selected Ames to replace her. Casey's counselor, Frederick Hutchinson, had pushed both Casey and Gates to give Ames the job. By the end of the year, Ames was director for intelligence in NESA, and the thirty-eight-year-old Gates was himself promoted to become deputy director for intelligence. As such, he was Ames's immediate superior. It was an amicable pairing. As Gates would later say, "I always considered my greatest recruitment in my whole life at the Agency was recruiting Bob Ames out of the clandestine service to be head of the CIA analytical office working on the Middle East."

Winston Wiley was a thirty-six-year-old analyst when Helene Boatner called him into her office soon after her dismissal. Ames was sitting across from her desk. "This is Bob Ames," Boatner said. "He's going to be taking over NESA." Ames shook hands with Wiley and said, "Helene has said great things about you." Ames then said he knew that Wiley intended to move on to another job. He added that he wanted to support what was best for Wiley but that he could use his help. "I wanted to work for him from the moment I met him," Wiley said. "He recruited me on the spot."

The DI was a wholly different world from operations. Ames was aware that some of his new colleagues wondered whether he could be objective. "Bob was more aware than his critics of the problems of someone like himself coming to the DI," said Bob Layton, who became his deputy in February 1982. "We talked frankly about this problem, and we struck a bargain. He agreed that I would first review the papers written by our analysts. And unless there was a problem, he would never interfere. He just wanted to be sure that each issue was respectfully argued." Helene Boatner had recommended Layton to Ames. Layton had spent his whole career as an analyst, working on Vietnam from 1965 to 1976. He knew nothing about the Middle East. But this didn't bother Ames. "Bob was very comfortable in his skin," recalled another analyst. He ran the DI office as if he were its coach. He made it clear that the Arab-Israeli issue was his bread and butter. But he also demonstrated that he could be detached.

"Bob defended his analysts," recalled Layton. "If the situation warranted it, he could stand up to the guys on the seventh floor. He stood up to Bob Gates. But he did it without confronting Gates. If there were a disagreement, Bob would just ignore Gates. And Gates would not challenge Ames, particularly about the Israeli-Palestinian issue." Ames was now in the business of analysis, but he didn't give up seeing his old sources. "Ames didn't talk about his DO contacts," said Layton. "But I know that even after Salameh's death, Ames continued to see PLO sources. He was willing to cut his own path."

"Bob was very excited about the NESA job," said Fred Hutchinson, who as counselor had an office in Casey's seventh-floor suite. He used to see Ames at least once a week in the Agency's executive dining room. "Bill Casey and I had a very warm relationship," Hutchinson said, "and I used to watch out for Ames." Hutchinson recalled vividly the first time he met Ames. "He was dressed in these very modestly priced Brooks Brothers jackets. He had a certain reserve and greeted you with a slight smile. He had a certain charisma. I had the impression that this guy was just very solid. Later, in our meetings with Casey, well, sometimes things could get a little overwrought with Casey. But Bob was imperturbable."

"Ames clearly had a formidable operational career," said Paul Pillar, who had worked with him in the National Intelligence Council (NIC). "But he was functionally comfortable in the analytical arena." Coming from the clandestine side had its advantages. Analytical intelligence estimates could be notoriously dry. "But," said Pillar, "Ames was someone who could illustrate the abstract estimates with his own personal experience."

As one of thirteen national intelligence officers, Ames had from time to time briefed policy makers in the Carter administration. But as the deputy director for intelligence for the Near East, he would have regular contacts with ranking officials in the White House, the NSC, and the State Department. "Bob liked the analytical side," said George Cave, a case officer who'd worked with Ames on the Iranian revolution. "He was damn good at it. He had finally found his home, and he was getting to the point where senior policy makers were seeking him out."

"It is a huge difference," *Lindsay Sherwin* said. "Instead of recruiting and running agents, he was having to do real policy support. It is also a big difference in terms of who you meet and greet." The conventional wisdom within the Agency was that there should be a wall between intelligence and policy. Ames thought this ridiculous. To be sure, everyone valued objectivity. "Don't contaminate the intelligence with policy" was a constant mantra within the Agency. But according to Hutchinson, Ames strongly believed that the intelligence should help shape policy. To that end, intelligence officers had to understand the needs, prejudices, and motivations of the consumers of their intelligence—the policy makers. Politicians by definition have a very short time frame. "Ames was very good at interpreting the long-term implications of the intelligence to the policy makers," explained Hutchinson. "But he did this well precisely because he took into account their biases and their short four-year time frame."

By early 1982, Bob Ames was the CIA's "Mr. Middle East" in the Reagan administration. He spent most of his time in Washington, but his staff noticed that he made regular trips to New York City. He told them he was seeing sources. But most of these trips were to see his old friend Mustafa Zein, who in January 1982 had finally decided to flee Lebanon's civil war and settle in New York. Zein had made a small fortune in the past decade, so he could afford to buy a lovely apartment at 372 Fifth Avenue. "Bob arranged for me to get a green card," Zein recalled. Ames was listed as a personal reference on Zein's green card application for permanent U.S. residency, and the green card was issued from the CIA's limited quota of one hundred individuals admitted to the country annually. A man Zein knew only as "Edward"—a CIA officer assigned to the United Nations—personally delivered the card. Whether he was in Reston, Kuwait, or Tehran, Ames had kept in frequent touch with Zein by mail or phone. And now Zein occasionally visited Bob and Yvonne in Reston.

Zein, Ames, and Bob's former mentor Dick Helms sometimes lunched together in Washington in these years. Helms always picked up the check. To make it up to him, one day Zein arrived at the luncheon table with a gift for Helms: a set of amber prayer beads he'd recently bought in Beirut for $2,000. "Helms loved them."

Ames had to keep abreast of developments all over the Middle East, but events in Lebanon were about to monopolize his energies. A lull had occurred in Lebanon's persistent civil war. But in July 1981 PLO forces in southern Lebanon launched hundreds of rockets into northern Israel. Israel retaliated by bombing PLO buildings in downtown Beirut, killing hundreds of people. Subsequently, on July 24 a cease-fire was negotiated and the PLO agreed to halt its cross-border attacks from southern Lebanon into northern Israel. Over the next ten months the border was relatively quiet, indeed, almost serene.

In April 1982, Ames invited three of his top analysts to meet with Mustafa Zein. Ames rented a large suite in the Hilton Hotel, just north of Dupont Circle in downtown Washington. He ordered a nice buffet lunch and then told everyone he wanted to hear them debate whether there was going to be another conventional war in the Middle East. After some back-and-forth, the three analysts said no, but "the Israelis are going to bleed Arafat" in a steady war of attrition. They pointed out that ousting the PLO from Lebanon would just free Arafat from having to deal with the Lebanese morass. Zein disagreed. "I have studied Sharon," he said, "and he is just waiting for an opportunity to invade Lebanon and push the PLO out. He will come with an armored column up along the seacoast and another column through the mountains— and he will rush all the way to Beirut."

Ames's analysts argued about this scenario and concluded that, if there *was* an invasion, Sharon would stop his advance north at the Litani River, well south of Beirut. At the end of the day, Ames told Zein that he should write up his prediction and hand it to Arafat. "Tell Arafat that Bob wants you to see this."

On June 3, 1982, the Israeli ambassador in London, Shlomo Argov, was shot and grievously wounded in an assassination attempt that the Israelis blamed on the PLO. In fact, the assassins proved to be employed by Abu Nidal. When Prime Minister Menachem Begin was told that the assassins were Abu Nidal's men—sworn enemies of Arafat and the PLO—he reportedly scoffed, "They're all PLO, Abu Nidal, Abu Shmidal—we have to strike at the PLO."

In retrospect, it's clear that for several years the Israelis had been looking for a pretext to eliminate the PLO from Lebanon. The right-wing Likud government of Prime Minister Begin had come to the conclusion that the 1979 Camp David Accords had removed the possibility that a military offensive against the PLO in Lebanon could escalate into a general war. Egypt was out of the game, leaving Begin free to move against the PLO. In December 1981, Begin and his defense minister, Gen. Ariel Sharon, actually discussed inside the cabinet an invasion plan, code-named "Big Pines" (a reference to Lebanon's famous cedar trees). The plan was rejected at the time. But Sharon was determined to use any future PLO provocations as an excuse to launch a decisive blow. He later wrote in his memoirs that the assassination attempt on Ambassador Argov was "merely the spark that lit the fuse."

On June 6, 1982, a massive Israeli ground force, including more than fifteen hundred tanks, invaded Lebanon. Begin and Sharon had assured the Israeli cabinet that the strike force would advance only forty kilometers into southern Lebanon, clearing out the PLO's militia and artillery encampments. But three days later, Sharon's men were on the southern outskirts of Beirut. As George Shultz later wrote in his memoirs, "Israel's real objective was the destruction of the PLO and its leadership of the Palestinian movement."

It later emerged that Sharon had received a tacit green light from Secretary of State Al Haig when they'd met in Washington on May 19 and 20. According to the authoritative Israeli historian Benny Morris, Haig characterized the Israeli plan to invade Lebanon and expel the PLO as a "lobotomy." Israel was going to take out the PLO, and when asked how far into Lebanon he intended to go, Sharon replied, "As far as we have to."

Ames had come to despise Secretary Haig. Giving Sharon tacit permission to invade Lebanon was, he thought, highly irresponsible. Lunching with Dick Helms and Mustafa Zein in a French restaurant in downtown Washington, Ames described the chaotic discord he was witnessing between the State Department and the White House. A few days later, Zein sent Ames a memo with his thoughts about the Lebanese crisis. "Israel, with its military might, is creating, as usual, new facts in the Middle East. The Arab regimes, whether they are conservative or radical, are different faces of the same coin. Corrupt, oppressive and impotent, they cannot in any way face the Israeli challenge politically or militarily." Zein feared there were only two political trends in the Arab world: the radical Left and Islamic fundamentalism. He argued that Israel's war in Lebanon was empowering the "religious zealots." He predicted that the Islamic fundamentalists would prevail and that this would ultimately "come back to haunt America and Israel." Israeli policy regarding the PLO was shortsighted, to say the least. "To eradicate the Palestinian question," Zein bluntly wrote, "the Israelis must eradicate every Palestinian." Washington faced a stark choice: "It can continue its unlimited support and accommodation of Israeli politics and objectives in the region, or it can forge an independent policy using the war in Lebanon as an opportunity to establish a just peace in the Middle East." Zein was a hardheaded idealist—just like Bob Ames. The two men agreed, and over the coming months they would try desperately to unchain Washington from its rote support of Israeli behavior.

◼

Gen. Ariel Sharon was soon to learn that laying siege to Beirut would come at considerable cost. The PLO's ragtag forces put up a fierce resistance and the Israelis lost more men than they expected. The war threatened to escalate, drawing in Soviet-supplied Syrian troops. Moreover, the Reagan administration soon made it clear that it was unhappy with the ambitious Israeli operation. President Reagan phoned Begin and complained that Israeli forces had gone "significantly beyond the objectives that you have described to me." The president urged an immediate cease-fire. Begin and Sharon stalled for time. Reagan sent out a seasoned Foreign Service officer, Phil Habib, to negotiate a cease-fire. But Israeli forces continued to lay siege to Beirut, and the cease-fire was always precarious.

In the midst of the June Lebanese crisis, President Reagan announced that George Shultz would replace Al Haig as secretary of state. At the time, Shultz was president of the Bechtel Corporation, a company with extensive interests in the Arab world. Some thought he might for this reason be more critical of Washington's perennial pro-Israeli tilt. "In contrast to 'pro-Israel' Haig," Shultz later wrote, "I was being stereotyped as an 'Arabist,' because Bechtel Corporation had big construction jobs under way in Saudi Arabia and around the Persian Gulf."

But Shultz was a conservative Republican through and through. His instincts were conservative with a small *c*. He was not the kind of man who understood the history of dispossession that drove Palestinian nationalism. He believed the PLO's use of political terrorism made it inappropriate, if not impossible, to have any kind of dialogue with its representatives. And he was surrounded by such early neoconservatives as Paul Wolfowitz and Douglas Feith, who believed that U.S. strategic interests in the Middle East were synonymous with Israeli interests.

Nevertheless, coming aboard in the midst of the Lebanon crisis, Shultz was open to innovative thinking. He thought of himself as a pragmatist. On July 16, 1982, President Reagan took Shultz out to the White House Rose Garden and swore him in as secretary of state. Afterwards, Shultz went to the State Department and made a few phone calls. His second phone call was to Bob Ames. Shultz had heard of Ames and knew that he was highly regarded. Just two weeks earlier, on July 2, 1982, Bill Casey had promoted Ames to SIS-4 (Senior Intelligence Service). Reagan's deputy secretary of defense, Frank Carlucci, told Shultz that if he wanted to understand the Middle East, he had to listen to Ames. "Please listen to him," Carlucci said. "He's good because he's balanced and he has no ego hang-ups." Within months, Shultz ran into Carlucci and told him, "One of the best pieces of advice you gave me was to listen to Bob Ames."

Shultz met with Ames several times in July. He thought of Ames as "the CIA's top specialist" on Arab affairs. "I was impressed by his understanding of the Arab political and cultural scene," Shultz wrote. "I once told Bob he reminded me of the engineers at Bechtel with their 'can do' approach to difficult challenges." But he was disturbed to learn that Ames "had been carrying on a dialogue with the PLO leadership through envoys and intermediaries for at least a year." (Obviously, Shultz was unaware that Ames had been doing this off and on since 1969!) Ames tried to impress on Shultz that the Beirut siege presented the Reagan administration with an opportunity to achieve a breakthrough. The PLO, he argued, was ready to meet Washington's primary demand: acceptance of UN Resolution 242, which specified Israel's right to exist and the "withdrawal of Israel armed forces from territories occupied in the recent [1967] conflict." Arafat had only one condition. In return, Washington would have to release a statement in support of Palestinian "self-determination." Shultz rightly regarded that as a code word for endorsing an independent Palestinian state. "That would be a gigantic step, not a gesture," he later wrote, "and I was unwilling to consider it." He told Ames that the PLO's messages were "all too slippery and vague." Further, when Ames indicated that he was about to see his PLO contact, Shultz recalled, "I instructed that there must be no such meeting."

But just days later, on July 19, Ames went ahead and saw his PLO contact. He did so with the specific approval of CIA director Casey. Both men believed there was just too much going on for the Agency not to be communicating with a key actor in the Beirut crisis. By then, Arafat had made it clear that he was willing to evacuate the PLO leadership and the bulk of his fighters. But no one at this point knew whether any other Arab nation would take in Arafat's men. Casey and Ames did what they thought was necessary. Shultz nevertheless discovered the next day that his explicit instruction had been ignored. It was his first lesson in interagency rivalry: "I saw then that Bill Casey and the CIA acted independently."

That summer Shultz scheduled a weekly luncheon with Casey,

whom he'd known casually for more than a decade. But the luncheons soon ended because the two men discovered they really didn't like each other. "He had too much of an agenda," Shultz told Tim Weiner, a reporter for the *New York Times*. "It's a mistake for the CIA to have an agenda. They're supposed to produce intelligence. If they have an agenda, the intelligence can get slanted." When the luncheons ended, Shultz relied on Ames as his conduit to the CIA.

Shultz blamed Casey, not Ames. In any case, Ames continued to see his PLO contacts. And Shultz in practice acquiesced to the necessity of keeping that channel open. Later in July, the cease-fire in Beirut all but collapsed. Israel began shelling the city again. Sitting in Beirut, the president's envoy Phil Habib called Shultz and shouted through the line, "Their guns are firing only a few hundred yards from me. I could have walked down the hill myself and told them to stop!" General Sharon had concluded that the PLO was stalling for time and did not intend to evacuate Beirut. He told his senior officers to plan for a full-scale assault on the city.

Ames's channel to the PLO at this point proved to be critical. As Israeli jet fighters targeted Arafat's command bunker, the PLO leader sent a message that reached Ames. The gist of it, as reported by Shultz, was a plea to negotiate the details of an evacuation: "Habib talks only about our going," complained Arafat, "never about how and where. Where are we to go? Syria will not take us. I am not interested in saving only my life."

Ames's contacts with the PLO now ran straight to Yasir Arafat and his chief of staff Abu Jihad. The main interlocutor was Hani al-Hassan, the PLO official who'd met with General Walters in Rabat in 1973. He and his brother Khalid were regarded as leading advocates of the "pragmatic" line within the PLO. Hani al-Hassan was well known to the dozens of foreign correspondents who hung out at the Commodore Hotel in Ras Beirut. Hani regularly came by the hotel's bar to brief the reporters on the siege. From his public pronouncements it was clear that Hani believed the PLO's survival depended on its ability to transform itself from a paramilitary organization into a political movement.

He was openly calling for a dialogue with the United States. Some of these messages between Ames and Hani al-Hassan and other PLO leaders were transmitted through Johnny Abdo, the Lebanese intelligence chief from 1977 through 1983. Abdo was a cultivated Maronite who nevertheless had wide-ranging friendships throughout Lebanon's sectarian mosaic. He was a personal friend of the Druze chieftain Walid Jumblatt but was also on close terms with Bashir Gemayel. Discreet and enigmatic, Abdo was regarded as an "honest broker" in wartime Lebanon. Abdo's sources were "good guys and bad guys high and low from all points on the spectrum."

Phil Habib was a consummate diplomat. But in Lebanon he was being forced to negotiate without being allowed to see the Palestinian leaders he was negotiating with. It was surreal. The prohibition against talking to the PLO was still in place. Habib was aware of the Ames back channel, but that was no substitute for what he had to do sitting on the Beirut battleground, trying to negotiate the terms of the PLO's departure from Lebanon. Habib decided he couldn't talk face-to-face with Arafat because he knew if Begin discovered he was in direct talks with the "terrorist," the prime minister would probably go ballistic. General Sharon bluntly warned Habib that if he learned that Habib was talking directly to a PLO official, he would send his army into West Beirut.

So Habib suggested what he called "proximity talks." Johnny Abdo had a safe house where Arafat and Habib could sit on separate floors. They would not actually meet face-to-face. Lebanese intermediaries would shuttle between the floors with messages. "They'll be on the first floor," Habib assured Begin, "and I'll be above. I will never even see them. There'll be no handshakes." Begin replied heatedly that this was unacceptable. Ironically, the man who had himself once been accused of being a terrorist for the 1946 bombing of the King David Hotel in Jerusalem—in which ninety-one people had died—understood that even "proximity talks" lent an unacceptable veneer of legitimacy to

Arafat the terrorist. It was a charade. But it was a charade that the U.S. government felt bound to carry out despite Begin's objections.

The crisis stretched on for weeks. Sharon kept threatening to invade West Beirut and the sprawling refugee camps of Sabra and Shatila. On August 1, 1982, Sharon escalated his assault, and some fifty thousand Israeli artillery shells landed in West Beirut in the space of only fourteen hours. Hundreds of civilians were dying. That day a reporter in Washington asked President Reagan, "Are you losing patience with Israel?" Reagan replied, "I lost patience a long time ago. The bloodshed must stop."

But finally, by mid-August, it was clear that the PLO was preparing to leave. Arafat had demanded that a Multinational Force (MNF) of peacekeepers first land in West Beirut. Only then would he and thousands of his fighters agree to board ships bound for Tunis, the capital of Tunisia, the smallest country in North Africa. Habib had promised in the name of the U.S. government that the MNF would protect the Palestinian civilians left behind in the refugee camps.

At one point, Phil Habib asked Johnny Abdo, the Lebanese intelligence chief, for his opinion on how many soldiers in the MNF would be needed to protect Palestinian civilians after the PLO left. Abdo replied, "Two hundred and fifty thousand men." Habib thought he was joking. "That's ridiculous." In the end, Habib decided that just eight hundred U.S. marines, eight hundred French Foreign Legionnaires, and four hundred Italian soldiers would constitute the MNF. These numbers would prove to be woefully inadequate.

Sitting in his perch at Langley, Ames watched the Beirut drama unfold. He found the battle images highly disturbing. But at the same time he realized that the crisis opened up an opportunity to create a new dynamic. He was seeing a lot of high-ranking Reagan administration officials, and he was hearing men like Secretary Shultz voice their anger and displeasure with the Israelis. "I was enraged," Shultz later wrote about Begin's and Sharon's duplicitous behavior.

Ames took advantage of Shultz's anger with the Israelis to gently encourage the new secretary of state to think about what he wanted to see happen in the Middle East after Arafat and the PLO left Beirut. By the end of July, Shultz had gathered a small core group of advisers to iron out what he called a "fresh start" on U.S. policy toward the long-term issues of war and peace in the Middle East. Shultz invited eight "informed, experienced and volatile" men to meet with him regularly in a conference room across the hall from his office in the State Department. The group included Bob Ames, NSC official Bud McFarlane, and veteran Foreign Service officers Lawrence Eagleburger, Charles Hill, William Kirby, Alan Kreczko, and Nicholas Veliotes. Shultz swore them to total secrecy. "Any premature hint that the United States was reconsidering its position on the Palestinian issue," Shultz wrote, "would have disruptive effects not only on Phil Habib's work in getting the PLO out of Beirut but also on the ability of the United States to make something positive emerge from this terrible war."

The problem was that Shultz wanted a "fresh start" that wouldn't reward Arafat with recognition of the PLO—let alone a Palestinian state. Neither did he wish to undermine King Hussein by doing anything that would replace the Hashemite kingdom of Jordan with a Palestinian state. Throughout late July and August, Shultz and his small team met regularly. In the interest of secrecy, they often met on weekends. Their discussions were sometimes heated. At one point, someone warned Shultz, "Anything we come up with will be unacceptable to Israel." Shultz replied, "Nothing that is worthwhile is acceptable to anyone in the Middle East, but everyone looks to us for ideas. It is up to us to set the agenda."

Shultz essentially wanted to square the circle. He wanted to offer hope that the Palestinians, like other people, could have "self-determination." But he knew that "self-determination" was code for a Palestinian state on the West Bank and Gaza. And Shultz was enough of a politician to know that a Palestinian state was not in the cards. So he told himself that a Palestinian state in the occupied territories was not economically viable. Shultz concluded that "self-determination" would have to occur within the political confines of the Jordanian state.

Various parties had kicked around the notion of a "Jordanian op-tion" for years. Ames and others familiar with the Black September civil war understood that satisfying Palestinian aspirations within a Jor-danian state would work only if Jordan became a democratic state. But because Palestinians represented a majority of Jordan's population, a "Jordanian solution" entailed the collapse of King Hussein's Hashem-ite monarchy. Yet Shultz had made it clear that he wasn't prepared to undermine King Hussein. Nevertheless, Ames saw great value in Shultz's determination to have President Reagan lend his administra-tion's prestige and influence to a grand American peace initiative. So he encouraged Shultz.

By mid-August Shultz and his secret group had the outlines of a plan. As specified by the Camp David Accords, the Palestinians in the West Bank and Gaza would acquire autonomy over the next five years. Local elections would be held. And during this period Israel would freeze all settlement activity. Ames knew this was the critical factor. With a freeze on new settlements in the occupied territories, Palestinian "self-determination" in the West Bank and Gaza could gradually become a reality. To be sure, Shultz was making it clear that the United States opposed the creation of a Palestinian state. The au-tonomous Palestinian entity would instead be linked to Jordan. Ames understood that Shultz was trying to finesse an intractable issue. And that was fine with him. Shultz's "fresh start" might not be so fresh, but it was nevertheless a step forward. As an intelligence officer, Ames understood that a policy maker like Shultz had to operate under politi-cal constraints.

Shultz was always suspicious of any memo that reeked of a contrived consensus. He thought most of the CIA's National Intelligence Esti-mates were boring "compromises." So periodically, he'd call up Bob Gates and ask him to stop by for an hour with several of his brightest analysts. Shultz would quiz them. "You find out the analysts have all kinds of different opinions," Shultz later explained, "and that's much more useful, much more interesting." Ames shone in these situations.

Bob knew he had the secretary's ear—and that was an invaluable thing. Some CIA officers spend their whole careers without ever really getting to influence a powerful policy maker. "It is a tricky business," recalled *Lindsay Sherwin*. "Do you try to stay true to your views or do you try to remain effective? At some point, people stop listening to you." *Sherwin* and other CIA colleagues thought that Ames was buying into some wishful thinking. "When it came down to it, they were proposing a Jordanian option," said *Sherwin,* "and everyone knew that was a nonstarter. But Bob argued that we should try to remain in the game. I would like to think that he had a broader view. He was telling himself that if we could persuade the Israelis to end the occupation, maybe down the road a real peace could emerge."

Bruce Riedel, an Agency analyst who worked with Ames on the peace initiative, thought it was the right thing to do. "Bob was a passionate believer in the idea that the Palestinian issue was a critical threat to U.S. national interests," Riedel said. "So he thought something had to be done. The initiative was a compromise between those saying we have to put forward an American peace plan and those who said we can't piss off the Israelis. It was a big step forward, even if it was a Jordanian option." Some of his colleagues nevertheless thought Ames was drinking the Kool-Aid. Some muttered that he was "getting too big for his cowboy boots." Even Ames's boss, CIA director Casey, was beginning to have some misgivings about Ames's close relationship with Shultz. "The fact that Ames was by then so much a part of Shultz's inner circle must have led to some tension," recalled Riedel.

On August 14, Shultz took Ames and several other members of his secret team up to Camp David to brief President Reagan on their progress. They had lunch with Reagan in a cozy dining room lined with knotted-pine boards. The president wore black cowboy boots, jeans, and a bright-red polo shirt. After lunch, the men adjourned to the living room, where Shultz outlined his peace initiative. He then asked Ames and Veliotes to "role-play" how the plan would be presented to Begin, King Hussein, and Egyptian president Hosni Mubarak—and how these leaders would react. "The actors were effective," recalled Shultz.

"The play was tense and presumed no sure outcome." The little drama appealed to the actor in Reagan—which was probably why Shultz put on this production. He knew the plan would inevitably attract intense controversy, so he wanted to be sure the president was on board and engaged—and that he would know his lines.

A few days later, Shultz called in Israeli ambassador Moshe Arens. Without revealing his still-secret initiative, Shultz suggested that with Arafat's departure from Lebanon imminent, perhaps it was time to revitalize the peace process. Arens vigorously disagreed. "Look," he said, "we have wiped the PLO from the scene. Don't you Americans now pick the PLO up, dust it off, and give it artificial respiration."

Ames was telling Shultz that Arens was wrong. Arafat, he said, was in the process of solidifying his political position even as he was being defeated and removed from the battlefield. "The PLO has plenty of life in it," Ames insisted. He predicted that after leaving Beirut, Arafat would take "a grand tour" of all the Arab capitals, drumming up political support. The PLO's new headquarters in Tunis was already being furnished. Operating out of Tunis would free Arafat from his previous dependency on Syria's dictator, Hafez Assad. And in an ironic twist, Ames argued, the PLO's defeat in Beirut had actually strengthened the hand of moderates within the organization. These political pragmatists in the PLO would now turn Arafat into a more effective leader on the world stage. Moreover, Ames said that from his meetings with his counterparts in Tel Aviv, he knew that Mossad's intelligence analysts agreed that Arafat had decisive control over the organization. Arafat was not going to disappear—and neither was the Palestinian conundrum.

Shultz didn't doubt Ames's analysis. But he did not regard the PLO as a reliable player. And he certainly did not see the PLO as moderate. That was why he thought it essential to bring King Hussein "back into the center of the scene." Shultz trusted and admired Ames. But a part of Shultz also discounted Ames's optimism precisely because of his Arabist credentials. On the afternoon of August 24, Shultz convened a meeting of his secret team to hear Nick Veliotes report back on his briefing of King Hussein. From Shultz's perspective, it was critical that he get Hussein firmly on board. But from Veliotes's account of his meeting with the king, it was clear that Hussein was covering his bases. Yes, he liked the Shultz plan—but Shultz could see from King Hussein's carefully worded written response that he really wanted the United States to negotiate directly with the PLO—and get the Israelis to withdraw from the occupied territories. "It's a very upbeat letter," Veliotes said, trying to put it in a good light. "The king is very interested; it's just that he has to cover his ass." Ames chimed in, "Hussein is always this way in first meetings. He'll come around."

Shultz knew he was being spun. "I also felt that I was seeing some of the professional optimism, even wishful thinking, for which the Arabists in the government were known. . . . My Arabist advisers did not appreciate my reaction and considered me lacking in the sophistication necessary to plumb the Arab mind."

He was right to be suspicious. The Arabists—Ames included—understood perfectly well why King Hussein was not willing to stick his neck out. Ames was the one man in the room who'd always had a jaundiced view of the Hashemite regime. But in this instance he no doubt kept that opinion to himself and tried to encourage the secretary of state to press ahead with what everyone knew would be a controversial initiative.

Shultz would have been shocked to learn that Ames had also arranged for Arafat to see a summary of the peace plan even before Reagan unveiled it. Four days before Arafat departed, Ames had Mustafa Zein fly into Cyprus from New York with a typed two-page summary of the plan. Beirut was still under siege and the airport was closed, so Zein had to take the ferry from Cyprus to the Maronite-controlled Lebanese port of Jounieh. Fearing that Israeli or Maronite soldiers would search him, Zein befriended an Egyptian doctor on the ferry and persuaded him to take his briefcase through customs. Zein had forged a press pass that identified him as an ABC News employee. The ruse worked: he sailed through customs, retrieved his briefcase, and emerged from the port. Ames had sent the new CIA station chief, Ken

Haas, to meet him. Haas was driving a weathered white Mercedes sedan. It was late at night, so Haas drove him to the Hotel Alexander, a hangout for journalists and foreign nationals in East Beirut.

As they pulled up in front of the Alexander, Haas groaned, "Oh, shit, here come a bunch of Mossad guys."

Mustafa turned to Haas and told him, "Here, take my briefcase and wait right here." He then popped out of the car and ran toward the Mossad men, shouting, "Hey boys, I am with ABC News. I'd just like to talk."

The Israelis hastily walked away, not wanting to talk to anyone from the press. Haas was incredulous. He'd never met Zein before, but he'd heard of his exploits. Ken later laughed about the incident and told Ames, "The last I saw Mustafa he was chasing Mossad officers in Jounieh."

The next morning Zein crossed over to West Beirut, leaving Haas behind. He paid a driver for the ABC News crew $500 to take him across the Green Line dividing the city between Maronite-controlled East Beirut and Muslim-controlled West Beirut. When they passed through the dangerous Museum checkpoint, Zein was greeted by Force 17 commandos, who escorted him to see Arafat.

Zein briefed Arafat on the peace plan, handing him a document titled "US Views Regarding the Future Settlement." The highlights included:

- "Self-government in the West Bank and Gaza for more than one million Palestinians."
- "Israeli military government and administration to be removed and replaced by a Palestinian government elected by the Palestinians in the West Bank and Gaza."
- "The United States considers Jerusalem as occupied territory as all other territories occupied in 1967, and all changes made in Jerusalem are illegal."
- "The United States does not recognize the PLO since it refuses to accept Security Council resolution 242."

Only the last point would have caused Arafat unhappiness. But Zein argued that the other points were a significant step in the right direction. Arafat was personally inclined to agree, but he correctly knew that most of his colleagues in the PLO would conclude that the plan didn't go far enough to satisfy their minimalist demands for a Palestinian state on some portion of old Palestine. Moreover, Arafat understood that the PLO's defeat in Beirut left him little political capital.

On August 30, 1982, Arafat finally boarded a ship in Beirut and sailed for Tunis. (Mustafa Zein was there at the dock to see him off.) All told, some 8,500 PLO fighters were evacuated under the eyes of Israeli sharpshooters. Habib was ecstatic. Nearly three months of excruciating diplomacy had finally triumphed.

Some people thought the PLO shouldn't have left. "Arafat muffed it," said David Hirst, a seasoned British reporter for the *Manchester Guardian*. "The PLO was on the verge of its first real heroic moment. People were ready to go on. He blew it."

Another reporter in Beirut, Janet Lee Stevens, agreed. Thirty-two years old, Stevens had come to Beirut in late 1981 and was freelancing for a number of magazines, including the local English-language weekly *Monday Morning* and a Japanese newspaper, *Asahi*. After the Israeli invasion of Lebanon, she published an article in *Monday Morning* titled "Slaughterhouse Lebanon." It described the "thousands of civilians who were maimed and wounded" in the invasion. She was also filing reports on human rights cases for Amnesty International.

Born in 1951, Stevens was trying to finish her doctorate at the University of Pennsylvania. A Fulbright scholar, she'd once been married to the Tunisian playwright Taoufik Jebali. By 1982, Janet spoke fluent Arabic and knew her way around the Palestinian refugee camps. That summer she had lived through the Israeli siege, stubbornly refusing to leave. She was an advocate. Other journalists thought of her as a partisan journalist. Some wondered if she was working for some intelligence agency. "I thought she was CIA," said the *Washington Post* reporter Loren Jenkins. "I had dinner with her a couple of times at the Commodore Hotel." But Janet was just a passionate young woman who felt strongly about the plight of the Palestinian refugees. She spent a lot of time in Sabra and Shatila, sometimes volunteering her time at the Akka Hospital and the Gaza Hospital, both located in the camps. She was a familiar figure. The residents of Sabra and Shatila knew her as Miss Janet. And because of her strongly voiced opinions, some called her "the little drummer girl." Anne Dammarell, a U.S. embassy official with the U.S. Agency for International Development (USAID), thought Janet "was not flashy. . . . She was a very serious young woman."

The British novelist David Cornwell, a.k.a. John le Carré, hired Stevens to serve as his "guide, interpreter and irrepressible philosopher" when he visited Beirut in 1982. Le Carré had visited the Middle East for three months in 1980 to conduct research for his novel *The Little Drummer Girl*—a title le Carré appropriated from Janet's moniker in the refugee camps. He was introduced to Yasir Arafat on this trip and also met with Mossad officers in Israel. He met Stevens when he returned in 1982 to scout out scenes for a movie based on the book. Le Carré later wrote of his friendship with Stevens: "We all loved Janet, and quickly appointed her to be our instructor and—even more—our moral and compassionate focus for the pain and devastation which we witnessed." Janet took le Carré into Sabra and Shatila so he could see for himself the conditions in which these poor people lived. "It was Janet's sensitivity which guided us through Sabra and Shatila, the Gaza hospital and the camps of the south; [it was] Janet's amazing capacity to reach the poor and bereaved and destitute that made us feel their plight, and her unswerving commitment."

Le Carré and Stevens clicked. The novelist admired her passion and her disarming irreverence. He once teased her that when she was old she would acquire "the venerability, if not the piety, of Mother Teresa." Janet scoffed at this. She thought the comparison was absurd. They also shared similar political views about the Arab-Israeli conflict.

"I think the Israelis have behaved disgracefully," le Carré told *Monday Morning*, "and I don't care who knows it."

Janet had interviewed Yasir Arafat on numerous occasions, and on August 8, 1982—three weeks before Arafat's eventual departure—Stevens walked into Arafat's bunker headquarters and begged him not to evacuate his PLO Fedayeen to Tunis. She urged him to stand and fight the Israelis. "You must launch a 'Stalingrad defense,'" she told the guerrilla leader. "The international public will support it. . . . You cannot believe the Reagan Administration, Abu Ammar! Women and children are terrified of what might happen if their husbands and brothers leave them alone." Arafat understood. He tried to console her. She became distraught and started to cry. Arafat actually wrapped his arms around her even as she began to beat his shoulders gently with her clenched fists. There were witnesses to this drama. One was a twenty-year-old Lebanese Shi'ite named Imad Mughniyeh. Four years earlier, Ali Hassan Salameh had recruited Mughniyeh into Arafat's elite intelligence unit, Force 17. By 1982, Mughniyeh was serving as one of Arafat's many bodyguards. When Arafat left Beirut he would leave his young Shi'ite bodyguard behind. The unemployed Mughniyeh would soon transfer his allegiances to a new underground militia called Islamic Amal. His presence that day in Arafat's bunker would become a deadly irony.

On the day Arafat left Beirut, Bob Ames was working with President Reagan's speechwriters. Reagan delivered the speech on the evening of September 1, 1982. He began by saying bluntly that the "military losses of the PLO have not diminished the yearning of the Palestinian people for a just solution of their claims." The president then endorsed the not very controversial notion that the Palestinian residents of the West Bank and Gaza should gain "full autonomy over their own affairs" over the next five years. According to the terms of the 1978 Camp David Accords, this should have happened long ago. But he specifically called for "the immediate adoption of a settlement freeze by

Israel in the occupied territories." That was controversial. Then again, he also specified that Washington "will not support the establishment of an independent Palestinian state in the West Bank and Gaza." But he also said that the United States would not support the "annexation or permanent control by Israel" of these occupied territories. Negotiations had to determine the final status of these lands. "But it is the firm view of the United States," said Reagan, "that self-government by the Palestinians of the West Bank and Gaza in association with Jordan offers the best chance for a durable, just, and lasting peace."

The speech was well received in every quarter but one. Begin was furious. He wrote an angry letter to Reagan: "A friend does not weaken his friend; an ally does not put his ally in jeopardy." Begin flatly rejected the Reagan peace initiative. Shultz, however, was unfazed. He knew that what Reagan had announced "must be shattering for Begin and the group around him. . . . As they see it, we have suddenly pulled the rug out from under them." Shultz's aide Ray Seitz told him, "Everything is going according to plan: the Israelis are very negative, the Arabs are very fuzzy, and we have a good strong defensible position." But not for long.

Bloody events would soon throw Shultz's finely tuned plan off course. Late in August 1982 the Phalangist warlord Bashir Gemayel was narrowly elected president of Lebanon. He was the only candidate. And everyone knew that he was Israel's candidate—but also America's. The State Department actually discussed drawing on its contingency budget for funds to give Bashir "in case he needs it to buy votes." The CIA thought this would not be necessary, but in any event the American ambassador Robert Dillon cajoled a couple of crucial Sunni Muslim members of parliament to cast their votes for Gemayel at the last minute. "We covertly supported the election of Bashir," Dillon later said, "because of all the realistic presidents who could emerge, Bashir was the best. . . . I used to see a lot of him. He was a young man. He would stop by my house late in the evenings, and we would spend hours talking."

The Americans believed the thirty-four-year-old Gemayel had matured and was the only Christian leader capable of working out a deal with the country's Sunni, Shi'ite, and Druze factions. The Israelis thought Bashir would restore Maronite supremacy in Lebanon and sign a full-fledged peace treaty with Israel. Just a week after his election, Prime Minister Begin demanded to see Bashir. An Israeli helicopter was sent to Beirut and ferried Bashir to the seaside resort town of Nahariya, just across Lebanon's southern border. Bashir found Begin in a rage. He berated Bashir for his ingratitude and demanded that he agree to sign a peace treaty as soon as he was inaugurated as president. Bashir emerged from the meeting shaken and angry. He told his associates that Begin wanted to turn Lebanon into a "puppet state."

Bashir returned to Beirut, determined to distance himself from the Israelis. The Americans encouraged him, believing that he could not acquire the credibility necessary to rule effectively if he was seen in the Arab world as a puppet. But by then Syria's dictator, Hafez Assad, had clearly decided that Bashir's ascendency had to be blocked because the young Maronite Christian warlord was too allied with the Israelis. On September 14, 1982, an agent of Syrian intelligence planted a massive suitcase bomb in the Phalangist party headquarters. When Bashir arrived for his regular Tuesday party meeting, the assassin detonated the bomb. Bashir and twenty-six other Phalangists were crushed to death.

By then, the U.S. Marines and the rest of the multinational peacekeepers had been pulled out of Beirut. Reagan's defense secretary, Caspar Weinberger, didn't think they were needed—even though the Reagan administration had promised Arafat that they would remain for a decent interval to protect Palestinian civilians after the departure of the PLO militia. So on the morning after Bashir Gemayel's assassination Israeli forces moved in and seized key checkpoints in West Beirut. Begin told Morris Draper, a high-ranking U.S. envoy, that Israeli forces were moving in "with the object of keeping things quiet and ensuring that there were no incidents to mar the peace." But when Draper arrived in Beirut three hours later to attend Gemayel's funeral, he could see that "the city was in flames." Israeli tank and artillery fire was decimating parts of West Beirut. Draper rushed to the Israeli army's headquarters outside Beirut, where he was told blandly, "Everything is fine."

"Begin told me as a representative of the United States government that the Israelis were not going to move into the heart of Beirut," Draper later said. "And within hours they were inside the heart of Beirut. He told a straight-out, 100 percent, bald-faced lie to the United States government." The next day Draper confronted Sharon and demanded to know why he'd violated the cease-fire agreement. Sharon said, "Circumstances changed, sir." He argued that the PLO had left 2,500 "terrorists" in the camps. Draper disputed this. A transcript of Draper's meeting with Sharon shows the two men arguing heatedly. Sharon insisted, "We went in because of the 2,000–3,000 terrorists who remained there. We even have their names!"

"I asked for those names," Draper responded, "and you said there was an enormous list, but what you came up with is a miniscule one. . . . The Lebanese will take care of those who have remained behind."

"You know the Lebanese," Sharon said dismissively. "We'll tend to our own affairs."

At this point, Gen. Rafael Eitan, the Israeli army's chief of staff, interrupted: "May I say something? They [the Lebanese army] are not up to it. Lebanon is at a point of exploding into a frenzy of revenge. No one can stop them. Yesterday we spoke with the Phalange about their plans. They don't have a strong command. . . . They're obsessed with the idea of revenge. You have to know the Arabs well to sense something like that. . . . I'm telling you that some of their commanders visited me, and I could see in their eyes that it's going to be a relentless slaughter. A number of incidents already happened today, and it's a good thing we were there, rather than the Lebanese army, to prevent it from going further."

Draper was shocked to learn that the Israelis were going to let the Phalangist militia into the camps. Even General Eitan seemed to understand what that could mean: "relentless slaughter." Draper thought it was pointless. The Israeli army should not be in West Beirut;

it should not be surrounding the camps. There was no threat to the Israelis. "There were a few armed men in the camps," he later said. "But they were all men sixty or seventy years old. They may have had old shotguns, but they were not a threat. Essentially, the camps were disarmed."

Even as Draper and Sharon were arguing, at 6:00 P.M. on Thursday, September 16, a squad of 150 Phalangist fighters was entering the Sabra and Shatila camps. They were under the command of Elie Hobeika, the chief of Phalange intelligence. Hobeika had served as Bashir Gemayel's personal bodyguard. He had a reputation for brutality. Ambassador Bob Dillon once described him as a "pathological killer." Hobeika supervised the operation from the Israeli forward command post, across from the Kuwaiti embassy. At 7:00 P.M. Hobeika received a radio communication from one of his officers inside the camp. An Israeli officer overheard the conversation: the Phalangist officer asked Hobeika what he should do with fifty women and children whom his men had detained. "That's the last time you're going to ask me," Hobeika yelled. "You know what to do." The Israeli officer immediately told his commander, Brig. Gen. Amos Yaron—who did nothing.

Over the next two days and nights Hobeika's men slaughtered somewhere between 1,000 and 2,500 people, mostly women, children, and elderly men.* Israeli troops guarded the perimeters surrounding Sabra and Shatila. Floodlights were set up by the Israelis to provide some light for the Phalangists as they did their work. Occasionally, the Israelis shot flares into the sky to illuminate the camps. Anne Dammarell was watching the light show from the U.S. ambassador's residence in Yarzi, a mountain village just southeast of Beirut. Dammarell, age forty-four, worked for USAID and had been in Beirut for two years. That evening she stood outside and watched the tracer firings. "A large number of flares were sent up," she wrote in a letter, "giving off their

---

* An authoritative study published in 2004 compiled the names of 2,463 victims. But there were also hundreds of people identified who disappeared and were never seen again.

particular yellow lamination. . . . I stared and stared, fascinated by the strange beauty. Why it charmed me so I did not know. I was mesmerized." Only later did she realize what she'd been watching. "That was the night that the Palestinian camp, Shatila, was invaded by Christian militia while Israeli troops guarded the entrances. Hundreds were murdered. Perhaps thousands. Killed just for being who they were. Unarmed. Vulnerable. Poor. Women and children. . . . Nothing justifies this revenge."

Robert Fisk of the London *Times* stood on his balcony in West Beirut the following evening, when the flares again lit up the evening sky. "It was bright daylight, silvery yellow," he later wrote. "I could read a book on my balcony by the light. The flares sprayed down slowly, almost all of them over the Sabra-Shatila district. . . . Dawn at midnight." Fisk had been based in Beirut since 1976. That Friday evening he'd run into Loren Jenkins, the *Washington Post*'s correspondent. "Fisky," said Jenkins, "something's going on in the camps. The Israelis have brought the fucking Phalangists with them." Jenkins and Fisk agreed they would investigate the rumors the next morning. Karsten Tveit of Norwegian radio joined them that Saturday morning, September 18, and they walked into the camps.

What they saw shocked these seasoned reporters. Corpses were strewn down every alleyway. They also came across hastily dug mass graves. Bulldozers had been used to bury the bodies. But hundreds of the dead were lying openly in the streets. As the three reporters stumbled in a daze through this dreadful scene, they could see Israeli soldiers watching them through binoculars from a tower block to the west. Jenkins cursed, "Sharon! That fucker Sharon!"

Ryan Crocker, the U.S. embassy's thirty-four-year-old political counselor, went into the camps with a handheld radio transmitter. As he walked around he spoke into the transmitter, describing to his colleagues in the embassy what he was seeing. He counted at least fifty bodies.

Later that day, Janet Lee Stevens, the American freelance reporter, also came to the camps. "I saw dead women in their houses with their skirts up to their waists and their legs apart," wrote Stevens. "Dozens of young men [had been] shot after being lined up against an alley wall; children with their throats slit, a pregnant woman with her stomach chopped open, her eyes still wide open, her blackened face silently screaming in horror; countless babies and toddlers who had been stabbed or ripped apart and who had been thrown into garbage piles." Stevens stood stunned and sickened as Red Crescent volunteers worked to bury hundreds of bodies in a mass grave.

Stevens was outraged, and she would spend the rest of her short life investigating the massacre and trying to help the survivors. She wasn't afraid to confront those whom she blamed for the murders. A few weeks later, she happened to see Joseph Haddad, a well-known Phalangist officer, outside his party headquarters in East Beirut. Stevens walked up to Haddad and screamed at him, "Butcher!" Haddad looked straight into the eyes of the young American and made the sign of the cross. Janet was, as John le Carré observed, "irrepressible."

The USAID worker Anne Dammarell also visited the camps the day after the massacre. She was walking around Sabra and Shatila taking pictures when she came across a wailing woman who had survived the massacre. Later, Dammarell wrote her family back in America, "I've spent the past four days working in and out of the Shatila camp to get the dead buried. After all of the visible bodies were taken care of [the] work stopped. The dead rotting under large slabs of cement had to stay put until the rubble was removed. . . . I think I'll become a Quaker and reject all violence. Love, Anne." Dammarell lobbied the embassy and Lebanese authorities to dig up the common grave where bulldozers had dumped many bodies. "It was clear that this was a mass grave," Dammarell said. "We wanted to know how many people had been killed." The Lebanese government denied her request. The authorities did not want an accounting.

Sharon would be blamed. But so too would America. When Arafat was shown a videotape of the massacre, he angrily told reporters that Phil

Habib had personally signed a paper pledging to protect the Palestinians living in the refugee camps. "What Arafat said is absolutely true," Habib said. "I signed this paper which guaranteed that these people in West Beirut would not be harmed. I got specific guarantees on this from Bashir and from the Israelis—from Sharon."

Secretary of State Shultz concurred. "The brutal fact is," said Shultz, "we are partially responsible." Shultz was stunned and angry. That morning he briefed President Reagan, who asked Shultz if he'd made a mistake in withdrawing the U.S. Marines. The two men were uncertain what should be done, but, as Reagan put it, "If we show ourselves unable to respond to this situation, what can the Middle East parties expect of us in the Arab-Israeli peace process?"

Shultz also went to see Bob Ames, who'd learned the news early Saturday morning Washington time and had rushed to Langley headquarters. There he found his colleagues deeply shaken and angry. Some were in tears. Carolyn Kovar was an analyst who was on weekend duty that day when the news came in of the massacres. She worked for Ames on Lebanese affairs. "I started phoning people to come in that morning," recalled Kovar. "And then I was crying, the reports were that bad. I heard a lot of anger directed at the Israelis that day. We also thought it showed that the Christian warlords were just destroying their country."

Ames told Shultz, "We need action quickly." If the administration didn't react strongly to this outrage, he argued, Washington would lose all support in the Arab world for the new peace initiative. "After Sabra and Shatila," said the NSC's Geoffrey Kemp, "everyone was saying, 'My God, we have to do something.'"

Reagan's defense secretary, Cap Weinberger, objected to sending the marines back, arguing, "A limited Beirut mission is too risky." But on Monday, September 20, 1982, Reagan announced that he was sending the marines back to Beirut as part of a multinational force. They arrived four days later and stationed themselves in a barracks near the airport. "It soon became clear," said Geoff Kemp, "that the marines were caught in the middle of the Lebanese morass."

The Israeli invasion of Lebanon was a disaster for all parties. Lebanon became Sharon's war. And Sabra and Shatila was Sharon's massacre, even though no Israelis murdered anyone in the course of those three terrible days. But as President Reagan noted in his diary, "The Israelis did nothing to prevent or halt it." Prime Minister Begin denied any responsibility for the massacre. But three hundred thousand Israelis rallied in the streets of Tel Aviv to protest the massacre. The protests forced Begin's government to accede to the creation of an independent investigative commission. Four months later, in February 1983, the Kahan Commission concluded: "The decision on the entry of the Phalangists into the refugee camps was taken without consideration of the danger—which the makers and executors of the decision were obligated to foresee as probable—the Phalangists would commit massacres and pogroms against the inhabitants of the camps." The Kahan Commission blamed Sharon for this decision and concluded that he "bears personal responsibility." The commission recommended that Begin "consider" firing the defense minister. Sharon initially refused to resign as defense minister. Eventually he was forced to, but Begin allowed him to remain in the cabinet without a specific portfolio. Nineteen years later, he would become Israel's prime minister.

The Sabra and Shatila massacre was by definition an event of tragic proportions. But it also became a historical marker, a turning point. It would come to symbolize everything that was wrongheaded about the Israeli invasion of Lebanon, an invasion that would turn into an eighteen-year occupation. The Israelis would not completely withdraw from South Lebanon until the year 2000. Sharon never achieved his goal of establishing a pro-Israeli Maronite regime in Lebanon. Instead, Lebanon became Israel's Vietnam War. More than 675 Israeli soldiers would die over the years. Nearly eighteen thousand Lebanese were killed in 1982 alone. And when the Israelis were forced to withdraw from central Lebanon in 1985, a new round in Lebanon's civil war resulted in the defeat of Maronite Christian forces. Lebanon would never sign a peace treaty with Israel. To be sure, the invasion expelled the PLO to Tunis. But that only served to create a new and in some ways far more deadly enemy in Lebanon. The Israeli invasion—and the camp massacre—created a new political force called Islamic Amal, an organization that later morphed into what we know today as Hezbollah, the Party of God. "The Israelis had assumed that they could invade Lebanon, restore Maronite supremacy, and throughout it all the Shi'ites would remain passive," recalled Bruce Riedel. "But in actuality, the Israeli invasion unleashed the Shi'ites."

Hezbollah's current secretary-general, Hassan Nasrallah, has said that he doesn't believe his party would exist today had the Israelis not invaded Lebanon in 1982. "I don't know whether something called Hezbollah would have been born," Nasrallah said. "I doubt it." The Shi'ites of South Lebanon had initially welcomed the Israelis, but the Israeli occupation was heavy-handed, and their indiscriminate use of tank and artillery fire led to many civilian deaths. And then many Shi'ites were killed in the Sabra and Shatila massacre. "I don't think there was any real understanding of what was going on in southern Lebanon," said *Lindsay Sherwin*. "We were focused on the Palestinians and the Maronites. But I remember thinking at the time, the Shi'a are a growing influence. It is hard to think ahead strategically. But it is even harder to get people to listen to you. No one wanted to hear about how unhappy the Shi'a were."

One of those unhappy Shi'ites was Imad Mughniyeh, the twenty-year-old bodyguard who'd witnessed Janet Lee Stevens's encounter with Arafat in his bunker just a month earlier. Mughniyeh was outraged by the massacre. He'd grown up in this part of South Beirut, and these were his neighbors who'd been butchered. That autumn, a rash of kidnappings and murders of Shi'ite and Sunni leftists in Lebanon further angered him. Hundreds of people living in non-Christian sectors disappeared that autumn, presumably at the hands of death squads organized by the right-wing Christian Lebanese Forces. Many of these murders were taking place in West Beirut and other parts of the city under the nominal control of the U.S. Marines. By one account, Mughniyeh himself was injured that autumn when the Maronite Christian forces unleashed an artillery barrage on his neighborhood in Beirut's southern suburbs. The artillery barrage took place while the multinational peacekeeping force stood passively by in its encampment nearby. In the eyes of Shi'a like Mughniyeh, the Americans and their "peacekeeping" forces were somehow complicit with the Christian Lebanese Forces.

Mughniyeh knew that several hundred volunteers from the Iranian Revolutionary Guard Corps (IRGC) had arrived that autumn in Lebanon's Bekaa Valley, near the Syrian border. These Iranians were fellow Shi'a and proselytizers for Ayatollah Khomeini's revolution. On November 21, 1982, Revolutionary Guards allied with some local Shi'a Lebanese calling themselves the Islamic Amal stormed a Lebanese army post in the ancient town of Baalbek. The tattered, dysfunctional Lebanese army gave up the Sheikh Abdullah Barracks without a fight, and the barracks became the IRGC's headquarters for the next decade. (One member of the Revolutionary Guards stationed in Baalbek was the future president of Iran, Mahmoud Ahmedinejad.) Soon afterwards, Mughniyeh made a trip to Baalbek to offer his services to the Revolutionary Guards. He allegedly met with an IRGC intelligence officer, a twenty-five-year-old Iranian named Ali Reza Asgari. It was the beginning of a long and ominous partnership. Asgari hired Mughniyeh and as his first assignment asked the young Lebanese to gather intelligence on Western expatriates living in Beirut.

Ames was heavily preoccupied by the Lebanese crisis. But his analytical job as director of NESA also required him to keep up with developments outside the Arab world. On October 1, 1982, he wrote his second-eldest daughter, Adrienne: "I'm off to India and Pakistan tonight and won't be back until 19 October. The troubles in the Middle East have been keeping me pretty busy. I'm almost a stranger in my own house!" Adrienne was then a freshman in college, and Catherine, his eldest child, had recently married. But Bob would still attend basketball games at Reston's South Lakes High School with his boys and watch them play soccer on weekends. His two other teenage girls were just beginning to express interest in boys, so he'd sit in the stands and make comments on the boys' characters based on how they played the game. His son Andrew later called him "my coach, my mentor. . . . He taught me everything about growing up." His daughters called him "gentle, and loving and kind."

■

On January 11, 1983, Ames stopped by the White House around 3:00 P.M. and had a long talk with the NSC's deputy for the Middle East, Geoffrey Kemp. Afterwards, Kemp noted in his diary that Ames had given him a "very pessimistic assessment of [the] state of play in our Mid-East policy. Simply not enough follow-up and not enough dynamics." Their conversation prompted Kemp to write another memo to Reagan's chief of staff, Judge William Clark, urging him to try a new approach.

On February 4, 1983, Ames participated in a two-hour-long meeting with President Reagan in the Cabinet Room. It was a tense, pessimistic meeting. President Reagan's "talking points" for the meeting had him saying, "We are increasingly seen as incapable of persuading our oldest friends in the area [Israel,] never mind convincing our newest partners on the need for progress toward a Middle East peace." The focus of the discussion was all about how to "persuade the Israeli Cabinet" to withdraw Israeli forces from Lebanon. It wasn't going to happen.

Ames returned again on Tuesday, February 22, to give the president a long briefing on the PLO. Afterwards, Judge Clark wrote Ames a thank-you note. Reagan, he wrote, "would like to compliment you on your incisive review of a complex and important issue." Judge Clark added his own special thanks for Ames's "continued help in support of the President's September 1 initiative. We shall certainly want to call on you in the near future as we press ahead with this vital foreign policy issue." Ames was called back less than a month later and gave

Reagan another briefing on Thursday, March 17. The topic was how and whether the Israelis could be coaxed to pull out of Lebanon. President Reagan was quite determined to try once again to impress upon the Israelis that they had to withdraw from Lebanon—but also to stop building settlements in the West Bank. Reagan was about to meet with the Israeli foreign minister, Yitzhak Shamir, and Reagan wanted to be sure that Shamir "cannot leave without hearing from me once again our deep concern over Israeli settlements policy and our determination to pursue the initiatives outlined in September 1." Shamir listened, and the Israeli Likudite government did nothing. This was to become a familiar script in Israeli-American relations.

Ames tried to be a little upbeat about it all. "I'm a little more optimistic about a solution than I was on Sunday," Ames wrote his mother afterward. "But I'm not holding my breath." He told her he was off on a four-day business trip to Paris the following weekend. Upon his return he hoped to "relax" a bit and perhaps drive up to Philadelphia for a visit. He never made the trip to visit his mother.

Ames was alternately depressed and exhilarated. The news from Lebanon was never good, and early that year it seemed highly likely that the civil war would once again resume. Yet Ames also felt empowered by his access to the Reagan White House. He was suddenly receiving high-level recognition for his work. On January 13, 1983, Casey issued Ames the CIA's "Distinguished Intelligence Certificate"—the "highest honor granted under the Senior Intelligence Service award system." Casey himself formally handed Ames the leather-bound certificate in a ceremony that month; the award came with a substantial stipend of $20,000. Yet some of his colleagues thought his opinions were markedly unrealistic. "I saw Ames in early 1983," said Clair George, the veteran DO officer whom Casey had appointed as the CIA's liaison to Congress. "He gave me a five- or six-minute sermon on how the Arab-Israeli conflict would be solved. I thought it was naive."

CHAPTER TWELVE

Beirut Destiny

Keep your head down.

— *Thomas Braman to Bob Ames, April 15, 1983*

In early March 1983, David Cornwell, a.k.a. John le Carré, the acclaimed British novelist, released a new book, *The Little Drummer Girl*. Ames usually favored nonfiction, but he knew that le Carré had set this spy story in Beirut—and naturally this aroused his interest. The novel tells the story of Mossad's recruitment of a young British woman as part of an operation to assassinate a Palestinian terrorist. Ames told his NSC counterpart, Geoff Kemp, that he really liked it. Ames was unaware that le Carré had taken the title for the novel from a young American freelance reporter, Janet Lee Stevens, who was known in the Palestinian refugee camps as "the little drummer girl."

Later that month, shortly after his March 17 meeting with President Reagan, Ames decided to plan a trip back to the Middle East. He hadn't been back there in some five years. That was too long an absence. He told one of his deputies, Bob Layton, that he felt out of touch with things. He needed to get a feel for the "ground truth." Initially, he planned to visit just his Mossad contacts in Tel Aviv. But then at the last minute he added Beirut to his itinerary. He wanted to see Mustafa Zein, who'd cabled him that he had urgent business to discuss. Mustafa had returned to Beirut from his Fifth Avenue apartment

in New York, just temporarily, to take care of business concerns—
but also to help Ames. Among other things, Zein wanted Ames to see
Lebanon's new president, Amin Gemayel—the brother of the assassinated president-elect, Bashir Gemayel. Amin was a drab, uninspir-
ing figure—nothing like his flamboyant younger brother. But when
Bashir had been assassinated, the Israelis had virtually dictated that
Amin take his place: "We Israelis said, 'This is a Gemayel era.'"

On Friday, April 15, the day before his departure, Ames had lunch
with his old friend and colleague Sam Wyman, who was then chief of
the Arabian Peninsula desk of the DO. Bob explained that he'd added
Beirut to his trip but claimed he really didn't have any other official
business to do there. He asked Sam if he thought he had to go into the
CIA station in the embassy. "Oh, you have to drop by the station,"
Sam replied. "Otherwise, they will consider it a snub."

He also had a long talk with *Lindsay Sherwin*. They argued. It was
nothing personal, just a firm debate about policy. "We had our differences," *Sherwin* said. *Sherwin* was very skeptical of the Reagan peace
initiative and thought it was a nonstarter, a "Jordanian solution" in
disguise. But *Sherwin* also knew Ames didn't mind a good argument.
"I told him he was going on a fool's errand, trying to push a Jordanian
solution that he knew was not viable. He was of two minds about it.
But when I look back on that conversation," *Sherwin* recalled, "well,
I regret it."

Ames was torn between his natural skepticism and his desire to see
things change for the better. Recently he'd told his mother, Helen,
"We think we can smooth the whole thing over, over there, and we
can't."

He expressed a similar feeling of pessimism to Bruce Riedel, the
young analyst who'd accompanied him on one of his Mossad liaison meetings in Tel Aviv. "He told me he thought, 'Things are falling apart,'" Riedel recalled. "He was skeptical of the idea that we
and the Israelis could impose a Maronite government on the Shi'ites.
He felt he had to go to Beirut and see if he could come back with an
idea that could turn the situation around." But he was well aware of

the perils. "We also discussed the fact that things were getting pretty dangerous."* Riedel mentioned the fact that a few months earlier a car bomb had destroyed an Israeli interrogation and prison facility in Tyre. It was only the second time this tactic had been used in Lebanon. (The first occasion had been when a truck bomb destroyed the Iraqi embassy in Beirut.) Riedel thought this was ominous, and Ames agreed. Seventy-five Israelis had been killed in the attack, along with a score of Palestinian and Lebanese prisoners. The Israelis had publicly announced that it had been an accidental propane gas explosion—but the CIA believed otherwise.

Before leaving Langley late that afternoon, Ames dropped by the operations center to say good-bye to a few people. He ran into Thomas Braman, whom he'd first met at the Farm twenty-three years earlier. Braman was then serving as Director Casey's intelligence officer. Ames and Braman had worked together on Iran in recent years; Braman had been posted to Tehran in late 1978, just as the revolution broke. Prior to his departure for Tehran, Ames had told him, "Keep your head down." Braman had been captured and roughed up in February 1979 when Revolutionary Guards briefly occupied the Tehran embassy. Ever since, whenever one of them was off on a trip, the other would jokingly tell him, "Keep your head down." It had become a mantra between two old friends. "When Bob came to see me that day," Braman recalled, "my parting words were, 'Keep your head down.'"

That evening, Bob called his mother in Philadelphia and casually told her that he was flying to Beirut the next morning. "He had this way about him," Helen Ames later said, "of letting you know that everything was alright."

That Saturday morning Ames said good-bye to his children. As usual, he told Andrew, "Take care of your mom." But the fourteen-year-old happened to be annoyed with his father that morning—later,

---

* When Bruce Riedel visited Beirut the following year, he clambered down from the helicopter and was asked, as if it was a routine question, if he wanted a shotgun or just a pistol.

he couldn't remember why—so instead of answering, Andrew turned away in silence. His ever-patient father ignored the adolescent slight and walked to his car.

Yvonne drove him to National Airport. She knew he'd be absent for about two weeks. She regarded it as a short trip—nothing compared to those two- or three-month TDYs to Beirut or Yemen. It seemed normal. In 1983, their eldest daughter, Catherine, twenty-one, was married. Adrienne, nineteen, was finishing her freshman year at Concordia Lutheran College in Austin, Texas. But the four other children—Kristen, eighteen, Karen, fifteen, Andrew, fourteen, and Kevin, eleven—were living at home. Bob was still very much the family man, always involved in his children's activities. "He coached their basketball teams," Yvonne recalled, "and always went to the soccer games. . . . He left at the same time every morning, and he was always home for dinner. And he was always there on the weekends. He was the cornerstone of the family."

Bob arrived in Beirut early Sunday morning, April 17, and checked into Room 409 of his favorite boutique inn, the Mayflower Hotel, near Hamra Street in Ras Beirut. It was an overcast, rainy day—not unusual for a Lebanese spring. "He was exhilarated to be back," said Susan M. Morgan, a CIA officer who was also visiting Lebanon that week. Morgan was an economist and a newly minted analyst on the Lebanon desk. She'd arrived in Beirut on April 11 for a short TDY assignment. It was her first trip abroad as a CIA officer. Ames was her office director, but she'd been unaware that he was flying into Beirut. She was "delighted to see Bob." That evening he saw Morgan and several other Agency officers at a dinner party hosted by James and Monique Lewis. Jim was the Agency's deputy station chief, and his Vietnamese-born wife had just passed her security clearance to become an Agency secretary. Monday would be Monique's first day on the job in the station.

The embassy phone book listed James F. Lewis, age thirty-nine, as a political officer. That was his cover. A former Green Beret, Jim Lewis was one of the Agency's most experienced covert operatives. He was fluent in French and Vietnamese, and his Arabic was more than decent. Lewis had an extraordinary résumé. During his years in Vietnam he'd led an elite guerrilla unit of Montagnards. He'd once guided a Special Forces unit on a reconnaissance mission deep into North Vietnam. He won four Bronze Stars, a Purple Heart, an Air Medal, and a Gallantry Cross. In 1970 Lewis was recruited by the CIA and sent back to Southeast Asia. On April 11, 1975—on the eve of Saigon's fall— Lewis was wounded by rocket fire and then captured by enemy troops. He spent the next six months in North Vietnam's infamous Sontay prison, where he was beaten and tortured. He was finally released in late October 1975—the last American prisoner of war to come home. By then, he'd spent nearly thirteen years fighting the North Vietnamese in a losing war.

Back in America, the Agency allowed him two years off to study French literature at George Washington University. He earned a bachelor's degree in 1977. He then met and married Monique Nuet, a beautiful Vietnamese woman who'd studied pharmacology in Switzerland and France. The newly married couple moved to Chicago, where the Agency assigned Jim to study Arabic. By 1982 the Agency considered Lewis proficient enough in Arabic to assign him to Beirut. They needed someone there with his paramilitary skills. Lewis arrived in Beirut on August 13, 1982. The city was under Israeli siege. Yasir Arafat was about to depart with his PLO militia.

Beirut was becoming a veritable hellhole, and not only for the Lebanese. Earlier that summer of 1982 David Dodge, the president of the American University of Beirut, was kidnapped by the Islamic Amal. (Dodge would not be released for a full year.) By the autumn of 1982 there were a dozen or more explosions in the city each week. Israeli soldiers patrolled some neighborhoods. Tensions remained high between the Israelis and the multilateral peacekeepers. In one incident a lone U.S. Marines officer, Capt. Charles B. Johnson, stepped in front of a column of three Israeli tanks, pulled out his loaded Colt 45, and ordered the Israeli officer driving the lead tank to turn it around. Pointing his pistol at the tank, Captain Johnson said the Israeli tank would pass only "over my dead body." The incident created headlines in the *New York Times* and elsewhere, underscoring the growing animosity between erstwhile allies.

Militias were everywhere. On his very first day in Beirut, Marine Sgt. Charles Allen Light Jr. glanced out his bedroom window in the U.S. embassy and saw a man suddenly assaulted and nearly beaten to death on the sidewalk. LCpl. Robert "Bobby" McMaugh, twenty-one, was walking down a street in West Beirut one day in early April 1983 when a car bomb exploded and knocked him flat on his back. McMaugh brushed himself off and walked away—this time. On April 14, someone fired a rocket-propelled grenade at the embassy. It crashed into an empty office and exploded. No one was hurt.

Though Beirut was clearly a dangerous city, Jim Lewis's wife, Monique, was allowed to join him in early 1983. Monique's first day on the job as a station secretary was scheduled for Monday, April 18. So the dinner party they hosted Sunday evening in honor of Bob Ames was also something of a celebration for Monique's new career in the Agency. Jim had learned to cook French and Vietnamese food during his years in Southeast Asia, and he'd spent hours preparing a gourmet meal. He had also invited the entire CIA station to his apartment, just a ten-minute walk from the embassy. They were a very close-knit group of friends.

At thirty-nine, Kenneth E. Haas was young to be a station chief. He had earned a doctorate in philosophy by the time he was twenty-five; he'd taught at Hamline University in Saint Paul, Minnesota, for a few years, but in the early 1970s he joined the CIA. He was considered a rising star. His son Alex was born in 1975 and several months later he was posted abroad. He served in Tehran some years prior to the revolution, and he also had a stint as chief of station in Oman. But his wife worried about the risks they were taking, and tensions in the marriage led to a divorce in 1980. In July 1982, Haas married his second wife, Alison, and days later left for Beirut. She joined him there in October. Despite the chaos and uncertainty, Alison thought of Beirut as an exhilarating adventure. "There was a lot of socializing," she later recalled. "You had maids and drivers and things, so socializing wasn't a big burden. It was really something almost every night, and because of the situation and the closeness of the embassy, it was like a family. You became close to people very quickly."

Frank J. Johnston, age forty-six, also came to the Lewis dinner party that evening, accompanied by his twenty-three-year-old bride, Arlette. Born in Nazareth, Israel, Arlette was a Palestinian-Israeli, and though her native tongue was Arabic, this was the first time she'd lived in an Arab country. Arlette called Frank her "first real love, her husband, her universe." She knew Frank was a veteran CIA operative. They'd met in a bowling alley in Germany, dated for six months, and then gotten married on October 26, 1982. They'd arrived in Beirut in January 1983. For security reasons, they had to drive around the streets of Beirut in a car with armor plating. But Arlette liked the city. "I spoke Arabic," Arlette recalled, "and Lebanon felt like home for me." Frank had served under Ken Haas in a previous posting in prerevolutionary Iran. They were good friends, and Frank was eager to work with him again.

Deborah M. Hixon, thirty years old, had just arrived in Beirut for a six-week TDY. "She was a lovely woman," said Clair George, the legendary DO officer who was her boss at the time. Hixon had grown up in Colorado and her father was an airline pilot. She was fluent in French. Alison Haas thought of her as a "very vivacious young woman." Hixon loved her work in Beirut and thought it so important that she'd recently asked for an extension.

Phyllis Faraci, forty-four, was a single woman who'd turned a secretarial career in the CIA into a life adventure. The Agency had sent her all over the world, including many years in South Vietnam, where she had been one of the last four Americans to be evacuated from the Mekong Delta when Saigon fell in April 1975.

William R. Sheil, fifty-nine, was a former Green Beret Special Forces officer who, like Jim Lewis, had melted into the Agency after his years in Southeast Asia. He was valued for his skills as an interrogator, a man who could gently and expertly extract information from foreign informants. He was stationed in Washington, D.C.—but he traveled all the time on short-term assignments for the Agency. He was a contract agent for the CIA—and in recent years his family had known that he spent a lot of time in Central America, working on missions to support the anti-Sandinista Contras in Nicaragua. His son assumed that was where he was. In fact, that April he'd just arrived in Beirut.

These and other guests at the dinner party savored Jim Lewis's Vietnamese cooking and the fine Bordeaux he served. But as the evening progressed, the conversation soured. "It was a very nice dinner," recalled Arlette Johnston. "But the atmosphere was very tense and very—there was something going on which I didn't really understand." Arlette later noted in a diary that "this guest [Ames] seems to have bad news, as if he was not happy with the work these people were doing.... The atmosphere was gloomy." Alison Haas, the wife of the station chief, remembered the dinner party "for a visiting dignitary from Washington" with the same misgivings. "There was tension because Washington saw things one way and the people in Beirut saw things another way." "Washington" in this case clearly meant Bob Ames. He was the visiting dignitary. Everyone in the room knew that Ames met regularly with Secretary of State George Shultz and President Ronald Reagan.

And all the CIA officers that evening knew that Ames was the ghostwriter of the Reagan peace initiative. It was his plan, his idealism, his innate optimism that had persuaded the president to put his prestige behind a plan for Israel to exchange the territories occupied in the June 1967 war for a comprehensive peace with its Arab neighbors. Yet seasoned CIA officers like Ken Haas, Jim Lewis, and Frank Johnston could not help but voice some skepticism about the practicality of persuading Lebanon's warlords to play that rationality game. And what about the Israelis, who were now prowling the streets of Beirut's outer suburbs? Was the Reagan administration truly prepared to force them out of Lebanon? They argued over the peace initiative's viability.

Lewis's guests lingered uncomfortably, drinking late into the night. They went home feeling troubled. Bob Ames went back to the Mayflower Hotel, knowing that the next morning he'd be hard-pressed by his colleagues to see the Beirut of 1983 through their eyes. It would be a difficult meeting. Beirut was no longer the cosmopolitan city he knew from the late sixties and early seventies.

That evening, as Frank Johnston crawled into bed, his Nazareth-born wife heard him muttering to himself. "What are you talking about?" Arlette said.

"I'm talking to him."

"Who?" said Arlette.

"I'm talking to God," Frank said. "When I'm going to die, I'm going to talk to him and tell him—"

"Stop talking like that," interrupted Arlette.

"Don't worry," Frank replied, "you'll be a nice, beautiful rich widow."

Arlette didn't sleep very well that night. She had cramps. But she also heard an owl screeching—and in Nazareth an owl was bad luck. She awoke the next morning to a dark, overcast day. It looked as though it might rain. Frank had risen earlier and was already dressed for work. He came over to her side of the bed and kissed her. They debated whether she should join him for lunch at the embassy, but Arlette finally said, "Maybe you can come home and I will fix you lunch." Frank said, "Okay, maybe," and kissed her again. As he walked out the door Arlette yelled out, "Come back! Kiss me again!"

While the party at the Lewises was taking place Sunday night, another party was occurring over at the apartment of Elizabeth "Tish" Butler, an embassy USAID official. She'd invited all the off-duty U.S. marines whose job it was to guard the embassy. The marines stayed late that night, eating spaghetti and drinking champagne. By the time they walked into the embassy at 1:00 A.M., they were raising a bit of hell. The marine guard on duty at Guard Post One nevertheless buzzed them in, and they took the elevator up to their apartment on the sixth floor. LCpl. Robert "Bobby" McMaugh had a beer in his room and then collapsed on his bed fully clothed. He knew he had to get up by 7:00 A.M.

the next morning and stand duty at Guard Post One. When he showed up on time, his face was white. Confessing that he felt hung-over, he told Cpl. Ronnie Tumolo, "I'll give you three hundred Lebanese lira if you stand my duty today." Tumolo was broke, so for a moment he considered the offer. But then he realized that he'd have to awaken the gunnery sergeant and ask his permission. So he told Bobby, "Well, I don't think that is going to happen, but we'll see how things go later on in the day."

Bobby McMaugh was the second-youngest marine guard in the embassy, and probably the most popular. He made a habit of handing a single red rose to any of the pretty secretaries as they made their way to work each morning. Despite his hangover, this morning was no exception. Bobby was a charmer. He'd grown up in Manassas, Virginia, and his father, Earl Vincent McMaugh, had worked most of his career for the Defense Intelligence Agency. That spring, Bobby knew his parents were probably headed for a divorce, and this worried him. In recent weeks he'd used a free phone at the embassy to call his family back in Virginia. He was particularly close to his younger sister, Teresa Ann McMaugh; he had, in fact, called her on an embassy tie-line phone the previous evening. They commiserated with each other about their parents' impending divorce. Bobby wanted to know if Teresa was okay. But as they were speaking, Teresa could hear loud noises in the background. "What is all that noise?" she asked. Bobby said they were explosions, followed by big flashes of light in the sky. Teresa was just eighteen years old; she had no idea what was happening in Lebanon, but she tried to ask her brother what it was like living in Beirut. Bobby just replied that he'd met a lot of "neat people." It was their last conversation.

At 7:00 the next morning—April 18, 1983—Bob Ames walked the short distance from the Mayflower Hotel over to the Commodore Hotel to have breakfast with Mustafa Zein in his suite. It was a dark, cloudy day. The sky was filled with black thunderclouds sweeping in from the Mediterranean Sea. The two old friends flinched momentarily when a loud clap of thunder interrupted their conversation. Bob mentioned the dinner party from the previous evening and explained that he and Ken Haas, the station chief, had gotten into an argument. Bob pulled a memo from his briefcase and asked Mustafa to read it. It was an unofficial summary of a proposed peace agreement between Israel and Lebanon. The agreement provided for a staged withdrawal of Israeli forces from South Lebanon. Bob explained that the whole agreement had a catch. The Israelis would withdraw their forces only if Syria actually withdrew all its military forces from all of Lebanon. Both men understood that the Syrians were not party to this agreement and probably would not withdraw their troops. Bob asked Mustafa what he thought.

Mustafa smiled mischievously and said, "These are very thick papers. It would be very practical and wise to type the agreement on very thin papers."

Bob said, "I know something is coming and I hate to ask why. But I am asking, why?"

"In case someone wanted to wipe his ass with it," replied Mustafa, "he doesn't get hurt!"

Bob laughed so hard he spit out some of his tea. But Mustafa was right about the agreement. A peace treaty with Israel would be highly unpopular with Lebanon's Shi'ite and Sunni Muslim citizens, who viewed the "Zionist entity" as a Western colonial outpost. Egypt's dictator, Anwar Sadat, had signed a peace treaty with Israel—and his 1981 assassination sent a clear message to Arab politicians everywhere that they risked the same fate. So Ames and Zein knew a Lebanese-Israeli peace treaty would never happen. And since the Syrians were not even a party to the agreement, and were unlikely to leave Lebanon, this meant the Israelis were unlikely to withdraw from South Lebanon. The so-called peace treaty would, in fact, fall apart within the year, and Israeli and Syrian troops would occupy portions of Lebanon for years to come.

After their breakfast, Ames walked down to the U.S. embassy on the corniche, just a ten- or fifteen-minute walk. Zein had tried to persuade him to have lunch at one of Bob's favorite restaurants, Al-Ajami—the name of which in Arabic refers to a non-Arabic-speaking Persian or "foreigner." Bob seemed doubtful. Shortly after noon, Zein dropped by the embassy and called Ames from the lobby. They talked briefly, and Zein again encouraged Ames to come with Haas and any other colleagues to the Al-Ajami. Ames said they were too busy and it would be better to meet for dinner. So Zein reluctantly walked out of the embassy at about 12:40 P.M. As Zein left, he passed by LCpl. Bobby McMaugh, still standing guard that morning at Guard Post One.

Ames had been meeting all morning with the entire CIA station on the fifth floor. It had turned into a "contentious" meeting. They argued. Station Chief Ken Haas was so disturbed by the meeting that he called his wife, Alison, and suggested they should have their usual lunch a little earlier. Alison was already in the embassy that morning. She wasn't on the payroll, but it was her habit to come into the office and help out on whatever anyone needed. Usually, she brought her husband a homemade sandwich and they'd lunch together. On this day they ate their sandwiches, and then at about 12:45 P.M. Alison produced an apple and began to peel it. Ken stopped her and said he was "too upset, and to put the apple away." He told her that he had to write a long cable to Washington, a cable known in the business as an AARDWOLF: "I don't know how I'm going to do it; you go ahead and go home and take a nap and I'll be home when I finish."*

As Alison rose to leave, Ken came over and took her head in both hands and gave her a "great big dramatic kiss." Alison left for home, but on her way out she dallied. She went to the embassy's travel section to see about tickets for a planned trip to Cyprus the following week. But the travel office was closed for the lunch hour. She then tried

---

* CIA station chiefs rarely write long personal assessments, but these occasional lengthy cables back to Langley are referred to in the Near East Division as AARD-WOLFS—perhaps because they are as rare as the termite-eating mammal native to Africa.

to get a cholera shot, but the health clinic was also closed. She then tried the commissary in the basement, but it too was locked. So rather reluctantly, Alison walked out of the embassy at about 12:55 P.M., got into her car, and drove home to their apartment. As she got out of the car at 1:04 P.M., she heard an explosion and muttered to herself, "That was a big one."

Downstairs in the first-floor cafeteria, Anne Dammarell and Bob Pearson were having lunch together. Both were USAID officials. Anne ordered a chef's salad. She was scheduled to rotate out of Beirut in a week for a new posting in Sri Lanka. Pearson wanted to talk to her about whom to invite to her farewell party. They ordered lunch and sat down in the back of the cafeteria, behind a supporting pillar.

Sitting at another table closer to the front of the cafeteria was William McIntyre, the director of USAID's Beirut operations. He was having lunch with Janet Lee Stevens, the freelance American reporter who, despite being pregnant, was immersed in an investigation of the Sabra and Shatila massacre. Two days earlier, she'd told a friend, Franklin Lamb, that she was working hard to unearth evidence to convict Gen. Ariel Sharon of war crimes. At lunch that day she intended to urge USAID director McIntyre to funnel some development assistance into the camps. She'd arrived at the embassy around 12:45 P.M. and was scheduled the next day to fly to Cyprus to see her friend the author John le Carré.

Another reporter was in the embassy late that morning. David Ignatius was the son of Paul Ignatius, a former secretary of the navy and president of the Washington Post Corporation. David was then working for the *Wall Street Journal*. He was a good reporter and had developed a wide range of sources. On April 18 he had an interview on the sixth floor with a U.S. Army officer with the Office of Military Cooperation. Ignatius wanted to learn more about the U.S. government's efforts to rebuild and modernize the Lebanese army. The officer gave him an upbeat briefing, claiming that the program was turning the Lebanese army into "a force for national reconciliation that will bring together Sunnis, Shi'ites and Christians." As he took notes, Ignatius thought, *It's almost believable. Maybe the good times are returning. . . . The city has been pounded by eight years of civil war, and then by the Israeli invasion, and then by the massacre of Palestinians at Sabra and Shatila. But now the United States has arrived as Lebanon's protector.* The interview ended and Ignatius was escorted down to the first floor by Rebecca J. McCullough, twenty-four, a newly married embassy secretary. Ignatius retrieved his American passport at the marine desk, Guard Post One. He noticed Cpl. Bobby McMaugh's imposing physique and the shiny brass buttons on his dress blues—the dark-blue pants with the long red stripes. And then he walked out of the embassy and up the hill, toward his hotel in Ras Beirut.

Corporal McMaugh had just returned at about 12:55 P.M. to Guard Post One after a short lunch break. He'd tried to talk Corporal Massengill into taking his duty for the rest of the afternoon. Massengill declined, saying he was too tired, and took the elevator up to his room on the sixth floor. Rebecca McCullough, the secretary who'd escorted Ignatius, lingered at the marine desk and joked with Bobby. She teasingly warned him that she was going to tell her husband that the corporal was flirting with her. They laughed, and then McCullough suddenly thought she should get back to work. It was almost 1:00 P.M. She said good-bye to Bobby and took the elevator back up to the sixth floor.

At that moment, a weathered black GMC pickup truck was passing by the pockmarked ruins of the St. George Hotel on Beirut's waterfront corniche. The young Shi'ite Lebanese man at the wheel was driving slowly. He wore a black leather jacket. The truck's tarpaulin-covered cargo, weighing two thousand pounds, made the vehicle run low on its springs and its tires bulge beneath the weight. A green Mercedes sedan was parked two blocks away from the embassy. As the truck passed by, the driver in the Mercedes flashed its headlights, a signal to proceed. Moments later, the driver of the heavy truck slowed and then suddenly turned sharply into the exit of the embassy's crescent-shaped driveway. The driver gunned the engine and swerved wildly around the ambassador's parked black armored limousine. Implausibly, the truck then bounced up six or seven steps and crashed through the embassy's glass front doors and sped partly into the building's central lobby, immediately adjacent to Guard Post One. At exactly 1:04 P.M. the driver detonated his cargo and an enormous explosion ripped through the salmon-colored building.

Ambassador Robert S. Dillon was standing beside his desk on the eighth floor, talking on the phone to a German banker about some J.P. Morgan investments. As he listened to the banker, Dillon was simultaneously trying to pull a thick red U.S. Marines sweatshirt over his head. He'd been intending to go out for a jog along the corniche. Just as he pulled the sweatshirt over his face, the Mylar-covered glass window abruptly flashed toward him. He never heard the explosion. The sweatshirt probably saved his face from cuts. But the next thing he knew, Dillon found himself flat on his back, half buried under bricks and debris from the ceiling. He began swearing to himself in between fits of coughing. The room was filling with smoke, dust, and the whiff of tear gas. Dillon thought to himself that a rocket-propelled grenade must have hit his office. "Damn it," he muttered, "they missed us four days ago, but this time they really got us." For a moment, Dillon thought he'd lost his legs.

The ambassador's deputy, Robert Pugh, experienced much the same thing in the adjoining room. The windows had blown in—but he and the ambassador's secretary hadn't been buried in rubble. Within a minute or two, Pugh stumbled into Dillon's office and found that one wall had collapsed on the ambassador. Ironically, he was draped in the American flag that had stood ceremoniously next to his desk. Pugh grabbed the flagpole and used it to leverage off the largest piece of debris from the ambassador's legs. Only then did Dillon realize that his legs were whole and he was even able to stand upright. He was still bruised and scratched and bloody. But he knew he was alive. Everyone then began retching from a cloud of tear gas that quickly enveloped the room—tear gas from canisters stored by the marines in their quarters. Finally, a breeze from the blown-out windows cleared the room and they were able to see and breathe. At first they tried to make their way out to the elevator in the center of the embassy, but they quickly saw it was simply gone. So they turned around and found an open stairwell at one end of the embassy's crescent-shaped building. Only when they managed to get down to the second floor did they realize how much damage had been inflicted on the building. Dillon stepped out onto the second floor and saw Mary Lee McIntyre, the wife of the acting chief of the USAID mission. She had such a bad cut over her tearing eyes that she couldn't see anything. Dillon lifted her into his arms and carried her to a window, where he could see someone was standing on a ladder. Dillon gently handed Mary Lee out to the stranger.

He then turned around and someone whispered into his ear, "My God, Bill McIntyre's dead. I've just seen the body." Only then did Dillon realize there were fatalities. McIntyre had been killed while eating lunch with the journalist Janet Lee Stevens. She died with him.* When Ambassador Dillon finally made his way around to the front of the embassy, he was stunned by what he saw: the entire center wing of the building had pancaked. Dillon knew there must be many dead, and some people were probably still alive, trapped under the rubble. It would be five hours before the last living person came out of the ruined embassy.

Anne Dammarell thought she was dead. The USAID official who'd been having lunch with Bob Pearson just remembered hearing a huge

---

* John le Carré flew in from Cyprus two days later, checked into the Commodore Hotel, and then visited the ruins of the embassy. On April 29, 1983, he wrote a moving letter to Janet's parents, mourning their loss. And when *The Little Drummer Girl* was released as a film in October 1984, he made sure the film was dedicated to her memory in the credits.

noise and feeling intense heat. And then there was just silence. Anne thought she'd been struck by lightning. "I thought—well, I'm dead. So I'm going to lean over and tell Bob that I'm dead." But she had no voice and she couldn't move. She felt as if an elephant had stepped on her. The next thing she knew Anne found herself lying on a stretcher, being carried outside. She heard voices yelling in Arabic, "*Yallah! Yallah!*"— "Go! Go!" Ambassador Dillon saw her being loaded hastily into an ambulance and thought, "*She looks like a piece of hamburger.*" He turned away, thinking that she wasn't going to make it. X-rays taken at the American University of Beirut hospital showed she had nineteen broken bones, including her pelvic bone, both arms, several fingers, and her collarbone. Shredded glass was embedded in her neck and arms. But Anne survived.

Staff Sgt. Charles Light had just left Cpl. Bobby McMaugh at Guard Post One and returned to his office on the first floor when the explosion blew him through a cinder-block wall into the adjoining room. He came to six or seven minutes later and heard ammunition rounds "cooking off" from the intense heat. He glanced to where his solid-oak desk had stood between him and the blast and saw that there was nothing left. "There wasn't a piece of wood on it as big as a match or a toothpick." When he got to his feet he noticed that his boots had been blown off. As Sergeant Light stumbled toward the front lobby, he heard a woman screaming. The blast had peeled off part of her face and she was bleeding profusely. Light wrapped his arms around the poor woman and tried to comfort her. At first, he wasn't sure how to get out. But as the smoke and debris cleared, he spotted a slice of daylight from a V-shaped opening through the collapsed floors. Because he could also see flames coming from this opening, Sergeant Light left the woman for a moment and went to see if they could safely escape the wreckage through this two-foot hole. Peering out into what was the circular driveway to the embassy, Light could see a severed human leg lying in the driveway. Beside it was a car in flames.

Sergeant Light ran back to the woman and guided her over to a place in the back of the lobby where water was gushing down from the upper floors. They stood under the water and thoroughly drenched their clothing. Only then did Light think it would be safe enough to crawl through the hole and out onto the driveway so near a burning car.

After squeezing through, Sergeant Light stood up and peered into the car, which he recognized as the black Suburban "chase" vehicle that always trailed behind the ambassador's limousine. The human leg on the asphalt belonged to Staff Sgt. Mark "Cesar" Salazar, a member of the Foreign Service National Guard. Salazar was one of the ambassador's bodyguards, and Sergeant Light could see him sitting in the Suburban engulfed in flames. "And just as I looked at him," Sergeant Light later testified, "his eyes popped out of his head." As Sergeant Light looked on in horror, Salazar's best friend, a senior Lebanese security guard named Mohammed al-Kurdi, was trying to pry Salazar out of the car with a long metal rod that had a little crook at one end. But every time Al-Kurdi tried to touch Salazar with the rod, a piece of flesh would drop off. Salazar was probably already dead, but just to be certain Mohammed pulled out his pistol and shot Salazar between the eyes.

Sergeant Light turned back to the injured woman he'd dragged out of the embassy. She was a Lebanese employee of the consular section. He helped her out onto the street in front of the embassy and waved down a Mercedes taxicab that happened to be driving by. Seeing the devastation, the taxi driver stopped and started to back out. Light had to draw his sidearm and point it at the driver before the cabbie stopped. He got the woman into the backseat, threw some money on the seat, and told the driver, "*Mustashfa,*" meaning "hospital."

When Sergeant Light turned around, he caught his first panorama view of the carnage. There were burning bodies lying on the sidewalk and in the driveway. Cars that had been driving by when the truck bomb hit were now charred hunks of burning metal. A Lebanese army tank that had been parked on the corniche across the street from the embassy had been blown into the ocean. There were bodies floating in the surf. All eight floors of the central wing of the embassy had collapsed. And then Sergeant Light suddenly remembered that after the initial blast, as he lay semiconscious on the floor, he'd heard loud slapping sounds, one after another. "It dawned on me that it was those floors coming down, one after another. One would hit a floor, and the weight of it would take another one down."

Sergeant Light then ran around to the side of the embassy, looking for survivors. He found what remained of the consular section, imploded into a crater of rubble. Looking down, he saw a woman who'd been blown through the air only to land with her legs slammed into an open filing cabinet. She was still alive. Sergeant Light had a Red Crescent volunteer lower him into the crater with his belt. He then went over to the filing cabinet and pulled the woman out. Her legs were broken and her right hand had been blown off and was dangling by a piece of skin. She had a chest wound and her face was pockmarked with glass and shrapnel. Sergeant Light held her in his arms: "She was talking to me, talking to somebody in Lebanese [Arabic]. I held her there until she died, and then I put her down and went on inside the embassy."

When the *Wall Street Journal*'s David Ignatius heard the explosion, he was nearly a mile away from the embassy. The windows rattled and he felt a "momentary feeling of vertigo, like fear but worse." He ran back down the hill toward the corniche. By the time he got there, U.S. marines were trying to cordon off the building. The smoke and dust had cleared. Ignatius looked up and saw the body of a man in a sports jacket dangling upside-down with his legs pinned between two collapsed floors.

Sergeant Light saw the same hideous image. He spent the next four hours on a rope with a Red Crescent worker trying to extract the body of William Sheil, the fifty-nine-year-old former Green Beret and CIA contract interrogator. Light failed. "There was nothing I could do," Light later said. "He was pinned, and there was no way I could get a bar or anything to pry him out of there. It took, I don't know, two or three days before we could get that poor man out of there." Sheil was caught between the fourth and fifth floors. They finally had to bring in two cranes, one with a chain tied to the floor that had crushed Sheil's legs, and the other with a chain wrapped around his body. Sergeant Light later testified that when the cranes yanked Sheil's dead body out, "the chain that was around him pulled his pants off, and he was hanging out there in public like that. I thought it was an absolute shame."

Back in America, Cheryl Lee Sheil was watching the television news because her sister had called to tell her that their father, William Sheil, was actually in Beirut. Concerned, Cheryl turned on the TV news and saw that the networks were airing clips of the damaged embassy. "I was watching them bring out dead bodies," said Cheryl. "I remember there was one gentleman hanging over a balcony, and [the networks] kept showing him again and again, and I said, well, gee, somebody should go get that guy. And it was worse because he was wearing a jacket that looked like one that my dad had bought when he was in Chicago visiting at Christmastime. I said [to myself], *Oh, I hope that's not Dad.*" It was.

The *Washington Post*'s Nora Boustany came running down to the corniche when she heard the explosion. "It was the only time I felt completely speechless," Boustany recalled. "I couldn't talk. I just stood there in shock, looking at the bodies on the sidewalk."

Alison Haas—the wife of CIA station chief Ken Haas—had heard the explosion, but it never entered her mind that Americans might have been targeted. A month earlier, she'd heard a blast just down the street from their apartment. Some of the debris had landed on their balcony, and many people had been killed. So Alison told herself this was just another Beirut explosion. She walked around the corner to her local grocery and bought Ken some cigarettes. As she returned she saw a crowd gathering and pointing at a huge plume of white smoke. Alison then heard someone say "American embassy" in Arabic. She ran home and immediately tried phoning Ken, but she kept getting a busy signal. Alison interpreted this as a good sign. She turned on the radio and was somewhat reassured when she heard a report that the explosion had hit the consular section and that "only" two or three people had been hurt. She waited until 3:00 P.M.—and finally she got in her car and drove back to the embassy. She had to stop the car and get out several blocks away because the road was blocked. She started running. Several marines tried to stop her, but she got past them and kept running. Finally, an embassy officer grabbed her and asked her who had been in the CIA office that morning. Alison said everyone except Frank Johnston. She hadn't seen Frank. By then, Alison was becoming hysterical. No one would let her around the corner where she could have seen the full extent of the damage to the front facade of the embassy. Someone took her by the hand and drove her to the ambassador's residence.

Early that evening Ambassador Dillon returned to the residence and gently knelt down on one knee before Alison and said that so far Ken had not been found. He explained that the CIA office on the fifth floor had taken the full force of the blast. Alison replied, "They could be in an air pocket, they could be trapped."

Later that night Alison was taken back to her apartment, where she saw that someone had brought Arlette, Frank Johnston's Palestinian-Israeli wife. Arlette had heard the explosion from her apartment. The blast was "so hard it shook the windows." She'd then run down to the embassy only to see that it was gone. She'd seen only darkness and black smoke. "The day seemed night," she later wrote in her diary. By the time Alison arrived home, Arlette knew her husband was gone. Someone had handed her his wallet—proof that he'd been found. They didn't tell her the grim story of *how* he'd been found. Soon after the blast, as the cloud of smoke and dust cleared, the marines could see someone trapped between two slabs of concrete. It was Frank Johnston, and he was still alive. Rescuers got to him fairly quickly and managed to pry him loose. But his body had been severely crushed. Just before he died, Frank managed to ask that his wallet be given to his wife.

Arlette was given a sleeping pill and codeine—and she eventually fell asleep. But Alison couldn't sleep, even when a marine doctor gave her another dose of codeine. Finally, around 3:00 A.M. on Wednesday, Murray McKann, one of three CIA officers who hadn't been in the

embassy late that morning, came and told Alison, "They found him."
Alison said, "Is he alive?" And Murray had to say, "No."

Deputy Chief of Mission Bob Pugh formally identified the bodies
of Jim and Monique Lewis, Deborah Hixon, Ken Haas, and Phyllis
Faraci. "They were not mangled," Pugh recalled. "They looked very
much like themselves. They'd been suffocated by the debris and dirt. It
looked almost as if they had died in their sleep."

Susan Morgan, the CIA officer on a TDY assignment to Beirut, was
having a leisurely lunch in the southern port city of Sidon when her
hostess casually mentioned that there'd been an explosion in the embassy. Morgan thought she was joking. Another guest at the luncheon
table reminded her that such things happened all the time in Lebanon:
"We're used to it." Morgan and another embassy official quickly piled
into their car for the hour-long drive back to Beirut. Bob Ames had
called Morgan early that morning to invite her to have dinner with him
and a "Shi'a businessman"—none other than Mustafa Zein. They'd
agreed to meet at the Mayflower Hotel at 7:30 P.M. Morgan felt nau-
seous on the drive back to Beirut. She knew Bob had been heading for
the embassy that morning.

Morgan arrived at the embassy at 4:00 P.M. The scene of devastation stunned her. Bulldozers were already at work, clearing the rubble.
"I see the walking wounded, and search for faces I know," Morgan
wrote a few days later in a "Beirut Diary" that the CIA classified "secret." She saw a Foreign Service officer who'd been in the building, but
when she asked about Ames, he just shook his head and said he didn't
know, but that "many people have died." Morgan went back to the
Mayflower, hoping to find a message from Ames; there was nothing,
so she left one for him in case he returned. It then occurred to her that
Bob might have been taken to the hospital, so she rushed over to the
nearby American University of Beirut hospital. The emergency room
was crowded with wounded people, but when Morgan scanned a list

of the admitted wounded, Ames was not on the list. "I ask nurses," Morgan wrote. "Nothing. In my heart, I know already."

By 9:00 P.M. Morgan returned to the embassy: "Nothing has changed except that tear gas canisters stored in the embassy are leaking. I approach the rubble to start searching only to drop back when I get a mouthful of gas." Floodlights had been erected so that rescue workers could see as they dug through the rubble. Standing on the perimeter, just outside the floodlights amid the wrecked cars and debris, Bob Pugh pointed up to a dangling body, pinned between two upper floors. "I fix my eyes on the body," Morgan wrote, "trying to see around it, to look for Bob Ames." As the hours passed, the night air grew so chilly that Morgan left briefly to find a coat at a friend's nearby flat. But she hurried back to the site, fearing that Ames's body would be found in her absence. In fact, no bodies had been found in the rubble since 6:00 P.M.

"Suddenly, at 0230," Morgan wrote, "there is a commotion at the rubble heap. People cluster around one spot. A body has been found. My heart skips and I know." Someone waved Morgan over and asked her to identify the body. "I look briefly. Yes. I am handed his passport and wallet." Oddly, there was not a mark on Ames's body or clothes, and Morgan later speculated that he'd died in the elevator from the concussion of the bomb.*

Bob Ames may have died alone. His daughter Karen later overheard someone at the memorial service saying that Bob had been found in a stairwell. "He looked like he'd just probably been leaving the cafeteria, heading up to a meeting, that he was facedown, that his eyes were already closed, and that he was killed by the impact of the explosion, not that anything had fallen on him, and that there was just a small cut on his neck."

An embassy officer reminded Susan Morgan that she should retrieve

---

* According to Ames's death certificate, Dr. Ahmed Harati noted that the cause of death was "fractures, burns, wounds, internal hemorrhage as a result of the explosion."

all of Bob's papers from his hotel room. But Morgan was determined to accompany the body to the morgue. She followed the ambulance, arriving at the morgue around 3:30 A.M. It was a grisly scene, and the morgue's guards tried to dissuade her from entering. Morgan ignored them and climbed a railing to get into the room. Upon entering, she saw that there were five other bodies lying on the floor. "I retrieve Bob's wedding ring, pray for his soul, and tell him goodbye," Morgan wrote. "I wonder why I do not cry." She had to get someone to cut off Bob's wedding ring, and she noticed that he was wearing a small chain around his neck. She took that too.* A half hour later, Morgan walked into the Mayflower, a regular venue for visiting Americans. The staff was in shock. "I tell them what I know of the dead and the living," Morgan wrote. And then she explained that she needed to pack up his belongings—and make sure nothing of a classified nature was left behind. Only then did Morgan find a phone to call Langley. It was around 5:00 A.M. Beirut time when she called to report that she'd made a positive identification of Ames's body. Back in Washington it was nearly 10:00 P.M. on Monday evening.

Mustafa Zein had expected to see Ames that evening. He had made dinner reservations at Al-Ajami restaurant for himself, Ames, Ken Haas, and Susan Morgan. That afternoon, as Zein was driving to his appointment with President Amin Gemayel's cousin, he saw the plume of smoke along the corniche, and he briefly worried about his American friends. But he nevertheless decided to show up at Al-Ajami on time—and he waited alone with growing anxiety until the restaurant closed at 2:00 A.M. "I really, really lost it that day," Zein later said.

Pete Gallant, a thirty-four-year-old State Department security officer, arrived on Tuesday afternoon on a flight from Athens. Gallant

---

* The wedding ring was eventually given to Yvonne Ames; it still had blood on it. Yvonne gave the necklace to Karen Ames, then fifteen. Twenty years later, Karen said, "I've never taken it off."

was charged with writing up a preliminary investigation of the bombing. "The smoke had cleared," he said, "but blood and body parts were everywhere. It is a smell you never forget." The charred engine block of the truck carrying the bomb was retrieved from the shallow waters of the fishermen's cove across the street from the embassy. Gallant learned from the embassy's resident security officer, Dick Gannon, that two Delta vehicular barriers had been sitting in storage for nearly a year. They were to have been installed on the embassy's driveway the following week.

Three days after the blast, Marine Sgt. Charles Light and Cpl. Brian Korn crawled back into the rubble. They'd been instructed to see if they could find a safe in the marine office on the ground floor where their diplomatic passports were stored. They found the safe and the passports, and on their way out Corporal Korn said, "Here's where Post One used to be. Robert's here, we need to get him out." Sergeant Light and Corporal Korn spent forty-five minutes digging through the rubble before they found him. "He was standing straight up, bent over," Korn later testified. "His head was smashed like a pancake, real flat, real long." Both his legs and his arms were broken—and, grotesquely—a steel rod had plunged through his chest. Corporal Bobby McMaugh had died instantly. Still, it was a terrible death.

Altogether, sixty-three people died and some 120 people were wounded, many with lifelong injuries. Seventeen Americans were killed, along with thirty-two Lebanese employees of the embassy and fourteen visitors or passersby, mostly Lebanese applying for American visas. Of the seventeen Americans, eight were CIA officers—an unprecedented number then or since.* The other dead Americans included one U.S. marine, four other U.S. servicemen, three USAID officials—and Janet Lee Stevens, the freelance American reporter.

* Three CIA officers survived the blast only because they happened to be out of the building. Susan Morgan was having lunch in the southern Lebanese port city of Sidon. Murray J. McKann had slipped out of the building to inspect a Persian carpet he was considering buying. And Alexander MacPherson was avoiding the embassy precisely because he was in Lebanon under deep cover.

The truck bomb had hit the embassy at 1:04 P.M., or shortly after 6:00 A.M. Washington time. Yvonne had risen early that morning and gone as usual to the local YMCA to swim. It was part of her new regimen. She returned a little later to get the children off to school. Around 9:00 A.M. someone from the CIA called and asked if she'd seen the news on television. Yvonne said no. She was then told that the embassy had been bombed but that they'd had no communication with Beirut. Yvonne didn't know what to think. It was "employee lunch day" at her office and she'd prepared some food for the potluck, so she decided to go in to work. She was then working full-time as an administrative assistant at the accounting firm of Arthur Young. "I continued through the day as though nothing had happened," Yvonne recalled. She mentioned her worry to only one friend at work. That evening, she received a phone call from Beirut. It was Mustafa Zein, asking rather plaintively if she'd heard from Bob. Mustafa was clearly concerned and upset, so Yvonne tried to reassure him that Bob was just out of reach. She still hadn't heard anything more from the Agency, but she nervously decided to keep a dinner appointment at a friend's house nearby. She left the children at home, giving them a number where she could be reached. The children hadn't heard about the bombing—and Yvonne didn't want to alarm them with what could only be speculation. So she went out.

Later that Monday evening, around 10:00 P.M., Kristen, eighteen, was upstairs watching television in her parents' bedroom. She came across a news report about the Beirut bombing and remembered thinking, "That's interesting." She knew her father was out in the Middle East, but she didn't know his itinerary. When she mentioned the news report to Kevin, eleven, and Karen, fifteen, they speculated that their father probably hadn't arrived, and in any case they would have heard something if he was there. A few moments later, Kristen heard the doorbell. When she opened the door, she saw two strangers, Thomas Braman and his wife, Lillian. They introduced themselves as colleagues of her father's. They asked if Yvonne was at home, and upon learning that she was out, Braman waited for Yvonne to return. Later, Braman asked Kristen if she'd seen the news about Beirut. When Kristen said yes, Braman said he thought Bob was in the embassy and that he might have been killed.

"I told them he wasn't there," Kristen said, "and that he wasn't killed."

Tom replied, "Well, we do think he was there, and he was killed."

Kristen said, "No."

Finally, Lillian Braman said, "No, we don't think. We know. He was killed." At this point, Kristen broke down and started screaming hysterically. Her brother Kevin was in his room upstairs. He'd heard Kristen answer the door and then heard her piercing scream. "It's the kind of scream you hear," he later said, "and you cringe inside, because you know something horrible has happened."

Moments before this, Karen had been sitting on her bed, trying to memorize a line from her French homework. "As I was staring at that page," Karen said, "trying to memorize that line, a chill came over me. And I just looked up, and my [elder] brother [Andrew] was standing in my doorway, and his hands were stuffed in his pockets. And I just said, 'He's dead.'" She remembers Andrew just shook his head and ran off. Karen picked up a phone and called a friend and told her, "What am I going to do? My dad's dead."

Andrew remembers the same scene a little differently. He was in his room upstairs and heard Kristen's screams, so he ran into the living room, where he saw two strangers standing with Kevin and Kristen. Everyone was crying. "I went immediately downstairs to Karen's room," Andrew said, "and I stood in the doorway. She looked up at me, and she saw it right away. She said, 'He's dead.' And I just nodded and ran back to my room."

Eleven-year-old Kevin had a hard time comprehending what was happening. He walked downstairs to the family's small study and sat in his father's rocking chair. He sat there for the longest time, just rocking back and forth. Unconsciously, as he rocked, he gripped one handle so tightly that his thumbnail wore a deep groove into the wood.

One of the children had called their mother at the phone number she'd left for them. When Yvonne got the call, she knew. She rushed home and walked into the house in tears. She remembers little. It was all a blur. She had to call Bob's mom, and his sisters and her own parents. "From that time on, the house was filled with people for about two weeks," Yvonne said. "But it didn't give us any time to be alone together and to grieve together and to come to some sort of closure." Her neighbors brought by home-cooked dishes, often walking past black government limousines parked in the cul-de-sac. CIA director Bill Casey came to the house and offered his condolences, as did many others.

The children were devastated—and also shocked to learn that their father had worked for the CIA and not the State Department. They felt both a sense of wonder and disbelief. Their father had lied to them all these years—but at the same time they felt a certain pride in what they were beginning to learn about what he'd done.

The news quickly spread through the hallways of Langley. Eight CIA employees were dead. "When I heard the news," Clair George said, "I ran out into the hall and screamed, 'Does anyone know what to do?'" Sam Wyman got a phone call from a friend in the DO Watch Office. He was informed that one of the three DO officers who hadn't been in the embassy had phoned from Beirut and reported that the station had been wiped out. "I broke down," Wyman recalled. "I called my wife and cried. I was dumbfounded and shocked. It was just unbelievable." Wyman was then chief of the Arabian Peninsula Branch for the DO, but he'd soon be tasked with supervising the bombing investigation. *Lindsay Sherwin* had heard the morning news reports about the Beirut attack but had thought Bob would be okay. As the day progressed, *Sherwin* began to feel sick. Late that evening he got the phone call. He too cried. The next morning he tried to go to work as usual. *Sherwin* made it to Langley's parking lot. "And then I had to turn around and go home," he said. "It was horrific. The Agency did not know how to deal with it."

In Tel Aviv that day *Dov Zeit*, a senior Israeli intelligence officer, had been awaiting Ames's scheduled visit later in the week. "The word spread that there had been an explosion," *Zeit* recalled. "The mood among those of us who had known him was of deep mourning. A certain melancholy settled in. We Israelis may be rough, but we can also be very sentimental."

The next morning, Ames's NSC counterpart, Geoff Kemp, noted in his diary, "Bob Ames among the dead in Beirut. We believe Iran involved. Felt very sad about Bob."

Five days later, on Saturday, April 23, President Ronald Reagan took a marine helicopter out to Andrews Air Force Base to meet a cargo plane containing sixteen coffins. (One of the Americans killed, Albert N. Votaw, a USAID official, was cremated in Beirut at the wishes of his family.) The sixteen flag-draped coffins were lined up in an airport hangar. Inexplicably, the mourners were not told which casket contained the body of their husband or son or daughter. The relatives of those killed stood nearby, weeping. Reagan spoke briefly and, visibly shaken, walked among the mourners. "It was a moving experience," Reagan wrote in his diary that night. "Nancy and I met individually with the families of the deceased. We were both in tears—I know all I could do was grip their hands—I was too choked up to speak." Reagan lingered for a few moments more with Yvonne Ames, who was wearing a short black veil to cover her eyes. Someone told the president that these were Bob Ames's widow and children. "There was definitely a marked sadness on his face and in his eyes," Karen Ames recalled. "They both gave us hugs."

Ames was the only one of the victims whom the president had known. They'd seen each other just a month earlier, on March 17, 1983, in the White House. When he heard that Ames was one of the victims, Reagan had noted in his diary, "We lost [name deleted] our top research man on Middle East." Afterwards, Reagan told an aide that the ceremony was one of the most difficult things he'd ever had to do.

The very next day, on Sunday, April 24, Ames's casket was loaded aboard a military funeral carriage drawn by four horses. A U.S. marine in dress uniform led a riderless horse up a hill in Arlington National Cemetery. Yvonne and the children sat under a canopy by the burial site. Mustafa Zein had hastily flown in from Beirut for the funeral; he rode in a black limousine with Yvonne and her brother to the cemetery and sat with the family at the grave site. A squad of marines fired their rifles in the air. After the casket was lowered into the ground, Yvonne remembers someone handing her an American flag, folded into a triangle. She remembered little else: "I was there in body, but it was like—it was just the body." Eighteen-year-old Kristen asked if they could put a flower on the casket, or just touch it: "We were told we couldn't do that." Afterwards, Yvonne had to return to her Reston home with her six children. She was numb with fear and grief. "Bob's death fractured our family," she later explained. "It's like when you take a photograph and rip it. You can try to piece it back together, but it's never the same."

That they'd never been allowed to see Bob's body made things infinitely worse. It had been surreal at Andrews Air Force Base, where they'd had to stare at sixteen flag-draped coffins without knowing which contained Bob's body. Later, Yvonne had asked if she or another family member could identify the body—and she was told this was not possible. "There was no closure for us," Yvonne said in 2003. "I think if we'd been able to see Bob . . . we could have had closure. I know I have spent these twenty years thinking, well, perhaps he was involved in something and for the safety of his family—I feel ridiculous saying this, but it is the truth—that he was alive somewhere."

All the children had the same thoughts. "I guess the way we put it in our minds," Kristen said, "was that he was doing something noble for us, and he's not really in there; he's just protecting us from whoever's trying to get him so that he's alive somewhere. . . . There's a hope."

On Tuesday, April 26, more than 3,100 diplomats, government employees, and private citizens gathered in the nave of Washington's National Cathedral to honor all those who had died. Vice President

George H. W. Bush attended the forty-five-minute memorial service, as did Defense Secretary Caspar Weinberger. Bush made a point of taking Yvonne aside and offered her his condolences.

The April 1983 Beirut embassy bombing is a largely forgotten moment in the history of America's presence in the Middle East. But it was a signal moment. It was the beginning of America's deadly encounter with a political Islamist movement. It was also the birth of a Shi'ite political entity that we now know as Hezbollah. As a 1984 declassified CIA document noted, "The [1979] Iranian revolution . . . and the Israeli invasion of predominantly-Shi'a southern Lebanon galvanized the Shi'a and set the stage for the emergence of radical groups prone to terrorism." Young Shi'ites in southern Lebanon traumatized by the Israeli invasion saw the Americans as allies of the Israelis. It's easy to see how America became a target. "We were very much identified with the Israelis," testified Ambassador Robert Dillon in 2003, "particularly among the Shi'as. There was huge resentment of the Israelis by this time in southern Lebanon."

Ambassador Robert Oakley read a flash cable about the bombing while standing in his office in the U.S. embassy in Mogadishu, Somalia. "I was not astonished," he later said, "because we'd seen the frenzy with which the Lebanese Shi'a responded to the United States following the Israeli invasion of Lebanon in 1982, and above all, the massacres of the Palestinians at Sabra and Shatila camp. The United States by that time had become identified with the Israelis and we were seen as an enemy of Islam and as an enemy of Iran because we were supporting the Iraqis in the war against Iran—and the Iranians had good reason to try to get us out of there. But we also were seen throughout the Middle East and particularly in Lebanon as sort of public enemy number one right after the Israelis themselves."

To be sure, Americans had lost their lives before in this troubled part of the world. Ambassadors had been assassinated. But April 18, 1983, was the first time a truck bomb was used against a high-profile target like an American embassy. President Reagan and Secretary Shultz tried to talk tough in the wake of the embassy tragedy. Reagan publicly called the bombing a "vicious . . . cowardly act." Shultz said, "Let us rededicate ourselves to the battle against terrorism." But these words were mere bromides. There was no talk of retaliation, because no one was quite sure who'd carried out the attack. Privately, Reagan confided in his diary, "Lord forgive me for the hatred I feel for the humans who can do such a cruel but cowardly deed." But he knew there was nothing to be done.

At a memorial service at CIA headquarters, Bill Casey described Ames as "the closest thing to an irreplaceable man." He intoned, "They did not die in vain."

But in reality, the truck bomb, driven by a single suicidal driver, demonstrated more than just America's political and military weakness in the Middle East. For some, it seemed to underscore that Americans were very much out of place in this part of the world. Shortly before Susan Morgan left Beirut, she ran into a young U.S. Army officer who'd been working on providing military assistance to Lebanon's national army. He was bitterly disillusioned and told Morgan that "his men had come out here John Wayne–style, believing that they could save Lebanon, only to find themselves being shot at by the Israelis and bombed by the Arabs." He said, "We should withdraw and let the people here fight it out among themselves. They deserve each other."

On Wednesday, April 27, Morgan got up in the middle of the night to catch her ride to the airport. It was 3:00 A.M. "I look out my hotel window to the Embassy on the seaside, less than a mile away. It is brightly and garishly lit up, the only visible building in the blackness and mist. From here it looks almost like a stage set. It seems right to turn my back and drive away from Beirut in the darkness."

Shortly afterwards, Morgan resigned from the CIA.

CHAPTER THIRTEEN

The Enigma of Imad Mughniyeh

When in doubt, and we are always in doubt about this, blame Mughniyeh.

— *A retired CIA officer*

In the days after the attack, Bill Casey was visibly angry. He ordered his officers to launch an investigation. He wanted justice for those who'd died in Beirut. But it wouldn't be easy. "Terrorist targets had shifted," said John McMahon, Casey's deputy director. "At one time, we had a PLO that was big enough to penetrate. But what we were getting now in places like Lebanon were small mom-and-pop operations. Unless you're practically a member of the family, you don't get in. These organizations are almost impossible to infiltrate."

The National Security Agency scoured its satellite data for any intercepts of phone conversations in the region that mentioned the embassy as a target. All it could find were some cryptic conversations between Iranian Foreign Office officials in Tehran and their diplomats in Damascus. The NSA may also have intercepted some phone calls from Revolutionary Guard officers in Baalbek and the Iranian embassy in Damascus. The intercepts merely hinted that someone might be striking at an American installation somewhere in the region. One intercepted cable from the Iranian Foreign Ministry reported that $25,000 had been sent to Lebanon for an unspecified operation.* Only in retrospect did it seem logical that they were talk-ing about the American embassy as a target.

Later that autumn, President Reagan was awakened at 2:30 A.M. on October 23, 1983, with a phone call informing him that another truck bomb had exploded—this time hitting the barracks near Beirut airport that housed U.S. marines serving as part of the Multinational Force. This bomb was much larger the one that had hit the U.S. embassy six months earlier. It created an explosion the equivalent of twenty-one thousand pounds of TNT—the largest non-nuclear event ever. It killed 241 U.S. servicemen. "We all believe Iranians did this bombing," Rea-gan wrote in his diary, "just as they did with our embassy last April."

In a generic sense, this judgment is probably accurate. But many aspects of both tragedies remained a mystery. The Reagan administra-tion really didn't know *who* had hit them. "We were too paralyzed by self-doubt," recalled Secretary of State George Shultz.

Casey asked his in-house counselor, Frederick Hutchinson, to su-pervise an investigation. "When Bob was killed," Hutchinson said, "Casey asked me to give him a full picture of what happened and why." Hutchinson had entered the Agency as a high-ranking GS-16 in 1974. Bill Colby had recruited him from the Defense Department. Born in 1933, Hutchinson was one of the officers who'd persuaded Casey to promote Ames to be head of the Near East and South Asia Division in the Directorate of Intelligence. Hutchinson ended up writing a twenty-five-page report on the embassy attack. The report remains classified. But Hutchinson recollects its substance: "It criti-cized the State Department's security policies. The embassy was wide open to attack." Within hours of the truck-bomb attack someone had called several media outlets in Beirut and claimed responsibility on behalf of the Islamic Jihad Organization (IJO). No one had ever

---

* The syndicated columnist Jack Anderson reported on these intercepts. Casey was furious over the leak of such highly classified information. Tipped off that their commu-nications were being intercepted, the Iranians fixed the breach, and soon this source of intercept intelligence dried up.

heard of this group. Hutchinson believes the IJO was actually a cover name for Islamic Amal, a recent breakaway faction from Amal, the Shi'ite Lebanese political party led by Nabih Berri. Hutchinson recalls that the Lebanese intelligence agency picked up four individuals who'd witnessed the attack. But they were released two days later. They merely told police that they'd seen a young man wearing a black leather jacket crash a black pickup truck into the front door of the embassy.

Eventually, a dozen people were arrested, including an Egyptian named "Harb," who Hutchinson believes was the "principal grunt on the ground who helped put the bomb together."

In a subsequent phase of the investigation, a CIA contract officer named Keith Hall, age thirty-two, was ordered to fly to Beirut to interrogate those arrested by the Deuxième Bureau, Lebanon's intelligence bureau, headed at the time by Johnny Abdo. Hall was a former U.S. marine who'd worked as a cop in California before joining the CIA in 1979. (He'd also earned a master's degree in history.) At the time, he was assigned to the CIA's investigative and analysis unit. He was called to Langley's seventh floor and told, "We want you to go to Beirut and find out who blew up the embassy and how they did it. The President himself is going to be reading your cables. There is going to be some retribution here."

Hall later told his story to author Mark Bowden in the *Atlantic* magazine. He flew to Beirut and occupied an office in the Deuxième Bureau. And he confessed to Bowden that he "took part without hesitation in brutal questioning" of the Lebanese men arrested. Clubs and rubber hoses were used. The suspects eventually fingered a man named Elias Nimr, whom they described as the "paymaster" of the bombing. Nimr was arrested, but he initially evinced no fear, thinking that his family and political connections would protect him. He was only twenty-eight years old, but he was already a feared man. Years later, *Newsweek*'s accomplished investigative reporter Christopher Dickey wrote that Nimr "appears to have been a double, triple, a geometric-multiple agent. He was a Christian Lebanese intelligence chief who was trained by the Israelis but allegedly worked secretly for the Syrians as a paymaster for agents from Iran."

The Lebanese allowed Hall to feed questions to Nimr's interrogators, and over the course of ten days Hall personally questioned Nimr alone. According to Bowden, on the first occasion Hall bluntly told Nimr, "I'm an American intelligence officer. You really didn't think that you were going to blow up our embassy and we wouldn't do anything about it, did you?" Hall warned him that his Lebanese compatriots were not going to let him go. "That's not going to happen," Hall said. "You're mine. I'm the one who will make the decisions about what happens to you. The only thing that will save your ass is to cooperate." When Nimr refused to talk, he was taken to a cell and made to stand for two days.

When he was brought back for another session, Hall kicked the chair out from under Nimr. He still refused to talk. "I sent him back to his cell," Hall said, "[and] had water poured over him again and again while he sat under a big fan, kept him freezing for about twenty-four hours. He comes back after this, and you can see his mood is changing. He hasn't walked out of jail, and it's beginning to dawn on him that no one is going to spring him."

In future sessions, Hall watched as a Lebanese captain used a wooden bat to hit Nimr across his shins. The torture worked—or at least it persuaded Nimr to tell Hall what he wanted to hear. Nimr confessed that he'd been part of the plot to bomb the embassy. He also confessed to having some complicity in the assassination of President-elect Bashir Gemayel the previous autumn. He admitted that he'd been taking orders from Syrian intelligence agents. Hall taped Nimr's confession and flew back to Langley, convinced that he'd broken the case.

Not long afterwards, however, Hall learned that Nimr had died in his jail cell. Hall assumed Lebanese security officials had ordered Nimr's death to silence him and protect other parties implicated in the embassy plot. Someone also leaked the fact that a CIA officer had participated in the kind of rough interrogation techniques that had led to the death of the suspect. This earned Hall the moniker "Captain Crunch."

Fred Hutchinson recalls that when Casey learned of Nimr's death he hit the roof. Hall hadn't been there when the man died, but he'd tortured the man. Casey thought this could embarrass the Agency, so he had Hall fired. "We had the Justice Department look into whether Hall should be prosecuted," said Hutchinson. "But they said there was no case, so we just dismissed Hall. He later sued the Agency for wrongful dismissal, but nothing came of it."

Hall remains bitter and disillusioned about his experience in the Agency. And apparently he's unrepentant about his rough interrogation of Nimr. He believes the Agency made a mistake by refusing to pursue the leads he developed. The Lebanese eventually released all the suspects they'd rounded up. "No one was punished for it," Hall said, "except me!"

Unfortunately, the evidence against Nimr is less definitive than Captain Crunch would have us believe. *Newsweek*'s Dickey reported that in 1985 a Lebanese judge named Nimr as responsible for the embassy bombing. But Dickey also reported that "some of Nimr's old colleagues say he was just a victim of bloody inter-service rivalries among Lebanon's covert warlords and had nothing to do with the case." And, of course, the very fact that Captain Crunch used torture devalues Nimr's confession. Aside from that confession, there's no other evidence tying Nimr to the embassy bombing. It was, in fact, a dead end.

Other Agency officers dismiss the evidence obtained by Hall against Nimr. Robert Baer was a CIA officer who joined the Directorate of Operations in 1976 and spent the next twenty years in India, the Middle East, and Central Asia. Baer never met Ames, but he made it his business over the years to investigate the embassy bombing. He wrote about his conclusions in his 2002 memoir *See No Evil*. The book doesn't even mention Captain Crunch. Baer has a wholly different theory. "Iran ordered it," writes Baer, "and a Fatah network carried it out." When he says "a Fatah network" he means Imad Mughniyeh, the elusive Lebanese Shi'ite operative who joined Fatah at an early age.

Baer makes a circumstantial case that Mughniyeh was still in touch with his old Fatah comrades when the embassy was attacked.

Soon after Ames was killed, his fellow Arabist Sam Wyman was appointed head of Arab-Israeli affairs in the Directorate of Operations. "I was asked to keep tabs on the investigation of the embassy bombing," Wyman said. "I went out to Beirut and met with officers from the Lebanese intelligence and police services. And I read the investigative reports. But I don't recall ever seeing any hard evidence on who did it." As late as 2001, former defense secretary Caspar Weinberger told PBS, "We still do not have actual knowledge of who did the bombing of the Marine barracks at the Beirut Airport, and we certainly didn't then." Yet over the years, a consensus has gradually emerged that places Mughniyeh as the key protagonist in any narrative on who was responsible for the 1983 embassy bombing. Still, the evidence is curiously opaque.

Mughniyeh lived in the shadows. Even his birth is in dispute. Some accounts say he was born on July 12, 1962, in the village of Teir Dibna, a mountainous region overlooking the southern Lebanese coastal city of Tyre. But Mughniyeh seems to have doctored any official records. He may have been born on January 25, 1962, in Al-Jiwar, a poor neighborhood in the southern suburbs of Beirut. He came from a poor Shi'a family who for generations had made their living from a small orchard of olive and lemon trees. He grew up in the slums of southern Beirut, bordering the largely Palestinian refugee camps of Sabra and Shatila. They lived in a simple cinder-block house with no running water. His friends described him as "very smart" and "always alert." In 1976—at the age of fourteen—Mughniyeh and some of his friends joined a Fatah student training camp near Damour, on the southern Lebanese coast. A Fatah intelligence officer named Anis Naqqash ran the twenty-day military training course. "Imad stood out from the others," Naqqash told Nicholas Blanford, the author of a history of Hezbollah, "because while everyone was looking forward to the end of the course when they would get to fire guns, Imad was more interested in learning about tactics. He was the only one, apart from a teacher and a Maoist, who wrote down notes during the course. He was not interested in shooting guns like the others."

Mughniyeh may possibly have spent a short time studying business at the American University of Beirut. But in the midst of the Lebanese civil war, probably in late 1978 when the Israelis invaded Lebanon for the first time, Mughniyeh was recruited into Ali Hassan Salameh's elite Force 17. At some point, he may have benefited from training provided by the CIA to "professionalize" Arafat's personal bodyguard unit. Mughniyeh served as a bodyguard for Yasir Arafat, and he fought as a sniper along the Green Line dividing East and West Beirut. He made his first visit to postrevolutionary Iran as early as 1979. Some accounts have him performing the Haj to Mecca in 1980 in the company of Ayatollah Mohammed Hussein Fadlallah, then a leading Shi'ite cleric. Like many young Shi'ite Lebanese, Mughniyeh was radicalized by the disappearance of Lebanon's charismatic Shi'ite cleric, Imam Musa Sadr, who vanished mysteriously on a trip to Libya in 1978. And he was further radicalized by the Israeli siege of Beirut in the summer of 1982. He'd witnessed the emotional scene between Janet Lee Stevens and Arafat in which Janet had pleaded with Arafat not to leave Beirut. And then, of course, Mughniyeh had been deeply affected by the Sabra and Shatila massacres in September 1982. He had plenty of motives.

But in April 1983 Mughniyeh was only twenty years old. As the CIA's Robert Baer asks in his memoir, "How did a poor boy from Ayn al-Dilbah rise out of the ashes of the 1982 invasion and in less than a year put together the most lethal and well-funded terrorist organization in the world?" Baer points out the obvious: it just didn't add up. Mughniyeh seems too young, at age twenty, to have been the mastermind for the embassy bombing. Yet in subsequent decades Mughniyeh was deeply implicated in all sorts of attacks. The CIA blames him for a long string of terrorist attacks over a period of twenty-five years:

- The marine barracks bombing in Beirut that took the lives of 241 U.S. servicemen on October 23, 1983

- The March 16, 1984, kidnapping of Beirut CIA station chief William Buckley, who died in captivity
- The September 20, 1984, bombing of the U.S. embassy annex in Beirut
- The June 14, 1985, hijacking of TWA Flight 847 and the murder of U.S. Navy diver Robert Stethem (Mughniyeh's fingerprints were found on the airplane)
- The kidnappings of dozens of Westerners in Lebanon during the 1980s
- The March 17, 1992, bombing of the Israeli embassy in Buenos Aires that killed twenty-nine people
- The July 18, 1994, bombing of a Jewish cultural center in Argentina that killed eighty-six people
- The June 25, 1996, bombing of the Khobar Towers in Saudi Arabia that killed nineteen American solders and one Saudi civilian

If you count the U.S. embassy bombings and the marine barracks attack, Mughniyeh was responsible for more American deaths than anyone until the September 11, 2001, attacks on American soil by Osama bin Laden's Al-Qaeda. But the notion that Mughniyeh had a hand in the embassy and marine barracks attacks really only arose after the June 1985 hijacking of TWA Flight 847. Mughniyeh was indicted that year in a U.S. court for his role in the TWA hijacking and the death of U.S. Navy diver Robert Stethem. It was Mughniyeh's long résumé of post-1985 terrorist operations that has led many to assume that he must have been the mastermind of the 1983 attacks. "When in doubt," said one retired CIA officer, "and we are always in doubt about this, blame Mughniyeh."

In any case, while there's much that *isn't* known about the elusive Mughniyeh, it *is* known that, sometime after Arafat's departure from Beirut in August 1982, he offered his services to Shi'ite Lebanese political forces. Hezbollah—the Party of God—didn't exist at the time, at least by that name. But a shadowy Shi'a resistance group known as Islamic Amal had formed that summer, inspired by the Iranian revolution. Another group, the Islamic Jihad Organization, was probably the same entity under another name. Both parties eventually morphed into what we today call Hezbollah. But in late 1982 any Shi'a resistance was an effective arm of Iran's Revolutionary Guard. By offering his services to Islamic Amal, Mughniyeh was going to work for the Revolutionary Guard.

According to the journalist Hala Jaber, who in 1997 wrote *Hezbollah: Born with a Vengeance*, Mughniyeh had become thoroughly disillusioned with the PLO and "turned to the newly arrived Iranian Revolutionary Guards." Jaber reports that the Revolutionary Guard initially tasked Mughniyeh to "gather information and details about the American embassy and draw up a plan that would guarantee the maximum impact and leave no trace of the perpetrator."

Mughniyeh was inventive. A well-known Lebanese member of Al-Fatah, Bilal Sharara, told the Beirut-based journalist Nicholas Blanford that Mughniyeh approached him in the autumn of 1982 with a novel and audacious plan. "He wanted some explosives," Sharara said, "and wondered whether I had some for him." Mughniyeh explained that he had someone who was willing to blow himself up to attack the Israelis. "I laughed," said Sharara, "and thought he was crazy. Who would want to blow himself up? No one had done anything like that at the time." Blanford writes in his history of Hezbollah, *Warriors of God*, that Mughniyeh persuaded a childhood friend—Ahmad Qassir, age seventeen—to drive a white Peugeot sedan into the entrance of the Israeli army headquarters in Tyre. The car exploded and seventy-five Israeli soldiers were killed. This occurred on November 11, 1982—five months prior to the U.S. embassy attack. If Mughniyeh organized the Tyre suicide truck bomb, he could certainly have also been the mastermind behind the embassy bombing. Mossad later came to a qualified conclusion about Mughniyeh's responsibility. "We knew Mughniyeh was later responsible for many other terrorist acts," said Yoram Hessel, a senior Mossad officer. "But he had to have had institutional backing."

In March 1983, Mughniyeh drove to Damascus for a meeting with

Iran's Syrian ambassador, Ali Akbar Mohtashamipur. By Jaber's account in her book about Hezbollah, the Iranian ambassador hosted the meeting in the presence of Syrian intelligence officers. On the agenda was a plan to expel the American, French, and other Multilateral Peacekeeping Forces from Lebanon. Mughniyeh proposed a series of truck-bomb operations modeled after the Tyre attack. If true, the result of this meeting was the April 18, 1983, suicide truck-bomb attack on the Beirut embassy.

Mughniyeh operated in the darkest of shadows. Eventually, he built a network of individuals he could absolutely trust because they were blood relatives. For decades, only two photographs of him seemed to exist, and they were of doubtful provenance. "Imad was a very handsome young man, and very thin," recalled Mustafa Zein, who knew him when he worked for Force 17. "I wouldn't have recognized him from the photographs decades later."

Unlike many of his Shi'a colleagues, Mughniyeh was not motivated by religiosity. The Israelis later recorded a phone conversation in which one of his friends said of him, "He's no great saint when it comes to religion, but his glorious military achievements make up for that and assure him a place in Paradise."

Some sources claim that Mughniyeh underwent plastic surgery to alter his appearance. But this piece of his legend is apocryphal. He lived in Beirut, but unlike Ali Hassan Salameh he rotated randomly between different apartments and cities. By the mid-1980s, he understood very well that he was being hunted. But he was the most elusive of agents. "Mugniyeh is probably the most intelligent, most capable operative we've ever run across, including the KGB or anybody else," said Robert Baer. "He enters by one door, exits by another, changes his cars daily, never makes appointments on a telephone, never is predictable. He only uses people that are related to him that he can trust. He doesn't just recruit people. He is the master terrorist, the grail that we have been after since 1983." A former director general of the Mossad described Mughniyeh as "very shrewd, very talented. . . . He was the liaison between Hezbollah and Iran—and he spent long periods of time in Tehran." Mughniyeh reportedly learned to speak Farsi like a native Persian. The Iranians even gave him citizenship.

Mustafa Zein knew Mughniyeh. They were fellow Shi'ites, both sympathetic to the Palestinian cause, and they shared an admiration for the late Ali Hassan Salameh. They crossed paths again after the March 16, 1984, kidnapping of the Beirut CIA chief of station William F. Buckley. When Buckley disappeared, the CIA's Sam Wyman implored Zein to fly back to Beirut from New York to negotiate his release. Zein knew going back to Beirut entailed obvious risks. But he did it, partly because the Agency told him the rescue effort was dubbed "Operation Bob Ames." Zein did his best. At one point, he had a face-to-face meeting with Mughniyeh in an effort to locate Buckley and other American hostages. Incredibly, he obtained photographs of the hostages posing with a contemporaneous copy of Newsweek magazine. He passed these photos to the CIA. Negotiations ensued. Those holding the hostages made it clear that their key demand was the release of twenty-two Shi'ite prisoners in Kuwait who had been convicted of terrorism. They were known as the Dawa 22.

In the spring of 1985 Zein came back to Beirut. He thought he was close to a deal for the release of American hostages. By then, there were a half-dozen Americans in captivity. But on March 8, 1985, Zein narrowly missed being blown up with Ayatollah Mohammed Hussein Fadlallah, the spiritual guide of Hezbollah. The two men were about to get in Fadlallah's SUV to drive a short distance when the ayatollah was detained at the last moment. But his car was nevertheless sent ahead, and just forty yards from Fadlallah's home a parked car bomb with 440 pounds of explosives ignited. A seven-story building collapsed, killing eighty people. Mughniyeh's brother—who was working as a bodyguard for Fadlallah—was killed along with many of his friends. But both Fadlallah and Zein escaped injury in what is known today as the B'ir al-Abed bombing. They just happened not to be in the SUV targeted by the assassins. According to Bob Woodward, the attempt on Fadlallah's life was a plot jointly organized by the Saudis and Bill Casey. The CIA director had been told that Fadlallah had "blessed" the suicide driver of the truck bomb that had killed Bob Ames. Woodward reported that Casey had a meeting in Washington with the Saudi ambassador Bandar bin Sultan, and the two men agreed on a joint operation funded with $3 million. "They knew that the chief supporter and symbol of terrorism," wrote Woodward, "was the fundamentalist Muslim leader Sheikh Fadlallah, the leader of the Party of God, Hizbollah, in Beirut. Fadlallah had been connected to all three bombings of American facilities in Beirut. He had to go. The two men were in agreement." According to Woodward, Casey got President Reagan to sign a presidential directive authorizing the covert operation. Lebanese operatives recruited from the Phalangist security forces were trained and funded by the CIA. This special force was designated the Foreign Works and Analysis Unit (FWAU). It was designed to launch retaliatory strikes against the terrorists who had blown up the U.S. embassy and the marine barracks in 1983.

But then it all went wrong. The FWAU unit targeted Ayatollah Fadlallah for assassination—but these Lebanese assassins didn't care how many innocents were killed. Casey and Prince Bandar did not intend to kill eighty people. As painted by Woodward, the operation went awry. "When Bandar saw the news account," Woodward wrote, "he got stomach cramps." Woodward reports that the Saudis took steps to blame the attack on other parties. Woodward quotes Bandar as saying, "I take a shot at you. You suspect me and then I turn in my chauffeur and say he did it. You would think I am no longer a suspect." (Prince Bandar later denied any Saudi involvement in the bombing.) Woodward, of course, has no footnotes, just incredible access to incredible sources. But Mustafa Zein also believes that Casey ordered the assassination attempt—and his source is Imad Mughniyeh, who he claims told him that he later found two men involved in the bomb attack that killed his brother, and they confessed that it had been a CIA operation. Again, as is the case with Woodward's account, there is only an oral footnote for this story. Robert Baer and other CIA sources criticize Woodward's story and blame the Lebanese security forces for the bombing.

The B'ir al-Abed bombing sealed the fate of the American hostages. Mughniyeh and his Hezbollah friends hung a white sheet over the bomb site, proclaiming in black letters, "Made in America." Zein's negotiations ended. Buckley was alive as late as July 1985—but he died later that year, probably of dysentery or pneumonia. The other American hostages were not released for months or years to come.

The twenty-year-old Mughniyeh certainly had a role in the Beirut embassy bombing—perhaps he came up with the idea—but many others carried it out. It was too technically complicated an operation for a twenty-year-old former Force 17 bodyguard to handle alone. Zein reports that in the spring of 1985—after Zein was nearly killed in the attempted assassination of Ayatollah Fadlallah—Mughniyeh told him that he hadn't been involved in the embassy attack. He claimed that he'd been told that the truck bomb's first target had been the U.S. marine barracks—but that at the last minute the suicide driver had been diverted to the embassy. He didn't know why. Mughniyeh told Zein, "It was [Ali Reza] Asgari's operation"—referring to the Iranian Revolutionary Guard commander who had recruited him in 1982.

American investigators eventually determined that the truck that plowed into the embassy was bought in Texas, was shipped to Dubai, and then somehow ended up in Beirut. It was packed with an estimated two thousand pounds of explosives. A suicide driver was found to steer the truck into the embassy. But who assembled the bomb? Who financed the operation? Who bought the truck and explosives? These questions were not rigorously explored in a court of law for many years to come.

Finally, in March 2000, Anne Dammarell, one of the pluckiest survivors of the Beirut embassy bombing, read in the newspapers that Terry Anderson, an American journalist kidnapped in Beirut, had won a civil suit against the Islamic Republic of Iran. A U.S. District Court in Washington, D.C., had awarded Anderson more than $41 million in compensatory damages for his six years in captivity. Dammarell called Anderson's lawyer, Stuart H. Newberger of Crowell & Moring LLP, and asked if he would represent her and other survivors and relatives of the victims of the embassy bombing. Stu Newberger agreed. In 2002, the civil suit was filed in the name of Anne Dammarell but also on behalf of Yvonne Ames, her children, and a dozen other plaintiffs. A trial was held, and in September 2003 U.S. district court judge John D. Bates ruled that the Islamic Republic of Iran was responsible for the April 18, 1983, bombing. The court determined that the bombing was carried out with technical assistance from the Iranian Revolutionary Guard Corps stationed in the Bekaa Valley. Chemical analysis of the explosives used in the attack determined that the truck was loaded with about two thousand pounds of PETN (pentaerythritol tetranitrate), a military-grade explosive. Moreover, investigators determined that the PETN in question was not commercially available in Lebanon—but that this raw, "bulk form" of PETN was manufactured in Iran for military purposes. This was not an easily assembled bomb. The materials came from a military factory in Iran.

Unfortunately, there is no declassified intercept intelligence available pertaining to the embassy attack. But there is such evidence for the truck bomb that struck the U.S. marine barracks (and the French barracks) on October 23, 1983, killing 299 American and French soldiers. The same PETN was used in the marine barracks as in the embassy attack. On September 26, 1983, the U.S. National Security Agency intercepted some form of an electronic message from the Iranian Ministry of Intelligence and Security in Tehran to the Iranian ambassador in Damascus, Ali Akbar Mohtashamipur. The message instructed Mohtashamipur to contact Hussein Musawi, the chief of the newly formed Shi'ite militia Islamic Amal, and ordered him "to take a spectacular action against the United States Marines." This September 26 message was not discovered until two days after the October 23 attack—but it seems to be incontrovertible proof of Iran's hand in the operation. Admiral James A. Lyons later described it as a "24-karat gold document."

Years later, a former Hezbollah member with the alias of "Mahmoud" gave videotaped testimony to a U.S. court in which he claimed that Ambassador Mohtashamipur gave orders to a Revolutionary Guard officer named Ahmad Kan'ani to organize an attack on the marine barracks. At the time, Kan'ani was stationed in the Sheikh Abdullah Barracks in Baalbek. (He was the commanding officer of the several hundred Revolutionary Guards living in Baalbek, serving there until late January 1984.) Mahmoud testified that Kan'ani then held a meeting in Baalbek with Hussein Musawi, Sheikh Sobhi Tufaili, and Sheikh Hassan Nasrallah—all early leaders of the nascent Islamic Amal that was later to become known as Hezbollah. Mahmoud claimed, "They got the order. They met and adopted the operation against the Marines and French barracks at the same time.... The cars were built, equipped, in Biralabin in a warehouse near a gas station."

Mahmoud's 2003 testimony thus directly implicates the current Hezbollah chief, Hassan Nasrallah, in the marine barracks bombing. The court heard testimony from yet another anonymous source, an unnamed U.S. intelligence officer, who vouched for Mahmoud's reliability and truthfulness. It is difficult to evaluate this anonymous evidence from the shadows. In 2003, and even today, Washington has a foreign policy predilection to discredit Hezbollah. On the other hand, everything we know about the Islamic Amal and the early Hezbollah suggests that in 1982–83 this nascent Shi'a movement was operating under direct orders from the Islamic Republic of Iran.

"The Beirut embassy operation was directed and guided by the Iranian Revolutionary Guard Corps and carried out by Hezbollah," says Vincent Cannistraro, a veteran CIA officer who once served as a clandestine officer in the Middle East division of the Directorate of Operations. Now retired, Cannistraro worked on the Mughniyeh case in the 1980s while chairing an interagency committee dealing with the problem of American hostages in Lebanon. Cannistraro believes Mughniyeh was somehow involved in the embassy bombing. But he says Mughniyeh was not alone: "So, was Mughniyeh at that young age totally responsible for the embassy bombing? No . . . Iran provided the explosives."

The bottom line is that both the U.S. embassy bombing and the truck-bomb attack on the marine barracks were operations directed by Tehran and carried out by Iranian Revolutionary Guard officers stationed in Baalbek. Ahmad Kan'ani was not the only Revolutionary Guard officer stationed in Baalbek at the time. Feridoun Mehdi-Nezhad and Hussein Mosleh were also in Baalbek. And Brig. Gen. Mustafa Mohammed Najjar was also reportedly a commander of the Revolutionary Guard in Lebanon sometime during the 1980s. All of these men later were implicated in a long list of kidnappings, hijackings, and car-bomb attacks. All of these men were known to have associated with Imad Mughniyeh.

In 2003, Ambassador Robert Dillon testified in federal district court, "I remember learning that there was a senior Iranian intelligence officer in the Bekaa who moved back and forth between the Bekaa and occasionally Damascus, and I would presume from Damascus to Tehran. I can't remember his name. Years later, I was told [by the CIA] that he was, quote, the chief terrorist." This strongly suggests that at some point in its investigation of the embassy bombing, the U.S. government had evidence implicating an Iranian intelligence officer. And yet, oddly enough, even thirty years later, this evidence has not been declassified.

Mughniyeh's name, in any case, was repeatedly linked to the embassy bombing and many other acts of terrorism. His name first surfaced in a highly public fashion when he was indicted for the June 14, 1985, hijacking of TWA Flight 847. (The hijacking was carried out by Hezbollah operatives, partly in retaliation for the March 8, 1985, B'ir al-Abed car bomb that almost killed Ayatollah Fadlallah.) In October

2001, Mughniyeh was placed on the FBI's list of the twenty-two most wanted terrorist fugitives.

The United States tried repeatedly to hunt down Mughniyeh. He was almost caught in Paris in 1988, but French authorities insisted that he'd "managed to slip away." In late 1994, Mossad assassinated another of Imad's brothers, Fuad Mughniyeh, a mere shopkeeper in South Beirut. The car bomb killed four people. Mossad had hoped that Mughniyeh would show up at the funeral for Fuad. But the long-sought-after terrorist may have sensed an ambush and never appeared.

On April 7, 1995, the CIA learned that Mughniyeh was aboard a Middle East Airlines flight from Khartoum to Beirut. The flight was scheduled to transit Riyadh, so the Saudis were asked to detain the plane on the runway. Fearing a political backlash from their own conservative Wahhabi constituency if Mughniyeh was arrested on Saudi soil, someone ordered Riyadh's air traffic controllers to wave off the plane. There seems to be good evidence that Mughniyeh had traveled to Khartoum for one purpose: to meet with Osama bin Laden. The Israeli journalist Ronen Bergman asserts, "Imad Mughniyeh came to Khartoum to meet him [Bin Laden], and told him about the enormous effect of suicide attacks against the Americans and French in the early 1980s in Lebanon." Bergman cites the confession of Ali Abdelsoud Mohammad, an Egyptian-born American citizen who was later arrested for his involvement in the 1998 bombings of the U.S. embassies in Tanzania and Kenya—Al-Qaeda's first terrorist attack. Mohammad claimed to have handled the security details for the Bin Laden–Mughniyeh meeting. Lawrence Wright, the Pulitzer Prize–winning author of *The Looming Tower: Al-Qaeda and the Road to 9/11*, also confirms that Mughniyeh met with Bin Laden in Khartoum. Wright credits Mughniyeh with persuading Bin Laden that "suicide bombers could be devastatingly effective." Later, Bin Laden sent his agent, Ali Mohammad, to Beirut, where he received training in explosives from Hezbollah.

In 2003 Hezbollah's charismatic leader, Hassan Nasrallah, dismissed American allegations that Mughniyeh was involved in terror attacks. He told *Time* magazine's Nicholas Blanford that the U.S. charges were "just allegations. . . . Can they provide evidence to condemn Mughniyah?" Nasrallah described Mughniyeh as a "freedom fighter" and said, "He had a very important role during the occupation of South Lebanon by Israel." Indeed, Mughniyeh had played a key role as a Hezbollah commander in the military operations that forced the Israelis to withdraw from South Lebanon in 2001. He reportedly pioneered Hezbollah's deployment of armor-piercing roadside explosive devices that killed hundreds of Israelis in South Lebanon. He also fought in the Israeli-Lebanese war in the summer of 2006; the war was a disaster for Lebanon, but Hezbollah could nevertheless claim a victory by merely surviving the Israeli onslaught.

On February 12, 2008, Mughniyeh, by then forty-five years of age, was in Damascus to attend a reception celebrating the twenty-ninth anniversary of the Iranian revolution. The party was hosted by Iran's ambassador to Syria in the wealthy Kfar Soussa neighborhood of Damascus. Mughniyeh left the party around 10:15 P.M. and walked to his parked car, a Mitsubishi Pajero. When he sat in the driver's seat the car's headrest exploded. A witness said Mughniyeh was blown across the road and his arms and legs were severed from his body. He died instantly. One of the CIA officers who worked on the Mughniyeh case in the 1980s, Vincent Cannistraro, bluntly said, "Mughniyeh was assassinated by the Israelis, with intelligence on his whereabouts furnished by the CIA." But another former intelligence official insists that it was an operation primarily controlled by Langley. This source, who must remain unnamed, says that Mughniyeh was killed by an explosive charge hidden in the spare tire of his SUV. He says that the Israelis provided the intelligence on Mughniyeh's location—but that it was actually a CIA "black ops" team that carried out the assassination in Damascus.

"The world is a better place without this man in it. He was a cold-blooded killer, a mass murderer and a terrorist responsible for countless innocent lives lost," said State Department spokesman Sean

McCormack. "One way or another he was brought to justice." Danny Yatom, a former director of Mossad, told reporters, "He was one of the most dangerous terrorists ever." A female Mossad officer who had a role in the operation to kill Mughniyeh later told an Israeli journalist that she respected Mughniyeh's spy craft and professionalism: "His was a rare case where one individual had changed history."

Hezbollah accused Mossad of killing Mughniyeh and released a statement on its website calling him a "great leader and a martyr." At a memorial service in Beirut, a mourner named Zahra told the *Washington Post*'s Anthony Shadid, "What they don't know is that today, by killing one Imad Mughniyeh, they will give birth to another hundred Mughniyehs. Every time they kill one of us, hundreds more will be born. They consider him a terrorist. For us, he is a hero who was fighting our enemy." Indeed, later that spring, the *New York Times* reported that the Iranian government was issuing a postage stamp in Mughniyeh's honor. And in the autumn of 2008, Hezbollah inaugurated a museum in the southern Lebanese town of Nabatieh celebrating Mughniyeh's life and death. "At first glance," reported the *New York Times*'s Robert F. Worth, "the exhibit could almost be taken for an outdoor children's museum. The green entrance awning is a huge replica of Mr. Mugniyeh's signature cap, and visitors then cross a 'victory bridge' made partly from artillery shells." A glass-encased box displays the bloodstained clothes Mughniyeh was wearing when he was assassinated. Visitors can see his belt, shoes, and cell phone. "His prayer mat is here, his slippers, even his hairbrush," reports Worth, "as if they were a saint's relics."

So for some people Mughniyeh was a hero of the Shi'a resistance, a soldier who died in battle. This narrative exists. It is not to be dismissed. Yet this narrative obviously collides with the bare facts of who died on April 18, 1983: not only Bob Ames, not only seven of his CIA colleagues, but also forty-six Lebanese civilians. They were innocents. But so too was Bob Ames.

Mughniyeh is dead. But the Iranian Revolutionary Guard officers implicated in the embassy attack all remain alive and free. Ahmed Kan'ani—who was the commander of the Revolutionary Guard unit in Baalbek at the time of the embassy attack—later became an Iranian ambassador to Madagascar. The former Iranian ambassador in Syria, Ali Akbar Mohtashamipur, later served as interior minister, and today he is the leader of one of Iran's political parties.

That leaves Ali Reza Asgari, the Revolutionary Guard officer who, according to Mustafa Zein, was the man who initially recruited and groomed Imad Mughniyeh to fight the Americans. Mughniyeh told Zein that the Beirut embassy attack was "Asgari's operation." The case of Asgari is an extraordinary one.

Ali Reza Asgari was born on January 10, 1957, in the small town of Ardestan, in the central province of Isfahan. (In Farsi, *Asgari* means "soldier.") He reportedly joined the Revolutionary Guard soon after the 1979 revolution. He arrived in Damascus on June 21, 1982, as a member of an official Iranian military delegation sent to discuss aid for the Lebanese in their war with Israel. Asgari accompanied Iran's minister of defense, Mohammed Salimi, and two other Iranian officers. Asgari was then a twenty-five-year-old intelligence officer in the Revolutionary Guard. At the time he was already a senior member of the Muhammad Rasoullah Twenty-seventh Brigade. This unit was deployed to Lebanon but never saw combat that summer. That autumn, most of these Revolutionary Guards were ordered back to Iran, where they were needed to fight the Iraqis. But some five hundred IRGC men from two units remained in Lebanon's Bekaa Valley. Asgari was one of several IRGC commanders who stayed behind in Lebanon. Corroboration of his presence in Lebanon comes from Brig. Gen. Esmaeil Ahmadi-Moghaddam, the current commander in chief of the Iranian national police. This high-ranking Iranian official gave a speech on December 15, 2012, in which he said that Asgari had been sent in 1979 to Iranian Kurdistan, where he helped to suppress the Kurdish uprising of 1979–80. Ahmadi-Moghaddam then explained that Asgari had been deployed by the Iranian Revolutionary Guard from Kurdistan to

Lebanon in the 1980s. Ahmadi-Moghaddam stated that Asgari had set up a program to train young Shi'a Lebanese recruits in the military arts. According to Ahmadi-Moghaddam, his longtime friend Asgari was deeply involved that autumn in the "establishment of Hezbollah as a complete party with all military, intelligence, cultural and political elements." And according to Mustafa Zein, that is when Asgari met Imad Mughniyeh.

Former Mossad director general Danny Yatom told the *Washington Post*, "He [Asgari] held a very, very senior position for many long years in Lebanon. He was in effect the commander of the Revolutionary Guards in Lebanon." Asgari was certainly in Damascus and Lebanon during the summer of 1982 and later that autumn. Iranian press accounts later described Asgari as the deputy chief of the "Qods Force"—the "Jerusalem Force"—a special foreign branch of the Revolutionary Guard. Its mandate was to export Ayatollah Khomeini's brand of Islamic revolution to other parts of the Islamic world. In 1985, Asgari was rewarded with a promotion within the Revolutionary Guard. He spent the entire decade between 1982 and 1992 shuttling between Baalbek and Tehran, directing Iran's political and military activities in Lebanon—and nurturing the nascent Hezbollah's military prowess. These were the years, of course, when scores of Americans, French, British, and other Europeans were held hostage, often in the Sheikh Abdullah Barracks, controlled by the Iranian Revolutionary Guard. Some of these hostages died in captivity. And some were held in solitary confinement for as many as six years. As the former CIA officer Robert Baer wrote in *Time* magazine, "Asgari was in the IRGC's chain of command when it was kidnapping and assassinating Westerners in Lebanon in the 1980s." Asgari was a manager, as such, of this hostage business. Asgari admitted as much when on April 11, 1991, he told the Lebanese newspaper *As-Safir*, "Iran has a desire to release the Western hostages as well as Palestinian and Lebanese prisoners held by Israel. But the United States refuses to enter into this issue through a humanitarian window. It wants only to manipulate political interests from this issue." That same year he was interviewed briefly on the BBC's *Voice of Lebanon*, where he was identified as "the Pasdaran commander in Lebanon." *Pasdaran* is the Farsi term for the Revolutionary Guard. He told the BBC on this occasion that the Revolutionary Guard "is not a militia; our mission is to train the people to fight Israel." As Baer has written, Asgari "knows dirty secrets.... Asgari knows a lot about other IRGC-ordered, Lebanon-based terrorist attacks, including the October 1983 Marine barracks bombing in Beirut and the 1996 bombing of Khobar Towers in Saudi Arabia." Baer also seems to corroborate Mustafa Zein's allegation that Asgari was Imad Mughniyeh's virtual control officer: "Asgari was the primary Iranian contact for one of the world's most lethal and capable terrorists, Imad Fa'iz Mughniyeh."

Oddly enough, Asgari's role in all these Lebanese events, and his relationship with Mughniyeh, remained shrouded from public view— until, that is, he defected to the West in 2007.

By 1997, Asgari had become a brigadier general and a deputy minister of defense in Tehran. He occupied this position until 2002, when he fell out of favor and left the Defense Ministry. For the next two years he worked inside the Kala-Electricity company, an entity deeply involved in Iran's nuclear energy program. But in 2004 Asgari was arrested and he spent eighteen months in prison. Upon his release he reportedly went into business trading olive oil, and he briefly wrote a Farsi-language blog. During these years he was clearly disaffected with the regime, and particularly with Mahmoud Ahmedinejad, his former rival in the Revolutionary Guard who became president in 2005. Asgari may have been recruited by a Western intelligence agency as early as 2003. In any case, on February 7, 2007, Asgari traveled from Tehran to Damascus and then on to Istanbul, where he checked in to a hotel. He then vanished. Various newspapers soon reported that the CIA and Mossad had whisked away the Iranian general first to Europe, and then to America. "It was an organized defection," said Uri Lubrani, a former Israeli ambassador to Iran. "Everything was prepared, and his family sought refuge abroad before he did." The *Washington Post* quoted a "senior U.S. official" as saying that Asgari was "willingly cooperating."

A former CIA clandestine officer, Vincent Cannistraro, told the London *Guardian* that Asgari was a "longtime Western intelligence agent." Cannistraro later elaborated that "[any] Iranian defector was highly valued because of the terrorism by Iran and the information one might have on the nuclear issue." The Israeli investigative journalist Ronen Bergman reported that in 2006 Asgari gave the Americans actionable intelligence that made possible the arrest of Revolutionary Guard officers in the northern Iraqi city of Irbil. A former European counterintelligence officer told *Le Figaro*, "This type of defection requires at least two years of preparation. . . . This is the coup that all agencies dream of."

The actual story of Asgari's defection may be more prosaic. Erich Follath and Holger Stark, two reporters from the German magazine *Der Spiegel*, wrote about the case in 2009. Their key source is another Iranian defector, Amir Farshad Ebrahimi, who fled Iran in 2003 and ended up in Berlin, where he became, according to a *Los Angeles Times* story, "a valuable asset for Western intelligence agencies and analysts seeking information on the Islamic Republic. He was in regular contact with Western officials and a circle of neoconservative activists." Ebrahimi and his friends established a "Salvation Committee" to aid Iranian defectors. Perhaps Asgari had heard of Ebrahimi's Salvation Committee. But he apparently had met the Iranian years earlier in Beirut. As a young man, Ebrahimi had briefly served as a press attaché in the Iranian embassy in Beirut. It was during this period that he first met Asgari. "We were at the [Iranian] embassy together in Beirut in the mid 1990s," Ebrahimi later told a reporter. "That's where we knew each other. That's why General Asgari called me when he was in Damascus. . . . He reminded me that we had been together in Beirut." Asgari told him he didn't want to return to Iran—so Ebrahimi set in motion a simple plan to extract the general. He told him to rent a car and drive to Istanbul. Asgari had to pay a Turkish border guard a

$1,500 bribe to get into Turkey without a visa. Ebrahimi then arranged for a U.S. embassy official to meet with Asgari.

The Iranian brigadier general was flown from Istanbul to the Rein-Main Air Base near Frankfurt. Greeted by Ebrahimi, he reportedly said, "I brought my computer along. My entire life is there." Just hours after his arrival in Germany, Asgari was whisked to Washington, D.C.

Asgari reportedly brought with him Iranian intelligence documents containing information about Hezbollah, Lebanon, and Iran's uranium-enrichment program. The CIA knew exactly whom they were getting. A Mossad officer, Ram Igra, said, "He lived in Lebanon and, in effect, was the man who built, promoted and founded Hezbollah in those years. If he has something to give the West, it is in this context of terrorism and Hezbollah's network in Lebanon."

Asgari was brought to a CIA safe house near Washington, D.C., and was extensively debriefed. Among other things, he revealed that Iran had built a new centrifuge enrichment plant near Natanz and that Iranian engineers were also attempting to enrich uranium using lasers, an expensive and time-consuming process. He also provided evidence that convinced some in the CIA that Iran was helping Syria to develop nuclear weapons. A German defense-ministry official revealed that Asgari brought evidence that Iran was financing the transfer of North Korean nuclear technology to Syria. This intelligence reportedly led to the September 6, 2007, Israeli air strike on a Syrian nuclear reactor. In short, Asgari was regarded by many in the intelligence community as an extraordinary source of intelligence on the Islamic Republic.

Asgari may also have provided the information the Mossad needed to assassinate Imad Mughniyeh. This information reportedly included Mughniyeh's cell phone numbers and recent photographs. "It may be no coincidence," Ronen Bergman wrote in the *New York Times*, "that the Damascus operation [meaning Mughniyeh's assassination] followed the apparent defection to the United States last year of an Iranian general, Ali Reza Asgari, who in the 1980s had helped Mr. Mughniyeh establish Hezbollah as a military force in Lebanon."

Washington intelligence sources refuse to confirm or deny that Asgari may have been paid a portion of the $5 million reward money offered for Mughniyeh's capture or death by the State Department's Rewards for Justice antiterrorism program. Asgari remains in the United States, probably living under a CIA agent-protection program—though a recent intelligence source claims Asgari is in the United States under the auspices of the U.S. Defense Intelligence Agency (DIA). Asgari made phone calls to his friend Ebrahimi on two occasions after his defection, once from Washington, D.C., and again from "somewhere in Texas." Asgari reportedly wanted Ebrahimi to assure his second wife that he was in good health. He has since disappeared.

The decision to give Asgari political asylum under the DIA or the CIA's Public Law 110 program was probably opposed by veteran CIA officers who had some knowledge of Asgari's alleged responsibility for Robert Ames's murder. But they and the Agency were reportedly overruled by the George W. Bush administration's National Security Council. This was not, however, the kind of decision anyone in the intelligence community, including the director of central intelligence, could have made on their own. Granting asylum to a man with Asgari's résumé was a political call that could only have been made in the White House. Some of President Bush's NSC advisers evidently believed that the intelligence Asgari brought to the table on the Iranian nuclear program was essential to the national defense. In effect, national security needs trumped whatever loyalty the U.S. government owed to the memory of Robert Ames and all of Asgari's other victims in the Beirut embassy and marine barracks bombings. It was a cold calculation. When one high-level intelligence official in the Bush White House was asked about Asgari's asylum, he responded, "At the unclassified level, I cannot elaborate on the issue."*

Finally, it is highly significant that in the spring of 2013 Asgari visited Leidschendam, in the Netherlands, where he gave secret testimony

---

* Later, when this book was first published, the CIA "categorically" denied that the agency had had anything to do with "arranging" the defection of Asgari. Taken literally, this was true because Asgari had indeed "arranged" his own defection.

before the Special Tribunal for Lebanon, authorized by the United Nations to investigate the 2005 assassination of Lebanese prime minister Rafic Hariri. If nothing else, this fact demonstrates that Asgari is now undoubtedly under the protection and sponsorship of a Western intelligence agency. When told that a man with Asgari's résumé was now living in America, one retired CIA officer—a man who'd known and deeply admired Bob Ames—shrugged his shoulders and said simply, "Well, it happens." Fred Hutchinson, the former CIA general counsel who'd urged Ames's promotion in 1981, had this observation: "The value of information that Asgari could provide and the symbolic importance of his defection to the CIA would have outweighed personal feelings about his involvement with the embassy attack."

But others were surprised and disheartened. *Schmuel Litani*, a veteran Mossad officer, observed, "When faced in life with the unexplainable, you can ascribe it to either stupidity or malice. But usually the better explanation is simple stupidity. Yes, Asgari is in America. Why? Well, you should ask the Americans."

No one in Washington wants to address this question. It's an official secret. But what happened to Asgari is a generic secret. Dealing with bad guys is part of spy craft. If you are seeking information about bad things, you necessarily seek out bad guys. But there's always a decision made about the trade-off. Bob Ames befriended Ali Hassan Salameh, someone whose résumé at the time spelled "bad guy." But most people would probably agree today that Ames's calculation was a moral one. He was bringing Salameh in from the cold to a place where he could end violence and bring some definition of justice for his people: a two-state solution to the Palestinian conundrum.

Dealing with Asgari is an entirely different equation. Unlike Salameh, this man is implicated in the deaths of hundreds of Americans and many others. No doubt, some intelligence officer somewhere is making the case that by dealing with Asgari, America can avert a war or save some lives. But it's also just as likely that Asgari's "intell" became stale almost as soon as he defected—so it may become yet another sad story from the wilderness of mirrors.

Epilogue

Yvonne Ames today lives in a comfortable, but decidedly modest, cottage in rural North Carolina. Two of her children, Adrienne and Kevin, live nearby. She spends her days taking care of her grandchildren. She has found some solace in her religious faith. At the dinner table, she says a simple grace. She rarely hears from any of Bob's Agency friends. After Bob's murder, the CIA offered her a choice between an annual pension or a lump-sum payment. Perhaps unwisely, she chose the lump sum. That money ran out a long time ago.

"I was overcome by the responsibility of having five children at home; and until then I had always thought I was very strong, but that's when I realized that the strength of the family came from Bob's presence. He was dependable. He was reliable. He was someone you could turn to, you could lean on, and whatever children's problems there were, I could go to him to get help. And that was gone, and it became my responsibility. It was frightening.

"I was raised in a military family, and I learned that you kept a stiff upper lip when things went wrong. And Bob also had that demeanor . . . and I just carried it through. To me, that was my coping mechanism. We did not take time to grieve.

"I went to work almost immediately afterwards. I lasted about a month when I realized it was just too much." Yvonne eventually went back to work on a part-time basis.

Sixteen months after Bob's murder, Yvonne married a man she'd known before she met Bob. She felt that with five children at home there should be a man in the house. Andrew asked her to wait until he graduated from high school. "He wanted to be the man in the house," Yvonne said. But she thought he needed to be "the young man, and not the man of the house." She later regretted her decision to remarry so quickly. The new husband was the "polar opposite of Bob," Yvonne said. "There were too many changes too soon." The marriage was rough going, and after twelve years it ended in divorce.

In retrospect, Yvonne believes she made a mistake in not confronting her grief. "So the stiff upper lip is not a good way to go. It is better to feel the pain and face the reality and heal. I think as a result of that, none of us have healed. None."

When Anne Dammarell wrote her a letter asking her to join the civil suit against Iran, Yvonne was initially opposed to the idea. She did not like the notion of a lawsuit. But after talking with Anne on the phone, and thinking about it for a month, she changed her mind. In 2003, she told Judge John D. Bates during the trial, "My reasoning for going ahead with it is that in order to deter or even hope to begin to deter the terrorists, the money has to be stopped." But she also thought that the act of publicly testifying might help her and her grown children heal. "Not only is it something that I now believe in, it is also a process of personal healing. And I thank you, Judge, for hearing us today."

In September 2003, Judge Bates awarded Yvonne Ames and her children a total of $38,249,000 in compensatory damages. But she hasn't seen a penny of this money. The Islamic Republic of Iran has ignored the U.S. court decisions in such cases, and the lawyer in the civil suit, Stu Newberger, has so far been unsuccessful in his attempts to seize Iranian assets in America or abroad. Newberger says he's still hopeful. So perhaps someday Yvonne and her children will be awarded this compensation.

When I first contacted Yvonne Ames about writing a book about her late husband, she was hesitant. She said she'd never spoken to any reporters or historians about Bob. She did not wish to divulge secrets. Instinctively, she was still the CIA spouse, reticent and protective of the Agency. In recent years she has occasionally accepted invitations to attend ceremonies at Langley marking the anniversaries of the Beirut embassy bombing. She knows that Bob devoted twenty-three years—most of his adult life—to the CIA. She bears no animosity toward the institution.

But thirty years have passed since the Beirut tragedy, and now she wants people to know what Bob Ames did with his life. More important, she wants her children to know what he did. "Bob appears in my dreams even now. He appears—initially, it was [as if] he had come back from hiding, and my concern was: But I've remarried. What do I do now? But lately, he appears, and it's just a comfort."

All six of the Ames children went to college. All married and have children of their own. But all live with a lingering sense of trauma. And all are intensely interested in whatever pieces of information they can find about their father's life in the Agency. "Like most of my siblings," said Adrienne, "I have collected all the articles and information written about him. And I have this habit. I like bookstores anyway, but when I go to bookstores, I always go to the historical section, and I flip through the indexes, and I look for his name."

■

Mustafa Zein is equally obsessed with Bob Ames's life and death.

Zein has spent much of the last two decades methodically investigating the Beirut embassy bombing. He wrote an unpublished memoir, "Deceit with Extreme Prejudice," chronicling his adventures with Ames. At great personal risk, he spent many months in Damascus in 2009, patiently tracking down Syrian intelligence officers who might have known something about who carried out the Beirut embassy bombing. Today, he's firmly convinced that the mastermind of the Beirut embassy bombing was Ali Reza Asgari, the Iranian Revolutionary

Guard officer stationed at the Sheikh Abdullah Barracks in Baalbek. He believes Bob Ames's primary killer has been found—and that he resides comfortably today in America.

■

Anne Dammarell now lives in Washington, D.C.'s lively Adams Morgan neighborhood, just two miles north of the White House. In September 2003, Judge Bates awarded her $6,774,602 in compensatory damages for the many wounds she sustained during the embassy bombing. Like Yvonne Ames and the other plaintiffs in the civil suit, she has yet to receive a penny of this award. She had countless operations to repair her nineteen broken bones, and months of physical therapy: "I had to relearn how to move my body, to walk, to write, and to focus on the printed word." In 1994, she wrote a master's thesis at Georgetown University titled "Hidden Fears, Helpful Memories: Aftermath of the 1983 Bombing of the United States Embassy in Beirut." Like all of the survivors of the Beirut embassy bombing, she has struggled to understand and cope with the long-term psychological scars of what happened. For a year after the bombing she experienced an unsettling "giddiness." She'd survived where others had not. "Paradoxically," she wrote in her thesis, "during this difficult period, my primary emotion was joy. . . . I was alive. I had not died." But later she had to cope with feelings of intense anxiety. She experienced violent nightmares that became "so commonplace that I could actually tell myself that I was having a 'bombing dream' and move on to something else without waking up." Talking to her today, she seems an altogether vivacious woman. She remains interested in the news from the Middle East and empathetic with the region's struggle to find a way toward lasting peace. Without Dammarell, there never would have been a civil suit; she was the catalyst who brought together the survivors and grieving relatives such as Yvonne Ames to create a legal record documenting their collective trauma.

■

Bob Ames's legacy is uncertain. His alma mater, La Salle University in Philadelphia, still displays a plaque with his photograph, and the caption reads, "Blessed are the Peacemakers."

"I hate to say it," said *Meir Harel,* a former Mossad director general, "but Ames's work was in vain." If the Oslo peace process was fated to fall apart, perhaps this is true. But if one believes that someday the endless Palestinian-Israeli conflict will end in a peace settlement, then perhaps the relationship Ames cultivated with Ali Hassan Salameh played a small role in opening the path to negotiations. In this sense, his legacy still resonates with hope.

But it would be altogether ungenerous to see Ames's life as bordered by—and defined by—the depressing narrative of the Palestinian-Israeli conflict. To be sure, Ames's story is emblematic of a struggle largely waged as a protracted, six-decade-long intelligence war. But his career as an intelligence officer also sheds light on the multibillion-dollar business of intelligence. Today, that business relies all too heavily on the technical ability of the CIA to gather information from a literal and metaphorical cloud. The Agency *used* to invest in clandestine officers who spent years acquiring foreign-language skills and learning to understand the history and cultural intricacies of a foreign society. Robert Ames was a model of this type of intelligence officer. But even in his day, many of his colleagues disparaged these qualities. Today, they are all too rare. In his time, Ames was accused of having "gone native." It was true. He fell in love with the Middle East, its languages, its rhythms, and its deep sense of history and place.

There was nothing complicated about the way Bob Ames learned to become a good spy. "There was no deep trick to it," Thomas Powers wrote of the art of intelligence. "You had to want to know, you had to do a lot of homework, and you had to listen." Ames was a listener. This is not to say that he listened without judgment. He listened as an American, and he was always skeptical. But he listened with a plain sense of human empathy. He listened to people who by any broad definition were easily labeled by policy makers back in Washington as terrorists. He listened to Ali Hassan Salameh and Yasir Arafat at a time when it was forbidden for American diplomats to talk with any Palestinians from the PLO. Not only did he listen, he befriended Salameh. He grew to like and trust Salameh because he found a way to empathize with the PLO operative's political dilemmas. Later, he learned to listen to his Mossad colleagues. He understood their dilemmas as well. He could see both sides, even if they stood incontrovertibly opposed to each other on grounds of history and moral imperatives.

Ironies inform Ames's life and death. Some may note the irony that he dealt with terrorists and died at the hands of terrorists. One of the men implicated in his murder, Imad Mughniyeh, was once trained and employed by Ames's friend Ali Hassan Salameh. Another, Ali Reza Asgari, allegedly recruited Mughniyeh to serve in the Islamic Republic of Iran's secret war against America. Asgari himself is implicated in the embassy attack that killed sixty-three people. And then there is the final irony that this Iranian agent, a man also deeply implicated in Iran's hostage taking of Americans in the 1980s in Lebanon, is now living in America, protected by the agency for which Bob Ames worked and died.

Robert Ames died during a tragic turning point in the Lebanese civil war. When the American embassy in Beirut collapsed, so too did Washington's enthusiasm for its peacekeeping mission. After 1983, it all went downhill. By early 1984, President Ronald Reagan ordered the U.S. marines who were hunkered down on the outskirts of Beirut to retreat. Lebanon's civil war resumed and further descended into six more years of bloody conflict. Thirty years later, the Shi'a political and military force we now know as Hezbollah dominates the Lebanese landscape and threatens to spark yet another Arab-Israeli war.

America retreated not only from Lebanon but also from any real responsibility for resolving what by any measure remains one of the world's most dangerous sectarian, national conflicts. President Reagan never insisted on having the parties to the conflict implement the 1979 Camp David Accords. And after Ames's death, Reagan virtually gave up on his own peace initiative. The Palestinian-Israeli dispute remains a dangerously destabilizing conflict. The events of 1983 led not so indirectly to the collapse of the Twin Towers. Specifically, the 9/11 Commission found that in the autumn of 1993 Osama bin Laden sent a delegation of Al-Qaeda operatives to the Bekaa Valley in Lebanon for training in explosives and intelligence practices: "Bin Laden reportedly showed particular interest in learning how to use truck bombs such as the one that killed 241 U.S. Marines in Lebanon in 1983." The 1983 suicide truck-bomb attacks on American targets in Lebanon quite literally inspired Bin Laden's suicidal assaults on America in 2001.

As the 9/11 Commission observed, "Americans are blamed when Israelis fight with Palestinians." The Palestinian-Israeli conflict still engenders angry emotions on all sides. Robert Ames believed that a real peace was possible. The Middle East need not remain a perennial battlefield. He used his intelligence and charm to begin the peace process in the shadows of Beirut. His clandestine work was a catalyst for that symbolic handshake on the White House lawn. He was the good spy. But his work remains unfinished.

ACKNOWLEDGMENTS

I wrote this book in Barranco, Peru. When I introduced Alonso Alegria—one of Peru's leading playwrights—to Susan Goldmark, he later remarked that she must be a "trophy wife." Alonso was surprised when I replied that Susan was indeed a "trophy"—but that she is my first and only wife of many years. Susan remains a treasured muse, a source of wisdom and street smarts in all things large and small. This book is dedicated to her and to two other strong women: my late mother, Jerine, and Yvonne Ames. Elsewhere I have written about the extraordinary experiences my parents, Eugene and Jerine Bird, gave me as a child throughout the Middle East and India.

My mother and Yvonne Ames were good friends in Arabia before traveling different roads. Decades later, I reappeared in Yvonne's life and asked to tell a small part of her story as well as the extraordinary story of her late husband. Yvonne understood that I was the historian, and that I would tell Bob's story in my own way, bringing to it my own subjective views and perspectives. I am forever grateful for her trust and kindness.

The *Washington Post*'s David Ignatius never met Bob Ames. But Ignatius was in Beirut the day Ames was murdered, and he came to know much about Ames's story. He wrote about Ames and his relationship to Ali Hassan Salameh in *Agents of Innocence*, the first of his many acclaimed novels. When in 2010 I first stumbled upon the notion of an Ames biography, I called upon David and asked for his counsel. He strongly encouraged me to tackle the subject and provided introductions to some of his sources in the intelligence community. Later, he took the time to comment on an early draft of the manuscript.

This book would not be what it is without the courage and generosity of Mustafa Zein. He was relentless. He gave himself up to hours and hours of my interrogations. He gave me unfettered access to his unpublished memoirs, letters, and documents pertaining to his friendship with Bob Ames. He is a *mensch* and a gentleman, a guide and a catalyst. I will forever be in his debt.

Stu Newberger, a partner at the law firm of Crowell & Moring in Washington, D.C., was the lead attorney in the civil suit brought by Anne Dammarell, Yvonne Ames, and other survivors and relatives of the Beirut embassy bombing. He shared with me the records pertaining to that civil suit. Newberger is intrepid and passionate and a wonderful raconteur. His career underscores the powerful utility of using the law as a weapon for the peaceful resolution of international disputes.

Tamar Prizan-Litani, an Israeli journalist and editor, was my guide, translator, and counselor during my research visit to Israel. She is a fount of wisdom and common sense—and a trusted friend.

Iradj Alikhani and Amir Hossein Etemadi helped me navigate Farsi language Web sources. Bart and Nancy Ames Hanlon gave me photographs from the Ames family album. Kristen Stevens provided me with letters and photographs from the estate of Janet Lee Stevens. Anne Dammarell, a survivor of the Beirut embassy bombing, gave me hours of her time and access to her diaries and her Georgetown University thesis. Steve Dryden, Joe Eldridge, and Lance Potter helped with other research. Thanks to Lokman Slim and UMAM Documentation and Research in Beirut for the Arabic-language newspaper image on the cover.

Claude Dunn and Dominique Hyde hosted me in their lovely home in Amman and listened patiently to my spy stories—as did many other friends, including Michele de Nevers and Branko Milanović, Stephen Frietch and Nancy Nickerson, Rita Giacaman, Charles Glass, Helma Goldmark, Deborah Harris, Aviva Kempner, Keith and Shakun Leslie, Victor and Annie Navasky, Paula Newberg, Rabbi Micha Odenheimer, William Prochnau and Laura Parker, Caleb Rossiter and Maya Latynski, Michael Schwartz and Emily Medine, Martin and Susan Sherwin, Nilgun Tolek, and Don Wilson.

My three sisters—Christina, Nancy, and Shelly—have distant memories of Bob Ames, and so I have hope that they will be entertained by this story. My only child, Joshua, is now a creative and charming young man finishing college. As always, my ambition has been to infect him with my love of history and storytelling. Maybe this spy story will finally succeed. As my father, Eugene Bird, approaches his tenth decade, he remains intensely interested in the fate of the Middle East. He knew Bob Ames, and I benefited enormously from my father's memories of both the man and the Agency.

I imposed on many friends and colleagues to read early versions of this manuscript. I am most grateful for the comments of Frank Anderson, Robert Baer, Brennon Jones, Arthur Samuelson, Odd Karsten Tveit, and Samuel H. Wyman. Henry Miller-Jones had his own illustrious career in the CIA as a clandestine officer. But as a friend and colleague of Bob Ames, Henry had invaluable insights into Ames's life and career. Henry read an early version of the book and prevented me from making numerous mistakes. I promise not to hold him accountable for any further errors of commission or omission.

More than two score retired intelligence officers spoke with me about Ames. Some spoke on the record and some chose to tell their stories without use of their true names. But perhaps all of these sources implicitly understood that at least some old secrets deservedly belong to history. I am grateful for their honesty and frankness.

I relied on the works of many other historians and journalists to explain the background and context of Ames's career in the CIA. I am particularly grateful to Ronen Bergman, Nicholas Blanford, Nora Boustany, Jon Broder, Avner Cohen, Robert Fisk, Mark Gasioroski,

David Hirst, Aaron J. Klein, David Landau, Yossi Melman, Benny Morris, Jonathan Randal, Dan Raviv, Martin Smith, Jeff Stein, Peter Taylor, and Joshua Wood.

I am particularly in debt to Adam Zagorin, my friend of more than three decades. Adam is a masterful investigative journalist with many years of experience in the Middle East and Washington. He was my sounding board on this project, and at a critical juncture he took time from his own work to help me marshal the evidence against the perpetrators of the Beirut embassy bombing.

My friends in Peru encouraged me to think that I could sit in Barranco and write about Beirut—while savoring Peruvian cuisine with them over many lovely luncheons: many thanks to Marie Arana and Jonathan Yardley of the *Washington Post*; Alonso Cueto, Peru's much acclaimed novelist; my high-tech neighbor "Roberto" Budge; and Lucho Bello, Mark Lewis, Adolfo Figueroa, and Mike and Beatrice Glover.

Gail Ross has been my friend and literary agent for nearly a quarter century. She has been patient during the lean years and exuberant whenever I managed to finish a book. She and Howard Yoon made it possible for Crown/Random House to publish this book. My editor at Crown, Rick Horgan, immediately saw the promise in the story of Robert Ames. Rick is an astute and discerning editor who always challenged me with the tough questions. His assistant, Nathan Roberson, and the copy editor, Elisabeth Magnus, have been indefatigable throughout a meticulous editing process. Many thanks to Mark Birkey, Penny Simon, Jessica Prudhomme, and many others on the Crown team who have brought this book to publication. I am also gratified that Crown's publisher, Molly Stern, has so strongly backed this project. May her enthusiasm be infectious.

Kai Bird
Barranco, Peru

NOTES

An italicized source name signifies an anonymous source, either a CIA officer or a Mossad officer who wishes to remain anonymous.

All interviews are my own unless otherwise specified.

Prologue

2 *"It was noted that this was a big day . . ."*: Charles Englehart, e-mail to author, May 20, 2012.
2 *"Okay, let's get a bus . . ."*: Ibid.
2 *"I'm proud to say that it was my idea"*: Frank Anderson, e-mail to author, May 17, 2012.
3 *"We the soldiers . . ."*: Thomas L. Friedman, "Rabin and Arafat Seal Their Accord as Clinton Applauds 'Brave Gamble,'" *New York Times*, September 14, 1993.
3 *President Clinton "took Mr. Arafat in his left arm . . ."*: Ibid.
3 *We were at Bob's gravesite"*: Frank Anderson, e-mail to author, May 17, 2012.
3 *"He was no Lawrence of Arabia"*: Henry Miller-Jones, "A Remembrance of Bob Ames," unpublished op-ed, ca. May 1983, courtesy of Miller-Jones.
4 *"He came to know kings . . ."*: Ibid.
4 *"Everyone credited Ames . . ."*: *Lindsay Sherwin*, interview, March 22, 2011.
4 *"There was a moment of silent prayer"*: Charles Englehart, e-mail to author, May 20, 2012.
5 *"We were all quietly excited"*: Ibid.

Chapter One: The Making of a Spy

7 *"rock-bottom American-ness . . ."*: Henry Miller-Jones, "A Remembrance of Bob Ames," unpublished op-ed, ca. May 1983, courtesy of Miller-Jones.
7 *People prided themselves*: Nancy Ames Hanlon, e-mail to author, June 12, 2013.

8   *"He used to devour books":* Philadelphia newspaper clipping, "Local Mother Mourns Hero Dead in Blast," n.d., ca. April 1983, Yvonne Ames papers.

9   *"There was no money for that":* Nancy Ames Hanlon, interview, September 7, 2011.

9   *"never one to travel in crowds":* Helen Ames, quoted in "Local Mother Mourns Hero."

10 *"Bob was always talking about Gola":* Jack Harmer, e-mail to author, September 21, 2010.

11 *"Ames was a great player":* Robert S. Lyons, "1954 La Salle NCAA Basketball Champions," speech delivered at the Second Annual Induction Ceremony of the Philadelphia Sports Hall of Fame, April 8, 2005.

11 *"I'm not talking to you . . .":* Bob Ames, "Don't Let the Shower Drip," short story, n.d., courtesy of Yvonne Ames.

11 *"The other sports can be fun":* Ken D. Loeffler, "I Say Basketball's Our Best Game," *Saturday Evening Post,* December 19, 1953.

12 *"to bring order out of chaos":* John R. Rasmuson, ed., *A History of Kagnew Station and American Forces in Eritrea* (Asmara: Il Poligrafico, 1973), p. 48.

12 *"I do not believe we have a more remote station . . .":* Ibid., p. 64.

13 *Top Secret Codeword:* George E. Matthias, e-mail to author, July 26, 2011. Matthias was a veteran of Kagnew. "Top Secret Codeword" was a security classification term in use in 1957, but it has been long since retired.

15 *Many of the men at Kagnew Station:* Rasmuson, *History of Kagnew Station,* p. 63.

15 *"Fine-looking soldier!":* Joel Wilson, e-mail to author, July 31, 2011, with attached handwritten memo from his father, John Wilson.

16 *"After a week or so of this bullshit":* George E. Matthias, e-mail to author, July 26, 2011.

17 *"and see the world":* "Local Mother Mourns Hero."

17 *"repo man":* Lindsay Sherwin, interview, March 22, 2011.

19 *Liv Ullmann:* Miller-Jones, "A Remembrance of Bob Ames."

Chapter Two: The Agency

20 *"Dear Mom, I have been offered . . .":* Ian Shapira, "At Memorial for Iran-Contra Figure Clair George, CIA Colleagues' Loyalty Endures," *Washington Post,* October 16, 2011.

20 *"Initially, I couldn't picture him as CIA":* Nancy Ames Hanlon, interview, September 7, 2011.

21 *"Nixon looked horrible":* Yvonne Ames, interview, November 19–20, 2010.

21 *one woman:* whn, veteran DO case officer, memo to author, part 1, January 12, 2011.

22 *some sixteen thousand employees:* John Ranelagh, *The Agency: The Rise and Decline of the CIA* (New York: Simon and Schuster, 1986), p. 21.

23 *"a high tolerance for ambiguity":* whn, memo to author, part 1.

24 *"It was the first time I learned . . .":* Henry Miller-Jones, e-mail to author, September 22, 2012.

24 *"The course was a relic . . .":* Robert Baer, *See No Evil: The True Story of a Ground Soldier in the CIA's War on Terrorism* (New York: Three Rivers Press, 2002), p. 32.

25 *Kirkpatrick made it clear:* Thomas Powers, *The Man Who Kept the Secrets: Richard Helms and the CIA* (New York: Alfred A. Knopf, 1979), p. 65.

26 *"Although we became almost intimately familiar . . .":* whn, memo to author, part 1, January 12, 2011.

27 *"But the other side of the coin . . .":* Henry Miller-Jones, e-mail to author, March 10, 2012.

28 *just in case "any questions arise . . .":* Secret CIA cable, Washington to Tehran, August 3, 1979, Documents from the U.S. Espionage Den, vol. 56, http://ia600409 .us.archive.org/10/items/DocumentsFromTheU.S.EspionageDen/v56_text.pdf.

29 *There had to be trust:* Powers, *The Man Who Kept the Secrets,* p. 115.

29 *"The successful and satisfactory conclusion . . .":* whn, memo to author, part 1, January 12, 2011.

31 *"Jungle Operations Course":* Yvonne Ames, e-mail to author, April 11, 2012.

31 *"the cowboy era":* Said K. Aburish, *A Brutal Friendship: The West and the Arab Elites* (New York: St. Martin's Press, 1998), p. 135. Aburish interviewed Critchfield in 1994.

32 *Washington "was terribly dependent . . .":* Duane R. Clarridge, e-mail to author, March 16, 2013.

32 *"the only man who ever used the CIA for cover":* Said K. Aburish, "Lost Victories: The CIA and the Middle East," 2004, p. 3, www.iiwds.com/said_aburish/a_lost victories.htm.

32 *"People tended to go there and stay there":* Peter Earnest, interview, March 16, 2011.

33 *When the CIA was established:* Ranelagh, *Agency,* p. 28.

34 *"Helms and Ames were very much alike":* Lindsay Sherwin, interview, March 22, 2011.

34 *Dick Helms was an enigma:* Powers, *The Man Who Kept the Secrets,* p. 290.

35 *"From the outside, espionage . . .":* Ibid., p. 23.

36 *"Friends said he carried away . . .":* Ibid., p. 24.

36 *"Just because a document is a document":* Kim Philby, *My Silent War: The Autobiography of a Spy* (New York: Modern Library, 1968), p. 200.

36 *"To do the best job he can . . .":* Powers, *The Man Who Kept the Secrets,* p. 140.

36 *"the soggy mass of morality":* Ibid., p. 141.

37 *"We're not in the Boy Scouts . . .":* Ibid., p. 143.

37 *"Our best Russian agents . . .":* Richard Helms, "We Believed in Our Work," speech delivered at the Veterans of the OSS Dinner, Washington Hilton Hotel, Washington, DC, May 24, 1983, www.foia.cia.gov/sites/default/files/document_conversions/ 45/we_belv_wrk.pdf.

Chapter Three: Arabia

38 *"Bob was a very complex person":* David Long, e-mail to author, June 12, 2011.

38 *"He was able to show empathy . . .":* Harry Simpson, e-mail to author, September 19, 2011.

39 *Their job in the Dhahran Base:* Henry Miller-Jones, e-mail to author, January 20, 2011.

41 *"All we could see for miles . . .":* Kai Bird, *Crossing Mandelbaum Gate: Coming of Age Between the Arabs and Israelis, 1956–1978* (New York: Scribner, 2010), p. 89.

41 *"The oil town at Dhaharan [sic] . . .":* Ibid., p. 90.

42 *"He said that he had plotted out a career path":* Ralph Oman, e-mail to author, August 10, 2011.

43   *one of Aramco's Saudi desert guides:* Henry Miller-Jones, "A Remembrance of Bob Ames."

43   *"When the Arabs did not know him well":* Ibid.

44   *"The house was small . . .":* Ralph Oman, e-mail to author, August 10, 2011.

44   *Ronald Irwin Metz:* Bird, *Crossing Mandelbaum Gate,* pp. 106–7.

45   *an easygoing and fruitful relationship:* Ambassador Patrick Theros, interview, October 6, 2011.

45   *"Ames' interest in the Bedu . . .":* Henry Miller-Jones, "Aden Assignment," e-mail to author.

46   *"I think we should leave":* Ambassador Patrick Theros, interview, October 6, 2011.

47   *"Bob tended to see humor . . .":* Ibid.

48   *Aramco told Ames he had a standing offer:* Ralph Oman, e-mail to author, August 10, 2011.

49   *"I felt as if my clients were running the Middle East . . .":* Said K. Aburish, *The St George Hotel Bar* (London: Bloomsbury, 1989), p. 5.

49   *"Beirut is one of the liveliest centres . . .":* Philby, *My Silent War,* p. 201.

49   *"It was an amazing listening post":* Aburish, *The St George Hotel Bar,* p. 8.

49   *"He knew everyone":* Loren Jenkins, interview, April 22, 2011.

49   *rumors dogged him:* A retired CIA officer told the Norwegian journalist Karsten Tveit that Abu Said's CIA cryptonym was PENTAD. Karsten Tveit, e-mail to author, May 13, 2013.

49   *"It was clear to me . . .":* Wilbur Crane Eveland, *Ropes of Sand: America's Failure in the Middle East* (New York: W. W. Norton, 1980), p. 165.

50   *"For those of us lucky enough . . .":* Aburish, *The St George Hotel Bar,* p. 4.

Chapter Four: Aden and Beirut

51   *"Israel could defeat . . .":* Richard Helms, "We Believed in Our Work," speech delivered at the Veterans of the OSS Dinner, Washington Hilton Hotel, Washington, DC, May 24, 1983, www.foia.cia.gov/sites/default/files/document_conversions/45/we_belv_wrk.pdf.

52   *"Why don't you ask me . . .":* Robert Hunter, interview, March 17, 2011.

52   *"no honey to convince me . . .":* Robert Ames to Yvonne, October 4, 1967, courtesy of Yvonne Ames.

53   *"Everywhere you look . . .":* Ibid.

53   *one of only seven officers in the tiny post:* Associated Press, "South Yemen Cuts Relations with U.S. for Backing Israel," *New York Times,* October 25, 1969.

53   *"If they get you here":* Robert Ames to Yvonne, October 10, 1967.

53   *"I saw one Brit get wounded . . .":* Robert Ames to Yvonne, October 14, 1967.

54   *"The situation in Aden . . .":* Robert Ames to Yvonne, October 22, 1967.

54   *"I was pure raw material . . .":* Henry Miller-Jones, e-mail to author, September 22, 2012.

55   *"It's a good thing":* Robert Ames to Yvonne, October 14, 1967.

55   *He preferred root beer:* Robert Ames to Yvonne, June 15, 1972.

56   *"I bet you'd like to be sitting in my office now":* Robert Ames to Yvonne, December 5, 1967.

56   *"He won't have to worry . . .":* Robert Ames to Yvonne, October 22, 1967.

56   *"Except for the aura of terrorism . . .":* Robert Ames to Yvonne, October 4, 1967.

56 *"ugly relationship"*: Dewey Clarridge, interview, November 26, 2011.
56 *"Most of them are quite friendly"*: Robert Ames to Yvonne, October 10, 1967.
57 *"Ames admonished me . . ."*: Henry Miller-Jones, "Aden Assignment," e-mail to author.
57 *Ames clearly didn't care for the Brits*: Yvonne Ames, e-mail to author, March 7, 2012.
57 *"The soldiers are arrogant . . ."*: Robert Ames to Yvonne, October 10, 1967.
57 *"I really feel frustrated . . ."*: Robert Ames to Yvonne, November 28, 1967.
58 *"American Lawrence of Arabia"*: William M. Freeman, "The American Lawrence," *New York Times*, December 5, 1975.
58 *"He fully grasped the irrationality . . ."*: Henry Miller-Jones, "A Remembrance of Bob Ames," unpublished op-ed, ca. May 1983, courtesy of Miller-Jones.
58 *"This is one of the most inaccessible kingdoms . . ."*: Robert Ames to Yvonne, October 14, 1967.
59 *Qaboos was allowed only a few books*: Henry Miller-Jones, e-mail to author, September 22, 2012.
59 *"The Sultan, of course, will succumb . . ."*: Robert Ames to Yvonne, November 1, 1967.
60 *"They've caught the killer"*: Robert Ames to Yvonne, November 22, 1967.
60 *"A great quiet has fallen . . ."*: Robert Ames to Yvonne, November 3, 1967.
60 *"We have a full scale civil war . . ."*: Robert Ames to Yvonne, November 7, 1967.
60 *"Well, it looks like the NLF . . ."*: Ibid.
61 *"I'm afraid some things must be put off . . ."*: Ibid.
61 *he'd seen Yvonne only 20 of the past 141 days*: Robert Ames to Yvonne, October 22, 1967.
61 *"I'm sure I'll be a stranger to them . . ."*: Robert Ames to Yvonne, November 1, 1967.
61 *"What good is a picture?"*: Robert Ames to Yvonne, November 7, 1967.
61 *"I love you and miss you . . ."*: Robert Ames to Yvonne, October 25, 1967, and November 7, 1967.
61 *"Give the girls a hug . . ."*: Robert Ames to Yvonne, November 22, 1967.
61 *"The new government appears to be quite leftist"*: Robert Ames to Yvonne, December 2, 1967.
62 *"sincere and hard working"*: Robert Ames to Yvonne, December 11, 1967.
62 *"I've been living and breathing the Arabic language . . ."*: Robert Ames to Yvonne, December 2, 1967.
62 *"pathetic"*: Ibid.
62 *"the whole independence bit . . ."*: Ibid.
62 *Ames found the press people he met "interesting"*: Robert Ames to Yvonne, November 19, 1967.
62 *"My Arabic is improving . . ."*: Robert Ames to Yvonne, November 28, 1967.
62 *the consulate was "one disorganized mess . . ."*: Robert Ames to Yvonne, November 25, 1967.
63 *"People are cautiously sticking their heads out . . ."*: Robert Ames to Yvonne, November 7, 1967.
63 *"I got it for under $250 . . ."*: Robert Ames to Yvonne, November 28, 1967.
63 *"Our contacts are so restricted"*: Robert Ames to Yvonne, November 3, 1967.
63 *"So far, I haven't made any real close Arab friends"*: Robert Ames to Yvonne, December 9, 1967.

63 *"lost in the obscurity . . ."*: Robert Ames to Yvonne, December 2, 1967.

63 *"I have been all over Aden . . ."*: Robert Ames to Yvonne, November 28, 1967.

64 *"I don't recall a lengthy or active list . . ."*: Miller-Jones, "Aden Assignment."

64 *"I used to say that Bob forgot more . . ."*: Stephen Buck, e-mail to author, January 19, 2012.

64 *"a real down to earth fellow . . ."*: Robert Ames to Yvonne, October 9, 1967.

65 *"Abd'al Fatah told Bob of his experience . . ."*: William Casey, speech delivered at the Metropolitan Club, New York City, May 1, 1985, Digital National Security Archive, George Washington University. See also Joseph E. Persico, *Casey: The Lives and Secrets of William J. Casey* (New York: Viking Penguin Books, 1990), pp. 314–15.

65 *"Most of them are just about my age"*: Robert Ames to Yvonne, December 13, 1967.

66 *"Ames told me"*: Casey, speech at the Metropolitan Club.

66 *Getting to know the right people*: Persico, *Casey*, p. 315.

66 *"Had Ames been a public man"*: Henry Miller-Jones, "A Remembrance of Bob Ames."

67 *One day at the Gold Mohur Beach Club*: A retired Foreign Service officer who wishes to remain anonymous, interview, January 21, 2012.

67 *Later, Ames casually thanked the Foreign Service officer*: Anonymous Foreign Service officer, e-mail to author, May 4, 2012.

67 *His 1971 thesis*: Basil Raoud al-Kubaisi, "The Arab Nationalist Movement, 1951–1971: From Pressure Group to Socialist Party" (Ph.D. diss., American University, 1971).

67 *Al-Kubaisi came from a wealthy and well-connected Sunni Muslim family*: Fadl Naqib, e-mail to author, May 23, 2012. Naqib was a friend and contemporary of Al-Kubaisi's.

68 *"Ames was good at recruitment"*: Richard Zagorin, interview, March 24, 2011.

68 *a top-secret British Foreign Office memo*: Research Department Memorandum, "Iraqi Nationalist Political Parties," Top Secret, September 26, 1963, LR6/19/G, Document Reference: FO 370/2719-0007, p. 6, Public Records Office, UK.

68 *They were a natural fit*: My source for the fact that it was Al-Kubaisi who was recruited by Ames is a retired Foreign Service officer who prefers to remain anonymous. He remembers that the young man he sent to Ames from the Gold Mohur Beach Club later became a ranking PFLP member and was killed in Paris by the Mossad in 1973. Only Al-Kubaisi matches this description. Furthermore, Al-Kubaisi's 1971 Ph.D. thesis establishes that he was interviewing ANM sources in Aden in 1967–68—which establishes that he was in Aden at the same time as Ames. Finally, it is interesting to note that Bob Woodward writes in his book *Veil* that "during the Helms era, Ames had been the first to make a real penetration into the PLO for the CIA, developing two key sources." Bob Woodward, *Veil: The Secret Wars of the CIA, 1981–1987* (New York: Simon and Schuster, 1987), p. 230. Ali Hassan Salameh was one source; Al-Kubaisi was most probably the other one.

69 *"the most depressing and un-Christmas-like Christmas . . ."*: Robert Ames to Yvonne, December 25, 1967.

69 *"Aden was spartan"*: Yvonne Ames, interview, November 19–20, 2010.

70 *"Her eyes got wide . . ."*: Robert Ames to Yvonne, December 10, 1968.

70 *"I think half of Aden is waiting!"*: Robert Ames to Yvonne, December 3, 1968.

71 *"A female police officer arrived . . ."*: Yvonne Ames, interview, November 19–20, 2010; see also *New York Times*, "South Yemen Ends U.S. Ties," October 25, 1969, and "U.S. Diplomats Quit Aden," October 27, 1969.

72 *"Most of us case officers worked at night . . ."*: Charles Englehart, interview, September 20, 2011.

73 *"We used to try to come up with Arabic puns . . ."*: Sam Wyman, interview, July 27, 2010.

73 *"I was in awe of Bob"*: Richard Zagorin, interview, March 24, 2011.

74 *The CIA station in Beirut:* Henry Miller-Jones, e-mail to author, December 16, 2010.

74 *"We case officers"*: Richard Zagorin, interview, March 24, 2011.

74 *the "Green Wog"*: Duane R. Clarridge, with Digby Diehl, *A Spy for All Seasons: My Life in the CIA* (New York: Scribner, 1997), p. 105.

74 *"a professional Irishman"*: Charles Waverly, interview, March 28, 2011.

74 *"Henry was an aggressive, talented, street smart and gutsy officer"*: Henry Miller-Jones, e-mail to author, May 18, 2012.

75 *"They really were very close"*: Betty Bretting, e-mail to author, May 16, 2012.

75 *the "White Whale"*: Yvonne Ames, e-mail to author, May 21, 2012.

75 *"Henry was a character"*: Loren Jenkins, interview, April 22, 2011.

75 *"There was a period"*: Richard Zagorin, interview, March 24, 2011.

75 *Ames met a twenty-seven-year-old Lebanese citizen:* David Ignatius, interview, July 28, 2010; Sam Wyman, interview, November 5, 2010.

76 *"Bob and June Beckman . . ."*: Mustafa Zein, e-mail to author, June 28, 2012.

78 *Zein was unfazed:* Mustafa Zein, e-mail to author, August 11, 2012.

78 *"Zein was a player . . ."*: Sam Wyman, interview, November 5, 2010.

78 *"This and many other incidents . . ."*: "Jordan's Exhibit Assailed by Jews," *New York Times*, April 25, 1964; Emily Alice Katz, "It's the Real World After All: The American-Israel Pavilion–Jordan Pavilion Controversy at the New York World's Fair, 1964–1965," *American Jewish History* 91 (March 2003): 129–55, www .thefreelibrary.com/It's+the+real+world+after+all%3A+the+American-Israel +Pavilion—Jordan . . . -a0119570011.

79 *"Bob opened the meeting . . ."*: Mustafa Zein, interview, Amman, October 4, 2012; Mustafa Zein, "Deceit with Extreme Prejudice," unpublished memoir, ca. 2005, p. 122, courtesy of Mustafa Zein.

80 *"knew who he [Ames] was . . ."*: Ibid., pp. 123–24.

80 *Zein made a good living:* U.S. Court of Federal Claims, *Mustafa M. Zein v. United States of America*, Civil Action No. 99-244C, April 29, 1999, p. 3.

80 *"He was never a 'paid agent' "*: Sam Wyman, e-mail to author, August 6, 2012.

81 *"When I met Bob in Beirut . . ."*: Mustafa Zein, e-mail to author, August 4, 2012.

81 *"You recruit a principal agent . . ."*: Jack O'Connell, with Vernon Loeb, *King's Counsel: A Memoir of War, Espionage, and Diplomacy in the Middle East* (New York: W. W. Norton, 2011), p. 22.

81 *"I was very fond of Mustafa"*: Sam Wyman, interview, November 5, 2010.

82 *"Bob really wasn't that great . . ."*: George Coll, interview, March 14, 2011.

82 *"He was very long on guts"*: Sam Wyman, interview, November 5.

82 *"the Catalyst"*: Mustafa Zein, interview, Amman, October 7, 2012.

Chapter Five: The Red Prince

83 *Force 17:* Peter Taylor, *States of Terror: Democracy and Political Violence* (London: Penguin Books, 1993), p. 38. Arafat's intelligence bureau was initially called Rasd. Force 17 did not emerge until the mid-1970s.

83 *they all should be fluent in Hebrew:* Mustafa Zein, interview, Amman, October 7, 2012.

84 *"He was a youthful Marlon Brando . . .":* Ibid.

84 *"explore the possibility of contact . . .":* Mustafa Zein, e-mail to author, August 11, 2012.

84 *"The man was a magnet":* Ibid.

85 *a very thin Swiss platinum watch:* Zein, "Deceit with Extreme Prejudice," p. 117. Photographs of Salameh in the 1970s show him wearing a thin silver-colored watch.

85 *Ali Hassan Salameh was born:* Nadia Salti Stephan, "Abu Hassan by Abu Hassan" and "After I Die," *Monday Morning* (Beirut weekly magazine), January 29–February 4, 1979, pp. 16–26. Ali Hassan Salameh says in this interview, "I was born in Iraq in 1942." Other sources report that he was born in Qula, Palestine, in 1940.

85 *"Salameh has turned Ramla [town] into a centre of disorder":* Michael Bar-Zohar and Eitan Haber, *The Quest for the Red Prince* (Guilford, CT: Lyons Press, 1983, 2002), pp. 28–30. Bar-Zohar and Haber seem to be quoting Haganah intelligence files, but their book has no source notes.

87 *the British never caught Salameh:* Klaus-Michael Mallmann and Martin Cuppers, *Nazi Palestine: The Plans for the Extermination of the Jews in Palestine* (London: Enigma, 2010), p. 201; "Three Nazi Air Officers Caught in Palestine," *New York Times*, October 28, 1944; Rick Fountain, "Nazis Planned Palestine Subversion," *BBC News*, July 5, 2001.

87 *Salameh's guerrillas allegedly carried out the attack:* Bar-Zohar and Haber, *Quest for the Red Prince*, p. 69; Benny Morris, *1948: The First Arab-Israeli War* (New Haven, CT: Yale University Press, 2008), p. 101.

87 *During the first six months of 1948, Salameh's force grew:* Benny Morris, *Righteous Victims: A History of the Zionist-Arab Conflict, 1881–2001* (New York: Vintage Books, 1999, 2001), p. 194; B. Morris, *1948*, p. 121.

87 *Salameh boasted to a reporter:* "Tel Aviv Seizure Planned," *New York Times*, March 25, 1948. "26 Jews Are Slain in Convoy Attacks," *New York Times*, March 25, 1948.

88 *On June 2, 1948, he died:* Bar-Zohar and Haber, *Quest for the Red Prince*, p. 89; Mahdi Abdul Hadi, ed., *Palestinian Personalities: A Biographic Dictionary* (Jerusalem: Passia, 2006), pp. 172–73.

88 *"We must mention two Palestinian commanders":* Bar-Zohar and Haber, *Quest for the Red Prince*, p. 89.

89 *"The influence of my father . . .":* Stephan, "Abu Hassan by Abu Hassan" and "After I Die."

89 *"I wanted to be myself":* Ibid.

89 *Ali studied engineering:* Abdul Hadi, *Palestinian Personalities*, pp. 172–73.

89 *Nasser offered scholarships:* Mohammed Natour (Abu Tayeb), "The Martyrdom of Ali Hassan Salameh," unpublished manuscript, courtesy of Mustafa Zein.

90 *Shortly afterwards he joined Yasir Arafat's Fatah:* Stephan, "Abu Hassan by Abu Hassan" and "After I Die."

90 *"I became very attached to Fatah":* Ibid.

90 *Salameh was sent back to Cairo:* Yezid Sayigh, *Armed Struggle and the Search for State: The Palestinian National Movement, 1949–1993* (New York: Oxford University Press, 1997), p. 180.

90 *He was methodical and patient:* In 1968, Ali Hassan supposedly called a press conference in Cairo and announced that he had exacted vengeance for his father's death twenty years earlier. He announced that he had smuggled himself into occupied Jerusalem and together with other underground Fatah cadres had bought a delivery van. He had then parked it near a crowded market and rigged a two-hour timing device to explode its cargo of gasoline bottles and dynamite. "The young guerrilla spoke with undisguised satisfaction," reported the *New York Post,* "of the explosion which killed twelve people and wounded fifty-three more." The only problem with this story is that the *Life* magazine account of the Cairo press conference cites a nonexistent *New York Post* story. Neither the *New York Times* nor any other media reported on this alleged Cairo press conference. So perhaps the story is Mossad disinformation, planted with *Life* magazine to burnish Salameh's credentials as a legendary terrorist. See Paul O'Neil, "A Charming Assassin Who Loved the Good Life," *Life,* April 1979, p. 102. The reports of Andreas Baader's dealings with Salameh can be found in Odd Karsten Tveit's *Alt for Israel: Oslo-Jerusalem, 1948–78* (Oslo: J. W. Cappelens, 1996). See also Stefan Aust's *The Baader-Meinhof Group: The Inside Story of the RAF* (New York: Oxford University Press, 2009), p. 72.

90 *Ali Hassan had married well:* O'Neil, "Charming Assassin," p. 102. O'Neil erroneously reported that Nashrawan was the granddaughter of the grand mufti of Jerusalem, Haj Amin Husseini. The families are unrelated. Nashrawan says the family still has the deeds to their property in Haifa. Her brother, Hisham al-Sharif, married Ali Hassan Salameh's sister, Jihad. Mustafa Zein, e-mail to author, March 17, 2013.

91 *David Ignatius's novel:* David Ignatius, interview, July 28, 2010. Ignatius explained to the author that these details of Ames's first meeting with Salameh were entirely factual.

91 *"Ali looked at Bob . . .":* Mustafa Zein, interview, Amman, October 8, 2012.

92 *"You Arabs claim your views are not heard . . .":* David Ignatius, "The Secret History of the U.S.-PLO Terror Talks," *Washington Post,* December 4, 1988.

92 *prime minister Harold Wilson:* Wilson arrived in Washington on January 27, 1970. Richard Nixon, "Remarks of Welcome to Prime Minister Harold Wilson of Great Britain," January 27, 1970, www.presidency.ucsb.edu/ws/?pid=2502.

92 *Ames's promising lead:* David Ignatius, e-mail to author, June 11, 2013; David Ignatius, *Agents of Innocence* (New York: W. W. Norton, 1987), pp. 82–86.

93 *"Bob had Ali Hassan over . . .":* Yvonne Ames, interview, November 19–20, 2010.

94 *"He moved like a panther":* Frank Anderson, interview, November 4, 2010.

94 *"Love Me Tender":* Taylor, *States of Terror,* p. 55.

94 *an IQ of 180:* O'Neil, "Charming Assassin," p. 101, and "Death of a Terrorist," *Time,* February 5, 1979.

94 *"People expect a revolutionary . . ."*: Stephan, "Abu Hassan by Abu Hassan" and "After I Die."

94 *"Professionally speaking"*: Frank Anderson, interview, November 4, 2010.

95 *"The PLO factions were the darling . . ."*: Hume Horan, interview by Charles Stuart Kennedy, November 3, 2000, Foreign Affairs Oral History Collection of the Association for Diplomatic Studies and Training, Georgetown University, Washington, DC.

95 *"I didn't think the king . . ."*: Harrison Symmes interview by Charles Stuart Kennedy, Box 1, Folder 460, Foreign Affairs Oral History Collection of the Association for Diplomatic Studies and Training, Georgetown University, Washington, DC.

95 *"I was virtually alone . . ."*: O'Connell, *King's Counsel*, pp. 99–100.

96 *"Bob was just very clearly anti-Hashemite . . ."*: Dewey Clarridge, interview, November 26, 2011. Another DO officer, Thomas Twetten, confirms that Ames's anti-Hashemite views were long-standing. Twetten was stationed in Amman in 1980 when he met with Ames in Washington: "I was pleased to meet with Bob Ames, who had a major effect on policy at that time. And I was quite shocked to have him accuse me of a pro-Hashemite bias. He seemed quite sure I did, based on my position. And I considered myself quite balanced, based on my reporting from Amman. His irritation seemed an unwarranted provocation." Thomas Twetten, e-mail to author, February 21, 2011.

96 *"misinterpreting his own personal experience . . ."*: O'Connell, *King's Counsel*, pp. 99–100.

97 *"Bob was prescient"*: Graham Fuller, interview, April 3, 2012.

98 *"Foreign Minister Eban told [U.S.] Ambassador [Charles] Yost . . ."*: Document 325, "Intelligence Memorandum Prepared in the Central Intelligence Agency, Washington, DC, September 24, 1970," in *Foreign Relations of the United States, 1969–1976, Nixon-Ford Administrations*, vol. 24, *Middle East Region and Arabian Peninsula, 1969–1972; Jordan, September 1970*.

98 *"any move to undermine Hussein . . ."*: Bird, *Crossing Mandelbaum Gate*, p. 285; Nigel Ashton, *King Hussein of Jordan: A Political Life* (New Haven, CT: Yale University Press, 2008), pp. 154, 398.

98 *"Like all of us who get to know anything . . ."*: George Cave, interview, March 14, 2011.

99 *"it was not as though there was a Palestinian people . . ."*: *Times* (London), June 15, 1969; David Hirst, *The Gun and the Olive Branch: The Roots of Violence in the Middle East* (New York: Thunder's Mouth Press, 2003), p. 392.

99 *"Palestinian guerrillas . . ."*: CBS *Evening News*, September 6, 1970.

100 *"betting all his chips"*: Bird, *Crossing Mandelbaum Gate*, p. 274; David Raab, *Terror in Black September: The First Eyewitness Account of the Infamous 1970 Hijackings* (New York: Palgrave Macmillan, 2007), pp. 138–39; Hume Horan, interview by Charles Stuart Kennedy, November 3, 2000.

100 *"It was very messy"*: Bird, *Crossing Mandelbaum Gate*, pp. 274–75; Hume Horan, interview by Charles Stuart Kennedy, November 3, 2000.

100 *"The fight goes on . . ."*: Bird, *Crossing Mandelbaum Gate*, p. 275; Peter Snow and David Phillips, *The Arab Hijack War: The Whole Story of the Most Incredible Act of Piracy in the Decade* (New York: Ballantine Books, 1971), pp. 104, 141.

101 *King Hussein sent a frantic message*: Bird, *Crossing Mandelbaum Gate*, p. 276;

"Black September Plea to Israel," *BBC News*, January 1, 2001, http://news.bbc.co.uk/2/lowmiddle_east/1095221.stm.

101 *"There were atrocities . . .":* Bird, *Crossing Mandelbaum Gate*, p. 277; Hume Horan, interview by Charles Stuart Kennedy, November 3, 2000.

101 *It was Salameh's idea:* Bassam Abu Sharif, *Arafat and the Dream of Palestine* (New York: Palgrave Macmillan, 2009), p. 34.

102 *"It left an indelible mark . . .":* Stephan, "Abu Hassan by Abu Hassan" and "After I Die."

102 *moved to write a poem:* Bob Ames, untitled poem, Yvonne Ames papers.

103 *Salameh was providing raw intelligence:* Timothy Naftali, *Blind Spot: The Secret History of American Counterterrorism* (New York: Basic Books, 2005), p. 78.

103 *"under a lot of pressure . . .":* Frank Anderson, interview, November 4, 2010. Helms confided this to Anderson in 1992 during one of their "mentoring" lunches. At the time, Anderson was chief of the Near East Division in the Directorate of Operations.

103 *"Headquarters in Langley wanted Salameh . . .":* Bruce Riedel, interview, March 30, 2011. Riedel says he was asked to review the entire Salameh-Ames file as part of a general review of Fatah's connection to terrorism: "Were they really clean or not?" He says it was not a security investigation of Ames or Salameh.

104 *"There is a lot that is just a matter of opinion . . .":* Henry Miller-Jones, e-mail to author, March 10, 2012.

104 *"Bob would say":* John Morris, interview, March 22, 2011.

104 *"My best sources were never recruitable":* Graham Fuller, interview, April 3, 2012.

105 *"Ali's ambition . . .":* Frank Anderson, interview, November 4, 2010.

105 *"I remember avidly reading . . .":* Charles Allen, interview, December 21, 2012.

105 *"I thought it was a mistake":* Charles Waverly, interview, March 28, 2011.

105 *"I was of the opinion . . .":* Sam Wyman, interview, March 28, 2011.

105 *"An agent does not always mean a paid agent":* Hillel Katz, interview, Tel Aviv, November 11, 2012.

106 *"A CIA officer would start the ball rolling . . .":* Zein, "Deceit with Extreme Prejudice," p. 160.

106 *Bob gave Mustafa handwritten instructions:* Ibid., p. 163-A. Zein reproduces the handwritten note in his unpublished memoir—and it quite clearly appears to be in Ames's neat handwriting. Ames misspelled Cairo's famed Shepheard Hotel as Shepard's Hotel.

107 *"a complete professional . . .":* Eveland, *Ropes of Sand*, p. 143.

107 *"The meeting did not go well":* Taylor, *States of Terror*, p. 70.

107 *"Ali told me everything . . .":* Mustafa Zein, interview, Amman, October 6, 2012.

107 *"It took a while to restore the relationship":* Charles Waverly, interview, March 28, 2011.

108 *"We, you and I":* Robert Ames to Mustafa Zein, August 4, 1971.

108 *"Bob had warned us . . .":* Mustafa Zein, interview, October 6, 2012.

108 *"I know he's suffered . . .":* Robert Ames to Mustafa Zein, August 4, 1971.

108 *"It sure was great . . .":* Robert Ames to Mustafa Zein, August 20, 1971.

109 *"Regarding our friend," Ames wrote, "if you see him . . .":* Ibid.

109 *"Regarding our friend," Ames wrote Zein, "I believe it is imperative . . .":* Robert Ames to Mustafa Zein, September 14, 1971.

111 *"I was opposed . . .":* Alan Hart, *Arafat: Terrorist or Peacemaker?* (London: Sidgwick and Jackson, 1984), p. 348.

111 *"spiritual godfather and chief":* Abdul Hadi, *Palestinian Personalities*, p. 111.

111 *"At the time," said Bella, "Arafat could not afford to speak . . .":* Hart, *Arafat*, p. 347.

112 *"I told Ali . . .":* Mustafa Zein, interview, Amman, October 6, 2012.

112 *"Ali Hassan Salameh, the hard-living Fatah intelligence expert . . .":* Eric Pace, "The Black September Guerrillas: Elusive Trail in Seven Countries," *New York Times*, October 12, 1972.

112 *Salameh was the "mastermind":* Sayigh, *Armed Struggle*, p. 307.

113 *"We are Black September . . .":* Bird, *Crossing Mandelbaum Gate*, p. 281.

113 *"The Jordanians were in an ugly mood":* Robert Ames to Yvonne, December 4, 1971.

114 *an elaborate Damascene ceiling:* Bird, *Crossing Mandelbaum Gate*, p. 7.

114 *"Today is the Jewish Sabbath":* Robert Ames to Yvonne, December 4, 1971.

115 *he "missed the oriental dignity that was Jerusalem":* Ibid.

Chapter Six: Secret Diplomacy

116 *they never locked their doors:* Karen Ames, civil suit testimony in *Anne Dammarell vs. Islamic Republic of Iran*, April 15, 2003, Federal District Court, Washington, DC, www.gpo.gov/fdsys/pkg/USCOURTS-dcd-1_01-cv-02224/pdf/USCOURTS-dcd-1_01-cv-02224-4.pdf.

117 *"He didn't like what alcohol did":* Yvonne Ames, interview, November 19–20, 2010.

117 *They owned a Kuwaiti chest:* Yvonne Ames, e-mail to author, January 22, 2013, with a photograph of the chest.

118 *His favorite poem was Rudyard Kipling's "If":* Yvonne Ames, interview, November 19–20, 2010.

118 *"Bob was reading five books . . .":* Charles Englehart, interview, September 20, 2011.

119 *"He didn't talk much about himself":* Adrienne Ames, interview, November 19, 2010.

119 *"He was a quiet, solid neighbor":* Ron Simmers Sr., phone interview, April 22, 2012.

119 *a GS-13, earning less than $20,000:* Lance Potter, e-mail to author, January 30, 2012. Potter is citing U.S. Office of Personnel Management, "Rates of Pay Under the General Schedule: Effective the First Pay Period Beginning on or After January 1, 1971," www.opm.gov/oca/pre1994/1971_GS.pdf.

119 *"Bob didn't tolerate debt":* Yvonne Ames, interview, November 19–20, 2010, and Yvonne Ames, e-mail to author, January 28, 2012.

119 *"Everyone in our neighborhood . . .":* Yvonne Ames, e-mail to author, January 28, 2012.

119 *Yvonne sang with the Sweet Adelines:* Ron Simmers Sr., phone interview, April 22, 2012.

120 *"It seemed all the planes took off . . .":* Robert Ames to Yvonne, May 27, 1972.

120 *"There's lots of activity . . .":* Robert Ames to Yvonne, June 19, 1972.

121 *"I hear all sorts of gory tales . . .":* Robert Ames to Yvonne, June 13, 1972.

121 *"Here everything is dust":* Robert Ames to Yvonne, May 27, 1972.

121 *"It's about time I relaxed . . .":* Robert Ames to Yvonne, June 21, 1972.

121 *"I still crack my head . . ."*: Robert Ames to Yvonne, June 7, 1972.

122 *"water problems, dust problems . . ."*: Robert Ames to Yvonne, May 27, 1972.

122 *"I just had some canned spaghetti . . ."*: Robert Ames to Yvonne, June 4, 1972.

122 *"Well, it's getting late for me . . ."*: Ibid.

122 *"I won't be bored"*: Robert Ames to Yvonne, May 22, 1972.

122 *He lived frugally*: Robert Ames to Yvonne, July 27, 1972.

122 *"I'm just an old homebody now"*: Robert Ames to Yvonne, May 22, 1972.

122 *"One good thing about being in Yemen"*: Robert Ames to Yvonne, June 13, 1972.

123 *a short, almost perfunctory trial*: As a young freelance reporter in Sana'a, I attended one of these trials of saboteurs in the summer of 1973.

123 *"so there would be cars in front of me . . ."*: Robert Ames to Yvonne, July 21, 1972.

123 *"Well, I've driven everywhere . . ."*: Robert Ames to Yvonne, June 29, 1972.

123 *more than two hundred applicants*: Robert Ames to Yvonne, July 15, 1972.

123 *"The thing is"*: Robert Ames to Yvonne, May 5, 1972.

123 *"People wanted to see me . . ."*: Robert Ames to Yvonne, July 10, 1972.

123 *"If I put out ten more reports . . ."*: Ibid.

124 *"Tehran might be a more plausible choice"*: Richard Helms with William Hood, *A Look over My Shoulder: A Life in the Central Intelligence Agency* (New York: Ballantine Books, 2003), p. 412.

124 *"two of his best case officers"*: George Cave, interview, March 14, 2011.

124 *"try to find time . . ."*: Amir Oren, "Top Secret, Eyes Only," *Ha'aretz*, March 10, 2008. Oren's article is based on declassified papers of Richard Helms, Center for the Study of Intelligence, CIA.

126 *"We had no choice . . ."*: Ali Hassan Salameh, interview by Nadia Salti Stephan, *Monday Morning*, April 26–May 2, 1976.

126 *investigative journalist Aaron J. Klein*: Aaron J. Klein, *Striking Back: The 1972 Munich Olympics Massacre and Israel's Deadly Response* (New York: Random House, 2005), pp. 219–20.

126 *"I am fully aware of the activities of our friend"*: Robert Ames to Mustafa Zein, March 26, 1972.

127 *Flattery: "Our friend should know . . ."*: Ibid.

129 *It was a very narrow escape*: Bassam Abu-Sharif and Uzi Mahnaimi, *Best of Enemies: The Memoirs of Bassam Abu-Sharif and Uzi Mahnaimi* (Boston: Little, Brown, 1995), p. 112.

129 *Half a million mourners*: Klein, *Striking Back*, p. 169.

130 *"the result of complete carelessness . . ."*: Taylor, *States of Terror*, pp. 73–74; Ali Hassan Salameh, interview by Nadia Salti Stephan, *Monday Morning*, April 26–May 2, 1976.

130 *"Okay, whatever Bob says . . ."*: Mustafa Zein, interview, Amman, October 6, 2012.

130 *an attack on the Olympics would serve three purposes*: Klein, *Striking Back*, p. 34; Abu Iyad, with Éric Rouleau, *My Home, My Land: A Narrative of the Palestinian Struggle* (New York: Times Books, 1981), p. 106; Michael Rubner, review of four books on the Munich massacre, *Middle East Policy* 13, no. 2 (2007): 176–92.

131 *"picked up the keys . . ."*: Klein, *Striking Back*, p. 33.

131 *"a tragedy for the Israelis and us"*: Hart, *Arafat*, p. 352.

132 *"Terrorism is theater"*: Steve Coll, *Ghost Wars: The Secret History of the CIA, Af-*

ghanistan, and bin Laden, from the Soviet Invasion to September 10, 2001 (New York: Penguin Books, 2004), p. 138.

132 "Dozens of senior ex-Mossad . . .": Klein, Striking Back, pp. 218–19.

133 "a forward command post . . .": Simon Reeve, One Day in September (New York: Arcade, 2000), pp. 46, 280. See also David Clay Large, Munich 1972: Tragedy, Terror, and Triumph at the Olympic Games (New York: Rowman and Littlefield, 2012).

133 he "was wide awake . . .": Bar-Zohar and Haber, Quest for the Red Prince, pp. 124–25, 132.

133 telephone conversations intercepted by the German government: Paul O'Neil, "The Charming Assassin Who Loved the Good Life," Life, April 1979, p. 104.

133 "Not to my knowledge was Ali Hassan in Munich": Meir Harel, interview, Tel Aviv, October 18, 2012.

134 "Ali Hassan was the tactical planner": Sam Wyman, interview, April 23, 2012.

134 "Initially, Bob thought Ali was behind the Munich operation . . .": Mustafa Zein, interview, Amman, October 6, 2012.

134 "I am not trying to portray him [Salameh] as St Francis . . .": Zein, "Deceit with Extreme Prejudice," p. 190.

134 "When I heard about Munich": Taylor, States of Terror, pp. 62–63.

135 "In counter-terrorism . . .": George Jonas, Vengeance: The True Story of an Israeli Counter-terrorist Team (New York: Simon and Schuster, 1984), p. 240.

135 "man with the imagination of the devil . . .": O'Neil, "Charming Assassin," p. 104.

135 "At the time, we were subjected to a blackout . . .": Ali Hassan Salameh, interview by Nadia Salti Stephan, Monday Morning, April 26–May 2, 1976.

135 "It has to be resolved . . .": Zein, "Deceit with Extreme Prejudice," p. 117.

136 "I saw somebody give him [Salameh] a cheque . . .": Taylor, States of Terror, p. 71.

137 "What hurt deepest were the comments of Ali": Robert Ames to Mustafa Zein, February 10, 1973, courtesy of Mustafa Zein.

137 "I happened to see many files on Ali": Ibid.

138 "There is much I would like to tell you . . .": Ibid.

139 "Khartoum had made its point . . .": Robert Ames, memo to Ambassador Helms, July 18, 1973, Richard Helms Papers, Center for the Study of Intelligence, CIA.

139 "I suppose we were . . .": Taylor, States of Terror, p. 69.

139 "Fatah leader Yasser Arafat . . .": Scott W. Johnson, "How Arafat Got Away with Murder," Weekly Standard, January 29, 2007. Professor Yezid Sayigh wrote that Khartoum was an Abu Iyad operation: "Arafat was implicated once the attack had taken place, but it is not clear that he or other members of the Fatah central committee had prior knowledge of it." Sayigh, Armed Struggle, p. 311.

140 "You sup with the devil": Benjamin Weiser, "Company Man," Washington Post, May 17, 1992, p. 25.

140 Ames passed an urgent message to Salameh: David Ignatius, "The Secret History of U.S.-PLO Terror Talks," Washington Post, December 4, 1988; Mohammed Natour (Abu Tayeb), "The Martyrdom of Ali Hassan Salameh," unpublished manuscript, courtesy of Mustafa Zein. Zein reports that the Libyan businessman Al-Khudairi later escaped to Rabat with the assistance of Moroccan intelligence. Mustafa Zein, signed note to author, October 6, 2012.

140 "After Munich": Uri Oppenheim, interview, Tel Aviv, October 14, 2012. Oppenheim spent ten years as a clandestine Mossad officer in Europe.

141 One Thousand and One Nights: An Arabic edition of this book was found in his pocket by the medical examiner.

141 *"Over the years"*: Klein, *Striking Back*, pp. 119–23.

141 *"As far as I remember . . ."*: Ibid., pp. 122–23.

142 *"Basil was an Arab nationalist . . ."*: Dr. Abdul Said Aziz, interview, April 4, 2012.

142 *"on a tour in Europe . . ."*: Walid W. Kazziha, *Revolutionary Transformation in the Arab World: Habash and His Comrades from Nationalism to Marxism* (New York: St. Martin's Press, 1975), p. 38.

142 *He lived modestly:* Kameel B. Nasr, *Arab and Israeli Terrorism: The Causes and Effects of Political Violence, 1936–1993* (Jefferson, NC: McFarland, 1997), p. 72. Nasr is citing the London *Times*, April 10, 1973, and *Le Monde*, July 24, 1982.

142 *"La! La! La!"*: Jonas, *Vengeance*, p. 192.

142 *"a revolutionary avant-garde intellectual . . ."*: "Iraqi, on a Guerrilla 'Mission,' Shot and Killed in Paris," *New York Times*, April 7, 1973.

143 *"looks very much like the execution of a secret agent"*: "Iraqi Is Killed in Paris; Israeli Agents Blamed," *Washington Post*, April 7, 1973.

143 *nine different passports:* Klein, *Striking Back*, p. 155. Klein doesn't give a source for the "nine different passports," but the Associated Press story published by the *New York Times* quotes a hotel employee saying that police found $1,000 in cash. "Iraqi, on a Guerrilla 'Mission,' Shot and Killed in Paris," *New York Times*, April 7, 1973.

143 *"quartermaster"*: Jonas, *Vengeance*, p. 191.

143 *"on a mission"*: "Iraqi, on a Guerrilla 'Mission,' Shot and Killed in Paris," *New York Times*, April 7, 1973.

143 *"roving ambassador"*: Jonas, *Vengeance*, p. 193. Abu Iyad described Al-Kubaisi as a "professor at the University of Baghdad" (Iyad, *My Home, My Land*, p. 103). The American scholar Harold M. Cubert later wrote that Al-Kubaisi "was an active ANM member and continued his association with its leadership as a PFLP operative after December 1967." Following Al-Kubaisi's murder in 1973, the PFLP published his dissertation in its weekly magazine, *Al-Hadaf*. "It also eulogized him as an important ANM and PFLP member." Harold M. Cubert, *The PFLP's Changing Role in the Middle East* (London: Frank Cass, 1997), pp. 49–50.

143 *"was probably not affiliated with Fatah's Black September . . ."*: Klein, *Striking Back*, p. 153.

144 *"The Mossad was not after the muscle . . ."*: Fadl Naqib, e-mail to author, May 23, 2012; Fadl Naqib, "Ghassan Kanafani: Questions and Answers," speech delivered at the Brecht Forum, New York City, May 8, 1999.

144 *"Kubaisi rings a bell"*: George Cave, e-mail to author, May 11, 2012.

144 *"Mr. K was a chattering contact . . ."*: Duane R. Clarridge, e-mail to author, May 11, 2012.

145 *"I know"*: Graham Fuller, e-mail to author, May 7, 2012.

145 *"interesting intelligence"*: Robert Ames, memo to Helms, July 18, 1973, Richard Helms Papers, Center for the Study of Intelligence, CIA, https://www.cia.gov/library/center-for-the-study-of-intelligence/index.html.

146 *"His is the first execution . . ."*: Adam Goldman and Randy Herschaft, "Papers Shed Light on Envoy's '73 Killing," *Boston Globe*, July 1, 2007. See also Fred Burton and John Bruning, *Chasing Shadows: A Special Agent's Lifelong Hunt to Bring a Cold War Assassin to Justice* (New York: Palgrave Macmillan, 2011), pp. 199–205.

146 *"had ordered the execution . . .":* Zein, "Deceit with Extreme Prejudice," p. 194.

146 *"Fedayeen senior official":* Goldman and Herschaft, "Papers Shed Light on Envoy's '73 Killing." See also Burton and Bruning, *Chasing Shadows,* pp. 199–205.

147 *"Israel is here to stay":* Robert Ames, memo to Richard Helms, July 18, 1973, Richard Helms Papers, Center for the Study of Intelligence, CIA, https://www.cia.gov/library/center-for-the-study-of-intelligence/index.html. See also David Ignatius, "PLO Rejects Role for Jordan's Hussein in Mideast Talks, Moderate Group Says," *Wall Street Journal,* March 11, 1983.

147 *"Arafat claims to have the agreement . . .":* Bird, *Crossing Mandelbaum Gate,* p. 286; Robert C. Ames to Ambassador Helms, July 18, 1973, Richard Helms Papers, Center for the Study of Intelligence, CIA; also quoted by Oren, "Top Secret, Eyes Only"; David Ignatius, "Secret Strategies," *Washington Post,* November 12, 2004.

149 *"When the USG says . . .":* Henry Kissinger, cable to Richard Helms, August 3, 1973, Richard Helms Papers, CIA, https://www.cia.gov/library/center-for-the-study-of-intelligence/index.html.

149 *"low-level intelligence channels":* Henry Kissinger, *Years of Upheaval* (New York: Simon and Schuster, 1982), p. 625.

150 *"My company is still interested . . .":* David Ignatius, "Penetrating Terrorist Networks," *Washington Post,* September 16, 2001.

150 *"But Valters, I'm No. 2, so you're going":* Robert Greenberger, "New Envoy to UN Has Long Advocated Going Underground," *Wall Street Journal,* June 21, 1985, p. 14.

150 *"We regard the King of Jordan as a friend":* Kissinger, *Years of Upheaval,* p. 628.

150 *"There are no objective reasons . . .":* Naftali, *Blind Spot,* p. 74. Naftali is citing a memo from Brent Scowcroft to Walters, "Talking Points for Meeting with General Walters," October 23, 1973, NSC CO: Middle East, "Palestinian [July 1973–July 1974]," Box 139, Nixon Materials Project, National Archives.

151 *"The dynamics of the movement . . .":* Kissinger, *Years of Upheaval,* p. 629.

151 *"potentially too explosive . . .":* Ibid., p. 629.

151 *Israel's ambassador in Washington, Simcha Dinitz, was briefed:* Naftali, *Blind Spot,* p. 348 n. 56.

152 *Salameh was somewhere in Europe:* O'Neil, "Charming Assassin," p. 104. Actually, by Mustafa Zein's account, the botched Lillehammer operation came about as a result of misinformation planted by the PLO. Zein says he asked Salameh what happened in Norway. Salameh replied, "I just can't believe it! They [the Mossad] swallowed the bait, hook, line and sinker in one gulp. I just implanted in their minds through informers that I was going to be in Norway on that date. I chose the most far away place that I could think of that no one in the Middle East would ever think of visiting." Zein, "Deceit with Extreme Prejudice," p. 218.

152 *"When they killed Boushiki":* Bar-Zohar and Haber, *Quest for the Red Prince,* p. 200.

152 *"The CIA deputy director said it was not possible . . .":* Gordon Thomas, *Gideon's Spies: The Secret History of the Mossad* (New York: St. Martin's Press, 1995), p. 280.

153 *to shoot his plane down:* Kissinger, *Years of Upheaval,* p. 1037.

154 *accompanied by Ali Hassan Salameh:* George Cave, interview, March 14, 2011;

Taylor, *States of Terror*, p. 38. Salameh met in Beirut with U.S. embassy officials to plan the details of the visit. See "Whereabouts of Abu Iyad," U.S. embassy cable, Beirut, November 12, 1974, Wikileaks, https://www.wikileaks.org/plusd/cables/1974BEIRUT13562_b.html.

154 *"Salameh begged for understanding and flexibility":* U.S. embassy cable, Beirut, November 8, 1974, Wikileaks, https://www.wikileaks.org/plusd/cables/1974BEI RUT13562_b.html.

154 *"I have come bearing an olive branch . . .":* Edward R. F. Sheehan, *The Arabs, Israelis and Kissinger* (New York: Reader's Digest Press, 1976), p. 153.

154 *Mustafa Zein was there to introduce Salameh:* Zein, "Deceit with Extreme Prejudice," p. 228; *Charles Waverly*, e-mail to author, July 27, 2012.

154 *They spent the night in the Waldorf:* Shafiq Al-Hout, *My Life in the PLO: The Inside Story of the Palestinian Struggle* (London: Pluto Press, 2011), p. 122.

155 *"Arafat and his Fatah wing . . .":* Ignatius, "Secret History of U.S.-PLO Terror Talks."

155 *"The PLO at the Waldorf Astoria!":* Taylor, *States of Terror*, p. 72.

155 *"We in Force 17 . . .":* Natour, "Martyrdom of Ali Hassan Salameh."

156 *"persuaded the PLO leaders . . .":* Rubner, review of four books on Munich.

156 *"I'm just a middle man in all this":* Robert Ames to Mustafa Zein, June 5, 1974; reproduced in Zein, "Deceit with Extreme Prejudice," p. 225-A.

158 *"In Tehran":* Bruce Riedel, interview, March 30, 2011.

158 *"The Shah in his early years . . .":* Classified secret letter from "John" to Ambassador Helms, August 1973, published in "Documents from the U.S. Espionage Den," vol. 8, p. 49, http://ia600409.us.archive.org/10/items/DocumentsFromTheU.s .EspionageDen.

160 *"Glad things have worked out so well":* Knight, cable to Kuwait, November 1, 1973, Richard Helms Papers, Center for the Study of Intelligence, CIA.

160 *"Bob frequently produced long think pieces . . .": David Reeve*, e-mail to author, January 1, 2012.

161 *"Bob had a keen instinct for the jugular":* Graham Fuller, interview, April 3, 2012.

161 *"He once told me":* Yvonne Ames, interview, November 19–20, 2010.

161 *"Henry was a mess":* Yvonne Ames, e-mail to author, May 21, 2012.

161 *"His pugnacious Irish temperament . . .":* Henry Miller-Jones, e-mail to author, May 18, 2012.

162 *"Henry got juiced":* Bill Fisk, interview, March 27, 2011.

162 *He became a potter:* Betty Bretting, e-mail to author, May 16, 2012. Betty was Henry McDermott's first wife. They separated in 1970 and divorced in 1977. McDermott died in the early 2000s.

162 *"Please let me know":* Ames, secret cable to "KNIGHT," June 10, 1975, Richard Helms Papers, Center for the Study of Intelligence, CIA, www.foia.cia.gov/helms/pdf/75_1503978.pdf.

162 "CounterSpy *magazine":* Philip Agee and Louis Wolf, eds., *Dirty Work: The CIA in Western Europe* (New York: Dorset Press, 1988), p. 52. More than ninety other chiefs of station were named in this magazine article, so it seems unlikely that Ames would be pulled from Kuwait for this reason alone. But perhaps the circumstances in Kuwait warranted his transfer.

162 *"His murder . . .":* Nelson, cable to Helms, December 26, 1975, Richard Helms

Papers, Center for the Study of Intelligence, CIA, www.foia.cia.gov/helms/pdf/
75_1504058.pdf.

Chapter Seven: Headquarters, 1975–79

163 *only about 2,500:* George Crile, *Charlie Wilson's War: The Extraordinary Story of the Largest Covert Operation in History* (New York: Atlantic Monthly Press, 2003), p. 156.

163 *"Get rid of the clowns":* Tim Weiner, *Legacy of Ashes: The History of the CIA* (New York: Doubleday, 2007), p. 323.

163 *he'd fired more than five hundred:* Powers, *The Man Who Kept the Secrets*, p. 323; Weiner, *Legacy of Ashes*, p. 325.

164 *"We predicted . . .":* Weiner, *Legacy of Ashes*, p. 329. By contrast, a prescient memo written by a State Department intelligence analyst predicted in May 1973 that there was a "better than even bet" that war between Egypt and Israel would occur "by autumn." See William Burr, National Security Archive Electronic Briefing Book No. 415, March 5, 2013.

164 *"In the context of the politics . . .":* William Colby, oral history, March 15, 1988, CIA Oral History Archives, http://www.foia.cia.gov/helms/pdf/reflections.

164 *"The Congressional investigations":* Ibid.

164 *"A lot of dead cats . . .":* Weiner, *Legacy of Ashes*, p. 338.

165 *thirteen times to testify:* Powers, *The Man Who Kept the Secrets*, p. 341.

165 *"wear this conviction like a badge of honor":* Ibid., p. 353.

165 *"If we could, we'd bury you":* Kai Bird, "The Captured Documents," 1985, Alicia Patterson Foundation, http://aliciapatterson.org/stories/captured-documents.

165 *"In my experience . . .":* Richard L. Holm, *The Craft We Chose: My Life in the CIA* (Mountain Lake Park, MD: Mountain Lake Press, 2011), p. 23.

166 *18,000 officers and staff:* Bird, "The Captured Documents," 1985.

166 *"I am sure there were those in the division . . .":* Clarridge, *Spy for All Seasons*, p. 153.

166 *"wog factor":* Ibid., p. 105.

166 *He had three pairs:* Bob Layton, interview, September 20, 2011.

166 *"Bob played with a pipe . . .":* Henry Miller-Jones, unpublished op-ed, ca. May 1983, courtesy of Miller-Jones.

167 *"Ph.D.s don't do well in the espionage business":* Duane R. Clarridge, interview, November 26, 2011.

167 *"liaison relationship with this murderer":* Duane R. Clarridge, e-mail to author, March 16, 2013.

167 *"In the 1970s":* Duane R. Clarridge, telephone interview, March 22, 2013.

167 *"Willi was a very cool guy":* Karin Assmann, Felix Bohr, Gunther Latsch, and Klaus Wiegrefe, "The Munich Olympics and the CIS's New Informant," *Der Spiegel OnLine*, January 2, 2013, www.spiegel.de/international/germany/how-willi-voss-went-from-abetting-terror-to-working-for-the-cia-a-875374.html.

168 *"The intelligence was valuable":* Terence Douglas, e-mail to author, March 18, 2013.

168 *"If the agent [Voss] can set up Carlos . . .":* Clarridge, *Spy for All Seasons*, p. 158.

168 *"lost his nerve":* Assmann et al., "Munich Olympics." Voss, sixty-eight years old, is today the author of dozens of crime thrillers and screenplays in Germany.

168 *"He and I got along well . . .":* Duane R. Clarridge, telephone interview, March 21, 2013.

169 *Alcohol, he wrote, "plays a major part":* Clarridge, *Spy for All Seasons*, p. 79.

169 *A CIA survey:* retired CIA officer, e-mail to author.

169 *"Recruiting agents is very hard":* Duane R. Clarridge, telephone interview, March 21, 2013.

169 *"the Agency would have been awash in spies":* Duane R. Clarridge, e-mail to author, May 11, 2012.

170 *"Dewey is a brilliant intelligence officer":* Clair George, interview, March 23, 2011.

170 *"Dewey was an ass, a showboat":* Lindsay Sherwin, interview, March 22, 2011.

170 *"If Dewey asks . . .":* Henry Miller-Jones, interview, March 19, 2011.

170 *"He once told me":* Miller-Jones, unpublished op-ed.

170 *"Alan looked like . . .":* Henry Miller-Jones, e-mail to author, "Assignment Aden."

170 *Born in 1928:* Department of State Biographic Register, 1974. Wolfe received a letter of reprimand in the mid-1990s when the Agency discovered he had failed to report that CIA officer Aldrich Ames had a drinking problem in Rome. Wolfe later died of brain cancer.

170 *"He had a low threshold for the dim-witted":* Clarridge, *Spy for All Seasons*, p. 153.

171 *advance man for Henry Kissinger's secret trip:* Crile, *Charlie Wilson's War*, p. 59.

171 *"Learning a wog language":* Henry Miller-Jones, e-mail to author, December 2, 2010.

171 *"Orientalists," liable to be critical: Hillel Katz,* interview, Tel Aviv, November 11, 2012.

171 *"Alan, I understand . . .":* Frederick Hutchinson, interview, December 5, 2011. Hutchinson served as chief counsel to DCI Casey.

172 *"Right away," recalled Zein:* Mustafa Zein, interview, Amman, October 6, 2012.

172 *"Clandestine officers are usually extroverts":* Charles Allen, interview, December 21, 2012.

172 *"Bob had a nice personality":* Lindsay Sherwin, interview, March 22, 2011.

172 *"I think sloppiness is contagious":* Robert Ames to Yvonne, July 2, 1978.

172 *He typed his own memos:* Bob Layton, interview, September 20, 2011.

173 *He never learned to type:* Miller-Jones, unpublished op-ed.

173 *green ink:* By some accounts, there is a tradition by which intelligence officers favored green ink. See the biography of Sir Claude Dansey by Anthony Read and David Fisher, *Colonel Z: The Secret Life of a Master of Spies* (London: Hodder and Stoughton, 1984), p. 234.

173 *"Salameh was perceived . . .": Charles Waverly,* interview, March 28, 2011.

173 *"Okay, why don't you give him a replica . . .":* Bruce Riedel, interview, March 30, 2011.

173 *"He would seek his 'out of school' take on an issue":* Henry Miller-Jones, e-mail to author, March 10, 2012.

174 *"They were constantly trying to recruit each other":* Naftali, *Blind Spot,* p. 76. O'Connell told this to Naftali in an interview on October 22, 2003.

174 *"They tell you in the CIA . . .":* Henry Miller-Jones, interview, March 23, 2011.

174 *Ames got Salameh to pledge:* Sam Wyman, interview, July 27, 2010.

174 *37 percent of the Agency's total budget:* Church Committee, *Foreign and Military Intelligence,* bk. 1 of *Final Report of the Select Committee to Study Governmental*

Operations with Respect to Intelligence Activities, U.S. Senate (Washington, DC: Government Printing Office, 1976), p. 123, www.aarclibrary.org/publib/contents/church/contents_church_reports_book1.htm.

175 *"I never thought of Lebanon as a country":* Aburish, *The St George Hotel Bar*, p. 201.

175 *"In Beirut everyone has an agenda and a gun":* Benjamin Weiser, "Company Man," *Washington Post*, May 17, 1992.

176 *According to Jonathan Randal:* Jonathan Randal, *Going All the Way: Christian War-lords, Israeli Adventurers, and the War in Lebanon* (New York: Vintage Books, 1984), p. 182.

176 *Salameh supervised the security arrangements:* Sam Wyman, interview, July 27, 2010.

176 *"I will get you through the Palestinian lines":* Sam Wyman, interview, November 5, 2010.

177 *Kissinger even sent Arafat an official letter:* David Ignatius, "The Secret History of the U.S.-PLO Terror Talks," *Washington Post*, December 4, 1988; Nasr, *Arab and Israeli Terrorism*, p. 108.

177 *" 'Oh, I killed him two days ago' ":* Charles Waverly, interview, March 28, 2011.

177 *"I told him that we had some intelligence . . .":* Charles Englehart, interview, September 20, 2011. Englehart was told this story by Frank Anderson.

177 *"It is a little hard to hear":* Charles Waverly, interview, March 28, 2011.

177 *a "barbarian" and a murderer:* Woodward, *Veil*, p. 186.

177 *"our brutal warlord":* Bob Layton, interview, September 20, 2011.

177 *Woodward got this wrong:* Sam Wyman, e-mail to author, March 31, 2013. Wyman checked with friends in the CIA, and he insists that "Woodward is wrong." Tim Weiner reports that Ames was the CIA officer who recruited Bashir Gemayel, but on the basis of Wyman this seems incorrect (Weiner, *Legacy of Ashes*, p. 389).

177 *"pimply-faced, overweight hooligan . . .":* Aburish, *Brutal Friendship*, p. 205.

178 *Salameh's daily routine:* Klein, *Striking Back*, p. 212.

178 *"Being outside Palestine":* Ali Hassan Salameh, interview by Nadia Salti Stephan, *Monday Morning*, April 26–May 2, 1976. Also quoted by Bar-Zohar and Haber, *Quest for the Red Prince*, p. 208.

178 *"There are no permanent enmities . . .":* Ali Hassan Salameh, interview by Nadia Salti Stephan, *Monday Morning*, April 26–May 2, 1976.

178 *When Dany Chamoun, the chieftain of the Christian right-wing Tigers militia, was captured:* Bar-Zohar and Haber, *Quest for the Red Prince*, p. 209.

179 *"Salameh played a large part . . .":* Thomas, *Gideon's Spies*, p. 281.

179 *"I spent a lot of my time coaxing him . . .":* Sam Wyman, interview, November 5, 2010.

179 *"We had an audio operation":* Duane R. Clarridge, interview, November 26, 2011.

179 *"I told Salameh":* Sam Wyman, interview, July 27, 2010, and March 28, 2011.

180 *"They [the Israelis] are not supermen":* Paul O'Neil, "A Charming Assassin Who Loved the Good Life," *Life*, April 1979, p. 104.

180 *"a playboy, a smuggler, a murderer . . .":* Ali Hassan Salameh, interview by Nadia Salti Stephan, *Monday Morning*, April 26–May 2, 1976, p. 12.

180 *"We are here for beauty, not politics":* Bar-Zihar and Haber, *Quest for the Red Prince*, p. 202.

181 *postage stamps with Rizk's image:* Daily Star, Beirut, January 11, 1975.

181 *"She is Lebanon's queen . . .":* Daily Star, Beirut, March 1, 1975.

181   *he wanted to "prove that he was not needed . . .":* Mohammed Natour (Abu Tayeb), "The Martyrdom of Ali Hassan Salameh," unpublished manuscript, courtesy of Mustafa Zein.

181   *"Bush would have favored Salameh's trip":* Duane R. Clarridge, telephone interview, March 21, 2013.

181   *Vance authorized the visit:* Mustafa Zein, interview, Amman, October 7, 2012.

182   *"Everything was arranged . . .":* Duane R. Clarridge, telephone interview, March 21, 2013.

182   *Ames's ranking superior at the time, Alan Wolfe flew down to New Orleans:* Ibid.

182   *"Abu Hassan was pleased":* Taylor, *States of Terror*, p. 73.

183   *a hidden tape recorder:* Mustafa Zein, e-mail to author, August 21, 2012, and interview, Amman, October 8, 2012.

183   *"He was scared to death of it":* Charles Waverly, interview, March 28, 2011.

183   *"It was kind of creepy, riding in":* Robert Ames to Yvonne, March 5, 1977.

184   *"I think they should just level the place . . .":* Ibid.

184   *"One good thing came out of this war":* Robert Ames to Yvonne, April 2, 1977.

185   *"I feel the Muslims are more eager . . .":* Robert Ames to Yvonne, February 27, 1977.

185   *"three radio friends":* Robert Ames to Yvonne, March 5, 1977.

185   *Half of his meetings:* Robert Ames to Yvonne, March 12, 1977.

185   *he had to hide inside the trunk:* Robert Hunter, interview, March 17, 2011.

186   *"Bob said it was high tension . . .":* Sanford Dryden, e-mail to author, May 18, 2012.

186   *"I guess none of us ever lose that strange feeling . . .":* Robert Ames to Yvonne, March 26, 1977.

186   *"doesn't know how to write":* Robert Ames to Yvonne, April 2, 1977.

186   *"has fixed it up as only a Lebanese male can do":* Robert Ames to Yvonne, March 5, 1977.

187   *solid-gold prayer beads:* Robert Ames to Yvonne, March 12, 1977.

187   *"I think they're trying to convert me!":* Robert Ames to Yvonne, March 19, 1977.

187   *"Especially since she is blonde":* Robert Ames to Yvonne, March 26, 1977.

187   *"Why he still has this thing going . . .":* Robert Ames to Yvonne, March 5, 1977, and March 26, 1977.

188   *"I'm doing something useful . . .":* Robert Ames to Yvonne, March 5, 1977.

188   *"The bottom line":* Duane R. Clarridge, e-mail to author, May 7, 2012. The German agent was a "walk-in" who volunteered to spy on Fatah. His alias was "Ganymede." Clarridge thought he was the best penetration agent the CIA had against the PLO in 1974–75 (Assmann et al., "Munich Olympics").

188   *"It is hard to believe our friend was what he was":* Robert Ames to Yvonne, March 26, 1977.

189   *"a homeland for Palestinian refugees":* Jimmy Carter, *White House Diary* (New York: Farrar, Straus and Giroux, 2010), p. 33.

189   *"I think we're finally making some headway":* Robert Ames to Yvonne, March 19, 1977.

189   *"a consummate liar and dissembler . . .":* Richard Parker, *Memoirs of a Foreign Service Arabist* (Washington, DC: New Academia, forthcoming, manuscript courtesy of Jeffrey Parker), p. 159.

189   *"I got pretty pissed off . . .":* Robert D. Kaplan, *The Arabists: The Romance of an American Elite* (New York: Free Press, 1993), p. 123.

189   "I think I'm getting on better . . .": Robert Ames to Yvonne, March 19, 1977.

190   "It makes for grim reading": Robert Ames to Yvonne, April 9, 1977.

190   "After his death was announced": Robert Ames to Yvonne, March 19, 1977.

191   "The fighting there is foolish . . .": Robert Ames to Yvonne, April 9, 1977.

191   "Again the Christians and Israelis started it . . .": Robert Ames to Yvonne, April 23, 1977.

191   "He reported my remarks to Begin": Parker, Memoirs of a Foreign Service Arabist, p. 156.

192   "When this happened": Ibid., p. 156.

192   "When I got to the usual place": Robert Ames to Yvonne, April 2, 1977.

192   "No one in the CIA": Duane R. Clarridge, e-mail to author, April 2, 2012.

193   "Had Ames met Arafat . . .": Ibid.

193   "I think it was most useful": Robert Ames to Yvonne, April 2, 1977.

193   "It is absolutely ridiculous": Carter, White House Diary, p. 352.

193   Memorandum of Agreement: This September 1, 1975, memorandum is quoted by NSC officer Douglas J. Feith in an August 28, 1981, memo to Norman A. Bailey, "U.S. Policy Toward PLO," Folder PLO 1981 (1 of 3), Box 90220, Kemp Files, Ronald Reagan Presidential Library.

194   "The loss of innocence comes in stages": Graham Fuller, interview, April 3, 2012.

194   "on some very sensitive stuff": Robert Ames to Yvonne, April 9, 1977.

194   "Maybe my sharp cables . . .": Robert Ames to Yvonne, April 23, 1977.

194   "job pressures": Robert Ames to Yvonne, March 12, 1977.

194   "I enjoy life too much not to get my full share": Robert Ames to Yvonne, April 2, 1977.

194   "I feel I should get a promotion . . .": Robert Ames to Yvonne, April 9, 1977.

194   "If John MacGaffin . . .": Ibid.

195   "I'm more and more convinced . . .": Robert Ames to Yvonne, April 2, 1977.

195   "I hear indirectly from people . . .": Robert Ames to Yvonne, April 16, 1977.

195   He wore a white suit: Klein, Striking Back, p. 216.

196   "She seduced Ali": Mustafa Zein, interview, Amman, October 7, 2012.

196   diplomatic passport, No. X135101: American Vice-Consul Lisa A. Piascik, "Report of the Death of an American Citizen Abroad: Robert C. Ames," May 10, 1983, courtesy of Yvonne Ames.

196   He hadn't been back to Lebanon in a year: Robert Ames to Yvonne, June 25, 1978.

196   "lousy housekeepers": Robert Ames to Yvonne, June 29, 1978.

197   killed an estimated two thousand Lebanese civilians: Robert Fisk, Pity the Nation: The Abduction of Lebanon (New York: Atheneum, 1990), p. 124.

198   "The murder was truly savage . . .": Robert Ames to Yvonne, June 18, 1978.

198   "there is enough hatred . . .": Robert Ames to Yvonne, June 25, 1978.

198   "Our friend sends his best": Ibid.

198   "lots on my mind": Robert Ames to Yvonne, July 2, 1978.

199   "Lebanon is still waiting": Robert Ames to Yvonne, June 25, 1978.

199   "It's getting nasty here in Beirut": Robert Ames to Yvonne, July 5, 1978.

200   "Both men acknowledged . . .": Henry Miller-Jones, e-mail to author, November 3, 2012.

200   "Bob had a reputation . . .": Lindsay Sherwin, interview, March 22, 2011.

200   "I really haven't enjoyed anything . . .": Robert Ames to Yvonne, July 2, 1978.

201   "After you have been around for a while": Graham Fuller, interview, April 3, 2012.

201   *"Well, I can't possibly do the job . . .":* Kai Bird, *The Color of Truth: McGeorge Bundy and William Bundy, Brothers in Arms* (New York: Simon and Schuster, 1998), p. 157.

201   *"Perhaps," he wrote Yvonne on June 29, 1978, "my malaise . . .":* Robert Ames to Yvonne, June 29, 1978.

202   *"I gather they're looking hard . . .":* Robert Ames to Yvonne, July 5, 1978.

202   *"I don't like to be on the streets after dark":* Robert Ames to Yvonne, July 2, 1978.

202   *Why, Zein wanted to know, were people surprised:* Frank Reynolds, "Terror in the Promised Land," *ABC News,* December 30, 1978, courtesy of Vanderbilt TV News Archive, Nashville.

203   *"Despite the fact that Bob had no background . . .":* Harry Simpson, e-mail to author, September 19, 2011.

203   *"monthly warning assessments":* Robert C. Ames, memorandum for Director of Central Intelligence, June 25, 1979, Top Secret, declassified June 5, 2007.

204   *"has that unique ability . . .":* Copy of redacted security report, Form 1125, on Robert Clayton Ames, October 30, 1978.

204   *"Possessing weapons is as important . . .":* *Daily Star,* Beirut, February 3, 1975.

205   *"clarify the mystery":* Fouad Ajami, *The Vanished Imam: Musa Sadr and the Shia of Lebanon* (Ithaca, NY: Cornell University Press, 1986), p. 192.

Chapter Eight: The Assassination

207   *"The Israelis knew full well . . .":* Clair George, interview, March 23, 2011.

208   *"No answer was an answer":* Charles Waverly, interview, March 28, 2011.

208   *"We won't answer the question . . .":* Bruce Riedel, interview, March 30, 2011.

208   *"I am sure there was a debate":* Duane R. Clarridge, interview, November 26, 2011.

208   *Ames also urged Alan Wolfe:* Frank Anderson, interview, November 4, 2010.

208   *"There was some talk . . .":* Sam Wyman, interview, November 5, 2010.

209   *Mossad officers confirm this:* Uri Oppenheim, interview, Tel Aviv, October 14, 2012. *Oppenheim* said, "It was a mistake for Kimche to ask the Americans about Salameh—because Mossad must have known that there was some kind of connection. So why ask?"

209   *Ames contacted Salameh in Beirut:* Mustafa Zein, e-mail to author, July 4, 2012.

209   *"If Ali Hassan had agreed . . .":* Yoram Hessel, interview, Tel Aviv, October 10, 2012.

209   *and no one else:* Taylor, *States of Terror,* p. 76.

209   *"I knew he was dead":* Mustafa Zein, interview, Amman, October 7, 2012.

210   *"ticking bomb":* Aaron J. Klein, interview, Tel Aviv, October 15, 2012. *Time* magazine reporter Klein said, "No Mossad officer ever told me that they saw evidence that Ali Hassan was in Munich or Berlin." Klein believes that by 1979 Salameh "was not a ticking bomb."

211   *Salameh decided to postpone his Washington visit:* Mustafa Zein, e-mail to author, July 4, 2012.

211   *"We followed Ali Hassan extensively":* Meir Harel, interview, Tel Aviv, October 18, 2012.

211   *Ali Hassan had stashed Kalashnikovs:* Klein, *Striking Back,* p. 216.

212   *"I know that I'll die":* Bar-Zohar and Haber, *Quest for the Red Prince,* pp. 212, 214.

212   *"They're the ones who should be worried . . .":* "Death of a Terrorist," *Time,* February 5, 1979.

213 *According to Peter Taylor:* Taylor, *States of Terror*, pp. 76–77. See also Reeve, *One Day in September*, pp. 206–7.

214 *"I think Bashir had some* crise de conscience*":* Taylor, *States of Terror*, pp. 75–76. Pakradouni was the cold, calculating political adviser to the Gemayel clan. "Pakradouni was a very sharp man," said a former deputy chief of Mossad. "I liked him very much because he was a bastard" (*Hillel Katz*, interview, Tel Aviv, November 11, 2012).

214 *"He told me":* Frank Anderson, interview, November 4, 2010.

214 *"The last time I saw him . . .":* Taylor, *States of Terror*, p. 74.

215 *"He asked me how I planned to celebrate . . .":* Mustafa Zein, interview, Amman, October 7, 2012.

215 *Chambers held her breath:* Two Mossad officers confirmed to me that it was Chambers who pushed the ignition button.

215 *thirty-four-year-old British secretary named Susan Wareham: Glasgow Herald*, January 24, 1979, p. 2.

216 *"It was like hell":* Taylor, *States of Terror*, p. 78; Bar-Zohar and Haber, *Quest for the Red Prince*, pp. 219–20; Reeve, *One Day in September*, p. 208; Klein, *Striking Back*, pp. 221–22.

216 *He died on the operating table:* Reeve, *One Day in September*, p. 208.

216 *Eight other people were killed:* Ibid., p. 208; Raymond Carroll with Ron Moreau and Milan J. Kubic, "Death of a Terrorist," *Newsweek*, February 5, 1979.

217 *"Dear Hassan":* condolence notes by Frank Anderson, copies courtesy of Mustafa Zein.

217 *twenty thousand people attended:* "Funeral Held for Salameh," *Leader-Post*, Associated Press, January 25, 1979.

218 *"We have lost a lion":* Reeve, *One Day in September*, p. 208; "Death of a Terrorist," *Time*.

218 *"It was an unforgettable day":* Mustafa Zein, e-mail to author, July 28, 2012.

218 *"Your friends could not protect my son . . .":* Zein, "Deceit with Extreme Prejudice," p. 5.

218 *"Reputed Planner of Munich Raid Killed in Beirut":* Newspaper headline, *New York Times*, January 23, 1979.

218 *she'd waited for this day for years:* "Israel Officially Silent on Death of Guerrilla but People Applaud It," *New York Times*, January 24, 1979; Taylor, *States of Terror*, p. 79.

218 *"The day Ali Hassan Salameh was killed . . .":* Lindsay Sherwin, interview, March 22, 2011.

218 *"I am surprised . . .":* Lindsay Sherwin, interview, September 15, 2011.

219 *"If Ali Hassan had lived":* Sam Wyman, interview, November 5, 2010.

219 *"We lost a very important diplomatic channel . . .":* Frank Anderson, interview, November 4, 2010.

219 *"A few weeks later":* Ibid.

219 *"When Mossad killed Ali Hassan":* Charles Allen, interview, December 21, 2012.

219 *"He was extraordinarily helpful . . .":* Nasr, *Arab and Israeli Terrorism*, p. 109.

219 *"It is an enormous investment":* Yoram Hessel, interview, Tel Aviv, October 10, 2012.

219 *"A backstage contact . . .":* Meir Harel, interview, Tel Aviv, October 18, 2012.

220 *"close professional relations with the PLO":* Dov Zeit, interview, Tel Aviv, October

10, 2012. Brig. Gen. Amos Gilboa, a military intelligence officer, refused to believe that Ames could have been that close to the notorious Palestinian terrorist.

220   *"Did it solve the Palestinian problem?":* Richard Girling, "The Real Story Behind 'Munich'—A Thirst for Vengeance," *New York Times Magazine,* January 15, 2006.

220   *"The Israelis had a policy . . .":* Frank Anderson, interview, November 4, 2010.

221   *"I want you to do this":* Mustafa Zein, interview, Amman, October 7, 2012.

221   *"We want to finish the job . . .":* Ibid. For his part, Mustafa was worried about the safety of Bob. Mustafa was not immune to an occasional conspiratorial turn of mind. Eighteen months after Salameh's assassination—on August 27, 1980—U.S. ambassador John Gunther Dean's motorcade in Beirut was hit by twenty-one bullets and two bazooka missiles. Dean escaped, but he later wrote in his memoirs that he had discovered that the serial numbers on the weapons left behind in the attack showed that these were American weapons that had been shipped to Israel. Dean became convinced that the Israelis had shipped these arms to their Lebanese proxy, the Phalangists, who had carried out the assassination attempt: "Undoubtedly, using a proxy, our ally Israel had tried to kill me." John Gunther Dean, *Danger Zones: A Diplomat's Fight for America's Interests* (Washington, DC: Vellum/New Academia Publishing, 2009), p. 134. Zein knew this story, and he says that Ames told him at the time that Dean suspected the Israelis were targeting him because he was meeting in secret with Basil Aqel, a special adviser to Arafat. That the Israelis would target an American ambassador is inconceivable. But it is entirely possible that the Phalangists could have tried to assassinate Dean, who was known for his outspoken views.

Chapter Nine: The Ayatollahs

222   *"Fuck the Shah":* Kai Bird, *The Chairman: John J. McCloy and the Making of the American Establishment* (New York: Simon and Schuster, 1992), p. 648.

223   *Hart pulled out his gun and shot them dead:* Weiner, *Legacy of Ashes,* p. 270. I spent several weeks in Tehran in the spring of 1979 as a reporter and can attest to the volatile atmosphere of those days.

223   *"It is not easy to sleep . . .":* James A. Bill, *The Eagle and the Lion: The Tragedy of American-Iranian Relations* (New Haven, CT: Yale University Press, 1988), p. 1.

224   *not one spoke Farsi:* Mark Bowden, *Guests of the Ayatollah: The First Battle in America's War with Militant Islam* (New York: Atlantic Monthly Press, 2006), p. 301.

225   *Iran, Afghanistan, and the Soviet Union:* Bill, *Eagle and the Lion,* p. 291.

226   *"Bob was basically trying to convince them . . .":* Bruce Riedel, interview, March 30, 2011.

226   *"We hope your organization will improve its ties . . .":* Secret cable from Tehran CIA station to director, August 23, 1979, Documents from the US Espionage Den, col. 56, http://ia600409.us.archive.org/10/items/DocumentsFromTheU.s.Espionage Den/v56_text.pdf.

226   *"they had considered" the briefing:* Ibid.

227   *"Alarmed about the prospect of war . . .":* Mark Gasiorowski, "US Intelligence Assistance to Iran, May–October 1979," *Middle East Journal,* Fall 2012. I wish to thank Prof. Gasiorowski for a prepublication copy of his journal essay.

228   *"They wouldn't dare":* George Cave, interview, March 14, 2011.

228 *"We went to the degree of actually sitting down with them"*: Weiner, *Legacy of Ashes*, pp. 369–70.

228 *After Cave got back*: George Cave, interview, March 14, 2011.

228 *"We can't get away from Iran . . ."*: Bird, *Chairman*, p. 646.

229 *"Khomeini probably sensed . . ."*: Bruce Riedel, interview, March 30, 2011.

230 *publicly hanged in 1982*: Bowden, *Guests of the Ayatollah*, pp. 297–99.

230 *"The tragic irony"*: Gasiorowski, "US Intelligence Assistance to Iran."

231 *Cave carried with him a chocolate cake*: Bill, *Eagle and the Lion*, p. 1.

Chapter Ten: Jimmy Carter and Hostage America

232 *"The attacks on our embassy in Iran"*: Richard Helms, "We Believed in Our Work," speech delivered at the Veterans of the OSS Dinner, Washington Hilton Hotel, Washington, DC, May 24, 1983, www.foia.cia.gov/sites/default/files/document_conversions/45/we_belv_wrk.pdf.

233 *Beheshti had recently defended Ghotbzadeh*: Bowden, *Guests of the Ayatollah*, p. 250.

234 *"This did two things"*: Dr. Thomas Braman to Jack Harmer, March 10, 1995, and Thomas Braman to Kevin Ames, July 27, 2000, courtesy of Yvonne Ames.

234 *"the commission would then have the moral authority . . ."*: Bowden, *Guests of the Ayatollah*, 328.

235 *"First I would lose my job . . ."*: Ibid., p. 361.

235 *"Ham, they are crazy"*: Ibid., p. 366.

235 *he fired 825 clandestine officers*: Weiner, *Legacy of Ashes*, p. 364.

235 *"Bob like myself was a problem-solver . . ."*: David Long, e-mail to author, June 14, 2011.

236 *Senior Intelligence Service*: Yvonne Ames, e-mail to author, April 11, 2012.

236 *"assessments of both Begin and Sadat . . ."*: Robert Earl, e-mail to author, March 18, 2013. Earl was Ames's deputy at the time.

236 *"It was one-stop shopping"*: Robert Hunter, interview, March 17, 2011.

237 *"In order to preserve operational security"*: Robert Earl, interview, December 5, 2011.

238 *"The effort relied very heavily on the CIA"*: Weiner, *Legacy of Ashes*, p. 373.

238 *"Getting everybody to agree . . ."*: Robert Earl, interview, December 5, 2011.

238 *"He always wanted to hear people's views"*: Lindsay Sherwin, interview, March 22, 2011.

238 *"Bob didn't have a hard edge to him"*: Robert Hunter, interview, March 17, 2011.

239 *"He was much in demand"*: Fred Hitz, interview, March 24, 2011.

239 *"Ames sought the company of revolutionaries"*: Dov Zeit, interview, Tel Aviv, October 10, 2012.

239 *"I traveled to Israel with him"*: Bruce Riedel, interview, March 30, 2011.

239 *"Our need was greater than yours"*: Robert Hunter, interview, March 17, 2011.

239 *"Bob enjoyed sparring with the Israelis"*: Graham Fuller, interview, April 3, 2012.

240 *"After the Camp David Accords"*: Lindsay Sherwin, interview, March 22, 2011.

240 *"Other than on the subject of terrorism"*: John Morris, interview, March 22, 2011.

240 *"Somehow the conversation turned ugly"*: Bob Layton, interview, September 20, 2011.

240 *"I was most certainly there"*: Yoram Hessel, interview, Tel Aviv, October 10, 2012.

241 *"But he understood that you do not make any inroads . . ."*: Bob Layton, interview,

September 20, 2011. Gideon Gera was another Mossad analyst who regularly interacted with Ames on his trips to Tel Aviv. Gera came out of academia, and after his long career in the Mossad he would return to academia. "I won't say that they liked each other," recalled Layton, "but Gera respected him. It seemed mutual."

241 *"He could tell stories": Uri Oppenheim*, interview, Tel Aviv, October 14, 2012.

241 *"We wouldn't be getting moralizing . . .": Schmuel Litani*, interview, Tel Aviv, October 18, 2012.

241 *"I remember one day . . .": John Morris*, interview, March 22, 2011.

241 *"Bob had incredible gravitas": Bill Fisk*, interview, March 27, 2011.

242 *"He really didn't want to give up . . .": Lindsay Sherwin*, interview, March 22, 2011.

242 *"He was very reluctant . . .":* Ibid.

243 *he'd flown to see Khomeini:* Associated Press, "Arafat Visits Iran's New Leader," *Observer-Reporter*, February 19, 1979.

243 *Arafat had also brokered the initial release:* Ambassador John Gunther Dean, interview by Charles Stuart Kennedy, September 6, 2000: "The 13 hostages were released for Thanksgiving 1979 and there is no doubt that this release was linked to Mr. Arafat's and Abu Jihad's personal intervention with the Iranian authorities in Tehran." Jimmy Carter Presidential Library, Oral Histories, www.jimmycarter library.gov/library/oralhistory/clohproject/Lebanon.pdf.

243 *"This man [Jack Shaw] is slated . . .":* Zein, "Deceit with Extreme Prejudice," p. 280.

244 *raising money for the Reagan presidential campaign:* Jack Shaw, e-mail to author, May 2, 2013. Shaw wrote that he "got to know Casey tolerably well at [the] end of [the] campaign and in his early tenure at the Agency." Shaw wrote that he also "had interesting ties to Arafat and met with him several times in Beirut and Tunis."

244 *"He confirmed to me that Casey knew . . .":* Mustafa Zein, e-mail to author, May 26, 27, and 28, 2013.

245 *"Palestinian interest lay with a strong president . . .":* Zein, "Deceit with Extreme Prejudice," p. 280.

245 *Thirty-three years later, Shaw says he has "no recollection":* Jack Shaw, phone interview, May 25, 2013; also e-mails to author, April 23 and May 14, 16, and 22, 2013.

245 *"Casey was famous . . .":* Jack Shaw, e-mail to author, July 10, 2013.

246 *"Shaheen confirmed to me":* Shaw says that John Shaheen was a friend. Jack Shaw, e-mail to author, July 10, 2013.

246 *"Double your efforts . . .":* Zein, "Deceit with Extreme Prejudice," p. 281. The audiotape of this Zein-Shaw conversation may still exist in the closed archives of the PLO in Tunis.

247 *Two books have been published:* Robert Parry, *Trick or Treason: The October Surprise Mystery* (New York: Sheridan Square Press, 1993), and Gary Sick, *October Surprise: America's Hostages in Iran and the Election of Ronald Reagan* (New York: Times Books; Toronto: Random House, 1991). See also Abu Sharif, *Arafat and the Dream*, pp. 65–66. Abu Sharif, an aide to Arafat, writes that an aide to Reagan approached him in Beirut with a similar request to delay the mediation efforts on behalf of the American hostages. Abu Sharif says that this Reagan aide was not Jack Shaw. But Abu Sharif says that he knew Shaw and once took him to see Arafat in Tunis.

247 *"Mr. President, there is something I want to tell you . . .":* Douglas Brinkley, "The Rising Stock of Jimmy Carter," *Diplomatic History* 20, no. 4 (1996): 512.

248 *"chaotic movie set"*: John L. Helgerson, CIA Briefings of Presidential Candidates, 1952–1992, Center for the Study of Intelligence, CIA, Washington DC, 1996, p. 129, https://www.cia.gov/library/center-for-the-study-of-intelligence/csi-publications/books-and-monographs/cia-briefings-of-presidential-candidates/cia-1.htm. Helgerson was Ames's deputy, serving as the assistant national intelligence officer for the Near East and South Asia.

248 *"The Afghan story had not yet leaked"*: Ibid., p. 130.

249 *"We could lose Sadat"*: Ibid., p. 133.

249 *"You can't capture his attention"*: Mustafa Zein, interview, Amman, October 8, 2012.

249 *"The problem with Ronald Reagan . . ."*: Peter Dixon Davis, interview by John Helgerson, April 26, 1993, quoted in John Helgerson, CIA Briefings of Presidential Candidates, p. 139.

Chapter Eleven: Bill Casey and Ronald Reagan

251 *budget of about $6 billion*: Rhodri Jeffreys-Jones, *The CIA and American Democracy* (New Haven, CT: Yale University Press, 2003), p. 235.

251 *"With the people fired . . ."*: Persico, *Casey*, p. 213.

251 *"He was not happy with his career"*: Lindsay Sherwin, interview, March 22, 2011.

251 *He hired a financial consultant*: Ibid.

252 *"Look, I just want you to know . . ."*: Geoffrey Kemp, interview, March 29, 2011.

252 *"This meant undermining the influence of religion"*: Coll, *Ghost Wars*, p. 98.

253 *"Did you understand a word he said?"*: Persico, *Casey*, p. 228.

253 *"People said he was the one guy . . ."*: George Shultz, interview by James Sterling Young, chair; Stephen Knott; Marc Selverstone, December 18, 2002, Ronald Reagan Oral History Project, Miller Center of Public Affairs, Presidential Oral History Program, University of Virginia and Reagan Presidential Library, p. 27.

253 *worth nearly $10 million*: Persico, *Casey*, p. 210.

253 *"capable of great kindness . . ."*: Ibid., p. 208.

253 *"I liked Casey"*: Clair George, interview, March 23, 2011.

253 *"Facts can confuse"*: Persico, *Casey*, pp. 219–20.

253 *"At the end of one meeting . . ."*: Yoral Hessel, interview, Tel Aviv, October 10, 2012.

254 *"Off we went through the streets of Heliopolis"*: Charles Englehart, interview, September 20, 2011.

254 *Israeli jets bombed the reactor*: Persico, *Casey*, p. 253.

254 *"One real problem of this trip"*: Geoffrey Kemp, diary, April 9, 1981, courtesy of Geoffrey Kemp.

255 *his true employment*: Yvonne Ames, e-mail to author, April 9, 2012.

255 *Bob had arranged for Cathy to have a summer internship*: Lindsay Sherwin, interview, March 22, 2011.

255 *"Children sense that there is something going on . . ."*: Meir Harel, interview, Tel Aviv, October 18, 2012.

256 *"too intellectual"*: Lindsay Sherwin, e-mail to author, April 9, 2012.

256 *"I have a notion . . ."*: Bob Layton, interview, September 20, 2011.

256 *"You have to understand the culture . . ."*: Persico, *Casey*, pp. 251–52.

257 *Ames called Mustafa Zein*: This story is in Zein's "Deceit with Extreme Prejudice,"

p. 286; Mustafa Zein, interview, October 6, 2012. One retired CIA clandestine officer expressed skepticism when told about Zein's story. John McMahon, the only other living witness to this incident, refused to comment.

258 *Boatner's firing:* Winston Wiley, interview, September 16, 2011.

258 *"an acquired taste":* Lindsay Sherwin, e-mail to author, April 9, 2012.

259 *"I always considered my greatest recruitment . . .":* Weiner, *Legacy of Ashes,* p. 651.

259 *"I wanted to work for him . . .":* Winston Wiley, interview, September 16, 2011.

259 *"Bob was more aware than his critics . . .":* Bob Layton, interview, September 20, 2011.

259 *"Bob was very comfortable in his skin":* Ibid.

260 *"Ames didn't talk about his DO contacts":* Ibid.

260 *"Bob was very excited about the NESA job":* Frederick Hutchinson, interview, December 5, 2011.

260 *"Ames clearly had a formidable operational career":* Paul Pillar, interview, September 14, 2011. "To become a national intelligence officer after a clandestine career was not that unusual. David Blee had done it before Ames, and Graham Fuller did it later. But to become the director of analysis for an entire region, well, that was unusual for a DO guy. It was a huge vote of confidence."

260 *"Bob liked the analytical side":* George Cave, interview, March 14, 2011.

260 *"It is a huge difference":* Lindsay Sherwin, interview, March 22, 2011.

261 *"Ames was very good at interpreting . . .":* Frederick Hutchinson, interview, December 5, 2011.

261 *"Bob arranged for me to get a green card":* Mustafa Zein, e-mail to author, August 9, 2012. Zein said "Edward" was a very elegant man with a British upper-class demeanor who wore $2,000 suits and occasionally invited him to lunch at the Carlyle Hotel.

262 *"Helms loved them":* Mustafa Zein, interview, Amman, October 8, 2012.

262 *"Tell Arafat that Bob wants you to see this":* Mustafa Zein, interview, October 6, 2012.

263 *"They're all PLO . . .":* Benny Morris, *Righteous Victims,* p. 514.

263 *"merely the spark that lit the fuse":* Lawrence Joffe, "Obituary: Shlomo Argov, Israeli Diplomat Whose Shooting Triggered the Israeli Invasion of Lebanon," *Guardian,* February 25, 2003.

263 *"Israel's real objective . . .":* George P. Shultz, *Turmoil and Triumph: My Years as Secretary of State* (New York: Charles Scribner's Sons, 1993), p. 44.

263 *"lobotomy":* Morris, *Righteous Victims,* pp. 513–14.

264 *"come back to haunt America and Israel":* Mustafa Zein, memo to Ames, "Some Thoughts from a Moderate Lebanese Muslim," June 25, 1982, courtesy of Mustafa Zein. Also quoted in Zein, "Deceit with Extreme Prejudice," p. 283.

264 *"To eradicate the Palestinian question":* Zein, memo to Ames, "Some Thoughts from a Moderate Lebanese Muslim."

265 *"In contrast to 'pro-Israel' Haig":* Shultz, *Turmoil and Triumph,* p. 13.

265 *His second phone call was to Bob Ames:* Ibid., p. 39.

265 *"Please listen to him":* Woodward, *Veil,* p. 230.

266 *"the CIA's top specialist":* George P. Shultz to Brother Patrick Ellis, President, La Salle University, December 4, 1986.

266 *"had been carrying on a dialogue . . .":* Shultz's account of his exchanges with Ames on this subject is in his *Turmoil and Triumph,* pp. 48–49. Earlier that summer, the

Los Angeles Times had broken the news that the CIA had been meeting periodically with the PLO's Ali Hassan Salameh throughout the 1970s. Bob Ames's name was not mentioned. Doyle McManus, "U.S., PLO: 7 Years of Secret Contacts," *Los Angeles Times*, July 5, 1981, p. 1.

266 *"I saw then that Bill Casey and the CIA acted independently":* Shultz, *Turmoil and Triumph*, p. 50.

267 *"He had too much of an agenda":* Weiner, *Legacy of Ashes*, p. 644.

267 *"Habib talks only about our going":* Shultz, *Turmoil and Triumph*, p. 52.

267 *the "pragmatic" line within the PLO:* Rashid Khalidi, *Under Siege: PLO Decision-Making During the 1982 War* (New York: Columbia University Press, 1986), p. 104.

268 *"honest broker":* Ze'ev Schiff and Ehud Ya'ari, *Israel's Lebanon War* (New York: Simon and Schuster, 1984), p. 287.

268 *"good guys and bad guys . . .":* John Boykin, *Cursed Is the Peacemaker: The American Diplomat Versus the Israeli General* (Belmont, CA: Applegate Press, 2002), p. 117.

268 *General Sharon bluntly warned Habib:* Ibid., pp. 150–52.

268 *"proximity talks":* Ibid., pp. 224–25.

269 *fifty thousand Israeli artillery shells:* Ibid., p. 225.

269 *"Are you losing patience with Israel?":* Shultz, *Turmoil and Triumph*, p. 53.

269 *"Two hundred and fifty thousand men":* Boykin, *Cursed Is the Peacemaker*, pp. 135–36.

269 *"I was enraged":* Shultz, *Turmoil and Triumph*, p. 70.

270 *"Any premature hint . . .":* Ibid., p. 85.

270 *"Anything we come up with . . .":* Ibid., p. 86.

271 *"You find out . . .":* George Shultz, interview by James Sterling Young, chair; Stephen Knott; Marc Selverstone, December 18, 2002, p. 27, Ronald Reagan Oral History Project, Miller Center of Public Affairs, Presidential Oral History Program, University of Virginia and Reagan Presidential Library.

272 *"It is a tricky business . . .":* Lindsay Sherwin, interview, March 22, 2011.

272 *"Bob was a passionate believer . . .":* Bruce Riedel, interview, March 30, 2011.

273 *Arens vigorously disagreed:* Shultz, *Turmoil and Triumph*, p. 91.

274 *Four days before Arafat departed:* Mustafa Zein, e-mail to author, July 4, 2012.

275 *"US Views Regarding the Future Settlement":* Mustafa Zein, private papers.

276 *"Arafat muffed it":* Quoted in Thomas L. Friedman, *From Beirut to Jerusalem* (New York: Farrar Straus Giroux, 1989), p. 152.

276 *"Slaughterhouse Lebanon": Monday Morning*, July 12, 1982; F. Najia, "Janet Lee Stevens: American Arabist in 'Slaughterhouse Lebanon,'" *Arab Saga* blog, January 28, 2012, http://arabsaga.blogspot.com/2012/01/cost-of-gagging-beirut-part-v.html.

277 *"I thought she was CIA":* Loren Jenkins, interview, April 22, 2011.

277 *"the little drummer girl":* Franklin Lamb, "Letter to Janet," *Intifada Palestine*, September 14, 2007, www.intifada-palestine.com/2011/09/a-letter-to-janet-about -sabra-shatilla-%E2%80%93-remembering-a-martyr-for-palestinian-refugees/.

277 *He was introduced to Yasir Arafat:* Profile of John le Carré, *Monday Morning*, April 1983.

277 *"We all loved Janet . . .":* John le Carré [David Cornwell] to Mrs. Stevens and Jo Ann Stevens, April 29, 1983, courtesy of Kristen Stevens.

277 *"It was Janet's sensitivity . . .":* Ibid.

278 *"I think the Israelis have behaved disgracefully":* Profile of John le Carré, *Monday Morning,* April 1983.

278 *"You must launch a 'Stalingrad defense'":* Franklin Lamb, "The Palestinians of Sabra-Shatila: 26 Years After the Massacre," September 16, 2008, www.the peoplesvoice.org.

278 *Reagan delivered the speech:* Quoted in Shultz, *Turmoil and Triumph,* p. 97.

279 *"A friend does not weaken his friend":* This and the responses of Shultz and his aide are in ibid., pp. 98–99.

279 *"We covertly supported the election of Bashir":* Ambassador Robert Dillon, civil testimony, *Dammarell v. Islamic Republic of Iran,* April 7, 2003, p. 102.

280 *"puppet state":* Shultz, *Turmoil and Triumph,* p. 99.

280 *"with the object of keeping things quiet . . .":* Boykin, *Cursed Is the Peacemaker,* p. 267.

281 *"Begin told me . . .":* Ibid., p. 268.

281 *"We went in because of the 2,000–3,000 terrorists . . .":* Schiff and Ya'ari, *Israel's Lebanon War,* pp. 259–60.

281 *"May I say something? . . .":* Ibid., p. 260.

282 *"pathological killer":* Boykin, *Cursed Is the Peacemaker,* p. 269.

282 *between 1,000 and 3,000 people:* Bayan Nuwayhed al-Hout, *Sabra and Shatila: September 1982* (London: Pluto Press, 2004), pp. 288, 296. Al-Hout's final estimate is that about 3,500 people were killed. Israel's Kahan Commission 1983 estimated that seven hundred to eight hundred people were massacred. Abba Eban, ed., *The Beirut Massacre: The Complete Kahan Commission Report* (New York: Karz-Cohl, 1983).

282 *"A large number of flares were sent up":* Anne Dammarell, correspondence, September 27, 1982.

283 *"Fisky," said Jenkins, "something's going on . . .":* Fisk, *Pity the Nation,* pp. 357–58.

283 *"Sharon! That fucker Sharon!":* Ibid., p. 360.

283 *He counted at least fifty bodies:* Shultz, *Turmoil and Triumph,* p. 104.

283 *"I saw dead women . . .":* Franklin Lamb, "Remembering Janet Lee Stevens, a Martyr for Palestinian Refugees," April 20, 2010, *The Palestine Chronicle,* http://palestinechronicle.com/view_article_details.php?id=15900.

284 *"irrepressible":* John le Carré to Jo Ann Stevens, April 29, 1983.

284 *"I've spent the past four days . . .":* Anne Dammarell correspondence, September 27, 1982.

284 *"It was clear that this was a mass grave":* Anne Dammarell, interview, November 12, 2010.

285 *"What Arafat said is absolutely true":* Fisk, *Pity the Nation,* p. 372.

285 *"I started phoning people . . .":* Carolyn Kovar, interview, March 18, 2011.

285 *"We need action quickly":* Shultz, *Turmoil and Triumph,* p. 108.

285 *"After Sabra and Shatila . . .":* Geoffrey Kemp, interview, March 29, 2011.

285 *"A limited Beirut mission is too risky":* Shultz, *Turmoil and Triumph,* p. 109.

285 *"It soon became clear":* Geoffrey Kemp, interview, March 29, 2011.

286 "The Israelis did nothing . . .": Ronald Reagan, *The Reagan Diaries* (New York: HarperPerennial, 2007), p. 155.

286 *"The decision on the entry . . .":* Eban, *Beirut Massacre,* p. 104.

287 *"The Israelis had assumed . . .":* Bruce Riedel, interview, March 30, 2011.

287 *"I don't know . . .":* David Crist, *The Twilight War: The Secret History of America's Thirty-Three-Year Conflict with Iran* (New York: Penguin Press, 2012), p. 125.

287 *"I don't think there was any real understanding . . .":* Lindsay Sherwin, interview, March 22, 2011.

287 *death squads:* Robert Fisk, a correspondent at the time for the *Times* of London, reported on these autumn murders: Fisk, *Pity the Nation,* p. 386. See also the memoir by the Lebanese Phalangist Robert Hatem, *From Israel to Damascus* (La Mesa, CA: Pride International Publications, 1999), pp. 23, 29.

288 *Mughniyeh himself was injured:* Hala Jaber, *Hezbollah: Born with a Vengeance* (New York: Columbia University Press, 1997), p. 115.

288 *Mahmoud Ahmedinejad:* Nicholas Blanford, *Warriors of God: Inside Hezbollah's Thirty-Year Struggle Against Israel* (New York: Random House, 2011), p. 45.

288 *Asgari hired Mughniyeh:* Mustafa Zein, interview, October 8, 2012, Amman. Zein says that Mughniyeh told him about his 1982 meeting with Asgari. Asgari was initially an intelligence officer stationed in Baalbek, but later in the 1980s he became the commander of the Revolutionary Guard Corps in Baalbek. "Mr Asgari was the commander in the 1980s of a small group of Revolutionary Guards sent to Lebanon to train and organize opposition to the Israeli occupation." Gareth Smyth, "Mystery of Former Iranian Minister Deepens," *Financial Times,* March 11, 2007. See also Jaber, *Hezbollah,* p. 82.

288 *"I'm off to India . . .":* Robert Ames to Adrienne, October 1, 1982, courtesy of Yvonne Ames.

289 *"very pessimistic assessment . . .":* Geoffrey Kemp, diary, January 11, 1983, courtesy of Geoffrey Kemp.

289 *Reagan's "talking points":* William P. Clark, National Security Planning Group Meeting, February 4, 1983, secret, declassified November 15, 2005, NSPG 0051, Lebanon, Box 91306, Ex Sec, NSC, Reagan Presidential Library.

289 *Clark wrote Ames a thank-you note:* William P. Clark to Robert Ames, February 22, 1983, MC 003 Box 18, #128971, Reagan Presidential Library.

290 *Shamir "cannot leave without hearing from me . . .":* "Talking Points for the President," 3/11/83, NSPG 0058, Lebanon, Box 91306, Ex. Sec. NSC, Reagan Presidential Library.

290 *"I'm a little more optimistic . . .":* Robert Ames to Helen Ames. This was Bob's last letter to his mother.

290 *"Distinguished Intelligence Certificate":* Yvonne Ames, e-mail to author, April 11, 2012.

290 *"I saw Ames in early 1983":* Clair George, interview, March 23, 2011.

Chapter Twelve: Beirut Destiny

291 *The Little Drummer Girl:* The novel had an advance print run in the United States of 450,000 (*Monday Morning,* April 1983).

291 *Ames told his NSC counterpart:* Geoffrey Kemp, diary, April 19, 1983, courtesy of Geoffrey Kemp.

291 *"ground truth":* Bob Layton, interview, September 20, 2011.

292 *"We Israelis said, 'This is a Gemayel era' ":* Hillel Katz, interview, Tel Aviv, Novem-

ber 11, 2012. *Katz* rose to become a high-ranking Mossad officer and was deeply involved in brokering Israel's relations with the Maronite warlords.

292 *"Oh, you have to drop by the station":* Sam Wyman, interview, March 28, 2011.

292 *"We had our differences": Lindsay Sherwin,* interviews, March 22 and September 15, 2011.

292 *"We think we can smooth the whole thing over . . .":* "Local Mother Mourns Hero Dead in Blast," Philadelphia newspaper clipping, ca. April 1983.

292 *"He told me he thought, 'Things are falling apart' ":* Bruce Riedel, interview, March 30, 2011.

293 *"Keep your head down":* Thomas Braman, e-mail to author, August 25, 2011.

293 *"He had this way about him":* "Local Mother Mourns Hero."

294 *"He coached their basketball teams":* Yvonne Ames, civil suit testimony, April 15, 2003, Washington, DC, *Anne Dammarell v. Islamic Republic of Iran,* Civil Action No. 01-2224, vol. 5.

294 *"He was exhilarated to be back":* Weiner, *Legacy of Ashes,* p. 391.

294 *"delighted to see Bob":* Susan M. Morgan, "Beirut Diary," Studies in Intelligence, CIA, Summer 1983, classified secret, declassified April 2003, p. 1.

295 *a dozen or more explosions:* Charles Allen Light Jr., civil suit testimony, April 10, 2003, *Anne Dammarell v. Islamic Republic of Iran,* p. 9.

296 *"over my dead body":* Richard Halloran, "A Marine, Pistol Drawn, Stops 3 Israeli Tanks," *New York Times,* February 3, 1983.

296 *On his very first day in Beirut:* Charles Allen Light Jr., civil suit testimony, April 10, 2003, *Anne Dammarell v. Islamic Republic of Iran,* p. 9.

296 *a car bomb exploded and knocked him flat on his back:* Earl Vincent McMaugh, civil suit testimony, April 10, 2003, *Anne Dammarell v. Islamic Republic of Iran,* p. 59.

296 *someone fired a rocket-propelled grenade at the embassy:* Robert Dillon, civil suit testimony, April 7, 2003, *Anne Dammarell v. Islamic Republic of Iran,* p. 112.

296 *"There was a lot of socializing":* Anne Dammarell, testimony, February 4, 2004, *Anne Dammarell v. Islamic Republic of Iran,* hearing, p. 34.

297 *"first real love . . .":* Arlette Johnston, e-mail to author, September 6, 2012, with attached diary notes.

297 *"I spoke Arabic":* Arlette Johnston, e-mail to author, September 10, 2012.

297 *"She was a lovely woman":* Clair George, interview, March 23, 2011.

297 *"very vivacious young woman": Anne Dammarell v. Islamic Republic of Iran,* hearing, February 4, 2004, p. 11.

298 *"this guest [Ames] seems to have bad news . . .":* Arlette Johnston, e-mail to author, September 6, 2012, with attached diary notes.

298 *"for a visiting dignitary from Washington":* Anne Alison Haas, testimony, *Anne Dammarell v. Islamic Republic of Iran,* hearing, February 4, 2004, p. 35.

299 *Arlette didn't sleep very well:* Arlette Johnston, civil suit testimony, *Anne Dammarell v. Islamic Republic of Iran,* February 4, 2004, p. 12.

299 *"Maybe you can come home . . .":* Arlette Johnston, e-mail to author, September 6, 2012, with attached diary notes.

300 *"I'll give you three hundred Lebanese lira . . .":* Ronnie Tumolo, civil suit testimony, *Anne Dammarell v. Islamic Republic of Iran,* February 6, 2004, p. 86.

301 *"These are very thick papers . . .":* Zein, "Deceit with Extreme Prejudice," p. 318; Mustafa Zein, interview, Amman, October 4, 2012.

302 *"contentious"*: Anne Alison Haas, civil suit testimony, *Anne Dammarell v. Islamic Republic of Iran*, February 4, 2004, p. 37.

303 *"That was a big one"*: Ibid., p. 38.

304 *It's almost believable*: David Ignatius, "A Blast Still Reverberating: 25 Years Ago a New Kind of War Began in Beirut," *Washington Post*, April 17, 2008.

304 *A green Mercedes sedan was parked*: Karsten Tveit, interview, Beirut, October 20, 2012. Tveit, a Norwegian journalist, lived just three hundred yards from the embassy. He was sliding his key into his car door when he saw the explosion. Like a good reporter, he started running toward the embassy.

306 *She died with him*: Karsten Tveit met with John le Carré two days after the embassy bombing. Le Carré autographed a copy of *The Little Drummer Girl* for him. See also Judy Huskey, "Tribute Paid to Venice Woman," *Sarasota Herald-Tribune*, November 1, 1984.

306 *It would be five hours*: Ambassador Robert Dillon, interviewed by Martin Smith and Peter Taylor in their BBC documentary *States of Terror*.

306 *Anne Dammarell thought she was dead*: Anne Dammarell, civil suit testimony, *Anne Dammarell v. Islamic Republic of Iran*, April 7, 2003, p. 38.

307 *Ambassador Dillon saw her*: Ambassador Robert Dillon, civil suit testimony, *Anne Dammarell v. Islamic Republic of Iran*, April 7, 2003, p. 115.

307 *Staff Sgt. Charles Light had just left*: Charles Allen Light Jr., civil suit testimony, *Anne Dammarell v. Islamic Republic of Iran*, April 10, 2003, p. 17.

308 *A Lebanese army tank that had been parked on the corniche*: Cheryl Lee Sheil Pienkowski, civil suit testimony, *Anne Dammarell v. Islamic Republic of Iran*, February 10, 2004, p. 57.

309 *"momentary feeling of vertigo . . ."*: Ignatius, "Blast Still Reverberating."

310 *"I was watching them bring out dead bodies"*: Cheryl Lee Sheil Pienkowski, civil suit testimony, *Anne Dammarell v. Islamic Republic of Iran*, February 10, 2004, p. 55.

310 *"It was the only time I felt completely speechless"*: Nora Boustany, interview, Beirut, October 19, 2012.

311 *"The day seemed night"*: Arlette Johnston, e-mail to author, September 6, 2012, with attached diary notes.

311 *the grim story of how he'd been found*: Ted Gup, *The Book of Honor: The Secret Lives and Deaths of CIA Operatives* (New York: Anchor Books, 2001), p. 280.

312 *"They were not mangled"*: Ibid., p. 281.

313 *"He looked like he'd just probably been leaving . . ."*: Karen Ames, civil suit testimony, *Anne Dammarell v. Islamic Republic of Iran*, April 15, 2003. Nevertheless, for years afterwards, a far more gruesome story became part of the Ames legend inside the CIA: it was said that Ames's severed hand was found floating in the Mediterranean Sea, and that it was identified by the wedding band on his finger. Baer, *See No Evil*, p. 67. Pete Gallant, a thirty-four-year-old security expert, arrived in Beirut the next day from Athens. Gallant says that navy divers found the hand and that it probably belonged to another victim. He confirmed that Ames's body was intact. Pete Gallant, interview, April 23, 2012.

314 *"I retrieve Bob's wedding ring . . ."*: Morgan, "Beirut Diary."

314 *"I really, really lost it that day"*: Mustafa Zein, e-mail to author, July 11, 2012.

315 *"The smoke had cleared"*: Pete Gallant, interview, April 23, 2012.

315 *"He was standing straight up, bent over"*: Brian Korn, civil suit testimony, *Anne Dammarell v. Islamic Republic of Iran*, January 26, 2004, p. 148.

316 *It was Mustafa Zein:* Yvonne Ames, e-mail to author, January 23, 2013; Zein, "Deceit with Extreme Prejudice," p. 320.

316 *Kristen, eighteen, was upstairs watching television:* Kristen Ames, civil suit testimony, *Anne Dammarell v. Islamic Republic of Iran,* April 15, 2003.

317 *"It's the kind of scream you hear":* Kevin Ames, "Remembering Bob Ames," *CBS News,* April 17, 2003.

318 *" 'Does anyone know what to do?' ":* Clair George, interview, March 23, 2011.

318 *"I broke down":* Sam Wyman, interview, July 27, 2010.

318 *"And then I had to turn around and go home":* Lindsay Sherwin, interview, March 22, 2011.

319 *"The word spread that there had been an explosion":* Dov Zeit, interview, Tel Aviv, October 10, 2012.

319 *"Bob Ames among the dead in Beirut":* Geoffrey Kemp, diary, April 19, 1983.

319 *"It was a moving experience":* Reagan, *Reagan Diaries,* p. 219.

319 *"There was definitely a marked sadness . . .":* Karen Ames, civil suit testimony, *Anne Dammarell v. Islamic Republic of Iran,* April 15, 2003.

319 *"We lost [name deleted] our top research man . . .":* Reagan, *Reagan Diaries,* p. 218.

320 *Mustafa Zein had hastily flown in:* Yvonne Ames, e-mail to author, January 22, 2013.

320 *"I was there in body . . .":* Yvonne Ames, civil suit testimony, *Anne Dammarell v. Islamic Republic of Iran,* April 15, 2003.

320 *"I guess the way we put it in our minds":* Kristen Ames, civil suit testimony, *Anne Dammarell v. Islamic Republic of Iran,* April 15, 2003.

320 *3,100 diplomats, government employees, and private citizens:* Ken Ringle, "Thousands Honor Beirut Dead at Memorial Services," *Washington Post,* April 27, 1983.

321 *"The [1979] Iranian revolution . . .":* civil suit testimony, *Anne Dammarell v. Islamic Republic of Iran,* John D. Bates, U.S. District Judge, Memorandum of Opinion, Findings and Conclusions, September 8, 2003, courtesy of Stu Newberger.

321 *"We were very much identified with the Israelis":* Ambassador Robert Dillon, civil suit testimony, *Anne Dammarell v. Islamic Republic of Iran,* quoted in John D. Bates, U.S. District Judge, Memorandum of Opinion, Findings and Conclusions, September 8, 2003, courtesy of Stu Newberger.

321 *"I was not astonished":* Robert B. Oakley, civil suit testimony, *Anne Dammarell v. Islamic Republic of Iran,* March 31, 2003, p. 15.

322 *"vicious . . . cowardly act":* Naftali, *Blind Spot,* p. 130.

322 *"Lord forgive me for the hatred I feel . . .":* Reagan, *Reagan Diaries,* p. 146.

322 *"the closest thing to an irreplaceable man":* William Casey, "Remarks of the Director of Central Intelligence at the Memorial Ceremony held at Headquarters on 29 April 1983," Studies in Intelligence, CIA, Summer 1983, classified secret, declassified April 2003, p. 11; Persico, *Casey,* p. 315.

322 *"his men had come out here John Wayne–style . . .":* Morgan, "Beirut Diary," p. 6.

Chapter Thirteen: The Enigma of Imad Mughniyeh

323 *"Terrorist targets had shifted":* Persico, *Casey,* p. 316.

323 *The intercepts merely hinted:* Ibid., p. 316; Ronen Bergman asserts, "The NSA also picked up phone calls from the Revolutionary Guards in Baalbek requesting a green light for the attacks from the embassy in Damascus." Ronen Bergman,

The Secret War with Iran: The 30-Year Clandestine Struggle Against the World's Most Dangerous Terrorist Power (New York: Free Press, 2008), p. 71. See also Woodward, *Veil*, p. 231. Woodward writes about Jack Anderson's scoop.

324 *twenty-one thousand pounds of TNT:* Steven O'Hern, *Iran's Revolutionary Guard: The Threat That Grows While America Sleeps* (Washington, DC: Potomac Books, 2012), p. 56. O'Hern is citing a Department of Defense commission report on the marine-barracks bombing.

324 *"We all believe Iranians did this bombing":* Reagan, *Reagan Diaries*, p. 278.

324 *"We were too paralyzed by self-doubt":* George Shultz, interview, Martin Smith and Peter Taylor BBC documentary, *States of Terror*.

324 *"It criticized the State Department's security policies . . .":* Frederick Hutchinson, interview, December 5, 2011.

325 *But they were released two days later:* Thomas Friedman, "Lebanon Holding 4 in Embassy Attack," *New York Times*, April 21, 1983, and "Lebanon Frees 4 Witnesses Held in Bombing," *New York Times*, April 22, 1983.

325 *"principal grunt on the ground . . .":* Frederick Hutchinson, interview, December 5, 2011.

325 *"took part without hesitation . . .":* Mark Bowden, "The Dark Art of Interrogation," *Atlantic*, October 2003.

325 *"appears to have been a double, triple, a geometric-multiple agent . . .":* Christopher Dickey, "Snowland: Calling Captain Crunch," *Newsweek*, April 17, 2003. See also *Captain Crunch*, a History Channel DVD released on November 25, 2005, in which Keith Hall describes his experiences in Beirut.

326 *Hall taped Nimr's confession:* Robert Baer says he read the Hall report and thought it "ludicrous." Robert Baer, e-mail to author, April 26, 2013.

326 *Nimr had died in his jail cell:* Baer, *See No Evil*, p. 71. Baer does not write about Captain Crunch, and he doesn't name Elias Nimr as the suspect who died. But he does confirm that "Lebanese investigators beat a suspect to death during questioning." Robert Hatem, an associate of Elie Hobeika, the intelligence chief for the Lebanese Forces, claims in his memoirs that Hobeika had Elias Nimr killed in his jail cell. Hatem, *From Israel to Damascus*, p. 31.

327 *"No one was punished for it":* Bowden, "Dark Art of Interrogation."

327 *"Iran ordered it":* Baer, *See No Evil*, p. 267.

328 *"I was asked to keep tabs . . .":* Sam Wyman, interview, July 27, 2010.

328 *"We still do not have actual knowledge . . .":* Roger Morris, "A Death in Damascus," *Counterpunch*, February 25, 2008.

328 *born on July 12, 1962:* Bilal Y. Saab, an academic who interviewed some of Mughniyeh's relatives, reports that Mughniyeh was actually born on January 25, 1962. O'Hern, *Iran's Revolutionary Guard*, p. 49; Bilal Y. Saab, "Imad Mughniyeh: Lebanese by Birth, Palestinian by Heart," Jane's Islamic Affairs Analyst, *Jane's Defense Weekly*, April 11, 2011; Bilal Y. Saab, "Israel, Hizb Allah, and the Shadow of Imad Mughniyeh," *Combating Terrorism Center Sentinel*, June 1, 2011.

328 *"very smart":* Blanford, *Warriors of God*, p. 28.

328 *"Imad stood out from the others":* Ibid., p. 28. Naqqash remained a lifelong friend of Mughniyeh.

329 *Mughniyeh was recruited:* Baer, *See No Evil*, p. 99; O'Hern, *Iran's Revolutionary Guard*, pp. 49–51; Saab, "Imad Mughniyeh"; Blanford, *Warriors of God*, pp. 27–29, 46, 73.

329 *first visit to postrevolutionary Iran:* Saab, "Imad Mughniyeh." Saab's source for Mughniyeh's 1979 trip to Iran is Ibrahim Al-Amin, editor-in-chief for the Lebanese newspaper *Al-Akhbar.*

330 *hijacking of TWA Flight 847:* O'Hern, *Iran's Revolutionary Guard,* p. 63. O'Hern reports that the FBI identified Mughniyeh's fingerprint from a bathroom on the plane.

330 *"When in doubt . . .":* Roger Morris, "Death in Damascus."

331 *"gather information and details . . .":* Jaber, *Hezbollah,* p. 82.

331 *"He wanted some explosives":* Blanford, *Warriors of God,* p. 53.

331 *"We knew Mughniyeh was later responsible . . .":* Yoram Hessel, interview, Tel Aviv, October 10, 2012.

331 *Mughniyeh drove to Damascus:* Jaber, *Hezbollah,* p. 82. See also Bergman, *Secret War with Iran,* p. 70.

332 *"Imad was a very handsome young man . . .":* Mustafa Zein, interview, Amman, October 8, 2012.

332 *"He's no great saint . . .":* Bergman, *Secret War with Iran,* p. 68. In 1983, Mughniyeh married Sa'ada Badr al-Din, a sister of Mustafa Badr al-Din, a Force 17 officer and later a military commander for Hezbollah. But he later acquired a second wife and set her up in a nice apartment in the Hamra district of Beirut.

332 *Mughniyeh underwent plastic surgery:* Thomas, *Gideon's Spies,* pp. 658–63.

332 *But this piece of his legend is apocryphal:* Blanford, *Warriors of God,* p. 355.

332 *"Mughniyeh is probably the most intelligent, most capable operative . . .":* David Kohn, "Shadow Warriors," *CBS News,* February 11, 2009.

332 *"very shrewd, very talented . . .":* Meir Harel, interview, Tel Aviv, October 18, 2012.

333 *The Iranians even gave him citizenship:* Jaber, *Hezbollah,* p. 119.

333 *"Operation Bob Ames":* Harry C. Batchelder Jr., "Sentencing Memorandum on Behalf of Mustafa Zein," 88 Cr. 99 (J.E.S.) United States District Court Southern District of New York, *United States v. Mustafa Zein,* p. 39.

333 *He passed these photos to the CIA:* Ibid., p. 46.

334 *"When Bandar saw the news account":* Woodward, *Veil,* pp. 396–98.

334 *Zein also believes that Casey ordered the assassination attempt:* Mustafa Zein, e-mail to author, June 12, 2013; For more on the B'ir al-Abed car bombing, see Persico, *Casey,* p. 443; Blanford, *Warriors of God,* pp. 74–75; Odd Karsten Tveit, *Goodbye Lebanon: Israel's First Defeat* (Oslo: H. Aschehoug, 2010, 2012), p. 101; Bergman, *Secret War with Iran,* pp. 71–73.

335 *"It was [Ali Reza] Asgari's operation":* Mustafa Zein, memo, March 2011. Asgari was brought to America in February or March 2007 and debriefed in a CIA safe house outside Washington, D.C. He was admitted to the United States under Public Law 110, which allows the CIA to bring into the country up to one hundred foreign nationals annually.

335 *A suicide driver was found:* Robert Baer makes a circumstantial case that the suicide driver was a young Shi'a Lebanese man named Muhammad Hassuna. Baer, *See No Evil,* pp. 120–22.

336 *The court determined:* Judge Bates cited the testimony of Ambassador Robert Oakley, who said it was "very clear that Islamic Jihad [Hezbollah] was behind the bombing in 1983." Civil suit testimony, *Anne Dammarell v. Islamic Republic of Iran,* quoted in John D. Bates, U.S. District Judge, Memorandum of Opinion,

Findings and Conclusions, September 8, 2003, p. 21, courtesy of Stu Newberger. Ambassador Oakley further expressed "confidence that the government of Iran was involved directly in the Hezbollah organization, which was created, armed, trained, protected, and provided technical assistance by the Iranian Revolutionary Guards." Another expert witness, Dr. Patrick Clawson, estimated that Iran had spent in the range of $50 million to $150 million in 1983 on various terrorist projects (pp. 5–8).

336   raw, "bulk" form of PETN: See Warren Parker, expert testimony, Deborah D. Peterson, Personal representative of the Estate of James C. Knipple, v. The Islamic Republic of Iran, Civil Action No. 01-2684, filed May 30, 2003, U.S. District Court for the District of Columbia, p. 17. Parker was testifying about the PETN used in the October 23, 1983, attack on the U.S. marine barracks, but the same type of PETN was used in the U.S. embassy attack.

337   "a 24-karat gold document": Admiral James A. Lyons, testimony, Deborah D. Peterson v. Islamic Republic of Iran, p. 13. See also Col. Timothy J. Geraghty, Peacekeepers at War: Beirut 1983 — The Marine Commander Tells His Story (Washington, DC: Potomac Books, 2009), pp. 181, 185–86.

337   in Baalbek, serving there until late January 1984: This key fact comes from the 2007 Farsi memoirs of Iran's ex-president Akbar Hashemi Rafsanjani, who reports that on January 24, 1984, Ambassador Ali Akbar Mohtashamipur complained to him about the "disorderly state of the Guards [in Lebanon] since Kan'ani left" (http://namehnews.ir/News/Item/19721/2). Courtesy of Ali Alfoneh, e-mail to author, February 18, 2013.

337   "They got the order . . .": "Mahmoud," testimony, Deborah D. Peterson v. Islamic Republic of Iran, p. 15.

337   "The Beirut embassy operation was directed . . .": Vincent Cannistraro, e-mail to author, March 1, 2013.

338   Mustafa Mohammed Najjar: Geraghty, Peacekeepers at War, pp. 199–201. Geraghty writes that Najjar was commander of the IRGC in Baalbek when a truck bomb struck the marine barracks in October 1983. But he also names Ali Reza Asgari as another IRGC officer who was involved in this attack.

338   "I remember learning . . .": Ambassador Robert Dillon, civil suit testimony, April 7, 2003, Anne Dammarell v. Islamic Republic of Iran.

339   "managed to slip away": Bergman, Secret War with Iran, p. 104.

339   On April 7, 1995, the CIA learned: Ibid., p. 244.

339   "Imad Mughniyeh came to Khartoum . . ." Ibid., p. 224.

339   "suicide bombers could be devastatingly effective": Lawrence Wright, The Looming Tower: Al-Qaeda and the Road to 9/11 (New York: Alfred A. Knopf, 2006), pp. 173–74.

339   Later, Bin Laden sent his agent: Ibid., p. 186.

340   "just allegations . . .": Nicholas Blanford, "Hizballah Mourns Its Shadowy Hero," Time, February 13, 2008.

340   Mughniyeh had played a key role: Blanford, Warriors of God, pp. 466–67.

340   He died instantly: Ian Black, "Profile: Imad Mughniyeh," Guardian, February 13, 2008; BBC News, February 13, 2008; Anthony Shadid and Alia Ibrahim, "Bombing Kills Top Figure in Hezbollah," Washington Post, February 14, 2008. See also Yossi Melman and Dan Raviv, Spies Against Armageddon (New York: Levant

Books, 2012), p. 303; Blanford, *Warriors of God*, p. 465; Bergman, *Secret War with Iran*, pp. 379–80.

340 *"Mughniyeh was assassinated . . .":* Vincent Cannistraro, e-mail to author, March 1, 2013.

341 *"His was a rare case . . .":* Ronen Bergman, interview, Tel Aviv, October 11, 2012.

341 *"What they don't know . . .":* Shadid and Ibrahim, "Bombing Kills Top Figure."

341 *postage stamp in Mughniyeh's honor:* "Iran: First-Class Stamp Honors Militant," *New York Times*, March 11, 2008.

341 *"His prayer mat is here . . .":* Robert F. Worth, "Hezbollah Shrine to Terrorist Suspect Enthralls Lebanese Children," *New York Times*, September 2, 2008.

342 *born on January 10, 1957:* Some sources say he was born on November 1, 1952. In the mid-1980s he married Zyba Ahmadi. Later, he acquired a second wife. He has four daughters and one son by his first wife.

342 *Asgari accompanied Iran's minister of defense:* Bergman, *Secret War with Iran*, p. 59. The two other officers were Col. Sayed Shirazi and Mohsen Rezai, the commander of the Revolutionary Guard.

342 *"from Kurdistan to Lebanon":* Brig. Gen. Esmaeil Ahmadi-Moghaddam, press statement, Fars News Agency, December 15, 2012: www.farsnews.com/newstext .php?nn=13910925001246 (in Farsi), www.mashreghnews.ir/fa/news/178155. See also www.ashoora.ir/archive-article/tarikhche-hezb-allah/vorode-sepah-enghelab -be-sahne-lobnan/menu-id-41.

343 *"establishment of Hezbollah . . .":* Fars News Agency, December 15, 2012, www .farsnews.com/newstext.php?nn=13910925001246. Farsi-language press sources also establish that Asgari was a close friend of Seyed Abbas Musavi, later secretary-general of Hezbollah. When Musavi was assassinated by the Israelis in April 1992, Asgari attended the funeral: http://webcache.googleusercontent .com/search?q=cache:http://www.mashreghnews.ir/fa/news/23943/ %D8%B9%DA%A9%D8%B3-%D8%B9%D9%84%D9%8A%D8%B1%D8%B6 %D8%A7%D8%B9%D8%B3%DA%AF%D8%B1%D9%8A-%D8%AF%D8%B1 %D9%84%D8%A8%D9%86%D8%A7%D9%86. I am in debt to Amir Hossein Etemadi for this research in Farsi-language sources. Amir Hossein Etemadi, e-mail to author, April 18, 2013. See also Bergman, *Secret War with Iran*, pp. 59–60. See also Gareth Smyth, "Mystery of Former Iranian Minister Deepens," *Financial Times*, March 11, 2007. Smyth reports, "Mr. Asgari was the commander in the 1980s of a small group of Revolutionary Guards sent to Lebanon to train and organize opposition to the Israeli occupation."

343 *"He [Asgari] held a very, very senior position":* Dafna Linzer, "Former Iranian Defense Official Talks to Western Intelligence," *Washington Post*, March 8, 2007.

343 *Asgari was rewarded with a promotion:* Bergman, *Secret War with Iran*, p. 61.

343 *"Iran has a desire . . .":* Ali Reza Asgari, interview, *As-Safir*, Associated Press News Archive, April 11, 1991.

344 *the Revolutionary Guard "is not a militia . . .":* Magnus Ranstorp, *Hizb'Allah in Lebanon: The Politics of the Western Hostage Crisis* (London: Macmillan Press, 1997), pp. 34, 84, 215. The BBC identified him as "Hadi Reza Askari." *Hadi* is an honorific title, meaning "guide" or "leader."

344 *Asgari "knows dirty secrets . . .":* Robert Baer, "Could a Missing Iranian Spark a War?" *Time*, March 22, 2007.

344 *"It was an organized defection":* Georges Malbrunot, "Passed Over for Promotion, Iranian General Defects," *Le Figaro,* March 13, 2007; Laura Rozen, "Where Is Ali-Reza Asgari?" *Politico,* December 31, 2010.

345 *"willingly cooperating":* Linzer, "Former Iranian Defense Official." See also Ivan Watson, "Understanding the Case of Ali Reza Askari," *All Things Considered,* National Public Radio, April 2, 2007. Watson interviewed Robert Baer.

345 *"longtime Western intelligence agent":* Julian Borger, "Defection or Abduction? Speculation Grows After Iranian General Goes AWOL in Turkey," *Guardian,* December 8, 2007.

345 *"[any] Iranian defector was highly valued . . .":* Vincent Cannistraro, e-mail to author, March 1, 2013.

345 *Asgari gave the Americans actionable intelligence:* Bergman, *Secret War with Iran,* p. 294.

345 *"This type of defection . . .":* Malbrunot, "Passed Over for Promotion."

345 *"a valuable asset for Western intelligence agencies . . .":* Borzou Daragahi, "Iranian Exile Speaks Out Against Militia He Once Supported," *Los Angeles Times,* July 9, 2009.

345 *"Salvation Committee":* Ebrahimi later said that this organization was renamed the "Rescue Committee," and that it was run by the U.S. State Department to encourage Iranian defections. He said he was the only Iranian who served on the committee. "Interview: Amiri Was Not Who He Pretended He Was," *Amir Farshad Ebrahimi* (blog), August 7, 2010, www.farshadebrahimi.com/2010_08_01 _archive.html.

345 *"We were at the [Iranian] embassy together . . .":* Kenneth R. Timmerman, "Iranian Defectors Provide Crucial Intel," *Newsmax,* April 1, 2008.

346 *"I brought my computer along . . .":* Erich Follath and Holger Stark, "The Story of Operation Orchard: How Israel Destroyed Syria's Al Kibar Nuclear Reactor," *Der Spiegel Online,* November 2, 2009.

346 *Asgari was whisked to Washington, D.C.:* Timmerman, "Iranian Defectors." Amir Farshad Ebrahimi was Timmerman's source for this information. Washington has still not officially acknowledged Asgari's defection. According to one CIA source, Asgari is not on the official list of declassified defectors.

346 *"He lived in Lebanon . . .":* Linzer, "Former Iranian Defense Official."

346 *Asgari was brought to a CIA safe house:* Bergman, *Secret War with Iran,* p. 351.

346 *Iran was helping Syria to develop nuclear weapons:* Ibid., p. 358.

346 *A German defense ministry official revealed:* Associated Press, "Iran Ex-deputy Minister Jailed in Israel," *NBCNews.com,* November 15, 2009, www.nbcnews.com/id/ 33951026/ns/world_news-mideastn_africa/wid/7/#.USZmVFriqKx.

346 *Israeli air strike on a Syrian nuclear reactor:* A lengthy Library of Congress report prepared by the Federal Research Division reported, "Asgari's defection was significant because he was deeply engaged in establishing Iranian links with Hezbollah. Asgari seems to have provided intelligence to the Israelis and may have been the source of the intelligence they used in Operation Orchard to strike Syria's nuclear reactor." "Iran's Ministry of Intelligence and Security: A Profile," December 2012, p. 34, www.iranwatch.org/government/us-congress-libraryofcongressreport-1212.pdf.

346 *Mughniyeh's cell phone numbers and recent photographs:* Daniel Byman, *A High Price: The Triumphs and Failures of Israeli Counterterrorism* (New York: Oxford University Press, 2010), p. 262.

346 *"It may be no coincidence"*: Ronen Bergman, "Bracing for Revenge," *New York Times*, February 18, 2008.

347 *"somewhere in Texas"*: Follath and Stark, "Story of Operation Orchard." In the spring of 2013 Asgari visited Leidschendam, in the Netherlands, where he gave testimony before the Special Tribunal for Lebanon, authorized by the United Nations to investigate the 2005 assassination of Lebanese prime minister Rafic Hariri.

347 *Public Law 110:* This 1949 law allows the CIA to bring in no more than one hundred essential aliens each year: "Whenever the Director, the Attorney General, and the Commissioner of Immigration and Naturalization shall determine that the admission of a particular alien into the United States for permanent residence is in the interest of national security or essential to the furtherance of the national intelligence mission, such alien and his immediate family shall be admitted to the United States for permanent residence without regard to their inadmissibility under the immigration or any other laws and regulations, or to the failure to comply with such laws and regulations pertaining to admissibility: Provided, That the number of aliens and members of their immediate families admitted to the United States under the authority of this section shall in no case exceed one hundred persons in any one fiscal year" (50 U.S. Code 403—Sec 403h).

347 *"At the unclassified level . . ."*: e-mail to author, April 17, 2013, from a former NSC official in the Bush administration. Fran Townsend, a former NSC official who worked on counterterrorism; Mike Singh, former NSC official; and Charles Allen, a former counterterrorism official with the Department of Homeland Security, all declined to respond to questions about Asgari.

347 *"The value of information that Asgari could provide . . ."*: Frederick Hutchinson, e-mail to author, February 28, 2013.

348 "When faced in life with the unexplainable . . ." *Schmuel Litani*, interview, Tel Aviv, October 18, 2012.

Epilogue

352 *"I had to relearn how to move my body . . ."*: Anne Dammarell, "Hidden Fears, Helpful Memories: Aftermath of the 1983 Bombing of the United States Embassy in Beirut" (M.A. thesis, Georgetown University, 1994), pp. 24, 30.

353 *"I hate to say it"*: *Meir Harel*, interview, Tel Aviv, October 18, 2012.

353 *"There was no deep trick to it"*: Thomas Powers, *Intelligence Wars: American Secret History from Hitler to Al-Qaeda* (New York: New York Review of Books, 2002), p. xv.

355 *"Bin Laden reportedly showed particular interest . . ."*: Thomas H. Kean and Lee H. Hamilton, *The 9/11 Report: The National Commission on Terrorist Attacks upon the United States* (New York: St. Martin's Press, 2004), pp. 90–91.

355 *"Americans are blamed . . ."*: Ibid., p. 76.

BIBLIOGRAPHY

Abdul Hadi, Mahdi, ed. *Palestinian Personalities: A Biographic Dictionary.* Jerusalem: Passia, 2006.

Abrams, Elliott. *Tested by Zion: The Bush Administration and the Israeli-Palestinian Conflict.* New York: Cambridge University Press, 2013.

Aburish, Said K. *A Brutal Friendship: The West and the Arab Elites.* New York: St. Martin's Press, 1998.

———. *The St George Hotel Bar.* London: Bloomsbury, 1989.

Abu Sharif, Bassam. *Arafat and the Dream of Palestine.* New York: Palgrave Macmillan, 2009.

Abu Sharif, Bassam, and Uzi Mahnaimi. *Best of Enemies: The Memoirs of Bassam Abu-Sharif and Uzi Mahnaimi.* Boston: Little, Brown, 1995.

Agee, Philip, and Louis Wolf, eds. *Dirty Work: The CIA in Western Europe.* New York: Dorset Press, 1988.

Ajami, Fouad. *The Dream Palace of the Arabs: A Generation's Odyssey.* New York: Pantheon Books, 1998.

———. *The Vanished Imam: Musa Sadr and the Shia of Lebanon.* Ithaca, NY: Cornell University Press, 1986.

Arnold, Jose. *Golden Swords and Pots and Pans.* New York: Harcourt, Brace and World, 1963.

Ashton, Nigel. *King Hussein of Jordan: A Political Life.* New Haven, CT: Yale University Press, 2008.

Aust, Stefan. *The Baader-Meinhof Group: The Inside Story of a Phenomenon.* London: Bodley Head, 1987. Originally published in German as *Der Baader-Meinhof Komplex* (Hamburg: Hoffmann und Campe, 1985).

———. *The Baader-Meinhof Group: The Inside Story of the RAF.* New York: Oxford University Press, 2009.

Baer, Robert. *See No Evil: The True Story of a Ground Soldier in the CIA's War on Terror-ism.* New York: Three Rivers Press, 2002.

Bakhash, Shaul. *The Reign of the Ayatollahs: Iran and the Islamic Revolution.* New York: Basic Books, 1986.

Bar-Zohar, Michael, and Eitan Haber. *The Quest for the Red Prince.* Guilford, CT: Lyon's Press, 1983, 2002.

Bar-Zohar, Michael, and Nissim Mishal. *Mossad: The Greatest Missions of the Israeli Secret Service.* New York: Ecco/HarperCollins, 2012.

Bergman, Ronen. *The Secret War with Iran: The 30-Year Clandestine Struggle Against the World's Most Dangerous Terrorist Power.* New York: Free Press, 2008.

Bill, James A. *The Eagle and the Lion: The Tragedy of American-Iranian Relations.* New Haven: Yale University Press, 1988.

Bird, Kai. *The Chairman: John J. McCloy and the Making of the American Establishment.* New York: Simon and Schuster, 1992.

———. *The Color of Truth: McGeorge Bundy and William Bundy, Brothers in Arms.* New York: Simon and Schuster, 1998.

———. *Crossing Mandelbaum Gate: Coming of Age Between the Arabs and Israelis, 1956–1978.* New York: Scribner, 2010.

Black, Ian, and Benny Morris. *Israel's Secret Wars: A History of Israel's Intelligence Services.* New York: Grove Weidenfeld, 1991.

Blanford, Nicholas. *Warriors of God: Inside Hezbollah's Thirty-Year Struggle Against Israel.* New York: Random House, 2011.

Blight, James G., Janet M. Lang, Hussein Banai, Malcolm Byrne, and John Tirman. *Becoming Enemies: U.S.-Iran Relations and the Iran-Iraq War, 1979–1988.* Lanham, MD: Rowman and Littlefield, 2012.

Bowden, Mark. *Guests of the Ayatollah: The First Battle in America's War with Militant Islam.* New York: Atlantic Monthly Press, 2006.

Boykin, John. *Cursed Is the Peacemaker: The American Diplomat Versus the Israeli General.* Belmont, CA: Applegate Press, 2002.

Brinkley, Douglas. "The Rising Stock of Jimmy Carter." *Diplomatic History* 20, no. 4 (1996): 505–30.

———. *The Unfinished Presidency: Jimmy Carter's Journey Beyond the White House.* New York: Viking, 1998.

Brzezinski, Zbigniew. *Power and Principle: Memoirs of a National Security Adviser, 1977–1981.* New York: Farrar, Straus and Giroux, 1983.

Bullock, John. *The Making of a War: The Middle East from 1967 to 1973.* London: Longman, 1974.

Burton, Fred, and John Bruning. *Chasing Shadows: A Special Agent's Lifelong Hunt to Bring a Cold War Assassin to Justice.* New York: Palgrave Macmillan, 2011.

Byman, Daniel. *A High Price: The Triumphs and Failures of Israeli Counterterrorism.* New York: Oxford University Press, 2010.

Cambanis, Thanassis. *A Privilege to Die: Inside Hezbollah's Legions and Their Endless War Against Israel.* New York: Free Press, 2010.

Cannon, Lou. *President Reagan: The Role of a Lifetime.* New York: Simon and Schuster, 1991.

Carter, Jimmy. *Keeping Faith: Memoirs of a President.* New York: Bantam Books, 1982.

———. *White House Diary.* New York: Farrar, Straus and Giroux, 2010.

Clarridge, Duane R., with Digby Diehl. *A Spy for All Seasons: My Life in the CIA.* New York: Scribner, 1997.

Colby, William, and Peter Forbath. *Honorable Men: My Life in the CIA.* New York: Simon and Schuster, 1978.

Coll, Steve. *The Bin Ladens: An Arabian Family in the American Century.* New York: Penguin Press, 2008.

———. *Ghost Wars: The Secret History of the CIA, Afghanistan, and bin Laden, from the Soviet Invasion to September 10, 2001.* New York: Penguin Books, 2004.

Cooley, John K. *Green March, Black September: The Story of the Palestinian Arabs.* London: Frank Cass, 1973.

Copeland, Miles. *The Game of Nations: The Amorality of Power Politics.* London: Weidenfeld and Nicolson, 1969.

Corn, David. *Blond Ghost: Ted Shackley and the CIA's Crusades.* New York: Simon and Schuster, 1994.

Crile, George. *Charlie Wilson's War: The Extraordinary Story of the Largest Covert Operation in History.* New York: Atlantic Monthly Press, 2003.

Crist, David. *The Twilight War: The Secret History of America's Thirty-Three Year Conflict with Iran.* New York: Penguin Press, 2012.

Crumpton, Henry A. *The Art of Intelligence: Lessons from a Life in the CIA's Clandestine Service.* New York: Penguin Press, 2012.

Cubert, Harold M. *The PFLP's Changing Role in the Middle East.* London: Frank Cass, 1997.

Dallek, Robert. *Nixon and Kissinger: Partners in Power.* New York: HarperCollins, 2007.

Dammarell, Anne. "Hidden Fears, Helpful Memories: Aftermath of the 1983 Bombing of the United States Embassy in Beirut." M.A. thesis, Georgetown University, November 1994.

Deacon, Richard. *The Israeli Secret Service.* New York: Taplinger, 1977.

Dean, John Gunther. *Danger Zones: A Diplomat's Fight for America's Interests.* Washington, DC: Vellum / New Academia Publishing, 2009.

Deeb, Marius. *Syria's Terrorist War on Lebanon and the Peace Process.* New York: Palgrave, 2003.

Dobson, Christopher. *Black September: Its Short, Violent History.* New York: Macmillan, 1974.

Eban, Abba, ed. *The Beirut Massacre: The Complete Kahan Commission Report.* New York: Karz-Cohl, 1983.

Eveland, Wilbur Crane. *Ropes of Sand: America's Failure in the Middle East.* New York: W. W. Norton, 1980.

Fisk, Robert. *The Great War for Civilization: The Conquest of the Middle East.* New York: Alfred A. Knopf, 2005.

———. *Pity the Nation: The Abduction of Lebanon.* New York: Atheneum, 1990.

Friedman, Thomas L. *From Beirut to Jerusalem.* New York: Farrar, Straus and Giroux, 1989.

Geraghty, Colonel Timothy J. *Peacekeepers at War: Beirut 1983 — The Marine Commander Tells His Story*. Washington, DC: Potomac Books, 2009.

Gilbert, Martin. *Israel: A History*. New York: William Morrow, 1998.

Glass, Charles. *The Tribes Triumphant: Return Journey to the Middle East*. New York: HarperPress, 2006.

———. *Tribes with Flags: A Dangerous Passage Through the Chaos of the Middle East*. New York: Atlantic Monthly Press, 1990.

Gup, Ted. *The Book of Honor: The Secret Lives and Deaths of CIA Operatives*. New York: Anchor Books, 2000, 2001.

Halevy, Efraim. *Man in the Shadows: Inside the Middle East Crisis with a Man Who Led the Mossad*. New York: St. Martin's Press, 2006.

Hammel, Eric. *The Root: The Marines in Beirut, August 1982–February 1984*. St. Paul, MN: Zenith Press, 1999, 2005.

Hamzeh, Ahmad Nizar. *In the Path of Hizbullah*. Syracuse, NY: Syracuse University Press, 2004.

Hart, Alan. *Arafat: Terrorist or Peacemaker?* London: Sidgwick and Jackson, 1984.

Hatem, Robert. *From Israel to Damascus*. La Mesa, CA: Pride International Publications, 1999.

Helgerson, John L. *CIA Briefings of Presidential Candidates, 1952–1992*. Washington, DC: Center for the Study of Intelligence, CIA, 1996.

Helms, Richard, with William Hood. *A Look over My Shoulder: A Life in the Central Intelligence Agency*. New York: Ballantine Books, 2003.

Hersh, Seymour. *The Price of Power: Kissinger in the Nixon White House*. New York: Summit Books, 1983.

Hirst, David. *Beware of Small States: Lebanon, Battleground of the Middle East*. New York: Nation Books, 2010.

———. *The Gun and the Olive Branch: The Roots of Violence in the Middle East*. New York: Thunder's Mouth Press / Nation Books, 1977, 1984, 2003.

Hitz, Frederick P. *The Great Game: The Myths and Reality of Espionage*. New York: Vintage, 2005.

Holden, David. *Farewell to Arabia*. London: Faber and Faber, 1966.

Holden, David, and Richard Johns. *The House of Saud*. London: Sidgwick and Jackson, 1981.

Holm, Richard L. *The Craft We Chose: My Life in the CIA*. Mountain Lake Park, MD: Mountain Lake Press, 2011.

Hout, Bayan Nuwayhed al-. *Sabra and Shatila: September 1982*. London: Pluto Press, 2004.

Hout, Shafiq al-. *My Life in the PLO: The Inside Story of the Palestinian Struggle*. London: Pluto Press, 2011.

Ignatius, David. *Agents of Innocence*. New York: W. W. Norton, 1987.

Iyad, Abu, with Éric Rouleau. *My Home, My Land: A Narrative of the Palestinian Struggle*. New York: Times Books, 1981.

Jaber, Hala. *Hezbollah: Born with a Vengeance*. New York: Columbia University Press, 1997.

Jeffreys-Jones, Rhodri. *The CIA and American Democracy*. New Haven, CT: Yale University Press, 1989, 2003.

Jonas, George. *Vengeance: The True Story of an Israeli Counter-terrorist Team.* New York: Simon and Schuster, 1984.

Jordan, Hamilton. *Crisis: The True Story of an Unforgettable Year in the White House.* New York: G. P. Putnam's Sons, 1982.

Kahlili, Reza. *A Time to Betray: A Gripping True Spy Story of Betrayal, Fear and Courage.* New York: Threshold Editions / Simon and Schuster, 2010.

Kaplan, Robert D. *The Arabists: The Romance of an American Elite.* New York: Free Press, 1993.

Katz, Emily Alice. "It's the Real World After All: The American-Israel Pavilion–Jordan Pavilion Controversy at the New York World's Fair, 1964–1965." *American Jewish History* 91 (March 2003): 129–55. www.thefreelibrary.com/It's+the+real+world +after+all%3A+the+American-Israel+Pavilion--Jordan . . . -a0119570011.

Katz, Samuel M. *Soldier Spies: Israeli Military Intelligence.* Novato, CA: Presidio Press, 1992.

Kazziha, Walid W. *Revolutionary Transformation in the Arab World: Habash and His Comrades from Nationalism to Marxism.* New York: St. Martin's Press, 1975.

Kean, Thomas H., and Lee H. Hamilton. *The 9/11 Report: The National Commission on Terrorist Attacks upon the United States.* New York: St. Martin's Press, 2004.

Kessler, Ronald. *Inside the CIA.* New York: Pocket Books, 1992.

Khalidi, Rashid. *Under Siege: PLO Decision-Making During the 1982 War.* New York: Columbia University Press, 1986.

Kissinger, Henry. *Years of Upheaval.* New York: Simon and Schuster, 1982.

Klein, Aaron J. *Striking Back: The 1972 Munich Olympics Massacre and Israel's Deadly Response.* New York: Random House, 2005.

Kramer, Stephen. *Surrogate Terrorists: Iran's Formula for Success.* Lanham, MD: University Press of America, 2010.

Kubaisi, Basil Raoud al-. "The Arab Nationalist Movement, 1951–1971: From Pressure Group to Socialist Party." Ph.D. diss., American University, 1971.

Lacey, Robert. *The Kingdom: Arabia and The House of Saud.* New York: Harcourt Brace Jovanovich, 1981.

Large, David Clay. *Munich 1972: Tragedy, Terror and Triumph at the Olympic Games.* New York: Rowman and Littlefield, 2012.

Little, Douglas. *American Orientalism: The United States and the Middle East Since 1945.* Chapel Hill: University of North Carolina Press, 2002.

Livingston, Neil C., and David Halevy. *Inside the PLO: Covert Units, Secret Funds, and the War Against Israel and the United States.* New York: William Morrow, 1990.

MacFarquhar, Neil. *The Media Relations Department of Hizbollah Wishes You a Happy Birthday: Unexpected Encounters in the Changing Middle East.* New York: Public Affairs, 2009.

Mackintosh-Smith, Tim. *Yemen: The Unknown Arabia.* Woodstock, NY: Overlook Press, 2000.

Mallmann, Klaus-Michael, and Martin Cuppers. *Nazi Palestine: The Plans for the Extermination of the Jews in Palestine.* London: Enigma, 2010.

Martin, David, and John Walcott. *Best Laid Plans: The Inside Story of America's War Against Terrorism.* New York: Harper and Row, 1988.

McDermott, Anthony, and Kjell Skjelsbaek, eds. *The Multinational Force in Beirut, 1982–1984.* Miami: Florida International University Press, 1991.

Melman, Yossi, and Dan Raviv. *Spies Against Armageddon.* New York: Levant Books, 2012.

Morris, Benny. *1948: The First Arab-Israeli War.* New Haven, CT: Yale University Press, 2008.

———. *Righteous Victims: A History of the Zionist-Arab Conflict, 1881–2001.* New York: Vintage Books, 1999, 2001.

Morris, Edmund. *Dutch: A Memoir of Ronald Reagan.* New York: Random House, 1999.

Naftali, Timothy. *Blind Spot: The Secret History of American Counterterrorism.* New York: Basic Books, 2005.

Nasr, Kameel B. *Arab and Israeli Terrorism: The Causes and Effects of Political Violence, 1936–1993.* Jefferson, NC: McFarland, 1997.

Norton, Augustus Richard. *Hezbollah: A Short History.* Princeton, NJ: Princeton University Press, 2007.

O'Connell, Jack, with Vernon Loeb. *King's Counsel: A Memoir of War, Espionage, and Diplomacy in the Middle East.* New York: W. W. Norton, 2011.

O'Hern, Steven. *Iran's Revolutionary Guard: The Threat That Grows While America Sleeps.* Washington, DC: Potomac Books, 2012.

Olson, James M. *Fair Play: The Moral Dilemmas of Spying.* Washington, DC: Potomac Books, 2006.

Parry, Robert. *Trick or Treason: The October Surprise Mystery.* New York: Sheridan Square Press, 1993.

Parsi, Trita. *Treacherous Alliance: The Secret Dealings of Israel, Iran, and the United States.* New Haven, CT: Yale University Press, 2007.

Paseman, Floyd L. *A Spy's Journey: A CIA Memoir.* Minneapolis: Zenith Press, 2004, 2009.

Pedahzur, Ami. *The Israeli Secret Services and the Struggle Against Terrorism.* New York: Columbia University Press, 2009.

Perry, Mark. *A Fire in Zion: The Israeli-Palestinian Search for Peace.* New York: William Morrow, 1994.

Persico, Joseph E. *Casey: The Lives and Secrets of William J. Casey.* New York: Viking Penguin Books, 1990.

Philby, Kim. *My Silent War: The Autobiography of a Spy.* New York: Modern Library, 1968.

Phillips, Wendell. *Qataban and Sheba: Exploring the Ancient Kingdoms on the Biblical Spice Routes of Arabia.* New York: Harcourt, Brace, 1955.

Powers, Thomas. *Intelligence Wars: American Secret History from Hitler to Al-Qaeda.* New York: New York Review of Books, 2002.

———. *The Man Who Kept the Secrets: Richard Helms and the CIA.* New York: Alfred A. Knopf, 1979.

Prados, John. *Lost Crusader: The Secret Wars of CIA Director William Colby.* New York: Oxford University Press, 2003.

Raab, David. *Terror in Black September: The First Eyewitness Account of the Infamous 1970 Hijackings.* New York: Palgrave Macmillan, 2007.

Rabinovich, Itamar. *The War for Lebanon: 1970–1985.* Ithaca, NY: Cornell University Press, 1984, 1985.

Randal, Jonathan. *Going All the Way: Christian Warlords, Israeli Adventurers, and the War in Lebanon.* New York: Vintage Books, 1984.

Ranelagh, John. *The Agency: The Rise and Decline of the CIA.* New York: Simon and Schuster, 1986.

Ranstorp, Magnus. *Hizb'Allah in Lebanon: The Politics of the Western Hostage Crisis.* London: Macmillan Press, 1997.

Rasmuson, John R., ed. *A History of Kagnew Station and American Forces in Eritrea.* Asmara: Il Poligrafico, 1973.

Raviv, Dan, and Yossi Melman. *Every Spy a Prince: The Complete History of Israel's Intelligence Community.* New York: Houghton Mifflin, 1990.

———. *Friends Indeed: Inside the U.S.-Israel Alliance.* New York: Hyperion, 1994.

Read, Anthony, and David Fisher. *Colonel Z: The Secret Life of a Master of Spies.* London: Hodder and Stoughton, 1984.

Reagan, Ronald. *The Reagan Diaries.* New York: HarperPerennial, 2007.

Reeve, Simon. *One Day in September.* New York: Arcade, 2000.

Rogan, Eugene. *The Arabs: A History.* New York: Penguin Books, 2009.

Roosevelt, Archie. *For Lust of Knowing: Memoirs of an Intelligence Officer.* Boston: Little, Brown, 1988.

Salhani, Claude. *Black September to Desert Storm: A Journalist in the Middle East.* Columbia: University of Missouri Press, 1998.

Sayigh, Yezid. *Armed Struggle and the Search for State: The Palestinian National Movement, 1949–1993.* New York: Oxford University Press, 1997.

Schiff, Ze'ev, and Ehud Ya'ari. *Israel's Lebanon War.* New York: Simon and Schuster, 1984.

Schmidt, Dana Adams. *Yemen: The Unknown War.* New York: Holt, Rinehart and Winston, 1968.

Sheehan, Edward R. F. *The Arabs, Israelis and Kissinger.* New York: Reader's Digest Press, 1976.

Shlaim, Avi. *Lion of Jordan: The Life of King Hussein in War and Peace.* New York: Alfred A. Knopf, 2008.

Shultz, George. *Turmoil and Triumph: My Years as Secretary of State.* New York: Charles Scribner's Sons, 1993.

Sick, Gary. *October Surprise: America's Hostages in Iran and the Election of Ronald Reagan.* New York: Times Books; Toronto: Random House, 1991.

Snow, Peter, and David Phillips. *The Arab Hijack War: The Whole Story of the Most Incredible Act of Piracy in the Decade.* New York: Ballantine Books, 1971.

Takeyh, Ray. *Guardians of the Revolution: Iran and the World in the Age of the Ayatollahs.* New York: Oxford University Press, 2009.

Taylor, Peter. *States of Terror: Democracy and Political Violence.* London: Penguin Books, 1993.

Theroux, Peter. *Sandstorms: Days and Nights in Arabia.* New York: W. W. Norton, 1990.

Thomas, Evan. *The Very Best Men: The Daring Early Years of the CIA.* New York: Simon and Schuster, 1995, 2006.

Thomas, Gordon. *Gideon's Spies: The Secret History of the Mossad.* New York: St. Martin's Press, 1995.

Timerman, Jacobo. *The Longest War: Israel in Lebanon.* New York: Alfred A. Knopf, 1982.

Tinnin, David B., with Dag Christensen. *The Hit Team.* New York: Dell, 1976.

Turner, Stansfield. *Burn Before Reading.* New York: Hyperion, 2005.

———. *Secrecy and Democracy: The CIA in Transition.* Boston: Houghton Mifflin, 1983.

Tveit, Odd Karsten. *Alt for Israel: Oslo-Jerusalem, 1948–78.* Oslo: J. W. Cappelens, 1996.

———. *Goodbye Lebanon: Israel's First Defeat.* Oslo: H. Aschehoug, 2010, 2012.

Van De Ven, Susan Kerr. *One Family's Response to Terrorism: A Daughter's Memoir.* Syracuse, NY: Syracuse University Press, 2008.

Vassiliev, Alexei. *The History of Saudi Arabia.* New York: New York University Press, 2000.

Vitalis, Robert. *America's Kingdom: Mythmaking on the Saudi Oil Frontier.* Stanford, CA: Stanford University Press, 2007.

Walters, Vernon A. *Silent Missions.* Garden City, NY: Doubleday, 1978.

Weiner, Tim. *Legacy of Ashes: The History of the CIA.* New York: Doubleday, 2007.

Wise, David, and Thomas B. Ross. *The Espionage Establishment.* New York: Random House, 1967.

Woodward, Bob. *Veil: The Secret Wars of the CIA, 1981–1987.* New York: Simon and Schuster, 1987.

Wright, Lawrence. *The Looming Tower: Al-Qaeda and the Road to 9/11.* New York: Alfred A. Knopf, 2006.

Wright, Robin. *Dreams and Shadows: The Future of the Middle East.* New York: Penguin Press, 2008.

Yaniv, Avner. *Dilemmas of Security: Politics, Strategy, and the Israeli Experience in Lebanon.* New York: Oxford University Press, 1987.

Zein, Mustafa. "Deceit with Extreme Prejudice." Unpublished memoir, ca. 2005. Courtesy of Mustafa Zein.

INDEX

ABOUT THE AUTHOR

KAI BIRD is the coauthor with Martin J. Sherwin of the Pulitzer Prize–winning biography *American Prometheus: The Triumph and Tragedy of J. Robert Oppenheimer* (2005), which also won the National Book Critics Circle Award for Biography and the Duff Cooper Prize for History in London. He wrote *The Chairman: John J. McCloy; The Making of the American Establishment* (1992), and *The Color of Truth: McGeorge Bundy and William Bundy; Brothers in Arms* (1998). He is also coeditor with Lawrence Lifschultz of *Hiroshima's Shadow: Writings on the Denial of History and the Smithsonian Controversy* (1998). He is also the author of a memoir, *Crossing Mandelbaum Gate: Coming of Age Between the Arabs and Israelis, 1956–1978* (2010), which was a Finalist for the 2011 National Book Critics Circle Award and a Finalist for the 2011 Dayton Literary Peace Prize. Mr. Bird is the recipient of fellowships from the John Simon Guggenheim Memorial Foundation; the Alicia Patterson Foundation; the John D. and Catherine T. MacArthur Foundation; the Thomas J. Watson Foundation; the German Marshall Fund; the Rockefeller Foundation's Study Center, Bellagio, Italy; and the Woodrow Wilson International Center for Scholars in Washington,

D.C. An elected fellow of the Society of American Historians and a contributing editor of *The Nation*, he lives in Washington, D.C., with his wife and son.

www.kaibird.com